WHEN WORDS LOSE
THEIR MEANING

JAMES BOYD WHITE

WHEN WORDS LOSE THEIR MEANING

Constitutions and Reconstitutions of Language, Character, and Community

THE UNIVERSITY OF CHICAGO PRESS
CHICAGO AND LONDON

JAMES BOYD WHITE is Professor of Law, Professor of
English, and Adjunct Professor of Classical Studies
at the University of Michigan. He is the author of
*The Legal Imagination: Studies in the Nature of
Legal Thought and Expression* and (with James E.
Scarboro) *Constitutional Criminal Procedure.*

The University of Chicago Press, Chicago 60637
The University of Chicago Press, Ltd., London
© 1984 by The University of Chicago
All rights reserved. Published 1984
Printed in the United States of America
93 92 91 90 89 88   543

Library of Congress Cataloging in Publication Data

White, James Boyd, 1938–
    When words lose their meaning.

    Bibliography: p.
    Includes index.
    1. Language and languages.   2. Criticism.
3. Language and culture.   I. Title.
P106.W574   1984   801'.95   83-9191
ISBN 0-226-89501-7

FOR MARY

Contents

Contents

Preface

Our life is a life of language, and this book is about what that fact has meant, and can mean, to us and to others. In form it is a book of essays about a set of texts that range rather widely in both cultural context and generic type. I begin with the *Iliad*, Thucydides' *History*, and Plato's *Gorgias*; then consider works by Swift, Johnson, and Austen; and end with Burke's *Reflections* and some American constitutional materials. As one would expect of such a book, it is in the first place—and perhaps in the last as well—about the particular texts with which it engages: what they mean, how they can be understood, what connections can be drawn among them, what force and life they can be seen to have in our present world, and so on. But to be about a text is also to be about the process by which we respond to it, and one aim of this book is accordingly to work out what I call a way of reading, a set of conceptions and questions and attitudes—a language of criticism, if you will—that the reader can learn, if he chooses, and put to work in his own life. To some extent, then, this book is about the method by which it proceeds. In this it has much in common with other works of literary and rhetorical criticism and also with certain forms of teaching, such as law teaching, that are also instructions primarily in process and method. One of my reasons for choosing a wide diversity of texts is to show that this way of reading can work to unite matters that are often thought to belong apart.

But to talk of method may be a bit misleading, for what I mean by a way of reading is not a value-free technique of investigation—one that can be applied, without itself being changed, to whatever text comes along. What I mean, rather, is a way of learning and responding that is itself deeply informed by, and in important senses derived from, the texts engaged with here. For in my view each of these texts teaches us how it should be "read" in the large sense in which I will use that term: it teaches us how it should be understood and lived with, and this in turn teaches us much about what kind of life we can and ought to have, who we can and ought to be. Reading is an engagement of the mind that changes the mind, and this book is about that change.

This book thus has an aspiration beyond the explication of texts and beyond the elaboration of a way of reading. It is concerned with a set of substantive questions that are suggested by and exemplified in these texts: about the nature of language, self, and community; about the character of literary and political action; about the ways in which culture is defined and transformed. It is about a set of processes that cut across everything we shall read: how we define ourselves and others in what we say, how we create community and reconstitute our culture in language. The three levels of aspiration I describe are not discrete; they are interconnected, for one set of questions grows naturally out of another, and discoveries at any level affect conclusions at the others; indeed, I think it is impossible to pursue one kind of question without at least implicitly addressing the others as well.

This book thus begins as a book of readings—and remains one to the end—but it also becomes a book of its own, with its own shape and significance, in large part constructed out of those readings. For the reader this means that this book will ask for, and is intended to reward, attention of several different kinds. One set of aims is addressed on the surface of the text, which is meant to be straightforward, expository, and directly accessible on a first reading; another set is addressed in the way the book is put together, in its repetitions and connections and juxtapositions, even in the voice in which it speaks. In some respects this book is thus performative, creative, even imagistic in character; for out of the materials selected, and in their arrangement, it intends to make something of its own, with its own claims to meaning. In these respects it will prove harder to summarize, and slower to read, than many books are; and it asks not to be read through once only but to be thought about and lived with.

I will both proceed from and seek to validate the premise implicit in the title of this book, that language is not stable but changing and that it is perpetually remade by its speakers, who are themselves remade, both as individuals and as communities, in what they say. The basic question asked of each text is how it performs as a response to this situation. We shall thus be interested less in what differentiates the genres represented here—poetry and philosophy and history and moral essays and fiction and politics and law—than in what unites them, in the tree of which they are several branches. For they are all species of the more general activity that is our true subject: the double activity of claiming meaning for experience and of establishing relations with others in language. Each of the texts we shall read proceeds by working upon a world it defines and leading its reader to a position within it. To put it in a single word, I would say that our subject is rhetoric, if by that is meant the study of the ways in which character and community—and motive, value, reason, social structure, everything, in short, that makes a culture—are defined and made real in performances of language. Whenever you speak, you define a character for yourself and for at least one other—your audience—and make a community at least between the two of you; and you do this in a language that is of necessity provided to you by others and modified in your use of it. How this complex process works, and can work well, is our concern. As the object of art is beauty and of philosophy truth, the object of rhetoric is justice: the constitution of a social world.

As for the intended audience of this book, I hope that the general reader can read it through without being confused or misled and also that each chapter can be read with interest by a specialist who regularly works with the text it examines. I have attempted to make this possible—with what success readers of both kinds must judge for themselves—by including more by way of background and summary than the specialist normally requires and by relegating to the notes most of my attempts to locate what I say in the context of what others have said.*

ALTHOUGH THIS BOOK may not appear to be a book about law, I am a lawyer and my intended audience includes lawyers among others. To them in particular I wish to say that this book, despite appearances, is really about law from beginning to end. Indeed, one of its objects, which does not become explicit until the last chapter, is to set forth a rather different conception of law from those that presently prevail in academic circles: as an art essentially literary and rhetorical in nature, a way of establishing meaning and constituting community in language.

I can perhaps make clear something of the nature of my claim by explaining its origins. When I went to law school after doing graduate work in English literature, I found a continuity in my work that I had not ex-

---

*At the end of the book I have collected notes of two kinds. The bibliographical notes present brief background information about the particular text and refer the reader to scholarly and critical works with which further reading might begin. In addition, when my position on a major point seems to be controversial, I there set forth in outline the arguments for and against what I say, together with references for the reader to pursue. The end notes, by contrast, contain references that elaborate or complicate particular points made in the text. In the chapters dealing with Greek texts I have presented more of both kinds of materials than I have in the other chapters, assuming that the Greek texts themselves and the relevant scholarship are less readily available to the general reader.

pected. The enterprises of law and literature are in obvious ways very different, but I was still reading and writing, after all—still trying to make sense of what other people said and to speak intelligibly myself, still trying to understand claims of meaning made against a background of tradition and the tests of experience. Indeed, in its hunger to connect the general with the particular, in its metaphorical movements, and in its constant and forced recognition of the limits of mind and language, the law seemed to me a kind of poetry.[1]

When I turned to the practice and teaching of law, I continued to read literary texts, not because they met an aesthetic need unsatisfied by the law but because I could not do law as I wished without the kind of education these texts continually offered and demanded. And I found the converse to be true as well: my literary reading was continually informed by my experience of law, by watching people struggle with language and fact and experience as they tried to make a language of meaning adequate to their needs, and by the exasperations and clarifications I myself experienced in using both legal and other languages to make claims of meaning and to establish relations with others. For me the activities of law and literature, usually thought of as separate, were in a deep sense the same thing, and I could not do one without the other. The study of certain ancient Greek texts has seemed to complete a field of activity for me, in part because such lines as those between law and literature, so sharply drawn in our contemporary academic discourse, are here rather blurry, if they exist at all.

As this book is about law from beginning to end, so also is it about literature and classical studies. To readers in each field it says that to fulfill the possibilities of what you do you must do something else as well. It is not enough, for example, to read Thucydides' *History* or Jane Austen's *Emma* as sacred and self-justifying texts; the question must be asked what these texts have to say to us, situated as we are in our world as it actually is. I am not saying that the critic or classicist should become a lawyer; I am suggesting that a full fidelity to the texts at the center of one's professional life requires attention also to the culture in which we live, which has formed us and which we form. The question, "What can these texts mean to *us*?" is an essential part of reading them, and it can be answered only by knowing who we are. This has another side as well, for reading texts of the sort examined here is a way of making us "who we are": in our choice of texts, in our responses to them, in what we learn from them, we perpetually remake ourselves and our world.

SUCH IS THE BACKGROUND of what may seem at first, but I hope not in the end, to be a rather fragmented set of interests. In this book I want to show how the texts I place before us can be read, and read together; and in doing this I hope to work out what I call a way of reading that can illuminate not only texts of such kinds as these but the texts that people make in the world whenever they claim meaning for what they see and do.

At one time I thought of calling this an essay toward the definition of a new subject, with a new method, linking the fields of law and literature and perhaps classics and anthropology as well. I might even have given it a name. And it is true that the reader of this book will acquire familiarity with new terms, and perhaps with new ideas, as he or she comes to share the language in which I describe and explain these texts. But perhaps the simple truth is that, as I read these texts, they constitute a world for me, a world I see as one, and in this book I invite the reader to share its life.

Acknowledgments

It is a great pleasure to acknowledge my good fortune in having many friends who have helped me with their criticism and support. I want especially to mention the painstaking assistance and good suggestions given me by Thomas Eisele, Lewis LaRue, and Mary White, each of whom read nearly every word of this manuscript, and to thank them warmly. I am also especially grateful to my colleagues Wayne Booth and James Redfield, who in different ways stimulated much of what I have to say here, and to the students at The University of Chicago with whom I have worked on these texts and ideas. Many others have also contributed or stimulated ideas or have been helpful in other ways, and I wish particularly to thank Arthur Adkins, Theodore Baird, Gerhard Casper, Homer Clark, John Comaroff, David Currie, Judith Davis, Matthew Dickie, D. T. Erwin, Paul Friedrich, Charles Gray, Robert Kaster, Craig Lawson, Alfred McDonnell, Herbert Morris, Nancy Mrazek, Richard Posner, Donald Quander, Lisa Ruddick, Donald Regan, Howard Sayetta, Patricia Sharpe, David Smigelskis, Cass Sunstein, Stanley Szuba, Stuart Tave, Peter Teachout, David Tracy, John Tryneski, Joseph Vining, Bernard Weissbourd, and Peter White. None of them, of course, is responsible for any of my errors.

In addition, I wish to thank The University of Chicago Law School and the National Endowment for the Humanities, who generously granted the support that made the task possible, and Sharon Mikulich, who typed and retyped the manuscript with accuracy and good humor. The translations are my own, but I wish to thank Stanley Szuba for his important assistance with them.

PARTS OF FOUR CHAPTERS of this book have been published elsewhere in somewhat different form and are reprinted here by the kind permission of the copyright holders. Parts of chapters one and nine appeared in my article "Law as Language: Reading Law and Reading Literature," in the *Texas Law Review*, vol. 60, no. 3 (1982), pp. 415–45, © 1982 by The Texas Law Review. Part of chapter two appeared in my article "Homer's Argument with Culture" in *Critical Inquiry*, vol. 7, no. 4 (1981), pp. 707–25, © 1981 by The University of Chicago. Chapter four appeared as part of "The Ethics of Argument: Plato's *Gorgias* and the Modern Lawyer," in the *University of Chicago Law Review*, vol. 50, no. 2 (1983), © 1983 by The University of Chicago.

Ἔοικε δέ . . . περὶ ταὐτὰ καὶ ἐν τοῖς αὐτοῖς εἶναι ἥ τε φιλία καὶ τὸ δίκαιον.

Aristotle, *Nicomachaean Ethics*

Il ne serait pas concevable que ce déchaînement de générosité que l'écrivain provoque fût employé à consacrer une injustice et que le lecteur jouisse de sa liberté en lisant un ouvrage qui approuve ou accepte ou simplement s'abstienne de condamner l'asservissement de l'homme par l'homme.

J.-P. Sartre, *Qu'est-ce que la littérature?*

1

A Way of Reading

When Thucydides wishes to express his sense of the internal chaos brought upon the cities of Greece by the civil wars that arose during the time of the Peloponnesian War, he tells us, among other things, that words themselves lost their meaning. The Greek terms for bravery and cowardice and trust and loyalty and manliness and weakness and moderation, the key terms of value in that world, changed their accepted significance and their role in thought and life.[1] What before would have been called something like idiotic recklessness, for example, was now called stouthearted loyalty to friends; what would have been praised as prudent foresight was now condemned as cowardice. Whether or not Thucydides' report is accurate, he speaks of changes that undoubtedly do occur, though usually more slowly, for others have spoken in similar terms about great changes in language and in life. Clarendon and Burke do so, for example, in lamenting the political transformations of their respective times, and so does Proust when, at the end of his life, he finds uprooted every understanding on which he had founded his social expectations and his sense of himself. Such changes in language may, of course, be felt not as deteriorations but as great advances. The Declaration of Independence, for example, claims to create a new world when it declares its new and self-evident truths; and Thoreau, in a different way, also claims to create a new life and a new language when he goes to live by the pond in the woods.

This book is about such changes in the meaning of language and of the world: about the ways in which words come to have their meanings and to hold or to lose them and how they acquire new meanings, both in the individual mind and in the world. This means, as we shall see, that it is also about the ways in which character is formed—and maintained or lost—by a person, a culture, or a community.

One way to see what is so terrible about the world Thucydides describes is to ask what place you would have within it. For the reader Thucydides addresses, who uses these Greek words of value to organize his experience and to claim a meaning for it, the answer is none at all: in this world no one would see what he sees, respond as he responds, speak as he speaks. Even worse than this imagined isolation for such a reader would be the threat, in some sense the certainty, that to live in this world would lead to central changes within the self. One cannot maintain forever one's language and judgment and feelings against the pressures of a world that works in different ways, for one is in some measure the product of that world.

An alteration in language of the kind I mean is not merely a lexical event, and it is not reversible by insistence upon a set of proper definitions. It is a change in the world and the self, in manners and conduct and sentiment. Changes of this kind are complex and reciprocal in nature. The change in language that Thucydides records, for example, is in part caused by events of another kind, which are only partly verbal— those of the civil war; but the changes in language in turn contribute to the course and nature of that war and do much to define its meaning. The process is reciprocal in another sense as well, for at every stage the change is effected, knowingly or not, by the action of individual people, who at once form and are formed by their language and the events of their world. When language changes meaning, the world changes meaning, and we are part of the world.

One response to the world is to make a text about it, a reorganization of its resources of meaning tentatively achieved in a relation, newly constituted, between reader and writer. This is a way of acting in the world and on the world by using the language of the world. Thucydides' *History* is a response of this kind; so are the other texts we shall examine, and so, indeed, is this book itself. Other activities are also texts in this sense, including the conversations that take place among us, at home or at the office or on the street, whenever we talk about what matters to us. We struggle to make our words work as we wish, to redefine them to meet our needs, and in doing this we remake, in ways however small, our language and our world. The reconstitution of culture in a relation shared between speaker and audience is in fact a universal human activity, engaged in by every speaker in every culture, literate or illiterate, and the texts we shall read in this book can be taken as extraordinarily powerful and instructive examples of this activity. While this book is in some sense about reading, then, it is also about "writing" in the most general sense of the term: about what happens whenever a person uses language to claim a meaning for experience, to act on the world, or to establish relations with another person.

As the title of this chapter suggests, I wish to exemplify what I call a way of reading: a way of engaging the mind with a text, and learning from it, that will affect the way one lives both with other texts, including those of one's own composition, and with other people. The rest of this chapter will present a general account of this way of reading, but I should say now that this can only be an introduction, perhaps something of a guidebook, to what follows; for the way of reading at work here will receive its real definition, and its justification, if any, only in the reader's own experience of this text and of those it speaks about. Perhaps the best way to read this chapter is quickly the first time through and then more deliberately, after one has read one or two of the chapters that follow.

ACTING WITH WORDS

The first stage in the process exemplified here is to expand our conception of "writing," as I have just suggested, to include all action with language that appears in these texts, including not only what the author says but what he represents others as saying. In reading the *Iliad*, for example, we shall examine such events as the interchange between Chryses and Agamemnon that begins the poem, in which the old man asks for the return of his daughter and the Achaean leader denies him, and the ensuing conversations among the Achaeans about the meaning of what has just been done; in reading Thucydides' *History* we shall analyze the speeches in which the cities seek to persuade each other to particular courses of action; in reading *Emma* we shall focus on the kinds of conversation and community that Emma herself establishes with other actors; and so on.

The kind of "action with words" that we shall examine thus covers an enormous range, including in principle all that goes into the management of social life in language, from relations of great intimacy to those of great publicity, such as those that constitute national politics in Athens, England, or America. This means that the kind of text-making that this book is about is not limited to the elevated forms of poetry and history and philosophy and law but includes what happens whenever any of us acts with words in our own lives to claim a meaning for experience or to establish a relation with another. The very activity of reading in which we shall now engage is itself a kind of action with words, in a sense a kind of writing; for the process is completed only in the organization and expression of our responses to what we have read.

The first step in working out a way of talking about both reading and writing, for me at least, is to recognize that these, like other human activities—such as dancing, quarreling, playing football, telling a story, even sleeping—are not susceptible to complete reduction to descriptive or analytic terms. Each of these activities engages parts of the self that do not function in explicitly verbal ways, and behind all of our attempts to describe or direct them remains an experience that is by its nature inexpressible. No one can fully explain what a person does when he writes a sentence or even when he holds out his hand in a signal to stop. Writing is never merely the transfer of information, whether factual or conceptual, from one mind to another, as much of our talk about it assumes, but is always a way of acting both upon the language, which the writer perpetually reconstitutes in his use of it, and upon the reader. Action of this kind can never be wholly explained, and our talk about these things should reflect that fact.

The basic question we shall ask of the texts we read, and of the particular performances within them, will thus be What kind of action with words is this? This question will be elaborated by being broken down into two others: What kind of relationship does this writer establish with his language? and What kind of relationship does he establish with his audience or reader? To put this in other words: What kind of cultural action is this writing? and What kind of social action is it?

The Writer's Relation with His Language

Whenever a person wishes to speak to another, he must speak a language that has its existence outside himself, in the world he inhabits. If he is to be understood, he must use the language of his audience. This language gives him his terms of social and natural description, his words of value, and his materials for reasoning; it establishes the moves by which he can persuade another, or threaten or placate or inform or tease him, or establish terms of cooperation or intimacy; it defines his starting places and stopping places and the ways he may intelligibly proceed from one to the other. Sometimes, of course, he can use words in new ways—can cast new sentences and make new moves—for the user of the language is also its maker; but for the most part his resources are determined by others. What does it mean that he has held out his hand, palm up, or broken a red feather, or looked down and to his right, or used the word "coward"? Such questions as these have objective answers. The ways we have of claiming, establishing, and modifying meaning are furnished for us by our culture, and we cannot simply remake to suit ourselves the sets of significance that constitute our world.

That the forms and materials of speech are established for a speaker by his culture is something we all know as a matter of ordinary experience. Take, for example, the experience of argument in a simple sort of case. Suppose one person touches another, and the second objects. What can possibly be said by the two people about this event, the one in remonstrance, the other in justification? In what sorts of argument might they engage, making what claims or appeals, accepting what modes of reasoning? Suppose the event takes place in each of the following situations: on a street corner in the black ghetto; at a university faculty meeting; in the vestibule of a church; at a labor union meeting; in a police station, one person being an officer, the other not; in a law school classroom; on a baseball field. One can quickly see how differently the arguments might go and can even imagine participating, more or less expertly, in them. Different questions would be asked of the event in each situation; the story would be told in different terms; and different feelings would be expressed, aroused, and countered. Different meanings would be claimed; different moves would be regarded as unanswerable claims to triumph, on the one hand, or as admissions of defeat, on the other. In each case the conversation would have its own shape and texture, its own kind of life; it would define a set of possibilities for asserting and maintaining meaning, for carrying on a collective life.

The resources that establish the possibilities of expression in a particular world thus constitute a discrete intellectual and social entity, and this can be analyzed and criticized. What world of shared meanings do these resources create, and what limits do they impose? What can be done by one who speaks this language, and what cannot? What stage of civilization does this discourse establish? When we ask such questions, the study of language becomes the study of an aspect of culture, and we become its critics.

The relationship that a speaker has with his language may range from the comfortable to the impossible. Sometimes one's language seems a perfect vehicle for speech and action; it can be used almost automatically to say or to do what one wishes. But at other times a speaker may find that he no longer has a language adequate to his needs and purposes, to his sense of himself and his world; his words lose their meaning. In the *Iliad*, for example, this happens to Achilles, who struggles with the language and values of his heroic culture, trying and failing to find a way to speak in a satisfactory way about himself and his experience. It happens also to the interlocutors in Plato's *Gorgias*, who are severely distressed when they are forced to face the contradictions among the platitudes by which they shape their lives. And it happens to Emma, whose language, while seemingly satisfactory to herself, is to the understanding observer utterly impossible; Emma's attempt to create a new world, based on a perverted form of a proper moral discourse, ends in fortunate failure. For each of these speakers, language loses its meaning, and the question is: What can be done about it? Can the speaker make a new language, remake an old one, or find a way to use old terms and understandings to serve new purposes? Can he somehow reconstitute his resources to make them adequate to his needs?

But to put the question that way is to oversimplify, for each speaker is in an important sense the product of the language that he speaks, and who then can he be to remake it? Where can he stand when he tries? In Emma's case, at least, there is the additional complication that the central defect is not in her language at all—not in the resources that her culture makes available to her—but in herself, and the same can in principle be true of anyone. The question, then, is not only how one can reconstitute one's language but how one can learn from it and, in the process, reconstitute one's character and one's life.

These are questions not only for actors within these texts but for the writers of them as well. How, for example, can Homer, composing in an inherited language, created over centuries for the purpose of making a certain kind of heroic verse, find a way to examine and criticize the culture that that language was meant to celebrate? Or consider Plato: if he shows the language of ordinary Greek morality to be impossible, as he does, what language can he speak, and with what claims to meaning?

Thinking about our relationship with our language becomes increasingly difficult as we increasingly recognize its deeply reciprocal character. For while a person acts both with and upon the language that he uses, at once employing and reconstituting its resources, his language at the same time acts upon him. Language is learned only by stages and only for use and by using it; and, as one learns it, one naturally but imperceptibly undergoes changes: changes in attitude and perception and sentiment by which one becomes "acculturated," or "cultured," or perhaps "cultivated."[2] But to learn a language is also to change it, for one constantly makes new gestures and sentences of one's own, new patterns or combinations of meaning. Language is in part a system of invention, an organized way of making new meaning in new circumstances. Some of these inventions are shared with others and become common property; others remain personal, part of the process by which the individual within a culture is differentiated from others who are similarly situated. Culture and the individual self are in this view to be understood not in isolation, as independent systems or structures, but in their reciprocal relations one with the other: the only way they ever exist in the world.

Reading by Imaginary Participation

To examine the relation that a speaker establishes with his language, we must have some sense of the language itself. In reading these texts we shall attempt to achieve this in part by a method that may seem at once naive and intrusive: it is to imagine for a moment that the world of this text is a real world, one in which we are to make our way and must ask how that can be done. This is how we shall read Book One of the *Iliad*, for example, where we are presented with a working culture very different from our own. We shall seek to understand the repertoire of claims and appeals and moves with which these actors define their motives, claim meaning for events, establish positions of their own, or otherwise act meaningfully in this world. This is reading of a reconstructive and participatory kind, an active engagement with the materials of the text in order to learn about the real or imagined world of which they are a part. The hope is that we can establish some sense of the relationship that exists between the speaker and the materials of his culture; that we can experience from the inside, with the intimacy of the artisan, if only in a tentative and momentary way, the life of the language that makes a world.

This is rather like the way in which law students learn to read cases as a way of learning about the world in which they will have to live, and perhaps a description of that process will make this one clearer. On his first day in school, the law student is given a case, or set of cases, just as they appear in the reports, without further guidance, and is asked to reconstruct them from the beginning. His job is to live over in his imagination the experience of the parties and of the lawyers, asking why this choice or that one was made, what he would have done, and how he would have explained himself. He is given a piece of the world in which he will one day have to make his way, and his task is to figure out what that world is like and how to function within it, all on the basis of extremely fragmentary evidence. His primary way of giving attention to a case is by arguing it in his head, by examining the resources for making appeals and claims on each side that constitute what we call the law. He or she tests each statement against other possibilities, wondering why it was not done this way or that, asking how things would go if the facts were changed in such-and-such a particular, suggesting a puzzle that will crack open a particular line of reasoning, proposing an innovation, imagining a way to put a point to jury or judge, and so on. "What would I do with this case?" is his constant question, and it is a complex one; for it is a way of asking simultaneously about many things: about the nature of the resources he is offered by his world; about the way in which he and others can put them to use; about the facts of a particular case; and about his capacity to imagine or to invent new ways of talking that will work in the world he lives in. When he has done, he has mastered the set of persuasive resources that his culture makes available for dealing with a particular situation, and in doing that he has defined their limits. Together, the arguments made on each side establish in the world an idealized conversation in which the resources of the legal culture for claiming meaning and arousing sentiment are at once defined and exhausted and, in this way, exposed to analysis and to criticism.[3] It is as though the sea froze for a moment and we could study the waves; when the argument is done, the waves roll on until the next time someone tries to claim an order for the materials of his or her world.

Analysis

As we reconstruct from a text the resources of meaning that its culture makes available to its members, what questions can we most usefully ask of what we discover? How, that is, can the language we are learning best be understood and analyzed? I will not attempt to set forth in this book a full schematic analysis of any set of resources, for our attention will repeatedly be drawn to other questions in addition to this one; however, it may be worth while to identify here four fundamental questions that will be constantly at work in the somewhat more illustrative and suggestive work that we shall be doing.

1. How is the world of nature defined and presented in this language? To choose examples from our texts, how can the talk we hear about the Aegean Sea, or the English Channel, or the landscape of England, or the stars of a summer night, or the great size of the American continent function as an appeal or as a claim in this world? Often, especially in the modern world, it may seem as though the speakers live in a world without nature, a fact not without its own importance. But nature usually appears after all, in the form, perhaps, of the river or desert that makes a "natural" political boundary; or of "resources" that are being depleted or conserved or of an "environment" that is being desecrated or saved; or of the "natural" fact that the fetus is a person or that gender cannot be changed. It is hard to make a language in which the facts of nature have no place.

Nature also appears in symbols and metaphors, often in ways that are obvious within the culture but not outside it. Thus we can ask What is the meaning, in this language, of the spider? Of the rose? Of the sprig of heather? Of the sow that eats her farrow? Of the north wind? Of the annual floods? Of the field of goldenrod?

2. What social universe is constituted in this discourse, and how can it be understood? One might start with the characters represented in the particular text, including the speaker, and simply ask who they are. What does it mean that we have a "vicar" here, or a "warrior," or a "cop," or a "priest of Apollo," or a "verray parfit gentil knight," or an "*anax andrōn*" or someone called Sir Thomas or Caesar Augustus or Chief Justice? Each of these names implies an identity that is defined by a relationship with others: the vicar is a cleric, but among clerics he is very low in status; a Chief Justice is a judge of a particular bench with a particular jurisdic-

tion, with a clearly defined relationship with other judges and lawyers; and so on.

Beyond the individual person are the practices and activities that make up the life of the social world. For example, Book One of the *Iliad* begins with a father who is seeking the return of his daughter from another man and demonstrating the way that his culture gives him to do this, by supplication and ransom. Likewise, the "Bookseller's Dedication" to Swift's *A Tale of a Tub* depends for its effect on our understanding in some detail the contemporary practice of dedicating a literary work to a wealthy patron.

Social and political institutions are such practices set up on a permanent basis. They are not objects, though that is how we often talk about them, but complex sets of understandings, relations, and activities. They are ways of talking that can be learned and understood, and they play their part in constituting a world. For example, when, in the first book of Thucydides' *History*, we see ambassadors come from Corcyra to Athens to seek an alliance against Corinth, we already know that it is here agreed that cities will at least sometimes be spoken of as if they were single entities, which can be represented by single speakers; as if they could make and break agreements, i.e., as if they were moral agents; and, as we quickly discover when we examine the speeches, as if they were capable of feeling gratitude and shame and of reasoning about justice and expediency. This is, of course, not the only way to talk about a collection of people in a place; it is a constitutive fiction, a way of talking and acting that creates a public world.

3. What are the central terms of meaning and value in this discourse, and how do they function with one another to create patterns of motive and significance?

When we look at particular words, it is not their translation into statements of equivalence that we should seek but an understanding of the possibilities they represent for making and changing the world. This can be done only by giving attention to the shape and working of the language itself. Think of such terms in our own language as "honor," "dignity," "privacy," "property," "liberty," "friend," "teacher," "family," "marriage," "child," "university," or "school." Such words do not operate in ordinary speech as restatable concepts but as words with a life and force of their own. They cannot be replaced with definitions, as though they were parts of a closed system, for they constitute unique resources, of mixed fact and value, and their translation into other terms would destroy their nature. Their meaning resides not in their reducibility to other terms but in their irreducibility; it resides in the particular ways each can be combined with other words in a wide variety of contexts. They operate indeed in part as gestures, with a meaning that cannot be restated.

Words normally acquire this sort of complexity and richness gradually, as the incremental effect of many uses by many speakers and writers. Of course, even the most powerful word may be used by a particular writer as a kind of empty cliché, while another writer may give new and complex significance to what had been an ordinary term. The text itself, that is, will often act on its language in such a way as to give its words a kind of significance within it that they would otherwise lack in the discourse of the reader. As applied to poetry this observation is commonplace, for we have long been trained to see the poem, among other things, as a pattern of images and words that acquire unique significance through their association, operating in several planes or dimensions at once. But, as we shall see, what is true of poetry can be true of prose as well, even of expository prose; and in this book we shall have a continual interest both in the nature of the resources that a particular language offers its users—in the special meanings of its words—and in the ways in which a particular writer manages to change those meanings, to good effect or bad.*

4. What forms and methods of reasoning are held out here as valid? What shifts or transitions does a particular text assume will pass unquestioned, and what does it recognize the need to defend? What kinds of argument does it advance as authoritative? What is the place here, for example, of analogy, of deduction, of reasoning from general probability or from particular example? What is unanswerable, what unanswered?

This line of inquiry is encumbered for us by that part of our own intellectual tradition that has sought to reserve the term "reasoning" for two forms of it: deductive reasoning, which is tautological in nature, and inductive, which is empirical. In this book we shall for the most part be concerned with passages that do not use these forms of reasoning, and we shall therefore need to employ different terms of description and analysis. It would be wrong, for example, to try to reduce every passage of reasoning to a scheme of propositions of which it could be said that such and such were the fact and value assumptions with which the writer worked and that such and such was his logic. For one reasons not only with "propositions" but with metaphors, analogies, general truths, statements of feeling and attitude, particular definitions of self and audience, certain fidelities or infidelities to tradition or consistency, and the like, and one moves not only by logic but by association and analogy and image, by what seems natural and right.†

---

*Consider, for example, the way Burke gives new meaning to the word "toleration" in the paragraph quoted below, page 217.

†These matters are discussed at somewhat greater length in the Note on Fact, Value, and Reason on pages 21–23, below.

Criticism

As one reads through a series of texts in the reconstructive and participatory way I have just described, trying to bring to life and understanding the culture enacted in each and to see the achievement of the particular text against that background, description will inevitably lead to comparison, and comparison to evaluation. Are there ways in which we can criticize and judge the cultures and texts we read, admiring the resources of one, deploring the kind of life achieved in another, and so on? This means judging both the resources that a culture makes available to its members and the particular reconstitution of those resources achieved by a text we are reading. Can we become in this double sense critics of civilization—judges of culture and of individual contributions to it?

This is a question to which the book as a whole is a response, and any answer will acquire meaning only as the reader comes to make and to share particular judgments in particular cases. We cannot expect to proceed by discovering and applying rules of excellence, for the judgments of which I speak are not simply intellectual processes but aspects of being and becoming. They begin as individual responses to particular moments of actuality in a text, tentatively made, which then become the object first of contemplation and reexamination, then of shared attention. What is called for is the self-education of perception and response, a process that cannot be systematized or hurried.

There are two reasons why it is difficult to talk in abstract terms, especially ahead of time, about the kinds of judgments to be made in this book. In the first place, these judgments are not purely rational or logical and therefore are not susceptible to summary at the purely conceptual level. But in the course of our work with particular texts I hope that we can gradually establish a common language in which generalization is possible. The summary in the final chapter will accordingly mean something quite different to the reader who has read his way through the book from what it would mean to one who might turn to it now. The second difficulty can be put in the form of a question. Since we are all products of our own culture, from what position can we possibly claim to make valid judgments about it, about other cultures, or about the contributions a particular writer makes to his culture, whatever it is? This is a central problem of modern thought, and one of the grander ambitions of this book is to provide a rather modest response to it. The basic idea is this: in each text the writer establishes a relation with his or her reader, a community of two that can be understood and judged in terms that are not bound by the language and culture in which the text is composed; this community can become a basis for judging the writer's culture and his

13

own relation to it; and, in my view, the texts examined here collectively establish a set of examples and standards by which such communities of two can themselves be judged.

But this is to get a bit ahead of ourselves. For the moment it is perhaps enough to say that many of the judgments invited in this book are akin to the judgments one regularly passes on literary or musical or other artistic works or to judgments traditionally made in legal or historical criticism. These kinds of judgments can in fact be regarded as special or particular cases of the kind of criticism with which this book is concerned, and perhaps I can call upon the reader's experience of them as a way of defining the expectations appropriate to the present work. All these are judgments, after all, about what is better and worse in civilization; they are not scientific and cannot be reduced to rules or criteria, yet they make up an immensely important part of our shared life. We make such judgments all the time, sometimes tentatively, sometimes with confidence. We share and elaborate these judgments with others and, in the process, often complicate or change them. We recognize that some of our judgments are better than others and that some of our friends are better judges than others. We have a sense of fallibility and an eagerness to improve. In this sense we are all critics of civilization already and are engaged in teaching each other how to be critics; our aim here is to learn more about something we already do.[4]

The Relation between the Writer and the Reader: Establishing a Community in Language

Our work will also have a second focus, rather different from the first. This focus is on two sets of human relationships: those established by speakers in these worlds with each other and those established by the writers of these texts with their readers. In the *Iliad*, for example, we shall see Achilles and Agamemnon, who are allies, establish an implacable hostility, and we shall see Achilles and Priam, who are enemies, establish a miraculous friendship. Plato's *Gorgias* is explicitly about certain kinds of relations established in language—the destructive flattery of what Socrates calls "rhetoric," the educative friendship of "dialectic"— and, in the conversations of which the text is made, we see examples of both. *Emma* presents a kind of taxonomy of friendships, both healthy and perverted, each of which is defined, established, and maintained in language. In Thucydides and Burke we see similar questions presented on a national or international scale. What kinds of relations can exist among the cities of Greece, for example, or among the people of England? And, to turn to our own country, what can it mean to establish a public world on the premise that "All men are created equal"?

We shall be equally interested in the relationship established between each of the writers of these texts and his or her reader. The idea of such a relationship may be somewhat novel or uncomfortable—a book is not a person after all—but I mean nothing mysterious or out of the ordinary. Every writer speaks to an audience and in doing so of necessity establishes a relationship with that audience based on the experience of reading that the text itself offers. The experience of reading is not vicarious—it involves no pretense that one is an Achaean or a Trojan—but actual and intimate, first occurring in the present, then living in the memory; and the community that a text establishes likewise has a real existence in the world. While a book is not a person, a writer always is; and writing is always a kind of social action: a proposed engagement of one mind with another.

To start with, a writer always gives himself a character in what he writes; it shows in the tone of voice he adopts, in the signals he gives the reader as to how to take that tone of voice, in the attitudes he invites his reader to have toward the world or toward people or ideas within it, in the straightforwardness or trickiness with which he addresses his reader—his honesty or falseness—and in the way he treats the materials of his language and culture. The reader is also a character in the world created by the text. For in acting on the reader as he does, the writer calls on him to function out of what he knows and is—for one who brings nothing to a text cannot be a reader of it—and to realize some of his possibilities for perception and response, for making judgments and taking positions. To engage with a text is to become different from what one was. There is a sense in which every text may be said to define an ideal reader, which it asks its audience to become, or to approximate, for the moment at least and perhaps forever.

When I say that a text asks its reader to become someone and that, by doing so, it establishes a relationship with him, I mean to speak literally, not metaphorically. Think, for example, of what happens when a person opposed to racism is told a successful racist joke: he laughs and hates himself for laughing; he feels degraded, and properly so, because the object of the joke is to degrade. He need not feel ashamed of having aggressive feelings or of the fact that they can be stimulated by racist humor, for something like that is true of anyone. Nor should he be ashamed that these possibilities are realized in him against his will, for a great work of literature might evoke such possibilities against the will of the reader in order to help him understand and correct them, and this would be an act of the deepest friendship. But the one who responds to the joke is ashamed of having this happen at the instigation of one who wishes to use those possibilities as the basis for ridicule or contempt; he is ashamed at who he has become in this relationship with this speaker. Literary texts can of course work the same way, by stimulating aggressive or destructive impulses, not in order to subject them to understanding, to an integration with a larger context of impulses and values, but in order to give them free rein. This is a momentary and uncorrected disintegration of the reader, and it is no act of friendship.

But in other cases the conception of the ideal reader can point to the central achievement of a great text. To consider a text discussed below, for example, one could say of Jane Austen's *Emma*—so little of which is understood the first time through or even the second—that it is meant to teach the reader how to read his way into becoming a member of the audience it defines: one who understands each shift of tone, who shares the judgments the text invites him or her to make, and who feels the sentiments proper to the circumstances. This takes time and rereading. The first time through the opening sentence, for example, the reader may not catch on to the fact that there is something wrong here:

> Emma Woodhouse, handsome, clever, and rich, with
> a comfortable home and a happy disposition, seemed to
> unite some of the best blessings of existence; and had
> lived nearly twenty-one years in the world with very
> little to distress or vex her.

But as the reader thinks about it, perhaps first alerted by the word "seemed" to a distance between the narrator and the character, he or she will come to understand that the "blessings" listed, while blessings indeed, are only "some" blessings, worth very little without other, more important blessings, chief among them the lessons to be learned by "distress" and vexation. Even on the third or fourth reading, however, even when he or she fully understands the spoiled and self-indulgent character of Emma's reverie, the reader may miss something that is essential to understanding the text as a whole, Emma's good sense and deep kindness in her treatment of her father in the passage that follows.

At the end, if the book has done its work and we have done ours, we have become better readers, and for Jane Austen this means better people as well. This is a moral fiction, not because it teaches us that vice is punished or anything like that, but by virtue of the capacities for perception and being that it realizes in its reader.

Sometimes the reader becomes a character of his own against the intention of the text, when he rejects or repudiates it. Indeed one element in the relationship between reader and writer is a kind of negotiation in which the reader constantly asks himself what this text is asking him to assent to and to become and whether or not he wishes to acquiesce. The reader's engagement with the text is thus by its nature tentative: while responding to the text he is always asking how he is responding, who he is becoming, and checking that against the other things he is. Sometimes he is fooled, as by the racist joke, when he becomes a momentary and chagrined racist, or by the style of Ernest Hemingway, perhaps, when he becomes a sentimentalist; but sometimes—and this is the central point— he is educated, for reading is a process in which the reader himself, through a process of assimilation and rejection, response and judgment, becomes more fully one set of the things that it is possible for him to be. Reading works by a perpetual interchange between the person that a text asks you to become and the other things you are.*

The true center of value of a text, its most important meaning, is to be found in the community that it establishes with its reader. It is here that the author offers his reader a place to stand, a place from which he can observe and judge the characters and events of the world he creates, indeed the world itself. When Burke writes about the constitution of Great Britain, for example, he offers us another constitution, in his text, between himself and his readers, by which the British constitution is to be measured, and the true "dialectic" that Plato celebrates is not the activity performed by Socrates in relation to his interlocutors but that performed by Plato's text with its reader; and so on.†

This means that all literature, fictional and nonfictional, necessarily has an ethical and political dimension, for it always entails the definition of at least two roles (writer and reader) and the establishment of a relationship between them that can be seen to have both political and ethical content. (Usually a text defines others roles as well, enacted by the real or

---

*It is of course something of an oversimplification to speak of an actual reader becoming "the" ideal reader of a particular text. Each of us brings his own set of experiences and presuppositions to the text, and each of us thus becomes, or refuses to become, his own particular version of the "ideal reader." The process of negotiation and judgment by which this happens is enormously complex, as various responses and opinions are contrasted with one another. The part of the mind that manages this process, deciding what to accept and what to reject, is what might be called the "central reader"; this is the part that a text ultimately seeks to reach and educate.

†There may of course be a disparity between the values a writer actually exhibits and those that he claims. We are all familiar, for example, with the self-righteous moralist who preaches love for all mankind but who in his talk and manners is far from loving, and we know the apostle of liberty who allows no room for argument from his reader or anyone else. What matters is who the writer actually is in his relationship with us, not who he pretends to be.

fictional people about whom it speaks, and it establishes relations with them too, performed in the ways it speaks about them.) Of course these textual relations are merely offered to us as readers, not imposed on us, and they require our cooperation if they are to become actual; but this does not mean that the offer, or the relations established by the offer, once it is accepted, are not real. To speak to another in a way that respects him or her as a source of experience and meaning and value different from oneself is to constitute a community based on values that have direct political significance; and the same can also be said of talk that reduces the reader to an object of manipulation, by appealing to one part of his experience or personality in denial of the rest. (Sentimentality is thus a political as well as an aesthetic vice.)

I hope to show that the textual community can be understood in ethical and political terms across the whole range of texts we shall read and the genres they exemplify, from epic poetry in the *Iliad* to the legal texts of our own constitutional tradition. If we can find a way to describe and judge the relations established by these texts with their readers, we shall have a ground for judging more formal and explicit political relations as well. It is such a standard of judgment that I think these texts, properly read, can be seen to offer us; it is this fact indeed, not their historical sequence, that explains their selection and arrangement.

What are the criteria of judgment these texts collectively establish? At the most general level, a statement of them will hardly surprise: recognition of the equal value of other people, and integration of the various aspects of self and experience into meaningful wholes. What I hope to show is how these conceptions arise from a reading of these texts and are given by them a vastly richer and more biting content than any summary statement can possibly have. I hope, too, to show how the logic of these values extends from the relationship of two with which we begin—the writer and his reader—to the largest political communities. These texts will, in my view, teach us how to judge our own political communities, their rulers and their policies, from the family to the nation and beyond.

THE IDEA OF READING at work in this book is not simply the old-fashioned one of the discovery of meaning, nor is it the new-fashioned one of the creation of meaning by a community of readers; instead, it is the idea of an interaction between mind and text that works like an interaction between people—it is in fact a species of that—and the expectations we bring to a text should be similar to those we bring to people we know in our lives. Just as one person does not have a fixed and identical meaning for every other person, even for every friend—even for the same friend—so a work as rich and varied as the *Iliad* does not have, cannot have, identical and fixed meanings for every reader, or every good reader, or even for the same reader all his life. But this is not to say, either of the text or of the person, that it has no actual identity of its own or that it has only the identity that some group decides that it should have. Both have real identities, but these are too complex ever to be completely known and too alive to be fixed in a single interpretation forever. One reason this is true is that the reader, both of texts and of people, changes as he reads: one is always learning to see more clearly what is there and to respond to it more fully, or at least differently, and, in the process, one is oneself always changing, in relation to friend or to text. It is in this process of learning and change that much of the meaning of a text or of a friendship resides; a text is in fact largely about the ways in which its reader will be changed by reading it. The reader who knows Jane Austen well, for example, will not be like every other reader who knows her well, but he will be deeply different from what he would have been had he never read her at all.

The meaning of a text is thus not simply to be found within it, to be dug out like a kind of mineral treasure, nor does it come from the reader, as if he were a kind of movie projector. It resides in the life of reading itself, to which both text and reader contribute. And in this process the readers of a text can assist one another. I know that your *Iliad* will never be identical with mine, and in my reading of it in chapter two it is not my object to make it so. What I do hope is that the process by which you check what I say against that text, both as you remember it and as you reread it, will help you establish a fuller understanding of it and a deeper relation with it; and I know that the understanding and relation will be yours, not mine. What is to be sought among readings of a text, whether readings by different people or successive readings by oneself, is not identity, for there can never be that, but consistency and mutual instructiveness.

I HOPE THAT THE READER will by now have a clearer sense of what I mean when I say that this book is about reading and is meant to exemplify a way of reading. It is about "reading" defined so generously as to include writing and speaking, indeed all the ways we have of living with language and with each other through language; and it is about a "way of reading" conceived of not merely as a method of analysis but as a way of attending and responding to a text and a situation, of acting and being in relation to language and to other people. Its subject is a complex one, including the ways in which we constitute selves and communities in language and how the character we give ourselves can be maintained or lost; the ways in which words acquire and lose their special meanings; the ways in which one person can act with words to recognize or deny, to diminish or enhance, another. It is, above all, about the nature of the struggle to establish and maintain a proper relationship with one's language and with other people when language, self, and community are in a constant process of reciprocal change.

NOTE

There are two matters treated above on which some readers may wish me to say a bit more: my expansive use of the word "language" and my view of the relation that exists among the domains of fact, value, and reason.

Language and Culture

In this book I use the word "language" as a partial synonym for the word "culture," and this usage should perhaps be explained. Of course it is not the words themselves, as sounds or writings, that constitute resources or impose limits of the kind that interest me; it is the expectations that govern the way words may be used, the understandings that define some uses as appropriate, others as shocking or impossible. And these expectations necessarily involve substantive questions. For example, what is an intolerable insult or degradation to a self-respecting Achaean warrior? What delicacy toward the feelings of others is required of an English gentleman? What ought to be the proper meaning of the words "patience" or "hypocrisy"? It is substantive understanding of this kind by which the famous paradoxes of Socrates—e.g., "It is better to suffer injustice than to do it"—can be seen as the cultural impossibilities that they are.

One might understandably wish to use a word like "culture" for such substantive systems of value and meaning, reserving the word "language" for the code in which they are signified, but I believe that such a distinction between language and culture, while useful enough for certain kinds of linguistic analysis, is for our purposes a false one. The language, after all, is the repository of the kinds of meaning and relation that make a culture what it is. In it, as I have suggested, one can find the terms by which the natural world is classified and represented, those by which the social universe is constituted, and those terms of motive and value by which action is directed and judged. In a sense we literally are the language that we speak, for the particular culture that makes us a "we"—that defines and connects us, that differentiates us from others—is enacted and embedded in our language.

For our purposes it is appropriate to use the word "language" to include the understandings by which linguistic terms and structures are put to use, including understandings that determine shades of social meaning and expressions of attitude. Understandings governing syntax and grammar are, after all, continuous with those regulating tone of voice, social character, ironic implication, and manners generally. The term "language" can easily include all the resources for meaning that a culture makes available to its members, and to conceive of language in such a way has the merit of naturally directing our attention not to an independent system or abstract structure called a "culture" but to the relationship between the individual person, living through time, and the inherited resources for meaning and action that he or she struggles to learn and to control. Another way to talk about the basic attitudes and resources that give shape to a particular world, and limit it, would be to use the word "ideology." But that term has figured largely in battles with which we have nothing to do, and it has overtones that are hard to control; in addition, its very abstractness and objective quality remove it even farther from individual experience than the word "culture" and so render it less susceptible to confident verification or falsification by the reader. When I speak of your "language," you can confirm or deny; when I speak of your "ideology," your denials may be treated as mere defenses.

In all of this I do not mean to suggest that every question is merely a question of language or that by speaking the right way we can make anything come to pass. Both within the self and in the world there are limits on what we can do, and this book is not only about language but what lies beyond it: Achilles' wrath, the Athenians' self-love and Emma's, the persistent self-deception of which Samuel Johnson speaks. The world of language mediates between the languageless within and the languageless without. But I do mean to direct attention to the fact that, whenever we speak or write, whether we know it or not and for good or ill, we contribute to the creation of a culture, and we do so both in the way we reconstitute our language and in the relation we establish with the other person who is our reader. Every way of reading is a way of being and acting in the world.

Fact, Value, and Reason

In discussing the analysis of a language or culture, I suggest in the text that we ought not to accept sharp distinctions between discourses of Fact, Value, and Reason. These distinctions, powerfully present in contemporary intellectual life, are drawn from the physical sciences as they existed at a certain stage, and they are essential to the structure of certain forms of thought that call themselves scientific, especially to certain forms of social science. The basic idea is that there is a world of fact—brute fact or raw fact—external to the observer and that what the scientist does is to observe or record that world; then, using the principles of inductive logic, he discovers the regularities by which its phenomena can be predicted. In doing this, he must obviously put his own values aside and apply only his reason to the external facts; for essential to the conception of this sort of science is the repeatable character of every discovery. This is indeed what gives these discoveries their special character as knowledge.

Obviously, this kind of enterprise has its value, but equally obviously, it is very different from the one in which I am here engaged; for my interest is in the ways in which worlds of meaning and value are constituted by people as they speak and write—in knowledge of another kind—and in these processes the lines between value and fact and reason cannot be rigidly maintained.

To start with the line between "fact" and "value": terms of what seem to be social "description" are often used as powerful terms of "value" in argument. Think of the force of such terms as "university" or "judge" or "family" or "teacher." It does not make sense to call these terms either factual or normative, for they are both at once, in a kind of shifting mixture. Sometimes they are used with one emphasis, sometimes with another, but (unless they are stipulatively defined for the purposes of a closed system) they always retain both possibilities. It would be hard to limit "poverty" or "disease" or "happiness" to purely factual uses. And, except for very limited purposes, one cannot remake the language by stripping away something called the "value component" of such terms, leaving only the factual element, or vice versa.

Likewise, there is no sharp line between "reasoning" and talk about facts and values. It is true that science has drawn such a distinction, seeking to rely exclusively on the two forms of thought, deductive and empirical, to which it gives a special standing. The appeal of these two forms of reasoning is at heart the same: each lays claim to the power of proof. Agreement with a proposition of mathematics or of science can simply be compelled by the force of a logical or empirical demonstration. But on the matters that really divide a community, agreement cannot be compelled by the force of logic or by the demonstration of facts; it can only be reached, by discussion and argument, and it is with these processes, not with the methods of science, that this book is concerned. The region that can be ruled by the methods of logic and science, and by the parts of the mind that function in these ways, is, after all, rather small; and, for good or ill, much the larger part of human life must proceed without the certainties these two forms of reasoning provide. What I mean by "reasoning" in this book is thus not pure rationality of these scientific kinds but a way of making sense in an actual situation in a particular culture.

It may illuminate my point to consider for a moment two common ways of talking about values, both of which seem to me inappropriate for our purposes. One is to regard "value-choices" as outside the zone of rational talk, as though nothing intelligent or persuasive could be said on such matters. In this view, value-choices are merely preferences that cannot be subjected to intelligent and shared examination. (This is what economics does as a matter of principle.) Of course it is precisely on such questions, where the critical and creative intelligence seems so often to stop, that it is most essential to our life and culture that it function well. To define the term "rationality" or "reason" to exclude reasoning about matters of value is to demean language and to be false to experience.

The other view is to assume that the proper way to talk about values is to treat them as concepts, that is, as stipulatively defined terms in a closed conceptual structure or analytic scheme. The central assumption of this form of discourse—an assumption that is indeed essential to its logical integrity—is that words shall have exactly the same meaning each time they are used and that a word's stipulated statement of meaning could be substituted for the word itself with no loss beyond the awkwardness this would entail. But this is to deny to our most important terms their actual force and nature. In actual life our central words are what Empson calls complex words, and our central mode of discourse is what Barfield calls poetic; to deny our language and minds these resources in favor of a mode of thought impossibly mathematical would be to diminish our intellectual and social lives beyond reason.[5]

2

Poetry and the World of Two

Cultural Criticism and the Ideal of Friendship in the *Iliad*

The *Iliad* begins by defining a working rhetorical world, an imagined civilization that is immediately apprehensible by us even across the barriers of time and language: we know where we are right away and with a remarkable kind of sureness. This is the heroic culture within which the characters of the poem will speak and act. Yet, as we shall see, the poet also finds a way to examine this culture by making a place outside it, from which it can be seen and criticized. He creates, that is, what I have called a textual community with his reader,[1] the life and terms of which provide the standard by which the culture is to be judged. What is perhaps most remarkable is that he does all this while working wholly within a language that seems to have been made for the celebration of the heroic culture he criticizes. In this chapter we shall direct our attention to the character of this heroic culture and its meaning for those who must live on its terms; to the kind of relationship that the poet establishes with the language that defines it; and to the nature of the community he creates with his reader, that is, with you and me.

The fact that the *Iliad* is entirely composed in the special language of Greek epic poetry has important consequences for the actors within the world of the poem, who must use its resources of speech and action to live by; for the reader of the poem, whose experience is for the moment constituted by it; and of course for the poet himself. These consequences are of two rather different kinds. First, the use of this language seems to commit its user at least temporarily to a particular set of heroic values and attitudes, indeed to a set of social facts as well, whether he likes it or not. Second, the formulaic and artificial character of this language, particularly as employed by this poet, has certain consequences that are in the first instance aesthetic but deeply affect the quality and texture of every aspect of life in this poem, both for the actor within it and for the reader of it. It is with consequences of this second kind that I shall begin.

The Culture of Book One

Clarity Bounded by Silence: The Epic Language of the Iliad

The language of the *Iliad* was developed over a period of several centuries—beginning perhaps in Mycenaean times and ending during the seventh century—as the special language in which heroic poetry was composed. The poetry of this tradition was oral and improvisatory, and this language, gradually put together by the poets, was appropriate to composition of that sort; for it established sets of terms and phrases that readily combined to meet the requirements of the meter, a syntactically reduced set of metrically appropriate patterns in which the poet's mind might work as he orally composed his verse. This is not to say that the use of this language was easy or mechanical, for, as this poem makes clear, it remains a real language, with remarkable resources for certain kinds of invention. But it remains true that the forms in which the poet of the *Iliad* speaks were established for him by an inherited language, artificial and formulaic in character, which was made to express in poetry an imagined world, drawn from an otherwise forgotten past.

This language gives a special quality to the world it creates, a quality difficult to describe but one that affects the texture and feel of every aspect of life in the poem, from the representation of the natural universe to the definition of character and the expression of thought and feeling. Perhaps I can best define the quality I mean by directing attention to the composition of the following passage from Book One, describing Apollo's response to Chryses' prayer for assistance, after he has been rebuffed by Agamemnon:

> So he spoke in prayer, and Phoebus Apollo heard him
> and came down from the peaks of Olympus, angered in
> his heart, carrying his bow and covered quiver at his
> shoulder; the arrows rang on the shoulder of the angry
> one as he moved; he came like the night. He sat down
> apart from the ships and shot an arrow. A terrible clang
> arose from his silver bow. First he went against the
> mules and flashing dogs, but then against the men
> themselves he let fly a sharp shaft and kept shooting.
> Always there were fires of corpses, burning thickly.
> Nine days along the camp went the arrows of the
> god, and on the tenth Achilles called the people to an
> assembly. [l. 43–54]*

---

*The translations throughout are my own.

This is not an attempted representation of the way life is lived in any real world, contemporary or ancient, but a world made and remade by art. Time and space can be collapsed at will, and point of view can be shifted dramatically, without excuse or explanation. The characters may be men, gods, or heroes, inhabiting a "camp" or "Troy" or "Olympus"; they may bound down mountainsides and shoot magic arrows or do whatever the occasion calls for, because this world is made for the purposes of the poem and can be whatever it requires. It is constantly before us that this world is made, not found, and this fact gives it an expressive quality of a kind we find in art, not life: it speaks to us directly.

One way that this directness is felt is through the absence of what might be called waste, such as passages telling us who the gods are or how they hear things or why the dogs are "flashing," as if we didn't know or as if such things could be explained. But the term can be given a wider range, for the poem as a whole has a quality, reflected at least in the Greek of the passage quoted above, of immediacy or presence, a kind of tactile life, that is achieved in part by one's sense of a bright edge beyond which the reader is not able to go. This quality of directness or immediacy is familiar enough in the plastic arts. A work of sculpture speaks to us directly through its mass and texture and form, but it speaks that way only; otherwise it is as silent as the stone or metal of which it is made as to what it means. So too with a painting or with a tapestry (such as the cloak Helen is weaving in Book Three) or with an artfully worked shield (like the one made for Achilles in Book Eighteen).[2]

Here, of course, the mode of expression and apprehension is literary, not visual; one could not happily draw a picture of Homer's Apollo shooting the mules and men any more than one could draw him playing the phorminx on Olympus in the scene that closes Book One. (Even Chryses' supplication, complete with staff and fillet, which seems so pictorial, would look false in any illustration one can imagine.) But this art works in much the same way as visual art: what we have before us is perfectly plain, as directly stated as one could imagine—Apollo comes down the mountain, his arrows clanging as he moves—but we also know that there are questions we simply cannot ask of this text. "How does Apollo move? Is he bigger than a man? Is he visible? What happens to the arrows he shoots? Does he collect them?" We are told here what a child working on an intellectual puzzle or riddle is told by his parent or teacher when he asks for more facts: "You have been given all you need to know." We are not to place this text against a social or natural world with which it can be said to be continuous in order to pursue questions about the poem in the other, real, world—the streets of London, say, or the mines or trenches of France. What we do know about this world we know as we know few other things: "He came like the night." But we will not be told what it means, and we cannot find out the answer to our questions elsewhere.

The epic language is so clearly shaped and firmly established that the text enacts a remarkable sense of assurance about the world it creates: this is the way to make epic poetry, and this is the world we make when we do so, it seems to declare, and in a tone that permits no questioning. But beyond what is said with such assurance there is nothing to say. The special quality that the epic language gives to the world it creates is thus a sense of clarity bounded by silence, of extraordinary certainty placed against the wholly unknown. The bright edge that shapes this world and makes it speak to us directly is also responsible for its enormous and expressive silence.

This silence—the strange reticence of the poet who seems to tell us everything about the universe he presents with such an uninterrupted surface, but who withdraws from what he has made, leaving us to make of it what we can—is one source of the magnificent life of this poem. For in leaving to us the task of making sense of what is before us, this silence forces our continuous and attentive engagement with the poem itself. Every detail, every shift, may matter.

The Uncertain Life of the Heroic World

There is another and perhaps more obvious sense in which the language of the *Iliad* gives shape to our experience; for this epic language is especially appropriate to the celebration of the particular heroic culture of the *Iliad*, which is defined for us in Book One and elaborated in the rest of the poem. One might sketch this culture by saying that within it the great aim of life is the acquisition and maintenance of honor, particularly in the form of battle-prizes—in Book One, women; in other places, gold, armor, and horses—which are of value both in themselves, as riches, and as marks of esteem and status. Excellence in this world consists of strength in battle and skill in counsel, that is, in the qualities that bring success to the self, to the household to which each man belongs and for which he acts, and to the common enterprise. Honor is primarily the reward of achievement, not of virtue. The basic unit of this culture is the *oikos*, or household, and it is to this that primary loyalty is owed; beyond it there is almost nothing a modern scholar would call social organization. This is a heroic culture, and its values seem to be clear, unquestioned, and coherent.

But this summary of the values and structure of the world of Book One, while in its way informative and, I believe, accurate enough, says little about the way the culture works, either in the imagined life of the poem or in the actual experience of the reader. For a culture, real or imagined, is not a scheme or a structure but a way of living, and, to be understood, it must be seen as offering a set of resources for speech and conduct: a set of things that it is possible on certain occasions to say—by way, for example, of appeal, command, claim, or argument; and a set of things that it is possible to do, a set of moves with force and shape and meaning of their own—such as the offering of a ransom for one's daughter or the calling of an assembly.

In the poem itself the world of the *Iliad* is presented not in theoretical summary or outline, as I have just done, but in the form in which the real world is always experienced, as a sequence of events taking place against an assumed background, as a narrative in a living world. The story, you will remember, is this: Chryses, a priest of Apollo, comes to the Achaean camp to ransom back his daughter, who is held by Agamemnon as his prize of battle. When Agamemnon refuses to return the girl, Chryses prays for assistance to Apollo, who sends a plague upon the Achaeans. After nine days of the plague, Achilles calls an assembly and suggests that a seer be consulted. The seer says that, to appease Apollo, they must return the girl to her father. Agamemnon hates this verdict but acquiesces in it; he claims, however, that his loss should be made good by the others. When Achilles resists, Agamemnon claims Achilles' prize, the girl Briseis. It is at this point, and over this issue, that the quarrel between Achilles and Agamemnon can be said to begin. Thus arises the wrath of Achilles, the career of which is the subject of the poem.

As this story unfolds, the reader is naturally full of questions. Who are the actors in this world? What, for example, does it mean to be a warrior, a priest, or a god? What practices make up the world the actors share— ransom, prayer, supplication, boast, assembly, and so on—and how do they work? When one actor appeals to another, in what terms of value, and subject to what procedures, does he do so? "Return to me my daughter, because . . ."? We are invited by the poem itself to ask what resources the culture offers for the definition of character, for social action, for reasoning and persuasion, and for claims of meaning. We are invited to ask, in short, what life would be like lived in such a world as this, and it is part of the work of the poem to offer us a response.

Consider, for example, the way in which Chryses appeals to Agamemnon for the return of his daughter. As an abstract matter the possibilities for expression here are almost endless. Chryses might make a claim for her as a matter of moral or legal right; or he might try to get her back by arousing sympathy, or fear, or by making promises or threats; or he might try to buy her back, by offering a price for her; and so on. What does Chryses in fact do, and what is its significance?

[H]e came to the swift ships of the Achaeans, seeking to
get back his daughter and bearing boundless ransoms
and holding the circlet of far-shooting Apollo in his
hands, on the golden scepter. He beseeched all of the
Achaeans, and especially the two sons of Atreus, leaders
of the people:
  "Sons of Atreus and you other well-greaved Achaeans, to you may the gods who dwell on Olympus grant
the destruction of the city of Priam and a prosperous
return; but may you set my daughter free and receive
these ransoms, revering Zeus's son, far-shooting
Apollo."
  Thereupon all of the other Achaeans spoke out their
approval, to respect the priest and receive the shining
ransoms. But this did not please Agamemnon, son of
Atreus, in his heart, and he sent him harshly away.
[1. 8–25]

We have here a world so clearly defined and understood that ritual, at
least in the loose sense in which such a term may be applied to Chryses'
act of submission, can take place. For Chryses' appeal does not take any
of the forms I suggested above, nor is it argument of any sort. It is instead
a kind of supplication through ritual obeisance, which in this world is a
comprehensible and expected gesture, a resource appropriate to a certain
kind of situation. This submission of course entails an implied threat, for
Chryses emphasizes his relation to Apollo; but in form it is unqualified: in
actually tendering (not merely promising) the gifts, which are in value
beyond any appropriate price,[3] Chryses gives up everything first, exposing himself to the power of the other as the defeated wolf bares its throat
to the victor. And the very structure of the address enacts submission, for
his prayer for Achaean success precedes his request and is not in any way
conditioned upon a favorable response to it. The form and meaning of
such a supplication seem plain to everyone: it is as clear and intelligible
as behavior can be.
  When Agamemnon rebuffs him, Chryses shows that he knows another equally clear, equally conventional, way of asking for something.
He prays to Apollo:

  "Hear me, Silver-bow, you who protect Chryse and
divine Killa and rule over Tenedos with your might.
Smintheus, if ever I roofed a temple pleasing to you, or
if ever I burned fat thigh-pieces of bulls and goats for

you, accomplish my desire: may the Danaans pay for
my tears with your arrows." [1. 37–42]

This prayer is as formal as the supplication, but it operates on different
principles. In the supplication and in the last clause of the prayer, the
mood employed is the optative ("may it happen that . . ."), but in the first
and main part of the prayer it is the intimate, intense imperative: "hear
. . . and grant me this desire."[4] And, unlike the supplication, the prayer is
in form and substance conditional ("if ever . . .") and thus operates as a
claim that, if the condition is true, the wish should be granted. It is not a
claim of right, as under a rule of entitlement, but a claim on a prior relationship. This claim is not a claim to recompense, nor does it imply a net
imbalance of benefits between the parties which should now be re-
dressed. Indeed, when Chryses does, finally, ask Apollo to stop the plague,
after he has received his daughter back, the prayer takes this form: "even
as once before you heard my prayer, and honored me, and greatly hurt
the people of the Achaeans, so now, once again, grant me my desire"
(1. 453–55).

In making both appeals, Chryses is represented simply as one who has
occasion to do these things and knows how to do them. There is nothing
individual about him, no self beyond the typical. He is not represented as
having any special competence as a speaker or actor, nor does one get the
sense that one course of action or speech is chosen, by art or instinct,
over another. His smooth, almost inevitable, performance is in this sense
not an achievement of any kind. It is the stuff of which this world is
made; it is simply an enactment of what the situation calls for. The formulaic language in which the appeals are framed, itself so conventional
and syntactically reduced, reinforces the sense that these things could be
said and done in no other way.

But this is not a mechanically determined world of stock responses to
stock situations, in which expected language has its expected effect, nor
can it be reduced to certain theoretical premises of which the action can
be called an elaboration. What we have here are the conditions on which
life will be led—a very different matter. For if they are looked at from another point of view, from the way they work in the world, the resources of
thought and argument displayed in Book One are most uncertain; in an
important sense they are unstable, despite their evident clarity. Chryses
knows exactly how to make these persuasive addresses; what he does not
know is whether they will work. In similar fashion throughout Book One,
one actor or another will make a claim or take a step with perfect assurance as to form but real doubt as to consequences. Beneath the surface certainties, the "knowing how to do" that makes the texture of the
poem so tangible and sure, there is the deepest uncertainty. And the un-

certainty of this world extends to its very existence: when Achilles half-draws his sword against Agamemnon, only to be stopped by Athena, the fabric of the community itself is in peril. A simple blow could end it all. This is a world that trembles on the edge of dissolution.

The clarity is bounded by silence, the uncertainty by danger, and this tension gives the material an enormous life, not only for the reader but for the imaginary participants, who must themselves be, among other things, alert readers and users of the clear marks of an uncertain and precarious world.

Doubleness

But there is more than uncertainty here; there is opposition as well, an organized or composed tension that repeatedly gives a certain active character to our experience of the text. The doubleness of aspect and perception that I mean here is not hidden in a tension between surface and depth, like the doubleness of symbolism or irony, but is so plainly exhibited on the surface of the poem that the reader can fail to know that he has seen it, as if something so exposed could not be art. The contrasting possibilities for expression and experience are not merely hinted at or suggested; they are made manifest before our eyes. The familiar bright edge shapes them, the poet places them, and the rest is up to us.

Consider, for example, the contrasting ways in which Agamemnon's rejection of Chryses is characterized. At line 11 it is said that he "dishonored" the priest, and that is of course the way in which the matter is ultimately talked about by everyone; but at the moment of rejection it is said merely that "it pleased not Agamemnon in his heart" to return the girl. These two phrases are from different systems of thought and feeling and meaning: the language of honor, of persuasion and gifts and submission, and the language of simple preference, of will and anger, which simply rejects, and does not answer, the former. It is the languages themselves that are placed in opposition: "I don't care whether it dishonors you, it pleases me to keep the girl"; "I don't care what pleases you, this dishonors me." Out of either language a responsive discourse could be built, with claims of will meeting claims of will or with a real argument about what "dishonor" should mean here. But the languages themselves do not permit a conversation across the line that separates them.[5]

The prize girls are talked about in a similarly double way. From one perspective they are the external symbols of the honor the hero's prowess has earned, almost a currency of honor, and they are often talked of in this way. But from another point of view they are seen as individual people, companions of the bed and otherwise, toward whom feelings extend and the men talk of them that way too. Or take such a simple thing as the

31

moment when the Achaeans urge Agamemnon to "honor the priest" and "receive the ransoms" by returning the girl. The two infinitive phrases are set side by side, paratactically not syntactically; no preference is given to one over the other, no causal or temporal connection suggested beyond simultaneity, no puzzle expressed as to how the same act can have two meanings. It is just there.

The opposition between Agamemnon and Achilles has a similar double quality. It is on the one hand a perfectly probable conflict between two men who occupy naturally contending positions, respectively of political and personal superiority; but it is also a conflict between two person-alities or psychologies, an antagonism that is natural in another sense. As the story unfolds, it is told both ways at once, and the result—the deep quarrel—is here, as such things are in real life and for much the same reasons, overdetermined.

These instances mark a division between what might be called two levels of discourse in this culture: between the language of social struc-ture and motivation, including talk about honor and prizes, on the one hand, and, on the other, a contrasting talk about the materials of life described in more nearly natural terms, about men and women, about anger ("it pleases not the heart"), and so on. The unsettling tension be-tween them casts continual doubt on the firmness with which character-izations of the first sort can be made. This not only contributes to the sense of uncertainty that characterizes this world but establishes a kind of argument internal to the culture, a sense that everything is to be de-bated; and this sense, as we shall see, also marks its political life.

A Politics of Persuasion

I

What we would call the public or political life of this world is rhetorical rather than bureaucratic in character, and it would be a mistake to think that there was here a political structure or organization that could be re-produced on a modern "organization chart." Formal questions of au-thority, competence, and jurisdiction, which are second nature to us, are neither asked nor answered here. This world has a life of a different kind.

Consider, for example, as simple a question as this: what can be said of the position of Agamemnon as leader of the expedition beyond the fact that it is somehow special? When we are told that it "pleases not the heart" of Agamemnon to grant Chryses' appeal, no one—neither Chryses nor any of the others—argues with Agamemnon, saying that it is wrong or imprudent to refuse the supplication or making any other claims against his denial. But is Agamemnon's power to refuse such an offer, against the expressed wishes of the others, an aspect of his special position, or would any of the warriors have been equally free to act on his own will in such a case? We are simply not told.[6] Chryses' speech to the Achaeans places the relationship between Agamemnon and the others very precisely, as it were, by placing it very ambiguously: we are told that he supplicated "all the Achaeans, but especially the two sons of Atreus, leaders of the people," and his address is double: "O sons of Atreus and you other well-greaved Achaeans." Chryses' method of address leaves this political question open, as he found it, and this ambiguity is part of his diplomacy.

Not only are we unclear as to what the nature of Agamemnon's position as leader may be; our next question, "What is that position grounded upon?" is never given an answer. We are never told with authority, for example, whether Agamemnon is the leader because he organized the expedition, because he brought with him the largest force, because he rules over the most people,[7] or because of oaths taken by the others, or, perhaps, because of certain unstated facts of custom or heredity—because, for example, he is the older brother of Menelaus. He is the leader, we are told, and we are shown how in this instance he and Achilles attempt to give conflicting meanings to that fact. But the life of this world cannot be reduced to a scheme or structure.

What is true of Agamemnon's position is true of virtually every question that we would call political. Consider, for example, the assembly called, at Hera's prompting, by Achilles. We do learn here that among the resources of this world is a certain kind of forum, a public meeting, which any man of a certain class may apparently call and, subject to certain procedures, address.

But understanding what use Achilles makes of this resource is more difficult. He suggests that a seer be consulted, and accordingly, after assurances of protection from Achilles, Calchas the seer tells them what everyone must already have known, that Apollo was punishing them for Agamemnon's treatment of Chryses. One way to read this obviously stage-managed performance—Calchas speaks right up on cue, without being asked—is as a sort of insult by false politeness. (Achilles could presumably have gone privately to Agamemnon, perhaps with other important men, and have avoided this confrontation.) On this reading the egregious specificity of Achilles' assurance of protection—"not even if you mean Agamemnon, who now declares himself to be the best by far of the Achaeans"—would be deliberately provocative. But we might read what Achilles says and does with a different emphasis and regard the calling of the assembly not as an insult but as a refusal to be seen to prejudge, as a form of what we would call due process.[8] However obvious the result may be, the forms of assembly and consultation do give a certain standing both to Achilles' assurances and to Calchas' proposed remedy. And the fury of Agamemnon's response to Calchas, revealing how close this world always is to violent disintegration, makes Achilles' specific assurances seem far less gratuitous. The calling of the assembly can be read as an attempt, among other things, to maintain and operate the culture under stress—as a fiction in aid of decorum and propriety.

A proper reading of this scene would reflect both possibilities, admitting an uncertainty of significance, a doubleness of meaning, that is by now familiar. But on either reading of the events one thing is plain: no one in the poem thinks of the assembly in the terms most familiar to us, of right and power and function and jurisdiction, nor is there in all of this any institutional language that could serve as the basis for argument about the propriety of the invocation of the assembly, about its powers or processes, or about its relation to Agamemnon as leader.

Argument on the merits of particular questions moves in much the same ambiguous, competitive, and unsettling way. Consider, for example, the central dispute between Agamemnon and Achilles. Agamemnon responds to Calchas by expressing his rage at him and his desire to keep Chryseis, the girl; but then he suddenly shifts: "But even so I will give her back if it is better" (1. 116). This is followed by his command (to whom it is given is not clear) that he be presented with another prize, "lest I alone of the Argives be without a prize, since that would not be fitting" (1. 118–19). Achilles meets this as follows:

> "How shall the great-hearted Achaeans give you a
> prize? We do not know of great heaps of common goods
> piled up anywhere; the things we have plundered from
> the cities are all distributed and it is not fitting for the
> people to collect these things back again. Do you now
> send her away, for the god's sake; we Achaeans will re-
> pay you three and four times over, if ever Zeus should
> grant that we may sack the well-walled city of Troy."
> [1. 123–29]

This sets off an argument on the issue: what is fitting to be done here? Someone must be deprived, for the moment, of a prize, the external sign of prowess that serves as the mark of one's honor. But who should it be? The issue is stated with the directness of a modern legal case: there are apparently two accepted conceptions of what is "fitting," only one of which can be satisfied. It is like what happens in law when two lines of precedent, both solidly established, are seen to point opposite ways when a case that no one ever thought of comes up or when two rules of law are suddenly found to be in conflict. It is as though the world had discovered a hole in our way of talking.

Notice that these speakers use their language to make more than one claim at once. For example, Agamemnon's command to "make ready a prize for me" addresses no specific audience, and this enables him to assert, "I can command about these matters and here is what I think," without running the risk of actual disobedience. When Achilles uses the first-person plural to say what "we shall give you," he not only identifies himself with the Achaeans but claims to speak for them. In the next passage, Agamemnon threatens to take a prize "from you or Ajax or Odysseus. And he shall be angry whom I visit. But we shall consider these things later; come, now let us launch a black ship, . . ." (1. 138–41). This shift, characteristic of Agamemnon, leaves the threat stated but not acted upon; he has established a precedent, of the weakest kind, perhaps, but a precedent. The fury of Achilles' response can be read in part as directed to this attempt, familiar in the politics of every age, to make a claim and exclude an answer.

It is remarkable that the culture provides the intellectual and rhetorical material by which an opposition such as this can be defined—what is "fitting"?—but apparently no material by which it can be authoritatively addressed and resolved. No conventions of argument exist, and no authoritative agencies, by which a settled meaning for the term might be established and the dispute be brought to a close; more than that, there does not even seem to be an impulse to solve the case in general rather than specific terms. The question is always particular, and the central issue is always this: Who shall dominate, and who shall submit?

II

In such a world the central political act is not to command from a position of authority or to invoke an agency with powers to decide but to claim that things should be seen and spoken of in a certain way, and this claim will succeed only when other people are persuaded: this is a politics of persuasion. One may say that its fundamental term is the complex word *peithō*, which is usually defined as "to persuade" in the active voice, "to obey" in the middle and passive. Consider, for example, the following uses of the term from the argument between Achilles and Agamemnon: "you will not persuade me" (1. 132); "how can any of the Achaeans obey you?" (1. 150). What these uses of the term bring home is that there is a felt continuity in this world between the moment of persuasion and the act of obedience, that what is at stake in an argument is nothing less than what we would call power and authority. To persuade is to compel obedience; to obey is to be persuaded. When examined from this point of view, nearly every speech in Book One can be said to have "persuasion" or "obedience" as its object.

Peithō has a rich set of associations even in the small sample of uses

35

that appear in Book One. It is, not surprisingly, connected with the existence of authority—Agamemnon is defined by Calchas as the "one the Achaeans obey" (1. 79)—and with the word *sēmainō*, which means "to give orders by making signs" (1. 289). It is also connected with "hear" or "respond to," as in Achilles' statement that "he who obeys the gods, him they especially hear" (1. 218), and with "fear," as in the line in which the abused and rejected Chryses "was afraid and obeyed the command [to depart]" (1. 33). But perhaps its most important association is with reconciliation, as we see, for example, in Nestor's speech proposing a compromise:

> "These people [in Nestor's past] listened to my plans
> and were *persuaded* by my word. Do you, too, *obey*,
> since to *comply* is better. Do not you, Agamemnon, take
> away his maiden, excellent though you are, but let her
> be, since to him, first, the sons of the Achaeans gave
> her as a prize. Nor do you, son of Peleus, wish to strive
> with the king, since never does a scepter-holding king,
> to whom Zeus has given glory, have an equal share of
> honor. If you are strong, and a goddess mother bore
> you, yet he is more powerful, since he rules over more
> men. Son of Atreus, leave off your anger. And I myself
> entreat you to lay aside your wrath against Achilles, he
> who is a great bulwark for the Achaeans against evil
> war." [1. 273–84. The italicized words translate various
> forms of the Greek verb *peithō*, "to persuade or obey."]

Here Nestor seeks to persuade the men to a form of reconciliation that itself operates by a kind of mutual persuasion: each man would give up what he most wants to the other, in an act of mutual submission, and be satisfied.

Persuasion can thus operate not only as a way of reducing another to one's dominion but as a means of establishing harmony. It is this sort of persuasion that the members of the embassy in Book Nine conceive of themselves as attempting when they seek to bring Achilles back into the community; it reaches its fullest form in the final scene, when Achilles, persuaded by his mother to return the body of Hector, achieves a momentary reconciliation with Priam.

Persuadability in this sense is the central value of Achaean collective life, the means by which the community maintains itself. Ajax as much as says so explicitly, when Achilles refuses reconciliation in Book Nine; he declares that "anyone" will receive appropriate compensation and be satisfied, even for the death of a brother or a child, but not Achilles

(9. 632). A disposition to be reconciled, to put in the past what belongs in the past, is important in any world, but it becomes absolutely necessary when there are no communal agencies to impose it. Without it the chain of reciprocating grievances could go on forever, in an eventually unintelligible sequence of perpetual violence.

Nestor's speech is important to us for still another reason, because it is an attempt to organize language and life in a new way.[9] The method of persuasion proposed here, by an act of submission, is of course traditional. But the suggestion that the submission be mutual is a highly inventive attempt to reorder the materials of the culture to deal with a conflict that could not otherwise be addressed in its terms. It is a proposal for cultural change.

As things work out, of course, the proposal fails; it is almost ignored by the disputants. This may suggest that the proposal is fatuous (what else should we expect from a garrulous old man?), that the proposed submissions are not really mutual (on the point that both care about most, their relative status, Agamemnon would win), or that there is an anger here that is simply not amenable to restraint. But it is plain that Nestor's attempt to reorganize the rhetorical material of his world fails, and this failure demonstrates the limits of the malleability of the language: this, at least, one cannot make it do. Where persuasion fails, the boundaries of the culture are defined; and what this means here is that the crisis that has emerged cannot be solved.

III

The narrative of Book One presents what seems at first to be a discrete and manageable problem: how to respond to Chryses' plea for his daughter's return. No one could foresee what, when it happens, is so natural a consequence, the direct and unresolvable conflict between Agamemnon and Achilles, leading, as it does, to the breakdown of the community. Just as often happens in life, steps are taken by one side or the other with no knowledge, indeed, with mistaken hopes, as to how things will turn out. Each of the actors—Chryses, Agamemnon, Achilles, Calchas, and Nestor—tries to manage the rhetorical resources of his culture to have things seen and felt his way, to achieve what he wishes, and each does so with considerable skill but with incomplete success. Each acts in understandable and natural—indeed, almost necessary—ways but, in doing so, contributes to a movement beyond his understanding or control. This story is like a war, both in its small and seemingly irrelevant beginnings and in the way things move; for what has happened no one thought of and no one wanted. The events have a life of their own.

In this way what begins as a secondary question—whether Agamemnon should be compensated now or later for the loss of the girl Chryseis—becomes by natural stages an intolerable confrontation. Agamemnon cannot bear Achilles' resistance, nor can he accept his compromise. Achilles cannot stand Agamemnon's threat, nor will he acquiesce in postponing the resolution of the issue, and he decides to depart. The dispute is unmanageable because it brings to the surface, where it cannot be avoided, the problematic character of Agamemnon's relation to the other warriors, especially to Achilles. Agamemnon is an equal among equals, for that is what it means to be an Achaean warrior. But he is also in some undefined sense the leader of the expedition. In still another sense, he is the inferior of Achilles, whose preeminence in battle is never questioned. Since the dispute involves the very question of supremacy or equality, it cannot be compromised.

Where Achilles' withdrawal leaves Agamemnon and the others is plain enough: they are now deprived of the man whom they need most of all. They can try to get on without him; but if they fail, as they do, Agamemnon must take the proper steps—including submission by excessive gifts—to bring Achilles back by restoring his honor. All this is intelligible from what we know of this world.

Achilles' situation, however, is very different. It is clear enough that in his anger he will withdraw, but it is most unclear what that will mean, for him or for us. Achilles at first threatens to return to his home in Phthia, which he has just called "fertile, hero-nourishing," and lying beyond "many shady mountains and the echoing sea" (1. 155–57). But in fact he does not go back to Phthia. The reason is that his goal in life is honor gained in a life of action, and honor, like language, is a function of community. He could never be honored in Phthia in a way that would redress the dishonor he has suffered here. He needs the Achaeans as much as they need him, although for different reasons.[10] He cannot be wholly part of his world, yet he cannot wholly leave it; it is by force of this necessity and not by plan that he becomes a figure on the edge of things, awaiting his moment between the unknown and the known.

The location of a self on the margins of a world, which happens here almost by accident—perhaps its significance was a surprise even to the poet—is a literary and intellectual invention of the first order. It runs from the *Iliad* straight through to such modern figures as Thoreau and Huckleberry Finn and is a literary idea as powerful as the other great Homeric form, the tale of travels. These are both ways of directing attention to the nature of a world from the outside, by comparison or denial. Not that Achilles will prove to be an alienated hero of the modern sort, who works his way out of his society to face the ultimate meaninglessness of things and to fashion an identity for himself. He is not critical of himself, and his criticism of others never purports to be disinterested; he is a creature of passion, not of intellect; he returns to and in a sense becomes a hero of his world. But, as we shall see, what the poet will make of Achilles' movement to the margin of his world is nothing less than the beginnings of social awareness and criticism.

THE POEM AS CRITICISM

The movement to the margin is of course only a beginning, and it would mean little without the development of a way in which our observation of the culture could be clarified and our judgment on it invited. But how can these things be done, especially in a poem composed entirely in the artificial epic language, which was made for the purpose of defining and celebrating this culture? The resources of this language are copious and varied, wonderfully suited to the creation of a heroic world and to the depiction of heroic character and action, and its conventionality in diction and phrasing is no doubt responsible for much of the certainty and clarity of expression that characterizes the surface of this poem. But the language certainly suggests no methods by which the imaginary culture it defines can be criticized or judged. Criticism requires both terms of judgment and a place to stand, and how can the poet offer us these? Yet out of such materials Homer made a poem of which we can say that its art is self-regarding; that it subjects to a special kind of criticism the world its resources were designed to create; and that in the way its traditional language is used we can see something very different from the tradition itself, the mind of Homer at work. How this happens is our subject.

Patterns of Meaning

The primary way in which Homer moves his reader from a position within his imagined world, and accepting of it, to an external position from which it can be seen and judged is by organizing the traditional epic materials into patterns of meaning that have a significance different from anything that is or could be said directly in the epic language itself. He works by an art of juxtaposition that at once distances the reader from the heroic culture and defines a central value by which it can be judged.

Simone Weil speaks to this point in a famous essay celebrating what she calls the "extraordinary sense of equity" in the *Iliad*.[11] Homer describes Achaean and Trojan deaths, she observes, in identical terms, expressive of identical feelings; and in doing this he enacts for us a central value of the poem—a value distinct from those expressed by any character in it: the recognition of the equal humanity of the people who must suffer on both sides. "One is barely aware that the poet is a Greek and not a Trojan."[12]

The characteristic of the Homeric style that Simone Weil identifies is not confined to the death passages but runs throughout the poem: it is that context seems to have little effect on statement. A death is a death, Trojan or Achaean; a feast or voyage is presented in similar terms whatever the occasion; the same language describes the same events. It is a little as if each item were a polished bit or shape that was placed, without itself being changed, next to others, themselves unchanged. One consequence of this style is that there is on the surface of things a remarkable equality of treatment, a lack of hierarchy or priority. This is an "equity" that goes far beyond impartiality between Achaean and Trojan. It is an acceptance of the conditions of existence so strong as to become a marvelous hospitality to life in all its forms and aspects, a love of the world itself.[13] This is one source of the great freshness of the *Iliad*, and perhaps it is the quality that led Samuel Johnson to say of Homer that he more than any other poet arouses a "restless and unquenchable curiosity" in the reader.[14]

But are these qualities of impartiality and freshness, and the implicit cultural criticism they make possible, merely happy accidents of this way of making poetry, unlooked-for benefits of the language in which the poem is composed? In some sense, after all, any user of the language would have done the same. Or are these qualities seriously meant and achieved by art?

I think that there is an art at work here and that it is responsible both for the particular kind of freshness and impartiality that we find in this text and for the way these qualities function as values central to the life of the poem. This is an art of arrangement and location, and it can be discovered in the way the poet orders his material, in the patterns or designs his pieces make as well as (perhaps more than) in the way the pieces themselves are made. Like a mosaic, the design so made means something very different from what any of the pieces, standing alone, would mean, something that in fact could not be expressed directly in the language of the poem.

At the end of Book Eight, for example, there is a passage that describes in a simile the Trojan watchfires seen on the plain; they are compared to stars seen on a clear, still night by a shepherd, whose heart they make glad. In an important article the late Adam Parry argues that the formulaic nature of Homer's language is responsible for what seems to Parry the inappropriateness of this simile; that is, the passage seems to contain no recognition that in this context, after a day of Achaean defeat and Trojan advance, the fires represent to the Achaeans a terrible threat of destruction. For Parry this is an instance of a general phenomenon: "the formulaic character of Homer's language means that everything in the world is regularly presented as all men (all men within the poem, that is) commonly perceive it."[15] Thus there is only "one best way" to describe a multitude of watchfires, one that expresses admiration at their beauty, and that way is used here notwithstanding its oddness of tone. Parry's choice of this passage is infelicitous, to say the least, for very little of it is repeated, in a formulaic way, elsewhere in the poem; in fact, Homer speaks elsewhere of watchfires in quite different language, expressing quite different feelings.[16] And the very qualities of the watchfires passage that seem to Parry inappropriate have in fact a plain artistic function, for this passage operates as an appeal to normalcy, to a world without war, where night is safe and beautiful. It speaks to us in a way that a passage likening the watchfires to a volcano, say, or the fires of Hades, could never do.

Much of the force of the appeal comes from what could be called its purity, itself an effect of the formulaic language: the night of the shepherd is seen in a kind of isolation, as if it were the only thing in the world. This invites an absorption into the feeling of the scene that clarifies the line between what the stars mean in the world of the shepherd and what the watchfires mean in the world of war. Homer's way of writing as if there were no context is in fact a way of sharpening the effect of context itself.

From beginning to end the poem is made of such relations as these, and they constitute a method of contemplation and criticism, a way of inviting the reader to think of one thing in terms of another. Consider, for example, Odysseus' trip to return the girl, Chryseis, to her father, in Book One, a passage I never read without surprise. In this tense and heavily charged world, in which everything seems to have been put into potentially violent contention, why are we given this slow and deliberate journey, so heavily formulaic in texture? The answer is that this is a ritual of reconciliation, a kind of healing that will receive its most ample performance at the great moment in Book Twenty-four when Achilles and Priam share their sorrows. A movement begins here that will run throughout the poem.

It is by such an art of arrangement, by placing one thing against another, that Homer subjects to criticism the world of Book One with which he began; he does not work, as we would expect of a writer today, by elaborating a competing language of motive and value but by ordering his materials into patterns of experience that teach the reader something different from anything the material itself seems to say.[17] In a way, the poem as a whole thus takes the form of an argument. By this I do not mean argument in the ratiocinative sense of a thesis supported by propositions, from which it can be said to proceed by the rules of logic or by the laws of probability, but argument as an activity of critical engagement, a definition of resources and a testing of limits that results in the creation of a new position, taken by the writer and offered to the reader. An argument goes on in the text, but its method is closer to that of music than debate.

It has long been noticed that many of the similes that occur throughout the poem invoke, as the watchfires passage does, a world of peace, of threshing and milk pails and stables and shepherds and the hunt.[18] The reader moves from one world to the other and back again, and the movement invites comparison and judgment. Similarly, in the Shield of Achilles, which encompasses, as it were, the whole universe of human life—marriage and law and vineyards and music and herding—war is but a single scene among many, and this placement is a form of teaching.

The patterns of larger narrative units work in similar ways. Consider, for example, what happens after Book One. This book seems to promise a story consisting of little more than a battle leading to severe Achaean losses, a successful supplication of Achilles followed by his return to battle, and finally the Achaean victory (or perhaps a story of defeat), all in a very few books. Measured by such expectations, the poem as actually composed seems to wander off to include all sorts of material irrelevant to its narrative and heroic core. But it is this very material that performs the central function of complicating the heroic premises of Book One and criticizing the world built upon them. Agamemnon's speech to the troops—though it does so by mistake, contrary to its conscious intention—gives us the voice of war-weariness, speaking out of years of exhaustion and loneliness away from home; the duel between Paris and Menelaus is regarded by the soldiers, sitting on the ground with their armor piled beside them, as holding out the possibility of peace at last, and their ritual of oaths and promises expresses a longing for what is not to be; the farewell between Hector and Andromache is a dramatized lament, a full expression of the cost of war; the chance meeting of Diomedes and Glaucus becomes an invocation of hereditary friendship, an institution of peace; the heralds halt and make harmless the duel between Hector and Ajax, and in doing so evoke a world of peace and order, of games not war; and so on. The fighting itself is described in ways that make a sort of reverse appeal against the activities of war and what can be earned by it. For the killings are terribly brutal, full of gruesome detail. They are, in addition, often marked as pathetic by a touch of gentleness; Homer may tell us, for example, where the victim came from, or how many of his brothers have been killed, or where his wife or father is. As for the world of the gods, it can be seen in part as a comic version of the *Iliad* itself, a world where strife and jealousy occur but without harm, where the central fact of the *Iliad*, the certainty of death, is missing, and this works as an invocation of an impossible hope. One could go on and on.

But the structure of the poem is more complex than a simple series of appeals away from the heroic world, for these appeals are themselves often highly qualified by what happens next. After Agamemnon's speech to his troops, for example, Thersites puts the case against the war in terms that no one can accept; this stirs feelings in favor of the war that are reinforced when Nestor and Odysseus make their inspired and forceful calls to arms. The desire for peace is aroused and then supplanted by the spirit of battle. Similarly, Paris (who could be said to represent a side of life not reflected in the heroic world of Book One) is made to seem despicable beside the soldiers who must fight for him. And when Pandarus breaks the truce, the wrongfulness of his act functions as a justification of the Achaean response by battle. The poem does not operate as a string of unconnected appeals from the bad to the good but as a process of statement and counterstatement, a series of appeals and qualifications by which one event or statement or attitude is placed in a context of others; and it is through the relationships so established that the poem gives meaning to its material. This is how the poet works on the expectations and feelings of his reader.

An important instance of the art by which Homer defines one scene in terms of another appears in Book Three, where the duel between Paris and Menalaus is proposed as a way of bringing the war to an end, making innumerable future deaths unnecessary, the winner to take Helen and her possessions. This is a promise of peace. Homer complicates it by directing our attention to that promise seen from another point of view, by taking us to Helen herself, regarded not as the object of the war, as a prize, but as a person. What can this duel between her two husbands mean to her? What victory can she desire? The scene on the wall, where at Priam's request she names and describes the Achaean heroes, enacts the impossibility of her predicament and, by implication, that of everyone. For who are those heroes to her? Are they friends or enemies? In what terms can they be spoken of? In placing her outside the world she observes and cares for, in a position of accidental neutrality, Homer leads the reader to share a point of view, for the moment, from which the activity and emotions of this war can make no sense at all. A somewhat similar complication occurs at the end of Book Five, where Ares, the god of war and the personification of its brutality, has been killing men. When he is caught and wounded by Diomedes in the very act of stripping a corpse, he howls with pain, and it is our disgust at Ares—at what he means—that makes us take satisfaction in what happens to him; but Diomedes' wounding him, the act in which we take such satisfaction, is itself an act of war, of "Ares." We are led to adopt inconsistent points of view simultaneously; we experience statement and counterstatement at the same moment.

The values enacted in this complex way thus go far beyond the sense of the terrible cost of war, for the reader is compelled to recognize, in the actors and in himself, the impulses that find expression and satisfaction in war. The poem is a movement of countering appeals, none of which is discounted or trivialized, including both the impulse to engage in battle and the awareness of its costs. In creating responses of these opposed kinds, one after the other, the poet puts the reader in a position where no single response can work for him. He is forced to attend to a reality larger than any that could be perceived by an actor in the poem or by a person in the real world, engaged, as each is, in meeting the demands of the moment. The poet has in this way placed his reader outside the world he has created, observant and critical of it.

The art of this poem is thus an art of composition in the literal sense, an art of putting together to make a design. It constitutes an original and creative kind of thinking about the world, one that proceeds by poise and contrast, that moves by placing one thing against another and making a third, and thus contemplates and criticizes what it makes. The meaning of the poem, which is different from the meaning of any of its parts or their sum, is found in the experience of its movement in sequence and in time. What starts out as one thing turns into another, and the life of the poem is in that movement.

For the pieces of this poem lie in designs that are more than patterns; they work shifts and surprises that engage the mind in new ways, that open up new possibilities. This is how the world that is presented so directly and immediately, in such established and polished ways—as if there were no other way to talk—becomes an object of contemplation and criticism. This is how it is that Homer, speaking in an inherited language, made to express one sort of world and value, expresses others. He finds a place for himself and for us outside the limits of the language he is using.

Book Nine: Rhetorical Breakdown

In Book Nine the narrative reaches a crisis, and the poem shifts to a more explicit and dramatic method of cultural criticism.

In accordance with the plan of Thetis and Zeus, the Achaeans have now been beaten back to their ships, and Agamemnon is forced to come to terms with Achilles. He seeks reconciliation in the conventional way, by submission through excessive gifts—gifts so opulent that Nestor, who is surely in this respect the voice of tradition, says that no one could scorn them. Yet Achilles does scorn them. He seems to be offered everything he had wanted, everything Thetis had wanted for him, but he rejects it all. Having withdrawn from the heroic world of warfare and prizes because of an injury defined largely in its terms, he now rejects the compensation that was his object; indeed, in much of what he now says he seems to reject the heroic world itself, the only world he knows.

For the reader, this is a surprising event, but the "surprise" is of a special kind; for it is, paradoxically, no surprise at all. It teaches us what we knew all along without knowing that we knew it: that Achilles' refusal is natural and appropriate. The reason we are not shocked or puzzled is that we have been prepared for this moment by the experience of reading the earlier parts of the poem. The shift exhibited by Achilles in fact fulfills the promise of that material and allows us to place it, afterwards, much more firmly than we could have done the first time through. Then the narrative may have seemed to slide a little out of control, to include a bit too much; but now we see, if we did not before, that this material started a new process in the life of the poem, a process that becomes explicit in Achilles' speeches of refusal. The surprise of Book Nine brings into the foreground what had been in the background: the desire to criticize and to reject.

It is remarkable that, although Achilles changes, we do not see him change. A writer using modern conventions would have shown Achilles responding directly to the events of the battle as he observed them himself or learned of them from others; we would have heard him express his feelings of pity or anger or disgust. All that would have been a way for the writer to talk to us, guiding our responses by defining an attitude toward those of Achilles. The refusal in Book Nine would then have been presented as the natural consequence of such responses. Homer cuts this process short and works on the reader directly, not through the imagined experience of Achilles. He prepares us for the change in Achilles not by showing us how the events of the war work on his perceptions and feelings, nor by explicit comment, but by controlling our responses to the events themselves as they are defined and redefined in the patterns of his making. It is by virtue of our own experience as readers that when Achilles places himself partly outside the heroic universe and struggles to speak about it, he speaks in part for us.

By doing things this way Homer achieves an astonishing merger of literary qualities we usually think of as wholly inconsistent. The intensity that comes from close involvement with the career of a single figure (of the sort familiar from tragic drama) is combined with the expansiveness, the variety of incident and character, that seem to belong by necessity to a completely different sort of writing—say, that of Herodotus' *History*. This structure creates a tension between the life of a self and the life of the world, a tension characteristic of what we call epic.

Nowhere is this tension more explicit than in Book Nine, in the confrontations between Achilles and the embassy of Achaeans who seek to persuade him to return to the war. In their speeches to Achilles the heroic culture is defined, and by implication criticized, in a new and dramatic way, as its resources are organized in a complex, self-conscious, and expert effort at persuasion. Everything that can be said in this world on such an occasion is said; everything that can be done is done. The resources of the culture are defined, as it were, by their exhaustion, and in the process a fundamental incoherence is exposed. In Achilles' speeches in response we see an attempt made to define new meanings and new motives; but this effort also fails.

Odysseus

Odysseus speaks first, offering Achilles the gifts of Agamemnon. These are stupendous: seven tripods, ten talents of gold, twenty cauldrons, twelve horses, seven women, and Briseis herself—sexually untouched—all to be delivered immediately. Then, after the fall of Troy, Achilles may fill his ship with gold and bronze, choose twenty women, and marry whichever of Agamemnon's daughters he wishes, with a dowry of seven cities, whose citizens will honor their ruler like a god and accomplish his gentle laws. These gifts and promises seem to constitute a perfect performance of a gesture of submission and reconciliation. If gifts define honor, the honor offered here is immense. The promise seems to be of felicity itself.[19]

This gesture is a ritual submission through excessive recompense, like the propitiation of Apollo by the Achaeans (they returned the girl Chryseis without ransom, and with hecatombs besides) and like Chryses' own submission to Agamemnon when he asked for the return of his daughter. Such a move is a completed statement that implies a reciprocal response. Nothing else need be said; indeed, nothing could be said that would be relevant to the gesture itself.

But in Book Nine much is added to the ritual performance, some of which is consistent with it, some not. Odysseus first appeals to Achilles' loyalty and sympathy by speaking of the peril of the Achaeans and of their need for him. In a way that is obviously meant to stir up Achilles' competitive rage, he describes Hector exulting in his strength and praying for dawn. He utters commonplaces about the incurability of error and the wisdom of self-restraint. All of this is consistent with the offering of gifts, for Odysseus is merely adding complementary reasons for accepting them. But when he has listed the gifts, he shifts to an entirely different ground: "But if the son of Atreus and his gifts are too hateful to you, at least pity all the other Achaeans, exhausted in the field, who will honor you as a god" (9. 300–303). Here Odysseus recognizes that Achilles may hate Agamemnon so much that he will return to battle not because of the gifts but only in spite or disregard of them. He steps out of his role as ambassador and speaks in a different and incompatible capacity. It is a little as if an actor on stage suddenly whispered to the audience in his own voice. He has undone everything he has done. How could Achilles possibly accept gifts offered in such a way?

Achilles' answer is a rich and powerful rejection. He says first that he will speak straight, that he hates a person who says one thing and hides another in his heart. Then:

> "I do not think that Agamemnon, son of Atreus, will
> persuade me, or the rest of the Danaans, since there
> was not any gratitude for fighting ceaselessly, forever,
> with enemy men. A man has an equal lot whether he
> remains behind or fights hard. In like honor are held
> the bad and the noble: he dies the same who does
> nothing as one who does much." [9. 315–20]

Nothing has been given him for the pains he has suffered, for the nights without sleep, for the cities he has sacked. (He compares his ceaseless activity with that of a bird feeding her young.) What he won by battle he took to Agamemnon, sitting back by the ships, who would divide it up, keeping much for himself. All the other warriors still have their prizes; from him alone has Agamemnon taken and kept a spirit-pleasing woman.

> "Let him enjoy lying with her. And yet why must the
> Argives fight with the Trojans? Why did the son of
> Atreus collect and lead these people here? Was it not
> because of Helen the fair-haired? Are the sons of Atreus
> the only mortal men who love their wives? Any good
> and sensible man loves and cares for his wife, as I loved
> this one from my heart, spear-won though she was.
> Now, since he has taken this prize from my hands and
> deceived me, let him not make trial of me. I know him
> well. He will not persuade me." [9. 336–45. The word
> "persuade" translates a form of *peithō*]

He advises Odysseus and the others to look to their safety, for without him Hector cannot be restrained. He says that he will leave on the morrow for Phthia, where there is enough for him. Agamemnon's gifts are hateful, and not if he gave ten times as much, or twenty, or as much as is in Egyptian Thebes, or as many as there are grains of sand or dust, would he persuade the spirit of Achilles, until he had made good this terrible wrong. Achilles would not marry his daughter if she were as beautiful as

Aphrodite, as skillful as Athene. Peleus, his father, will find him a suitable wife.

> "Not worth my life is as much as they say Troy, the well-
> inhabited city, possessed in peacetime, before the sons
> of the Achaeans arrived, or all that the stone threshold
> of the Archer holds within, that of Phoebus Apollo in
> rocky Pytho. Cattle and fat sheep are proper booty, and
> tripods may be acquired, and tawny heads of horses.
> But the life of a man cannot come back again, captured
> or taken, once it has passed the barrier of his teeth. For
> my mother Thetis, the silver-footed goddess, tells me
> that I bear a double fate of death: if, staying here, I
> fight round the city of Troy, my voyage home will per-
> ish, but my glory will live forever; but if I reach home
> and the beloved land of my father, my noble glory will
> perish, but I shall live for a long time." [9. 401–16]

Achilles closes by saying that the ambassadors should announce all this to the Achaeans, except that he invites Phoenix to remain with him, to go home on the morrow, if he chooses: "for I will not compel him to go."

That this is an extraordinary speech—full of metaphors, rhetorical questions, and imagined scenes—even this summary should make plain. Its swift shifts of mood and repeated returns to the burning fact—"he has taken her from me"—enact an insistent rage. So too do its inconsistencies and confusions. Achilles is angry because of an impairment of his honor, yet he rejects the one way in this world in which such an injury can be appeased: submission, expressed by excessive gifts. Injury implies redress, but redress is here rejected. His language goes further and rejects the very enterprise of battle by which honor is won: no prize is worth the hazard of his life. Yet it is essential to his sense of himself that he, the only one who can resist Hector, remain the ultimate hero. Agamemnon's attempt to make things up does not give Achilles what he wants, as one might expect and as Thetis had planned, but is taken almost as an additional insult, the occasion for his decision to depart. Achilles says he will never be persuaded until Agamemnon has made good the injury, but he allows for no way in which that can be done. The anger of Achilles, in short, cannot be contained within or dealt with by the system that gave rise to it. It overwhelms everything: Achilles rejects Agamemnon, his gifts, his daughters, what can be won by battle, the war against Troy, honor itself—everything, in fact, that in the past has moved him to action.

48

Especially interesting is the broken or confused quality of this speech. Not that Achilles is anything but clear and eloquent in expressing his rejection. The problem is that he has, as it were, no other place to go, no language other than his inherited one in which to establish himself and his motives. He lacks the resources with which to make a coherent and intelligible statement, one that will be adequate to his situation. The statement he does make is one of anger and rejection rather than invention and reformulation. A position so defined is held by the feeling of anger, not by the mind or character; it cannot be held firmly, for coherence is essential to stability.

Phoenix

The resolve of Achilles does indeed bend in response to the appeals made by Phoenix and Ajax. After Odysseus' speech, Achilles announces his plan to depart the next morning; but, as we shall see, when Phoenix has spoken, Achilles invites him to stay the night and to decide with him whether or not to go; and after Ajax's speech, Achilles says that he will not fight until the fire has reached his own ships, implying that he will stay after all. While the part of the embassy managed by Odysseus proves to be a complete failure, what the others say reaches and moves Achilles. How can this success be explained, and what does it mean?

Phoenix makes two appeals, the first logical, the second ethical. The logical appeal reinforces Odysseus' argument, and Achilles confidently rejects it. It is this: if Achilles acts now, he will receive the gifts that constitute the mark of his honor, whereas, if he delays, he will fight anyway but perhaps without the gifts. (This is the point of the Meleager story.) Achilles' answer is a clear reiteration of his earlier position: "I do not need such honor" (9. 607).

Phoenix's more effective appeal is ethical, based on his special standing in the household and life of Achilles. For as he now reminds Achilles in detail, Phoenix was welcomed as a suppliant to his father's house and became Achilles' nurse and teacher. He thus combines the attributes of father and mother, and, in addition, he makes a claim that rests on his status as a suppliant to whom the house has been opened. This is an appeal to a culture that is prior to the warrior culture of Book One and constitutive of it, the culture of the household (*oikos*). Phoenix's appeal stirs the deepest loyalties possible in this world, and Achilles is powerless to resist it. But claims of loyalty work both ways, and Phoenix is likewise unable to resist when Achilles responds in a way that acknowledges Phoenix's claim but does not require Achilles to return to battle: he says that Phoenix should remain with him and that together they can decide what to do. Phoenix crosses over, changing sides in affirmation of his own appeal.

Ajax

It is the appeal of Ajax that proves the most successful. He begins by addressing not Achilles but Odysseus, saying that an appeal to Achilles will accomplish nothing and that they should go back and deliver their bad news to the Achaeans.

> "As for Achilles, he has put a wild and proud spirit in
> his breast, obstinate, nor does he care for the friendship
> of his companions, with which we honored him by the
> ships so much above the others. Pitiless; for a man ac-
> cepts compensation even from the murderer of his
> brother or of the child who has been killed; the one,
> after he has paid much, remains there in the district,
> while the other restrains his spirit and manly pride
> when he has received the penalty. But as for you, the
> gods have put a harmful and unceasing spirit in your
> breast on account of a single girl—and we now offer
> seven, by far the best, and much else besides. Put on
> a gentle spirit, respect your own house: we are under
> your roof, sent from the multitude of the Danaans, ea-
> ger to be your best friends and supporters among all the
> Achaeans." [9. 628–42]

As Odysseus spoke for Agamemnon and Phoenix for the family, so Ajax speaks for the community of warriors. His turning first away from and then toward Achilles is a performance of separation and belonging, an invocation of community by gesture. This community is the sole source of honor and friendship, and Achilles cannot reject the claim that he belongs to it; for who would he be without his world? He has no language of individuality, no system of value and motive, on which he could base an existence apart from it. Nor can he incorporate Ajax and the others into his own sphere, as he does Phoenix, for the heroic community is a community of equals.

The central value invoked by Ajax is what I earlier called "persuadability," a willingness to put in the past what belongs in the past and to be reconciled after all. This is the fundamental way in which this community is maintained, a way as central to it as we might say the rule of law is to our own. It underlies the practices of ransom, supplication, and giftgiving; it is essential to the existence and identity of the community itself. The appeal is to social necessity, and Achilles cannot wholly resist it.

His position shifts again: he will not fight until the fire has reached his own ships.

IN BOOK NINE, then, the poem performs the breakdown of the culture in two ways. First is the failure of persuasion: the most expert orchestrations of the culture's resources for making appeals to action and to community, for claiming meaning and stating motive, fail to bring Achilles back. The central resources of this culture are its ways of bringing about reconciliation through honorable persuasion, and these do not work. Second, and even more dramatically, Achilles demonstrates that these appeals can be broken into parts that do not fit together. The appeals of Agamemnon and Odysseus are rejected; that of Phoenix carries him over to Achilles' side; that of Ajax moves Achilles back, not to the Achaean community, but to his original position of irresolution. This fragmentation denies a unity that each of the ambassadors had assumed. It exposes a lack of relation, an incoherence, in what had to us been an intelligible and functioning culture.

But the claims of Achilles have undergone a similar breakdown: for him, as for the others, words have lost their meaning. He can no longer credibly say to himself or to others that he is trying to force Agamemnon and the Achaeans to restore his lost honor, for that offer has been made and rejected. But if he is not to say that, what can he say? He can no longer make a coherent statement about his motives for withdrawal or about what he hopes to gain from it. His wrath has become a fact of nature to which the language of the culture can give no meaning, except as an unexplained and threatening force. As for the Achaeans, their peril is now felt as real in a new way, for we can no longer see the Trojan superiority as a merely temporary part of Zeus's plan to bring honor to Achilles. The battle has become, in a way it was not before, a real battle, out of anyone's control. In this way, Book Nine has broken the expectations that were established in Book One, and at its close the poem makes a new beginning into the unknown.

THE MOVEMENT TO THE END: LIFE BEYOND CULTURE

From this point on, the poem takes Achilles through another reversal of attitude and brings him back to the battle again. But this time he does not fight for honor and prizes but for something new, and he does not so much come back to an old position as go on to a new one. How can this movement of the poem, from here to its end, be described and explained? What relationship does it have to the definition and criticism of culture achieved in the first nine books?

51

WE BEGIN in Book Ten with the remarkable nighttime expedition of
Odysseus and Diomedes across the corpse-strewn battlefield to the Trojan camp. This story involves the reader in the events with a cinematic
sense of immediacy; we are given a constant sense of the scene, of the
night and the bodies and the plain, and through it we follow the heroes
from one place to another and back again, almost with the eye of a cam-
era.[20] This establishes a new method; for as the narrative proceeds, the
reader continues to be brought into the story, and brought into it on the
Achaean side. It is now the Achaean heroes, one by one, whose valor and
energy are exhausted in vain, who are wounded and retire; it is the
Achaean wounded we visit, following Patroclus into the Achaean tents.
Patroclus is now a responding and directing presence of exactly the sort
that was missing in the earlier battle scenes. He suffers at what he sees,
and he speaks his suffering. This works on the reader, stimulating and
guiding his sympathies, and it works on Achilles as well, who cannot sus-
tain his position of withdrawal against these powerful claims on his loyalty and humanity. He agrees at last not to return, himself, but to send
Patroclus in his stead, dressed in his armor. This foolish action, which at
once commits Achilles to the Achaean cause and leads to the death of his
friend, is in no intelligible way explained by Achilles, who is unable to
make sense of his own situation or to come to a clear judgment about it.[21]
He does not wish to be reconciled, yet he cannot reject the claims of loyalty, either as these were first made by Ajax or as they are intensified now
by Patroclus. Neither course of action is authentic to him. His wrath has
led him out of the heroic culture that gave rise to it and into an impossible
predicament.

As for us, we participate naturally enough in the sympathies and loyalties evoked by the narrative and by the responses of Patroclus, but in
doing this we forget what we should have learned in the first battle sequence: the equal humanity of those who must die. For the appeal to battle made here is a paradoxical one: Patroclus invokes the very cost of war,
its terrible suffering and loss, as precisely the reason why Achilles should
return to it. He points to the sorrow of war and of death and urges Achilles to be angry no longer, to soften his heart—and to return to battle. As
we respond to the appeal, we momentarily share a complicity in the return and in its emotional basis: an incapacity to remember what we once
knew of the meaning of the death of a Trojan. The remainder of the poem
will expose this failure for what it is, as the present victors become the
losers and we are forced to see what we for the moment forgot. When
Hector puts on the armor of Patroclus with a crowing boast, we suddenly
see him both ways, as victor and as vanquished. We learn something in
the early books, we forget it, and learn it again; and this time we learn
something else as well, about our own susceptibility to circumstance, our
own incapacity to keep solidly to what we know.[22]

For Achilles the death of Patroclus changes everything. He will return to the battle, dressed in Hephaestus' armor and with a wounded heart, but this is not a return to the values and world of Book One. Achilles shows no interest in the traditional forms of reconciliation (a quick statement to the effect that "we should put our quarrel behind us" is all that he requires) and treats as meaningless Agamemnon's almost comically persistent efforts to give him the gifts of reconciliation. He is driven instead by his fury at the death of his friend, a fact that seems to relieve him of the uncertainties and confusions he has been experiencing and to offer him a role he can accept, that of avenger. The wrath of Achilles, which first was directed toward Agamemnon and then carried Achilles himself to a position of paralysis is now turned on Hector and the Trojans.

Patroclus' death has this effect on Achilles because it operates as the death of a part of Achilles himself.[23] It is a forced recognition, an actual experience of his own mortality, and it releases energy that was formerly spent in denying or resenting the fact that he must die. Energy formerly blocked in a kind of paralysis is now available for action, action based not on social expectations and rewards, not premised on a desire for honor, but rooted in the solitary hatred and frustration of his heart. The terrible force of Achilles is released upon the world.

THE POEM'S FUNDMENTAL VALUE is its recognition of the equal humanity of those who must die. Yet it seems that none of the characters shares this value. Near the end of Book Twenty-two, for example, Achilles is able to turn from the incredibly cruel slaughter and mutilation of Hector to his lamentation for the death of Patroclus without recognizing that the two deaths can be regarded in any way as similar. Later he kills twelve Trojans on the pyre without a thought for them. As for the Trojans, after Hector's death Hecuba says that she would gladly eat the liver of Achilles. For the Achaeans and the Trojans, though not for us, there is not the slightest connection between the two who are dead: one is a friend, the other an enemy.

All this changes in the great scene that closes the poem. Here, under the protection of the gods, Priam comes in the night to Achilles' tent to ask for the body of his son (which has been miraculously preserved despite its mutilations by Achilles), and Achilles, prompted by Thetis, grants his wish. Both figures are suffering a sense of ultimate loss, and they meet on that ground. They realize their common humanity, sharing their sorrows, almost confusing their sense of who is the dying son, who the mourning father. They form a precarious and momentary society of two in an alien world, two who understand what no one else understands. Achilles urges Priam to sleep outside lest one of the Achaeans find him, and in doing this he allies himself with Priam, not the Achaeans. When, on Achilles' urging, Priam has eaten food, he is able to say, "I had not eaten since you killed my son" (see 24. 642). The calmness with which this is said enacts an acceptance that puts the events of the war, even the death of Hector, as far into the distance as if they were woven into the tapestry of Helen. Priam and Achilles come to see and to express what Homer has led us as readers to see, to forget, and to learn again. They have moved to a new understanding of life, fully expressed, an understanding that seems to make the heroic civilization impossible for them. The world of Book One is left wholly behind.[24]

The poem ends in a moment of reconciliation, in an extraordinary recognition of common humanity. But what sort of ending is this, and how are we to take it? It is beyond the capacity of the human mind to imagine Achilles and Priam moving out of this moment as reformers of their world, trying to change their culture or to alter the nature of man. The poem does not contain the material out of which such a wish could even be formulated. Nor can one imagine Achilles, knowing what he now knows, returning to the battle, either for the motives of Book One— prizes and honor—or for those of Book Eighteen, anger at the death of Patroclus. Nor can one imagine any other life for him in this world. As has been the case since Book One, it is impossible for Achilles to return, impossible not to return. The poem has been the deepening story of what that impossibility has meant, from near murder and isolation to the transcendent moment of Book Twenty-four, a moment without a future. The ending of this poem is an ending indeed; what it enacts is that life itself, for Achilles and Priam, has come to an end.[25]

IN ENDING THE POEM as he does, without pretending to resolve the impossibility he has defined, the poet makes his reader share the predicament he has brought his characters to face. The relationship between Priam and Achilles at the end offers, at last, the standard by which the heroic culture is judged and found impossible. But by that standard all cultures are impossible, for none is rooted in the sense of common humanity and fidelity to what is real that marks this moment. Reforms cannot change the human heart, and it is at last with man's nature, not his culture, that this poem is concerned. Man will always forget what he has known, will always kill and always die. Like Achilles and Priam, we are left with a new knowledge, facing the fact that what ought to be will never be.

Yet that is not quite true. The impossible community that the poem defines and honors at the end is given in fact a real existence in the reader's experience of the poem itself. The poem constitutes a kind of culture of its own, and we can be part of it if we read the poem rightly and become our own versions of its ideal reader. Though it is a culture enacted in a text, not in the physical world, it is an actual part of life, and our experience of it is real. The imagined community between Achilles and Priam has a real counterpart in the community between the poet of the *Iliad* and his reader

This community is constituted by our experience of the poem, which moves us by a mosaic of countering appeals to a position outside the heroic world, and critical of it, where we can see, for the moment, what no one in the poem sees, the common humanity of those who must die. Book Nine directly enacts the fragmentation and breakdown of the culture, from which point the poem leads us back, against what we know, into the world of the battle, where we share the condition of the actors in it and of all men in the world: we cannot maintain our knowledge and feelings against the pressure of circumstance, against the force of our own sympathetic imagination. The poem ends in a position of rest, in a community of sympathy that establishes both a place of contemplation and a standard of judgment. This community is disciplined by the knowledge that, men being what they are, it can have only an unstable and momentary existence in the world. But it has a permanent existence in the life of the text, where, by the readers of this poem, it is continually created anew.

* * *

This, then, is what happens, at least this time, when we bring to the *Iliad* the way of reading set forth in the opening chapter and ask: What is the language that constitutes the world in which these actors live? How do they, and the writer himself, come to terms with its resources and its limits? What kinds of communities are established in this language, both within the imagined world of the poem, among its actors, and, in the text itself, between the poet and his reader?

In the *Iliad* the language is that of heroic poetry, and its terms and implications are so sharply defined and firmly established that it is easy to see it as a resource external to the individual self, who must find a way to come to terms with it. The best analogue in our own experience might be the language of the law, which from some points of view may seem similarly discrete and bounded, similarly constitutive of a certain set of clear social relations and expressive of a certain set of clear values. But the very clarity of the Homeric language is somewhat misleading; for as we saw when we examined it in our reconstructive and participatory way—as the imagined material for life—its use is also associated with great uncertainty. The paradoxical combination of certainty and uncertainty, of clarity and silence, makes the world at once intelligible and alive with tension, both for us as readers and for the actors within it. No simple print-out of a cultural pattern, this is a world of contention and struggle in which everything can be put into question, a moral and rhetorical universe in which the actors constantly claim meanings for what is said and done and do so in competition with each other. It lives by a politics of persuasion, upon a premise of instability. In this it may be a model of all politics, and its central term *peithō* may capture as well as anything could the connections among persuasion, community, and power.

It is in part by the silence that surrounds it that the reader's attention is directed to this language and to the culture it expresses. But this is achieved in another way as well, by narrative: the poem tells a story that brings to the surface, where it must be faced, a problem that had been avoided and for which the culture affords no solution, the tension between Agamemnon the leader and Achilles the preeminent warrior. This is in fact how narrative characteristically works in literature and life, by shifting positions so that the unseen becomes the seen, the unimaginable becomes real. Think, for example, of the way a story works in law, to present a question no one has ever thought of: a contradiction between two cases of equal authority, for example, or one more deeply hidden in our language. In Book One Homer stimulates two central kinds of understanding and establishes between them a tension that is still with us: the synchronic understanding of where we are and the diachronic understanding of how things move. Reading Book One is a lesson at once in reading the world and reading its stories.

In these ways Homer makes real for his reader, and for the actors in his poem, our second question: What relation can the individual mind establish with its language, with the values and methods of its culture? For some people there is a perfect fit between self and culture. The priest Chryses is such a one; he knows exactly how to do what is called for, and in these transactions he expresses—needs—no sense of individuality whatever. But for Achilles the fit is highly imperfect: he is forced by circumstance to take a new position on the margin of his community, a position of which he can make no sense. Indeed, he comes to discover in Book Nine that what he had aimed at he no longer wants. When his ambition is realized, the feeling that drove it—his wrath—no longer has a statable object in the world. The origins of the change are of course internal, not external, for it is Achilles, not his culture, that has changed. But from his point of view, it is as though language itself had lost its meaning, since he no longer has his accustomed materials for expressing motive and sentiment, for defining the self in action. The breakdown of the relation between self and culture threatens both. This is a version of a universal experience, for it is a repeated and surprising discovery for all of us— if, in no other way, as a part of growing up—that the terms upon which life has been led have changed, changed utterly, and that one must make one's own way in an unknown world.

For Achilles the story is a breakdown of his relation with his language and culture and a movement beyond it, to a point from which he has nothing to say. The self depends on its culture and community, and, when these relations collapse, an enormously destructive energy is loosed upon the world, an energy that might in other circumstances have found culturally appropriate expression. Achilles' wrath is so destructive in part because it has no social form. We can now see how perfect it is for the poet in his opening words to have made the "wrath of Achilles" his subject, for that wrath is occasioned by an insult within the culture but it carries Achilles outside it, where it has a career of its own that cannot be expressed in cultural terms at all. This career ends in a reconciliation of a universal kind, not merely with Agamemnon but with Priam: the enemy, the essential other. To make "wrath" a subject in this way is to engage in a process of radical abstraction in a language that does not seem to allow for it.

The heroic language is as problematic for the poet as it is for the actors. Homer comes to terms with it by a kind of ironic control: he arranges its materials in patterns that criticize the culture it is meant to celebrate, and in doing so he creates, in the relation he establishes with his reader, a new world operating on altogether different premises.

The center of this achievement is a kind of friendship. In the imagined world of the poem this takes the form of the momentary recognition of the equality and humanity of others even across the lines of enmity. We see this especially in Book Twenty-four and in the way our sympathies are repeatedly drawn across the lines of opposition. Friendship is given an even more complex definition in the relation between Homer and his reader, and the heart of it is a special kind of teaching: this poem teaches us by moving us from a position within the heroic world to another external to it, based on the recognition of the common humanity of all who must die. This is at once the simplest and most profound of truths, and it is the center of value in the poem. But no sooner do we attain it than we lose it; we are led back against what we know into the world of the battle, where we cannot maintain our knowledge and feelings against the pressures of circumstance. Having extended sympathies of one kind in the first nine books, we now engage them in a different way, in a kind of loyalty to what we now accept as our side. The poem teaches us that, by imaginative disengagement from the world, our sympathy may be extended universally throughout it and that, by engagement with it in action, real or imagined, we shall forget what we knew in our moment of disengagement. It thus establishes a kind of dialectic between different modes of conceiving of the world and acting within it, each of which informs the other; at its center is a tension between two kinds of friendship, two kinds of meaning.

All human experience is at once unique and collective: during a war, a child dies of cancer, an old man of a bad heart; another baby is born; a scientist discovers a new compound and the infidelity of his wife; one soldier is killed in an accident, another by the enemy; one man's bravery leads to his death, another's to the rescue of a friend; and so on. The full reality of these times is not the story of the war only, or of these private events only, but of all of them together, seen and felt simultaneously from every human point of view. The *Iliad* instructs us in the reality of such a universal vision, while at the same time teaching us that it is imperfectly attainable by man.

At the end of the poem we do return to a position of knowledge, but this time it is different; for now we learn that learning itself is always relearning and that it will always be followed by forgetting. In this sense the reader himself becomes the subject of the poem, and the process of life to which we are introduced is the continual reconstitution of knowledge and self, against a part of our own nature and the necessary conditions of our life. In these ways Homer teaches us that we can define ourselves as different from our language and that we can establish in our relations with others a ground on which it can be criticized; he insists on the reality of the world and the reality of our own conflicting responses to it; he instructs us in our ineradicable disposition to forget even the most important of lessons and hence in our need for art of the kind that this poem offers us. He thus teaches us a method of cultural analysis and criticism. This instruction is not informational or conceptual but ethical: the poem teaches us by the way it constitutes us. The ideal reader of this poem will be newly aware of the contingency of language and culture, of his responsibility for how he speaks and what he is, and of his own need for a life of continual self-education.

But for us there is a missing element here as well; for this poem is made out of a language, a culture, that does not change, and we live in the midst of cultural change. The text presents a culture with great clarity and then criticizes it, using its materials to create a new community between poet and reader; but the materials themselves, the language and attitudes of the heroic culture, remain unchanged. The poem moves us out of its imagined world into its own created one, but then, in a sense, it leaves us, all of us—actors, readers, and the poet himself—without a future. Homer's own response to the problem of life was not to reconstitute his language but to make a poem, and his implicit advice to us is to read it, to learn it well, and, by extension, to make such poems in our own lives. But how are we to do these things, especially in a world that constantly changes? How are we to maintain and live within the culture that we know? It is with questions of this sort that we turn to Thucydides, who took as his central subject the way his culture and its language changed and what that change meant for those who lived within his world.

3

The Dissolution of Meaning

Thucydides' History of His World

Thucydides begins his narrative, as Homer does, by immersing his reader in the workings of a complex rhetorical universe which then becomes a central subject of his text. In this case the primary actors are the city-states of Greece, and the culture consists of the discourse, the conventions of argument and action, by which they maintain and regulate their relations with each other. At the beginning of the *History* this culture of argument, if it may be so called, is shown to work in coherent and intelligible ways; but as the events of the war proceed, the terms of discourse shift and change, and both the language and the community constituted by it deteriorate into a kind of incoherence.

We shall first examine in some detail the culture of argument that Thucydides takes as his subject, asking: What are its central terms and procedures? What world of action and meaning does it create? How does it change over time? Since the *History* is the story not only of language but of events of other kinds—battles, social processes, lucky chances, the manifestation of individual character in action, and so on—we shall also examine the relationship between that discourse and what happens in the "real" world of battles and trade and politics. For example, are the people to whom arguments are addressed in fact shown to be persuaded by what they hear? If so, how and why? If not—as is perhaps the case in the opening debate—why do the speakers bother to make the arguments they do? And why does Thucydides reproduce them? What importance, indeed, does either a particular argument or the culture of argument as a whole have in this world? And, to look at it the other way around: What causes the changes that occur in the culture of argument? Why does the deterioration take place, and why can't it be successfully resisted? Thucydides' own relation to the language in which these speeches are composed is in one way plain enough, for he takes it as part of his material and part of his subject. But from the point of view of the actors, we can ask what place this language has in their world and what relations they variously establish with it; and, from our own point of view, we can ask what function this language and these speeches have in our experience of this text and in the community Thucydides creates with us.

DEFINING THE CULTURE OF ARGUMENT: THE CORCYREAN DEBATE

Thucydides begins his narrative of the war between Athens and Sparta by explaining how it arose. He spends little time on what he calls its "truest explanation" or deepest cause, for that is easily stated: it is Sparta's fear of Athens' growth. His primary concern is with its "causes" in a different sense: the grounds or claims, the "causes of action," that the two sides had against each other. He is interested, that is, in explaining how it all happened as well as why; or, to put it more accurately, he is interested in making it possible to ask "why" in a way that calls for an answer that is at once more complicated and more useful than a simple statement of Spartan apprehensions.

The first of the precipitating causes Thucydides identifies is a dispute between Corinth, one of the Peloponnesian powers, and Corcyra, one of her western colonies, which leads by gradual stages to a meeting at Athens at which a representative of Corcyra asks that his city be admitted into an alliance with Athens and a Corinthian representative opposes him. Our initial concern will be with these speeches; but to understand them, it is necessary to know something of their background.

Background

When the dispute between Corinth and Corcyra arose, in 435 B.C., Athens and Sparta had already established two contending organizations of Greek city-states with themselves as the leaders. Athens was the head of a league of cities, situated mostly on the coasts and islands of the Aegean Sea, that had originally been formed after the conclusion of the Persian wars (in about 478 B.C.) for the several purposes of maintaining a common defense, liberating Greek cities still held by Persia, and carrying out raids for booty on foreign territory. Each city in the league contributed to the maintenance of a common naval force, at first by providing ships but ultimately (except in the case of two cities) by payments of money. The shift in method of contribution had large consequences; for after the change Athens no longer led a force made up of independent contingents but had an enormous navy that was effectively its own, even though it was paid for by the allies. In 454 B.C., as its power then permitted it to do, Athens moved the treasury of the league from Delos to Athens, where it would be more completely subject to Athenian control, and it discontinued the council in Delos at which members of the league had met. In this way the league gradually acquired the character of an empire.

Sparta dominated the Peloponnesus through a system of alliances of which, owing to her invincible land forces, she was the undeniable chief. She maintained her hegemony over her allies by ensuring that they were governed oligarchically and in accordance with her interests. After a brief period of warfare, Sparta and Athens, in 445 B.C., concluded a treaty providing for a thirty years' peace. This treaty listed the allies of each city, and it provided that neither could form an alliance with the allies of the other, though neutrals could be admitted as allies by either side. This was the context in which the dispute between Corcyra and Corinth arose.

Corcyra, located on the island now known as Corfu, was one of the wealthiest cities in Greece and a colony of Corinth. She had no alliances. Epidamnus, farther up the Adriatic coast, was a colony of Corcyra, though her founding citizen had, according to custom, come from Corinth (because Corinth was the mother city of Corcyra). A civil war arose in Epidamnus, in which the popular side expelled the oligarchs, who then joined with local barbarians and attacked the city. The popular party sought assistance from Corcyra, which was refused,[1] whereupon, after consulting the oracle at Delphi, they asked Corinth for assistance, delivering the city to her as a colony. Partly owing to her preexisting antagonism toward Corcyra (which had failed to accord her the ceremonial honors due a mother city by her colony), Corinth agreed to help and sent out settlers and troops to Epidamnus. When Corcyra learned that a Corinthian garrison had arrived, she demanded that the city expel the Corinthians and receive back the oligarchs. When this demand was refused, Corcyra joined the siege of the city. Corinth then announced that a colony would be sent to Epidamnus. This was a political act of considerable significance, for it involved a commitment of protection to those who chose to go out from Corinth, who would share in the distribution of the land that had belonged to the now-dispossessed oligarchs. Corcyra sent envoys to Corinth, offering to resolve the dispute, either through arbitration or by appeal to the oracle at Delphi, and, if those offers were rejected, threatening to seek help elsewhere. Corinth refused to talk unless Corcyra would withdraw from the siege; Corcyra said she would withdraw only if Corinth would, but she was also willing to negotiate from the status quo, which Corinth refused.

At this point Corinth sent out a large fleet, which was soundly defeated by the Corcyreans. (On the same day it happened that Epidamnus fell to the oligarchs.) Corinth then spent the winter building a fleet and preparing for further war.

As even this brief account should make plain, this was a highly structured world, rich in resources for argument and action. The very fact that the cities could jockey for position as they did, each seeking to place the other in the wrong, shows that they operated on terms established by a shared and comprehensible discourse and that each was acting in part for an audience, internal or external, who would use that discourse to judge what it did. Thucydides now gives us the opportunity to learn something about the nature of that discourse, for at this moment Corcyra sends a delegation to Athens to ask for an alliance, and Corinth sends a representative to resist them. Thucydides presents their speeches in considerable detail.[2]

This is a highly literary moment, of which we can ask: Of all the things that might be said here, what will the speakers choose to say? How will they try to persuade the Athenians to do what they want them to? To what values will they appeal, for example? What pleas, what charges, what veiled or explicit threats or promises, will they make? Will they call on the gods, on compassion or justice, or on tradition or the law? Will they appeal to the Athenians' economic or military self-interest, and, if so, how will they define these things? Or will they appeal to the Athenians' sense of their own character, say, as virtuous or brave or generous, and how will they do that? In what terms will they tell their stories? With what actors, what motives, what events? Each speaker will define for the moment himself, his audience, and his culture. How will he do so?

The Speeches

The Corcyrean representative[3] speaks first, and the argument he makes is both complex and assured, reflecting a tradition of argument so clear that he knows not only how to make his own case but the case the other side will make and how to answer it in advance. The speakers are represented as being equally and perfectly competent at managing their resources; like Chryses, they know exactly who they are and what to say, and, like him, they engage not in invention but performance. Their speeches make a true pair, for neither side raises an argument that is not met or anticipated by the other.

I

Corcyra's first task is to meet an anticipated Corinthian claim[4] that her prior conduct demonstrates a character so untrustworthy that her offer of alliance should not be taken seriously by Athens. For Corcyra has no allies, and she knows that Corinth will say that the reason for this policy is that it enables Corcyra, in her remote position, to act unjustly without being exposed to others, as she would be if allies were witnesses or learned of it later when called on to help. In particular, in the absence of the usual treaty provision that requires disputes to be submitted to neutral tribunals, Corcyra can act as an unjust judge in her own cause and that of her citizens when disputes arise with merchants engaged in the extensive western trade that passes through her waters. In other words, according to Corinth, Corcyra is a kind of pirate state, which means that she has shown herself to be beyond the discipline of the community of cities constituted by the practices of this discourse, including the practice of alliance. Athens could have no rational confidence that Corcyra would honor any agreement she made about the use of her large navy.

This argument must be met by the Corcyreans, for if it were accepted by Athens and by others it would effectively exclude her from membership in the community of city-states, denying her the right even to speak the language of treaty and alliance.[5] She would be an outlaw, without alliance, without even a voice, a prey to anyone stronger than she. But how can it be met?

The Corcyrean speaker begins by conceding that, since the Corcyreans have no prior relationship with Athens, they must demonstrate both that what they ask is initially advantageous to Athens and that they will in the future have a firm sense of gratitude for her assistance and can therefore be counted on as allies. Their prior lack of alliance is explained as a policy of avoiding foreign entanglements, a policy originally based on considerations of prudence but now shown to be mistaken. Instead of the character of an outlaw state, they claim to have that of one who makes an honorable but foolish mistake and learns from the experience.

On the merits of the proposed alliance, the speeches of the two sides are built primarily on three topics—justice, expediency, and gratitude—and they are characterized by an extraordinary symmetry; for each point made by one side is squarely met by a point of seemingly equal force the other way. For example, when Corcyra argues that the alliance would not violate the treaty between Athens and the Peloponnesians, which expressly permits alliances with neutrals, Corinth responds with an appeal to the purpose rather than the letter of the treaty, saying that its language cannot possibly be intended to authorize alliances with neutrals who are already engaged in a conflict with the other side, for this would directly lead to hostilities between the signatories. Similarly, when Corcyra says that Corinth is at fault for having refused arbitration, Corinth replies that Corcyra's offer of arbitration was specious, since it was not made until the Corcyreans were engaged in a siege which they refused to lift. The proper occasion for invoking the practice of arbitration is before, not after, a resort to arms. In addition, both sides make stock and evidently flimsy arguments from probability to show that the other is at fault: Corinth points to her good relations with her other colonies to demonstrate that she must have behaved well toward Corcyra; Corcyra points to the natural disposition of the colony to honor its mother city as a way of showing that the breach must have been the fault of Corinth. As for the Corcyrean claim that they will be grateful to the Athenians for rescuing them, the Corinthians implicitly claim that such protestations are inherently unbelievable and that, in any event, the Athenians owe them, the Corinthians, a debt of gratitude for supporting them during the Samian revolt and the war with Aegina.

Both sides, in addition, make appeals to pure self-interest as a ground on which action can be based, apparently without regard to its justice or injustice. Corcyra, for example, speaks this way when she tells Athens that she can be counted on because she has the same enemies as Athens; that the best security is to do as little as possible to aid one's enemies; and that, if Athens is afraid of breaking the treaty with Sparta, she should remind herself that, if she remains strong by breaking it, that will be better for her than if she becomes weak by keeping it.[6] Corinth responds in kind when she appeals to Athens as another dominant power, saying that each of them should be free to punish its own allies and that Athens should not establish it as a precedent that those who revolt from one sphere of influence should be received by the other. The plain implication is that these principles are valid whatever the rights and wrongs of the particular case may be. Corinth concludes in this vein by saying that to refrain from doing an injustice to an equal power is a greater source of strength than to choose a risky course based on present appearances of advantage.

II

In these speeches we are thus given, in outline at least, a piece of a rhetorical universe, indeed, of a legal system. What can we make of it? To start with, it is apparent that the principal figures in this world are the individual cities, regarded as units, which can speak to each other through representatives in certain established places and modes. They are capable of making agreements and breaking them, hence of moral action; they have reputations for which they are concerned, and they are supposed to be capable of feeling gratitude and shame and of reasoning about justice and expediency. These premises, artificial as they are— every community, for example, is in some fashion divided[7]—are wholly unchallenged by the speakers, for it is these very premises that make possible the challenges they do make to each other, by creating the world in which they can occur.

The actors in this world are related to each other in several overlapping and competing ways, each serving as a check on the other: through alliance, through colonial status, and through spheres of influence estab-

lished by the greater states. In this way premises of equality and autonomy[8] are both affirmed and qualified. These cities have a remarkably
wide range of practices by which to manage their relations with each
other: negotiated treaty, arbitration, appeal to the Delphic oracle, and,
perhaps most important, the conventions of argument exhibited in debates such as this one.

The topics of appeal—justice, interest, and gratitude—are not fragmented, like the appeals made in Book Nine of the *Iliad*, but deeply related, and for the most part they work together to form a highly coherent
discourse. An alliance will be expedient only if the ally has a proper character, after all, and justice calls for different treatment of the good and the
bad. The Corinthian attack on the character of Corcyra is thus an attempt
not only to deny the Corcyreans standing to participate in the practices of
the culture but to meet their claim to be the victim of injustice and to
counter their argument from expediency (for the Corcyrean navy will be
of value only if Corcyra is herself reliable). The topics of justice, expediency, and gratitude are apparently related in another sense as well,
namely, that they are all obligatory; for it appears that a speech that omitted any of them would be starkly incomplete, a confession of failure.

But the relationship among these topics is also to some degree troubled; it is marked, as we have seen, by an explicit tension that leads both
sides to suggest that Athens should, if necessary, pursue expediency
against the claims of justice. This tension may not be serious if (as it
seems) each speaker, while conceding the priority of expediency over
justice should the two conflict, is required to maintain, as each of the
speakers here does, that there is no such conflict in the course he is rec-
ommending but harmony instead; for each maintains that the claims of
justice, expediency, and gratitude all point the same way. But whether
the tension in this discourse is great or small, how is it to be regarded? As
a kind of incoherence, like the unresolved and unresolvable question of
Agamemnon's status in the *Iliad*, which will naturally lead to the dissolution of the discourse? As a way in which the discourse maintains a congruence with the reality it seeks to constitute and regulate? Or is the very
unsettled quality of the discourse to be regarded as a sign of health, evi-
dencing a capacity for change? Such are the questions with which these
speeches leave us, and to them the rest of the *History* will offer a response.

III

What was the actual effect of these elaborate and symmetrical
speeches? We are told quite briefly that the Athenians, after two meet-
ings, decided to offer the Corcyreans a defensive alliance, for the reason
that they expected war to come in any event and did not wish to give up

the Corcyrean navy to Corinth; but it was to be a defensive alliance only, not a general one, because otherwise, should Corcyra attack Corinth, Athens would involve herself in an open breach of her treaty with Sparta.

Upon reading this we may well wonder why we are not told more about the deliberations of the Athenians that led to their decision, for it is presumably these—not the speeches—that determined their conduct. And in light of the grounds in fact asserted for the Athenians' judgment we may also ask what the long speeches we have just worked through were for in the first place. Why did the representatives of Corcyra and Corinth choose to include all those appeals to justice and character and gratitude and right, to which the Athenians paid so little attention? And however that question is answered, why did Thucydides include the speeches, when they seem to have had so little to do with the way in which the decision was actually made? The Corcyreans could simply have said, "We are here to offer you an alliance. We will not insult your intelligence or waste your time by pretending that either you or we are motivated by considerations of justice or gratitude. We will merely point out the reasons why such an alliance is in your interests and in ours." Why, instead of this, did the Corcyreans say what they did?

At least part of the answer is this: even if neither Athens nor the other two cities feel much interest in doing the just thing because it is just, all of them have a very real interest in refraining from behavior that is "unjust" in the special sense that it cannot be justified in the terms of the discourse spoken here. That is, as Thucydides implicitly presents it, it is not particularly important to Athens that what she does actually be right, but it is important that she be able to claim that it is right by saying, for example, that it is the proper act of an ally or a colony, or is authorized by the treaty, or is motivated by gratitude. While the talk about expediency is meant to persuade the Athenians directly to a particular course of action, then, the talk about justice has another kind of persuasive function as well: it is meant to demonstrate what can be said in the future for and against the justice of the recommended courses of action. "If you act in the way we wish, you will be able to say such and such on your own behalf; but if you act the other way, this is what we and others will say about you." The arguments are in this sense less about justice than about justifiability and less about gratitude itself than about avoiding the dangerous charge that one is to be regarded as incapable of it.[9]

The main interest a city has in being able to justify herself in this language arises from the fact that the next time she wishes to speak this language (in asking for an alliance, in trying to compel adherence to a treaty, in seeking arbitration), she will have to defend what she does now, which may be held against her either as a wrong committed or as having established a new precedent, to the invocation of which she at least, will not be able to object.[10] In such ways her rhetorical position may be impaired; if she cannot make even a superficially plausible claim of justification, she will no longer be able to use the language to obtain what it alone can offer, for no one will listen. Her interest, in other words, is in continuing to be a member of the community that is defined by this language. The cost of a failure to justify is not punishment in any usual sense of the term but rather exclusion or outlawry, the very sanction that Corinth tries to invoke against Corcyra. And Corcyra shows how terrible it would be; for, as she says, it would mean that Corinth could draw allies from all over Greece, Corcyra none. She would be eaten up.[11]

The fact that this language works here as a language of justification, not justice, explains something else about it, which for want of a better term I shall call its flexibility. What I mean is the peculiarity, noted above, that every move within this language seems to have a countermove, that every argument can be met by another, apparently valid, argument. Does it follow that anything at all can be justified in this language, that its symmetry renders it essentially empty of content? That this is not quite the case is demonstrated in this episode; for Athens is here led to form a defensive alliance partly by the recognition that a full alliance would almost certainly require conduct that could not be justified under the terms of her own treaty with Sparta.[12] But in general it is not so much the function of this language to direct conduct in a particular way, or to compel a particular result, as to permit the justification of a very wide range of behavior. I think that this feature is essential to the survival of a language of justification, at least of this voluntary kind—and in a sense all such languages are voluntary—because such a language will be used only so long as it meets the needs of its users. If it were to impose intolerable restraints, it would be disregarded; on the other hand, if it imposed no restraints at all, no one would bother to invoke it. It is a characteristic of such a language that its life and strength depend on a balance between its flexibility and its bite, and this balance Thucydides is careful to capture.

I think we can now explain why Thucydides includes these speeches in such detail. They are not meant to state the motives of the actors, which can adequately be summarized in brief terms, as was done with respect to Athens; rather, the speeches define the conditions imposed on the actors by the language that constitutes their community. This language defines a culture—a culture of argument—of which it is Thucydides' object to tell the history. Of course people are moved by self-interest, in this and every age, as the Athenians are here; but for Thucydides the more important and interesting question is this: What is the language in which this self-interest is given definition and reality and expression? What kind of community does it constitute, and how does it succeed and fail?

IV

The Corcyrean debate thus enacts a culture of argument that works, and works under pressure. Indeed, we are shown here that it works even when one of its central premises, the unity of each city, is challenged by the civil war in Epidamnus. And notice how it works: the civil war reduces Epidamnus to factions, depriving her of an identity from which she can speak or which can be recognized by the others; but the other cities move into the vacuum she creates by making competing efforts to establish and defend a unified city in her place. The premise of unity is thus maintained. I say that this culture of argument "works" even though the immediate result of these speeches is the beginning of a war, for it is not the purpose of the cities to eliminate war but rather to organize and control their relations so that war, when it comes, will be manageable. The Athenians' adoption of the defensive alliance and even the battle that follows, so far from being destructive of the community, are part of its life.[13]

But in the *History* we will learn that this culture of argument deteriorated and finally collapsed. The question Thucydides poses and tries to answer is how and why this happened. The short response is that Athens and her empire presented a problem that the language of this community could not contain or manage. But that only restates the question. What was there about Athens, and about this language, that made that true?

THE PROBLEM OF ATHENS: THE CULTURE COLLAPSES

Sparta

The alliance with Corcyra not unexpectedly brings Athens into a battle, inconclusive in result, against the Corinthians. At a congress of Spartan allies held to discuss this and other grievances against Athens, the Corinthians attack the Spartans for their sluggishness and urge war against the Athenians, whom they represent as restless, daring, and ambitious. "If, in sum, someone were to say that their nature was neither to have rest themselves nor allow others to do so, he would speak the truth" (1. 70. 9). An Athenian embassy present in Sparta on other matters is granted permission to address the assembly and chooses to speak, not to the charges that Athens has violated the treaty or to the question of their daring character, but to the fundamental question presented by the existence of their empire. That is, they explicitly address the question how Athens and her empire can be talked about in the language of this community.

The problem is a formidable one, for an essential premise of the culture of argument—the culture by which this world is constituted—is the nominal equality and autonomy of the cities; upon it depend the practices of alliance, gratitude, and debate itself. But Athens is more powerful than any other city, and she holds other cities in a subjection of a unique kind. If anything is an intolerable anomaly in this discourse, her empire is. How, then, can the Athenians describe and justify[14] themselves and their empire in this language?

I

Certain of the claims made in the Athenians' speech at Sparta are directly continuous with those of the earlier Corcyrean debate. The Athenians begin, for example, with an appeal that belongs to the topic of gratitude: they claim that they are entitled to recognition for their essential role in the great battles of Marathon and Salamis, by which Greece was saved from Persia. Similarly, they make an appeal to justice of a familiar kind when they say that their empire has its roots in the free choice of autonomous cities to band together and choose a leader. The empire is just because it is an alliance based on treaty, a contract that reflects the autonomy and freedom of the cities.

But this can be only the beginning of Athens' case, since it establishes at most that she had no imperial motives in fighting Persia and that the Delian League was justifiable at its inception. The Athenian speakers know that the empire in its present form cannot be justified as a treaty (or they choose not to advance such a justification), and they appear to concede that it is inconsistent with the premises of autonomy, equality, and freedom essential to the discourse of the Corcyrean debates. Instead they make a claim of quite another kind: we cannot be blamed, they say, because what we did was natural; it was motivated by the common human desires for safety, for honor, and for interest. Athens has done nothing strange or out of the human pattern in accepting power when it was offered and not letting go of it upon request.

> "For it has always been established that the weaker be
> kept down by the stronger; and at the same time we
> thought we were worthy of rule, and used to be thought
> so by you until, considering your own advantages, you
> began (as you do now) to use the argument from jus-
> tice, which no one, when he had a chance to get some-
> thing by force, ever put before it and refrained from
> taking the advantage. Those are worthy of praise who,

69

> while following human nature in ruling over others,
> have been more just than the extent of their power re-
> quired them to be." [1. 76. 2]

The Athenians here seem to repudiate the very practice of appealing to justice; argument from justice never persuaded anyone to give up what he wanted and was able to take, they say, and the way of the world is that the weak should submit to the strong.

Part of Athens' justification of her empire thus seems to be consistent with the set of appeals and arguments made in the Corcyrean debate, but part of it is inconsistent. Yet, even the inconsistent arguments are not wholly invented by Athens, for their seeds are present in the earlier discourse. Compare, for example, the attitudes toward justice here expressed by the Athenians with the earlier Corinthian observations (1) that the best security lies in refraining from injustice to equals in power (which defines justice as a topic that has its place in talk between equals) and (2) that each state ought to be free to punish her own allies (which recognizes the dominance of the weak by the strong as a fact that should be respected). Compare, also, Corcyra's statements that true security lies in helping your enemies least and that she herself can be relied on by Athens because she has the same enemies (an argument that suggests that the proper way to predict behavior, and to behave, is by assessment of self-interest without regard to relations established by treaty, alliance, or colonial ties). Moreover, Athens' view that talk about justice has a place only where the use of force is uncertain, i.e., only among equals, is the obverse of something we noticed before: that one premise of this discourse of justification is the equality of the speakers. Athens, perhaps rightly, characterizes this not as a value of the discourse but as a factual precondition to it. Notice also that Athens does not actually reject justice as a value. She redefines it, saying that justice as a virtue is properly understood as a species of mercy or lenity, a kind of grace, belonging to one who gives more than he is compelled to; and to this virtue Athens lays claim, saying that it costs her dearly, for it gives rise to more resentment than simple tyranny would.[15] And she closes by saying that Sparta and Athens should resolve their differences through arbitration under their treaty, not by resort to war.

Thus the Athenian speech is less a repudiation of the resources of justification enacted in the Corcyrean debates than a reshaping and reorganization of them, a fact that explains much of its force. Athens redefines and limits a part of that discourse, its appeals to justice, by making other appeals of a more or less established kind: to human nature, to commonly accepted motives and values, to a sense of reciprocal benefits, and to the facts of the world. The heart of her position is not that she will refuse to justify herself but that she will justify herself only in terms that respect the reality of her situation. This argument has precedent in the earlier appeals to self-interest over justice, and it has great force analytically, for it is hard to refute; in addition, it establishes Athens as a formidable power indeed, for in making it she claims to be unrestrained by certain bonds of culture that others respect.

II

But what will happen when Athens tries to act out of the language she has modified in this way? In what terms, for example, can she offer to establish relations with others or propose that those relations be regulated? In the present speech it seems to be her primary object not to persuade the Spartans to delay the war, as she pretends, but to define the terms on which Athens is willing to talk, then or later, about settling it: she will not give up her empire or admit that it is wrong.[16] But how could a settlement be cast in the terms she now insists upon? It is hard to see how the language she uses could be the basis of a community of cities, for it denies a tolerable place to any others who do not also lay claim to empire. No one else could accept it. Despite its continuities with the earlier speeches, the language of Athens seems to make use of the culture only to destroy it and to offer no workable substitute.

The use of this language has internal as well as external consequences, for a coherent sense of self is essential to coherent deliberation and action, and how can Athens speak of herself in a sensible way in terms such as these? Out of what conception of herself and others can she formulate intentions and make policies in pursuit of them? Pericles' celebrated Funeral Oration will provide one answer, but the definition of Athens enacted there contains no principles of limitation, no recognition of the proper place of other states or of Athens' need for them.[17] And when Pericles speaks to the people at a less auspicious moment, after the plague, he tells them that they fight not just to remain free but for an empire from which they cannot withdraw. For their empire is "like a tyranny, which it seems wrong to have taken, but is dangerous to let go" (2. 63. 2). The problem is not that Athens is self-interested—for the practices of this world assume the self-interest of its actors—but that she is unwilling, or unable, to speak the language of justification that constitutes her community. Her ambition seems limitless, even to herself, because it is undefined; and she seems to have no materials with which to define and limit it. Like the wrath of Achilles in Book Nine, it has no cultural form to give it shape and direction; it has become elemental and chaotic.

But this is to get ahead of ourselves, for it assumes the end of our story, which, as Thucydides tells it, is in large measure the history of the language of Athens. The stages of the development can for our purposes be marked by the way Athens talks on three occasions: in the debate over Mytilene, in the Melian dialogue, and at the congress at Camarina.

Mytilene

Three years after the beginning of the war in 431 B.C.,[18] several of the cities on the island of Lesbos, led by Mytilene, revolted from the Athenian alliance. By this time Lesbos was (with Chios) one of the two independent members of the Athenian alliance; that is, she contributed ships rather than money. The Athenians, being distressed at home, sent a small force against Lesbos and, after inconclusive fighting, placed Mytilene under blockade. The famine caused by this blockade led the oligarchs to arm the people for a mass assault on the Athenians; but, once armed, the people demanded food, threatening to make terms with the Athenians if their demand was refused. The oligarchs, realizing that they had better join any capitulation that was made, surrendered the city on the terms that the city of Athens should decide the fate of Mytilene.

When the question is first presented in the Athenian assembly, the Athenians decide to put to death all the adult males of Mytilene and to sell all the women and children into slavery. The reason for this harsh decision is that the Athenians are enraged at the Mytileneans for revolting, despite their favored status, and for doing so not impulsively but deliberately. A messenger is sent to the Athenian general in Mytilene with orders to carry out the decree. But the next day there is some feeling that the judgment had been too harsh, and another meeting of the assembly is called. It is the two reported speeches made at this meeting that are of interest to us. In them we see Athens not justifying a course of action to others but choosing one for herself, and the opposing speeches define two contrasting ways in which she might conceive of herself and her situation, two languages of motive and value, of character and choice.

The first possibility is presented by Cleon, whom Thucydides calls the most violent of the citizens and the most persuasive with the people (for Pericles had died in the plague of 429), and it is not very attractive. Cleon says that to reconsider the question is a terrible mistake; it is an instance both of the deplorable lack of firmness that is characteristic of a democracy and of the Athenian love of oratorical display, novelty, and paradox. Athens should simply adhere to the judgment already made, which is the more likely to be right because it was made when the Athenians were full of the feeling occasioned by the wrong. And the merits are clear: Mytilene has inflicted a greater wrong on Athens than any other state and so deserves greater punishment; for she revolted despite her position of privilege, without provocation,[19] and under no threat of compulsion from a third party. Athens should not spare the people but should punish them all, for they all revolted together. If she does not punish deliberate revolt more seriously than revolt under external compulsion, which of her allies will not find a pretext to rebel? And if the people had resisted the revolt, they would now be in power. Athens should not be led into clemency through compassion, for compassion should be shown only to those who will reciprocate it, not to those who are of necessity permanent enemies.

> "If you are persuaded by me, you will do what is just
> to the Mytileneans and at the same time what is of ad-
> vantage to yourselves; but if you decide otherwise, you
> will win no gratitude from them but will rather convict
> yourself of wrong; for if it was right for them to revolt, it
> would be wrong for you to rule. If, nevertheless, you are
> resolved to maintain your empire, even if it is not fit-
> ting, you must punish them according to your interest,
> in disregard of the equity of it, or you should resign
> your rule and play the honest man in a place of safety."
> [3. 40. 4]

He closes by saying that the Athenians should not soften their hearts but should remember how they felt when they first experienced the wrong and act on that. Teach the allies that revolt means death and the less will Athens in the future be compelled to turn from her enemies to fight with her allies.

Cleon's speech has its unattractive aspects, but it does offer an intelligible response to the question that has been defined above: In what terms can Athens talk about herself and her relations with others? Cleon starts from the observation of Pericles that the empire is a tyranny, but he puts that observation to work in a way that Pericles did not. What it means is that the allies are permanent enemies, to be ruled by force, not members of an alliance to be managed through claims of justice, expediency, and gratitude. The practices of reciprocity, of agreement, and of argument about justice, indeed of compassion and gratitude, can have no place where one city rules the others, for those practices are all premised on equality. But Athens can still use a language of justice, though of a primitive kind: repayment of injury by injury.[20] This way of thinking and talking may not accord with every possible ideal, but it has roots in Greek culture (in the world in which Aeschylus' *Oresteia* begins, for example),[21] it is required by the very nature of the empire itself, and it provides an intelligible basis for action. It permits coherent and consistent judgment, and it makes use of the feelings and thoughts that naturally arise.

In this way, Athens can fashion and maintain a character intelligible to herself and to others.

The argument of Diodotus, made in response, is a *tour de force*. In a passage that may remind the modern reader of English and American statements in favor of freedom of speech, he defends repeated debate, both as a general matter and on the present question, on the grounds that it will lead to right judgment and overcome the effects of haste and anger.

With respect to the merits of the Mytilenean question, Diodotus says that Athens should decide what to do not from considerations of justice (or compassion) but according to her own interests. And Cleon's argument that it is in the interest of Athens to punish the Mytileneans as an example to others is fallacious. Who was ever deterred at the moment of committing a crime, when his hopes were high? The motives for crime are universal; poverty breeds necessity, for example, and wealth breeds greed. And, led by Hope and Desire, and deceived by Fortune, men have done, and will always do, what they strongly desire; they will not be restrained by laws or any other terrors. And if the punishment for revolt is death, what city will not persevere in its rebellion to the end? But if lenity be the rule, a revolted city may come to terms while it still can. Under Cleon's doctrine, Athens would always have the cost of war-to-the-end, with the possibility of defeat; and, even if she were to win, she would get a damaged city, of less value to her than if it had been reconciled earlier.

In particular, Diodotus says, it is against the interest of Athens to punish the people along with the oligarchs. This would not serve as a deterrent to keep others from rebellion and would in fact harden the people to continue with a revolt once it had begun. But if the people are pardoned now, that will serve in the future as an incentive to others who rashly engage in revolt to break from their leaders. What is more, to punish the people would alienate the populace in other cities, who are at present well disposed toward Athens and might be of assistance in case of war. He concludes by saying that, irrespective of their guilt, the people of Mytilene should not be punished; only those Mytileneans whom the Athenian general in the field deemed responsible for the revolt should pay the penalty.

This is brilliant work. Instead of arguing for justice and compassion, as Cleon had evidently expected, Diodotus concedes that arguments from justice and compassion for the Mytileneans are irrelevant; he rests his case solely on rationality and self-interest.[22] But in this case a proper calculation of interests shows that the right course is the one that would usually be called merciful. This is an example of the sort of paradox and novelty that Cleon says infatuates the Athenians, and one can see why it enrages him. In this case the Athenians are persuaded by Diodotus and send a ship to countermand the first set of orders. Sped by the promise of reward from Mytilenean ambassadors, the second ship arrives just in time to prevent the general massacre.

It is all too easy for one in sympathy with Diodotus' position of lenity to overlook the profound revolution in the discourse he proposes: this is the first time in Thucydides that any speaker has suggested that any of the established topics (here, justice) can simply be ignored.[23] Both the Corcyreans and the Corinthians apparently felt obliged to claim that considerations of justice and expediency and gratitude all supported them; even in the Athenian speech at Sparta it was at most said that there were occasions when talk about justice was inappropriate, and the Athenians were in fact careful there both to make a claim on the gratitude owed them by the other cities and to assert that their practice of the virtue of justice, properly understood, was exemplary.

The convention by which the three main topics of this discourse are always asserted to be coherent has the effect of ensuring both that its criteria of justice are adequately congruent with the facts of the world (for justice may not demand too often what expediency forbids) and that the terms in which expediency is defined will continue to acknowledge the practices of justification by which the community of city-states is constituted. Although Cleon modifies his definition of justice, he adheres to this convention in two ways: he claims that justice and expediency unite in supporting the course of action he advocates, and he explains why gratitude is not in the case. Diodotus splits the topics up and asks that considerations of expediency alone be taken into account.

What happens when someone tries to do that with this language? What solution, for example, does the speech of Diodotus offer to the problem Athens faces, of finding an intelligible and coherent way to talk about herself? In the present instance this reasoning leads to a humane result, but in the next it may lead to deliberate and conscious injustice and inhumanity. Cleon's appeal to the simple instinct of revenge provides a basis for action in both thought and emotion; in this sense it offers its ideal reader an integration of different aspects of the self, as Diodotus' speech does not. In addition, Cleon's speech implies its own limits (for punishment is proper only upon injury), as again Diodotus' speech does not; Cleon's rhetoric leaves Athens open (in another case) to claims that cut against her self-interest—"don't hurt us if we have not hurt you"—and thus makes possible the constitution of a community in which others can have a place. What the two speeches constitute is not a single rhetoric of competing moves, as the Corcyrean argument did, but competing rhetorics, entailing very different intellectual and social consequences. Thucydides' point in placing them against each other is to make plain the position in which Athens finds herself. Since she can no longer use the traditional language of justification, as we saw it presented in Book One, her choice is between talking like Cleon and talking like Diodotus. Of these, Cleon's way is unattractive, primitive, and punitive but coherent and intelligible; that of Diodotus is elegant and rational but without limits or standards or permanent values. To give up the practice of redressing felt injuries and the language of rights and wrongs, of blame and mercy, for a language of pure self-interest is to give up a very great deal.[24] Such a discourse can have no basis in sentiment and no stable commitment to ideas; it must rest on what seems best at the moment.

What Thucydides will show us in this text is that it is as irrational, then as now, to talk about self-interest or expediency without regard to justice as it is to talk about justice without regard to self-interest. The reason is that a doctrine of self-interest requires a language in which the self and its interests can be defined, and this language, like all language, will be social in its origins and in its terms. For it is only in a social universe, cooperatively constructed and maintained, that the motive of self-interest (or any other motive) can be a rational or coherent basis for thought and action. The language that makes ambition possible, by giving it form and object, at the same time imposes limits on it; it commits the individual to the culture that can alone give meaning and reality to his desires.

But in the rhetoric of Diodotus anything can be said, and it invites one to think that anything can be done. To speak that way is to lose the capacity to form a community with others or to claim a consistent character for oneself; indeed it is to lose the power of practical reason. This is what Thucydides will show in the Melian dialogue, to which we now turn.

Melos

Much later in the war (416 B.C.) the Athenians sent a force against the island of Melos, a Spartan colony not far from the Peloponnesus, to compel its submission to Athenian rule. They offered to negotiate with the Melians before attacking them, but upon extremely limited terms, since the only alternatives they offered were capitulation or destruction, and they simply refused to discuss the justice or injustice of their demand.

This notorious position is the natural next stage in the development of the rhetoric employed by Diodotus and accepted by the Athenians when they were persuaded by him, for its central premise is that considerations of justice ought never to interfere with calculations of interest. Cleon's rhetoric, by contrast, would have offered a ground on which the justice of the Athenian demand could be attacked or defended: the Athenians could say that the Melians had injured them and explain how; the Melians could respond by saying that they had never hurt the Athenians, indeed, that they had actually helped them, and so on. The Melian dialogue[25] is meant to show us what it means for Athens to have chosen to think and speak in the language of Diodotus.

At the outset the Athenians say that they will not speak a language of justice and that the Melians should not do so either, "since you know as well as we that justice is a subject of determination in debate among men only where each is under equal compulsion, and that otherwise the strong do what they can and the weak yield what they must" (5. 89). The Melians respond that Athens' own self-interest should lead her to maintain the practice of appealing to justice when in danger (because the temporary superiority that Athens now enjoys will someday disappear, and the equality that is the condition for talking about justice will exist once more); to respect the status of Melos as a neutral (for to do otherwise would be to alienate all other neutrals); to respect the Melians' refusal to submit to a dishonorable capitulation; and to recognize that the Spartans, or the gods, or luck might help the Melians in battle. Athens responds that she does not need the practice of calling on justice; that she will run the risk of offending the neutrals; that honor is not an issue for the Melians (since honor, like justice, is in question only between equals); and that the Spartans are slow to fight, while the gods follow the same law as men: "wherever they have the power, they always rule" (5. 105. 2). They close by saying that the Melians have put forth nothing in which men who planned to save themselves would trust; they have offered only statements of empty hope.[26] Melos should not be ashamed to be considered less than the greatest state. "Those would be most successful who do not yield to their equals, who treat their superiors well, and who are moderate to their inferiors" (5. 111. 4).

But after deliberating in private, the Melians refuse to end, by capitulation, "the liberty of a city that has existed for 700 years" (5. 112. 2), and they declare that they will resist. The Athenians accordingly besiege Melos, and, the next winter, that city, distressed by the war and by division within, capitulates. The Athenians kill the adult males and sell the women and children into slavery.

What the Athenians say and do here is not only brutal but irrational. The burden of their argument to the Melians is that they should avoid false hopes and ground their conduct on a realistic assessment of circumstance and probability. Yet when they themselves are asked by the Melians to consider what the impact of the destruction of Melos will be on presently neutral states and, moreover, what their own fate might be should their empire be destroyed, the Athenians dismiss the questions, saying in effect that they will run those risks; but they do not seriously assess them. Similarly, their explanation of why they need to bring Melos into their empire at all (instead of respecting her as a neutral) is circular and empty. Athens, they say, will not distinguish between neutrals and members of the alliance because such a distinction would be regarded as weakness by her allies; but that would be true only if the allies knew that Athens made no such distinction. Athens thus destroys the distinctions between friend, colony, ally, neutral, and enemy, the distinctions by which her world is constituted, and in doing this she makes the world a universal enemy; in a shocking phrase, she says that the friendship of Melos would be an injury to her (5. 95). And in her dependence on the views of her subjects Athens shows that her power is, like the kind of power offered by the culture of argument with which we began, rhetorical in kind, a species of persuasion to which the cooperation of others is essential; but the rhetoric she now employs is far less stable and coherent than the rhetoric she has rejected.[27] In an attempt to create a new ethic that will be appropriate to the new circumstances, Athens says, as we have seen, that moderation toward inferiors is the wisest policy; yet her own behavior is as far from her announced principle as could well be imagined. Such is the reasoning by which a limitless and incoherent ambition works in the world.

Could Athens have said anything else to persuade Melos to join her alliance? Could she, for example, have offered Melos a genuine alliance of the traditional kind, promising mutual benefits (including protection from Sparta)? It seems plain that she could not, for one premise of the practice of alliance in this world is rough equality of power. The legitimacy and force of this kind of contract rest, that is, on the fact that it is an expression of free choice and autonomy. This means that even had Melos chosen to enter such an alliance, she could have left it at will and said to the other cities of the community that she was doing no wrong. She could say that the alliance she was breaking was no alliance because, when it was made, Melos was so much weaker than Athens. We know that she could say this because, when Mytilene went to Sparta to seek assistance against Athens, she made exactly that argument (3. 9–14).

Equality is the central premise not only of alliance by treaty but of almost every practice that constitutes this rhetorical community.[28] It is essential, for example, to action based on gratitude and compassion, as Cleon said in explaining why no compassion should be shown the Mytileneans: owing to their subservient status, neither they nor anyone else would consider them open to charges of ingratitude for continuing to resist. Similarly, when the Athenians say that the topics of honor and justice assume equality of the parties, and can have no place where there is none, they can be taken as describing not necessarily what they prefer but what is, in this world, factually true. Athens cannot talk to the Melians in a language based on premises of equality because no resolution expressed in those terms would have any force.

Can Athens find some other way to characterize what she offers? She says that the proper thing is to recognize the fact of inequality and to build an ethic on that: of moderation to inferiors, of sensible compliancy to superiors, of unyieldingness (of the traditional sort) to equals. But in saying this, as in saying that Melos should no longer be moved by honor and shame, she says what is not possible. For the materials of the language that define their public world start from the premise that each city is an independent and equal unit. The Athenians are thus asking the Melians to give up their identity as a community, which they cannot do. (What community can?) The resistance of the Melians defines the ground of their culture, for it shows what they would die for rather than yield; or, more precisely, it defines what leads them to act on an unreasoning hope, for that is how men respond when everything that matters to them is in peril.

In this dialogue, then, Athens is much less free to choose the terms of her argument than is commonly supposed, and Thucydides perhaps does not so much show a new stage in her moral decay as demonstrate the consequences of her situation. She cannot talk the old way, but she cannot find a satisfactory new way to talk. Like Achilles, she is outside her culture, incapable of coherent social action or thought. The ultimate sanction of outlawry, which Corcyra feared in the earlier debates, has been brought by Athens upon herself.

What is wrong here is not that Athens is so self-interested, for, as I observed above, the earlier language operated on the premises of self-interest. What is wrong is that the culture through which self-interest could intelligibly be expressed has been destroyed.[29] Athens is left with self-interest alone, the desire for power without a culture to give it bounds and meaning. Not only is ambition of this sort unlimited, it is incoherent and irrational; for without a comprehensible world there can be no way of reasoning about it or acting within it. One cannot be self-interested without a language of the self; one cannot have power without community. In this sense, then as now, the language of pure self-interest proves to be parasitic upon the culture it destroys. Athens indeed had an interest in the culture of argument she rejected, as the Melians said, for it gave her an identity in relation to others, both constituting a world and establishing ways of functioning within it. Without this language of social definition or some substitute for it, there is no social order at all, and there can be no rational definition or pursuit of self-interest. The essential emptiness of the argument between Melos and Athens over the likelihood of Spartan assistance shows how inadequate a language of pure self-interest is. The argument by itself is structurally inconclusive; it therefore requires, if it is to mean anything, that it be included in a larger assessment of the situation, made by an actor with a character of his own, with his own values and willingnesses to risk. And the prediction itself, on both sides, is based on a judgment about Spartan character that acknowledges just the kind of distinction—between the reliable and the unreliable, between friend and neutral—that Athens has effectively obliterated for herself.

The Melian dialogue thus enacts a kind of tragedy, for Athens is caught in circumstances, partly of her own devising, from which she cannot extricate herself. She now learns in a new way what it meant for her to build an empire, which "anyone would do," and to talk about it as she has done.

Camarina

But the rhetorical movement has not quite reached its end. That comes in the next year, at a conference in Sicily, when Athens seeks to renew an alliance with Camarina against Syracuse. Having said and done what she has, how can Athens now possibly try to make an alliance with another city? What character can she claim for herself? What credible offer can she make?

The envoy from Syracuse, Hermocrates, makes the obvious case against Athens (6. 76–80). He attacks her as the insatiable imperial power that has destroyed the liberty of Greece. If Sicily is to remain a community of free city-states, maintaining the culture of equality, its cities must unite to defend their collective self-interest. Athens cannot meet this argument by denying any of the facts, saying that she is a friend of liberty, for example, or claiming to have any sense of fidelity to the culture of argument by which alliances can be made and talked about. Athens in fact has the character attributed to her. But it is paradoxically upon that character that she says Camarina may rely. For while it is in Athens' interest to rule a united empire in Greece proper and in the Aegean, it is also in her interest that Sicily remain divided, that it not become united against her under the leadership of Syracuse. Her imperial interests at home thus lead her to favor liberty abroad. It is Syracuse, not Athens, who threatens liberty in Sicily.

Athens here gives up entirely the practice of self-justification—something she had not quite yet done at Melos. To the world of Sicily she is what Persia was to Greece, a threat to the culture that constitutes Hellas. She makes no effort to justify her empire or to claim commitment to any principle other than self-interest. This makes a kind of sense, but it cannot serve as the basis for an alliance. On what ground can Camarina believe that Athens' interest is limited to dividing Sicily rather than ruling it? Or that Athens will honor her obligation to come to her assistance if Syracuse attacks her? For Athens has declared herself immune to the sanction of community opinion, the only sanction an alliance has in this world.[30] Camarina understandably refuses to align herself with either side.

THE SPEECHES WE HAVE EXAMINED, from the Corcyrean debate to Athens' response at Camarina, mark successive stages in the deterioration of a culture of argument. The process is perhaps not inevitable, but it is natural, each containing the seeds of the next. The way the Athenians talk at Melos and Camarina, for example, is an advanced version of the way Diodotus talked, which was in turn a development of the Athenian speech at Sparta, which itself built on materials in the original Corcyrean debates.

But this is not the story of words alone, for, as language deteriorates, so does everything else. At Melos the Athenians do not merely talk in an objectionable way; they also slaughter the people. The interaction between speech and conduct is one of Thucydides' deep themes, perhaps nowhere more explicit than in the famous excursus on the effects of the wave of civil wars that swept through Greece as a consequence of the Peloponnesian War, beginning with the civil war successfully fomented by Corinth at Corcyra. As observed in the opening paragraph of this book, Thucydides says that in these times even the meanings of words were altered. "Irrational boldness was considered as manly loyalty to one's partisans; prudent delay as specious cowardice, moderation as a disguise for unmanliness, and a well-rounded intelligence as a disqualification for action" (3. 82. 4). And, along with the words, all standards of thought and behavior collapsed. To punish for a wrong was a greater good than to be without injury; oaths were meaningless, for they were disregarded as soon as made; the leaders used fine-sounding political slogans but were interested only in what they could get for themselves; and so on. Their warfare knew no rules. "The citizens who had not joined either faction were destroyed by both, either because they would not join or through envy that they might survive" (3. 82. 8).

Thucydides explains why the wave of civil wars broke out at this time and not before. They were the direct result of the war between Athens and Sparta, because without such a war the factions within a city would have no pretext for calling in outsiders, nor were outsiders necessarily ready to act; but now the disaffected party could always appeal to the power with whom their city was not allied, who would always be eager to intervene. The stimulation of faction, against the central premise of the integrity of the city-state, it will be recalled, was part of the policy of Diodotus; Thucydides here exhibits its consequences.

For Athens the deterioration of language has meant an increasing loss of the capacity to speak and act coherently, and this led ultimately to the

81

loss of a coherent sense of self and aim. Thus in the Melian dialogue we saw the rational proponents of pure self-interest talking irrationally about their interests, and in the disastrous Sicilian campaign, which immediately follows, Thucydides shows us an Athens incapable of fitting action to plan. Here the Athenians not only abandon Pericles' policy of prudent restraint; they mismanage everything, putting Nicias in charge of a campaign he disapproves of and recalling Alcibiades, who favored the campaign, to answer charges of crimes against religion. But Athens could have survived even these things, says Thucydides; what she could not survive was her own internal divisions, which destroyed her sense of herself and her capacity to act (2. 65. 12). She lost at the end what the men of Melos died to try to save, her sense of her own identity.

We have come full circle. In his introduction (which will be discussed more fully below), Thucydides says that Athens originally grew great because she first established political identity and stability. The most fundamental assumption of the culture of argument defined in the Corcyrean speeches is the integrity and unity of the cities who are the actors within it. As we saw, the language can work on this basis even during a civil war, for it organizes others in relation to that event. The Peloponnesian War created the circumstances in which civil war became endemic, in a modified form at last striking Athens herself. Athens' attempt to define herself as outside the culture of argument that defined her relations with others thus led first to incoherence and ultimately to her own destruction.

THE EXPERIENCE OF THE TEXT

I have thus far devoted most of my attention to one aspect of Thucydides' *History*, its treatment of the culture of argument that is established in the early debates and shown thereafter, with such terrible consequences, to deteriorate. This is an important part of Thucydides' work, but it is not all of it. We must ask what place this story has in the *History* as a whole, and this, in turn, is to ask about the nature and meaning of the text itself. What is the experience that this text offers its reader, and what, if anything, unites and organizes it? Is there a place of central value, like Book Twenty-four of the *Iliad*, where the author and reader may stand together to view and to judge the world before them? If not, how are one's perceptions and judgments given direction here? Or is Thucydides' aim more scientific (and seemingly more modest)? Does he seek merely to define the world and to explain what happens within it? If so, what kind of explanation does he offer? On what premises does the text function, and what sort of understanding does it hold out? What is its method, and what is its point?

When we turn to the text with such questions as these, we find at work within it several different ways of doing history: different ways of telling a story, different modes of explanation, different kinds of meaning. The problem is not that the text makes no sense of the events it presents but that it makes sense of too many different and incompatible kinds. As Thucydides tells his story he seems to invite us to conceive of the world he presents in a wide range of ways, but these, though intelligible enough when regarded independently, do not fit together into a coherent whole.

The rhetorical history I have summarized above, for example, makes a certain kind of sense. It proceeds naturally and plausibly from stage to stage, and it has a certain kind of self-evident meaning, for it is the story of the collapse of culture, and we know how to respond to that. But the very fact that this story can be abstracted from the rest of the *History* suggests that it is just one of many different stories, each of which operates on different principles and by different methods.

The Archeology

One important kind of history that is placed in opposition to the rhetorical history I have summarized above is exemplified in the initial section, usually called the Archeology. Here Thucydides begins by saying that "he wrote down the history of the war between the Athenians and the Peloponnesians, starting right when it began, because he expected it to be a great one and *axiologōtaton* [far more worthy of being spoken about, analyzed, made sense of] than any that had preceded it" (1. 1. 1). There then follows a dense and powerful history of earlier times, designed to show their comparative insignificance. Thucydides' method here is remarkable, a social thought of an extraordinary kind that anticipates the most modern conceptions of social process and change. What he writes here is not a political or military narrative but an explication of the relationships among the social and natural realities that at once constitute and explain events. The interest is in process and structure, and the mode of explanation is systematic.

His account goes this way. In the beginning it appears that what is now called Hellas [31] was not inhabited in any fixed way. Migrations were the rule. Each group moved on when forced by another that was stronger. There was no trade, and only subsistence agriculture; for there was no capital and no planting of olive trees and vines, which were vulnerable to destruction. Since the people could meet their needs pretty much anywhere and left little behind them when they moved, migration was relatively easy. It was the richest land that was the most subject to such changes, for both internal and external reasons: where the land was better, some men became more powerful than others, and this led both to civil wars and to invasions from outside. Owing to the poorness of her soil, Athens was free from civil war and invasion and became as a result so politically secure that refugees from other cities wished to come there in large numbers. In this way her population grew so great that she began to send out colonies. The material poverty of Athens paradoxically became her political wealth.

Under such circumstances there could be no united action, and there was none before the Trojan War. What made that possible was the use of the sea, which arose in the following way. Minos, in Crete, was the first to establish a navy, with which he ruled many of the islands of the Aegean, driving out the inhabitants, establishing colonies, and putting down piracy. Once these things were accomplished, it became possible for the first time to acquire wealth. Men began to wall their cities. "Moved by desire for gain, the weaker submitted to dependence on the stronger, and the more powerful, with greater resources, made the weaker cities their subjects" (1. 8. 3).

Power is here seen as a human artifact, made partly by agreement, for the weak submit to the strong for their own gain, whether one speaks of cities or of men. The nature of power is social, not material, and the realities of power should never be confounded with such appearances as the monuments a city chooses to build. (If the power of Sparta and Athens were to be judged by their monuments, for example, the one would be thought far weaker, the other far stronger, than was actually the case.)

Thucydides uses this method both to explain particular events and to show how one way of life was changed into another. He tells us, for example, that the reason the Trojan War lasted so long was not that the resources engaged were so great but that they were so small. Lack of supplies meant that the Achaeans were constantly obliged to employ some of their men in farming and pillaging and in going back to Thrace for food. If they had been able to supply their entire force and use it in battle without interruption, Troy would surely have fallen more quickly.

After the Trojan War there was a conversion from ancient to contemporary ways, which worked this way. At first there were upheavals, arising from the return of the forces from Troy and the Dorian invasion of the Peloponnesus. When conditions became stable, cities were able to send out colonies; trade grew, and this necessitated the development of fleets, for transport and for war. There was some conquest of the islands by naval powers, but on land there were no wars beyond border wars, and there were no foreign wars, for there was no organization of the cities, either under the leadership of the more powerful or by alliances of equals. With the increase of wealth the cities came to be ruled by tyrants, who naturally made their own safety, not expansion, their first priority.

After the tyrants were put down (largely by the Spartans) and the Persians were repulsed, Athens turned the Delian League into an empire by converting the contribution of ships into the payment of tribute. Sparta led her allies without demanding payment, but she saw to it that they were governed oligarchically and in her interest. Such, says Thucydides, was the state of affairs at the beginning of the war.[32]

IN THESE WAYS the Archeology identifies the essential elements of a social system and shows how they are related to one another, and it does this dynamically as well as structurally, for it shows how changes in one place produce changes in another. It is a polished and achieved piece of work; one could readily find materials in it for an advanced course in social analysis and explanation. Here is someone doing something new— new even to us—and doing it beautifully.

But Thucydides abandons the method as inadequate for the task he has set for himself. At the end of the Archeology he explains that the "truest explanation" of the Peloponnesian War, "though least expressed in speech," was Sparta's fear of Athens' growth.[33] This is a sensible statement and of a piece with what has gone before. What we would expect to follow, if the method of the Archeology were continued, is a rather short text analyzing process and structure in the war. But for Thucydides all this serves only to introduce the story he has to tell, and now he begins to operate in a number of very different ways. Instead of stopping with a true but relatively uninteresting statement about causation, he launches into his detailed account of the Corcyrean debate, taking as a central subject the culture of argument enacted there.

The Ambivalence of the Text

In telling the ensuing story of the way one event leads to another until a larger phenomenon, the war, has been described and, in this way at least, accounted for, Thucydides continues to exhibit fundamentally contrary tendencies and thus to make a text that is ineluctably ambivalent.

Consider, for example, this question, which I mentioned earlier but then slid over: Was Athens compelled by circumstances to talk as she did at Sparta, at Melos, and at Camarina, or could she have talked in other, less destructive ways? The importance of this question for the meaning and nature of the text could hardly be exaggerated, for if Athens was free to choose how she talked, she can be held responsible for the results of her choice: for what happens to her language, her community, and her own identity. On this view, the story would be one of culpability and consequence, a kind of moral drama. But if we are to see Athens as compelled by circumstances to talk as she did, she cannot be held responsible in the same way, and the story would be one in which events work by a remorseless logic to an inevitable conclusion, with Athens as the victim. What our question raises, then, is whether it is the object of this text to hold its actors responsible for what they say and do—to praise and blame, to admire and condemn—or whether, by contrast, its object is merely to describe and explain in some scientific fashion the chain of events that make up its narrative. This question affects the meaning of the text in the deepest way, yet it plainly has no answer.

Such irresolution on matters of greatest importance is a structural characteristic of the text as a whole. Again and again it suggests a question, or forces it upon the reader, and then offers grounds for conflicting responses. Consider, for example, how the following questions might be answered. Is it Thucydides' view that this world is governed by broad social forces and processes, in a regular and discoverable way, or does he think one should look rather to individual judgments and policies for the explanation of events? And, whatever the mode of explanation, are the events of this world in his view subject to regularity, or are they subject to fluke or chance? Is this a scientific history, in which events are reduced to their causes so that one may see more clearly how things happen in the world and learn to manage them? [34] Or is its structure closer to that of a tragedy, in which a great actor, Athens, careens out of control, destroyed by its very greatness? Is the central value of this book admiration for the genius of Athens, respect for the culture she destroyed, or, perhaps, neither of these but an attitude of scientific objectivity?

Much could be found in the text to support each of the views implicit in these questions, and in fact each has seriously and credibly been advanced as the way to understand the *History*.[35] For example, to some extent its events are clearly shaped by policy, and Thucydides plainly implies that, if Pericles' defensive and cautious policy had been followed, Athens would have survived (2. 65. 7). It has even been suggested that his dominant purpose in writing the *History* was to vindicate that policy,[36] and of course throughout the *History* we see people pursuing policies and making judgments that prove in the event to be wise or foolish. (The Sicilian expedition is but the most dramatic example.) From a related but distinct point of view, the story can be seen as the expression of character in action: the timid Nicias, the reckless Alcibiades, the prudent Archidamas, and so on, all stamp with their character the events for which they are responsible. One might even say that the central work of the book is the definition of individual character and the tracing-out of the consequences of character in action. Or, as suggested above, one can see the events as shaped by broad social and economic forces, perhaps inevitably so. The war was caused by Sparta's fear of Athens' growth, we are told, and what could have changed that? One can also find much in the text to support the view that the *History* has the form and meaning of a tragic drama, in which Athenian *hubris*, exemplified, for example, by Athens' behavior at Melos, is properly punished with destruction. Add to this the fact that the story is told in units of yearly campaigns, one after the other, and we have yet another way in which the material is conceived and organized: as a kind of chronicle. And there is a sense in which it may be wrong to call this a history in our sense at all, for it is the study not so much of the past as of the present: its events are contemporary ones, inquired into as they occur. Only one piece of it functions as we expect history to function, that is, as a chronological and orderly account of the facts, without much rhetorical characterization or narrative shaping. That piece is the Pentekontaetia, the history of the fifty years just preceding the war, and it is both dull and inaccurate.[37] One might almost think that it is inserted to show just how limited and uninteresting this mode of history is.

Finally, it is essential to see that the discontinuities among the various modes of doing history that can be found here are not merely differences in the method of explaining the same events but differences in defining, in constituting, the events themselves. For the mode of explanation largely determines what shall have standing as a fact or event to be explained. If social process is the mode, questions of individual character are irrelevant, and vice versa. The events of the *History* are thus constructed in incompatible ways as well as subjected to incompatible modes of explanation.[38]

How ARE WE TO READ a text that functions in such apparently conflicting and contradictory ways? What sense can we make of a mind that proposes, almost simultaneously, such a variety of ways both of making a world and of making sense of it? The worst response is to patronize Thucydides, saying, for instance, that his *History* has inconsistent strains because it is unfinished or because he had not yet worked out a resolution of the conflicts.[39] This is wrong, not only because his is not a mind to be patronized, but because the inconsistencies of language and method are not incidental but structural. I think that, had he ever finished the *History*, they would still be there, perhaps in even more marked form; for they seem essential to his object in making this text. For the same reason, it is wrong to try to harmonize them by producing some Thucydidean concept of causation, for example, or of rules of political life. The opposition is deliberate; in fact it is this that gives the text its central life and meaning. For the experience this text offers its reader at its center is that of trying repeatedly to make sense of its events, first one way, then another, and always, in the end, failing. Whenever the reader thinks he has found a way to render this text and its events coherent, it presents him with something he must explain away but finds that he cannot. In this respect the text is like the world itself, and that, in my view, is its very point. For it is not Thucydides' purpose in this text to present a narrative of events and to explain them, as today we expect a historian to do; his purpose is to make a text that, by reduplicating them in clarified and intensified form, will force upon the reader the difficulties Thucydides himself faces in describing and making sense of the "text" that is his real world. His object is not to explain events but to make them problematic, and this is how his text teaches us: it gives to us the problem it defines and elaborates, the problem of trying to reconstitute and comprehend collective experience. The modes of presentation and understanding Thucydides employs are the ways in which we still try to make sense of our own world.

The text that makes sense of its material in so many conflicting ways is a first-class instruction in each of them, for Thucydides performs each mode beautifully; but it also qualifies the confidence one can have in any one way of presenting facts and understanding them. The story can be told and analyzed in many different ways, each one of which makes sense but none of which makes the only kind of sense. Taken together, they define what it means to try to reconstitute the world in words and to make sense of it, an attempt that will always in some sense fail. That is the condition of life that this book makes real and upon which it insists.

It is because the text mirrors the world in this way that it can be said to offer an education in statesmanship. It does not demonstrate rules of prudence or generalship or establish a program for success or anything like that; instead it offers the experience of a part of life. The experience of this text is like the experience of the world, and this is how it relates to the future, not through the promulgation of lessons. This is why we need not be troubled by the obviously crafted and artificial quality of Thucydides' text or by the uncertain relationship between this world that he has made and the real world of fifth-century Greece. For the book asks to be tested not against that world, not against Thucydides' sources, but against the reader's experience of his own world. Thucydides is thus not a historian in any modern sense of the word,[40] for it is not his object merely to narrate and explain events. Rather, he is the maker of a text, the architect of an organized experience for his reader that is meant to instruct him in the nature and limits of his understanding, at once increasing his powers and qualifying them.

I asked above whether this text offers its reader a resting place like Book Twenty-four of the *Iliad*—a central place from which to perceive, to understand, and to respond to the events of this world. The answer is that it does not; indeed, what the text is ultimately about is the impossibility of either discovering or making such a place, and its life is in its perpetual restlessness. One might say of Thucydides what the Corinthians said of the Athenians, that it is his nature "neither to rest himself nor permit rest to others."

*   *   *

IN THIS TEXT Thucydides draws a sharp line between words and speeches (*logoi*), on the one hand, and deeds and facts (*erga*), on the other. This enables him, among other things, to break out of the culture as a whole one part of it, the culture of argument exemplified in the Corcyrean debate, and to make it an object of conscious attention. (One might do much the same thing with legal discourse in our own world or the discourse of religious argument in the seventeenth century.) This language is a way of constituting a world: it defines a set of actors and gives them roles and relations; it establishes practices in which they can engage—alliance, arbitration, colonization, and so on; and it creates a set of topics to which they must appeal in justifying their conduct—justice, expediency, and gratitude.[41]

This language has a remarkable flexibility, for it can be used to justify a very wide range of conduct. Such flexibility is essential to the continued existence of any language of this kind, for, if it requires more than an actor can give, it will lose his participation. But not everything can be justified: the language has some actual effect on conduct. And the requirement of justification is the essential idea of what we mean by the rule of law: we insist that a police officer explain in terms of his legitimate needs and goals the reason why he made a particular search;[42] we require that legislation be justified in terms of legitimate state interests;[43] and we discover that an institution of this kind imposes limits on those who use it, even when the powerful use it to oppress the weak.[44]

This language can be learned, in a rough way, by Thucydides' modern reader, who finds that he or she can ask what arguments will be made in a new situation and then check his or her judgment against what Thucydides offers, in this way becoming a judge of rhetorical appropriateness in this world.[45] In the text, its speakers use it instrumentally, not to say what they actually think justice requires in a particular situation but to make the best case they can in its terms. This language, and the world it constitutes, are thus in a sense artificial, for they are made by man and can be destroyed by him; but they nonetheless have a reality that cannot be denied.

The culture presented in Book One can be, as Thucydides teaches us, an object of history[46] and of concern. Without it, or some substitute, we would have no world at all, no medium for the organized definition and expression of motive, for action shaped by motive, but a formless chaos like that experienced by Achilles when his connection with his culture broke down. If a demythologizer were to claim of such a discourse, ancient or modern, that it was only words, mere words—*logoi*, not *erga*—he would have to substitute for it other words of his own, other ways of defining actors and relations and practices and motives, and he, like the Athenians, would find that these had a social and cultural reality of their own.

The discourse of the Corcyrean debate is, as we have seen, marked by deep and unsettling tensions, especially between the claims of justice and those of expediency. It would be a great mistake to think of it romantically as a language without a flaw, expressing a wholly stable and coherent tradition. But the tensions within this language are in fact a strength of it; for, as Thucydides shows, the world is constantly changing, and its language must therefore change too, and these tensions provide the occasions and means for change. For him it would be foolish as well as impossible to try to maintain with rigidity the conventions of a discourse that no longer fit its world. Life with this language in this world must reflect the possibility of change.

As it happens, of course, the kind of change that occurs is not adaptation but collapse, a failure of order and meaning. When the language in which the world is constituted falls apart, it becomes impossible, as Thucydides shows us, not only to act rationally within it but to make satisfactory sense of it. The end—for the historian and reader, as well as for the cities of this world—is a loss of language, a loss of the world, that threatens to become a loss of identity as well.

How is one to live on conditions such as these? Thucydides' text is addressed only in part to that question, for much of it was written in the process of discovering these conditions, against the writer's wish, not in responding to them. The unfinished character of the text may mean that for him there was no answer. But his text nonetheless exists, and its achievement is to reproduce for the reader, in distilled and clarified form, the conditions that make meaning impossible. To do that is to assert the possibility of meaning of another kind, in the world he creates with his reader, where he acts as tutor and friend, schooling our expectations against the intolerable fluctuation and chaos of life and creating a community of two with a life and order of its own. At the very least, the reader who later watches his own world fall apart will know that he is not alone.

But Thucydides goes beyond this, beyond the conditions of his own life as he represents them, and raises a hope that things could somewhere, sometime, be different. For he teaches us something about what a world that worked and maintained itself would be like, and in doing so he teaches us to be critics and users of our own public language. Of course it is not clear that in his view any person has much power to affect the course of things—that question he leaves wide open—but he teaches us at least to attend in new ways to the meaning of what we say and to understand our inheritance with different eyes.

For example, one of the lessons of this text—and I for one think this is a universal truth—is that it is as irrational to speak of self-interest without recognizing the claims of justice as it is to speak of justice without recognizing the claims of self-interest. What might be called the field of justice-talk can in fact be said to live in a tension between two contrary tendencies, each acting on the other: the claims the self makes on the world and those the world makes on the self. One part of the lesson is that the language of justice cannot demand from the self what it cannot give. This is the Athenian claim at Sparta, and it is unanswerable. But the other part of the lesson is equally unanswerable: it is that the self cannot function without a language in which it and its interests can be defined; the self is nothing without a culture and a community that establish others and their interests. The most self-interested person in the world thus has an interest in maintaining a language that alone can give reality and meaning to his wishes.

Justice and self-interest can indeed be seen as two sides of the same thing, as topics each of which necessarily implies the existence and validity of the other (as "form and substance" do, or "straight and curved"). There is a structural tension between them and a temptation to abandon one in favor of the other, as we saw the speakers in the Corcyrean debates start to do. But it is only in the tension between them that a coherent world of social action and meaning can be made. It is that tension—that reciprocal recognition of claim and limit—that makes possible the adjustments by which a culture can change without collapsing.

A second lesson of a similar kind, equally important to us, also emerges from the text. It begins with the Athenian claim that talk about justice can meaningfully go on only between equals in power, as a kind of compelled substitute for the exercise of force, since superior power will not be restrained except by power. This kind of remark makes us uncomfortable, but it is hard to refute; and it is supported by the demonstration in this text that the related practices of alliance, gratitude, and compassion, even honor, also have equality as their premise. This seems to mean what Athens makes it mean: that in a world of unequal power, talk about justice has no place. But could equality be seen not as the factual precondition of the discourse of justice but as its product, as something that it creates and makes real in the world? Could Athens, that is, have recognized that even cities unequal in power may have an equal interest in maintaining the discourse that gives them identity and community, that indeed makes their life and competition possible? This recognition would have led Athens to think very differently of herself and of her situation at Melos, for example, and to talk differently to the Melians and herself; it would have been the invention of a new idea, equality under law.[47] That invention would make real in the world of law and politics something analogous to what the *Iliad* creates in the mind of its reader: a recognition of the common humanity and equal value of all people.

IN THE LAST TWO CHAPTERS of this book we shall return to the examination of such possibilities, looking especially at the language of American law. For the present we turn to Plato's *Gorgias*, which examines the relation between a speaker and his language, not from the outside, as Thucydides does, but from the inside, and sees new and important possibilities for the life of the individual mind in relation to its language and in community with another mind.

4

The Reconstitution of Language and Self in a Community of Two

Plato's *Gorgias*

In the *Gorgias*, Plato (like Homer and Thucydides) is interested in examining the relationship between the individual and his language, in this case the language of ordinary Greek morality. His point of view is for the most part internal—that of the language-user—and his central concern is in a literal sense ethical,[1] for the main issue to which he returns again and again is the kind of character a person defines for himself and offers to others—the kind of life and community he makes—when he chooses to think and talk one way rather than another. This is Plato's concern from the very beginning, when Socrates gives Chaerephon the seemingly innocuous but in fact deeply threatening direction to "ask Gorgias who he is" (447d); and it runs through to the very end, where Socrates defends his own way of life, despite its terrible costs.

The great difference between this and the other two texts we have read is that for Plato language can be consciously and deliberately changed by the individual mind. When that happens, the mind and its life change too; this means that we are responsible in a new way for what we say and are, and Plato is accordingly interested in the ways in which changes in language and self can and should be made. Thus, instead of telling the story of the disintegration of language and the world, as Thucydides did, and instead of making out of his resources something new and seemingly inexpressible in inherited terms, as Homer did, Plato writes a text that seeks to involve the reader directly in the processes by which language and character are broken down and remade. His interest is in the possibilities of life we can give ourselves, in the possibilities of meaning we can give our language.

In this dialogue he focuses on two contrasting ways of speaking, of being, and of establishing community with others. These are "rhetoric," which he attacks, and "dialectic," which he defends and intends to exemplify. Of rhetoric there are three representatives: Gorgias, a Sicilian visitor to Athens and one of the first teachers of rhetoric; Polus (the name means "colt"), his brash young student; and Callicles, a mature practitioner of the rhetorician's art. Opposed to them are two exemplars of dialectic: Socrates, in relation to these interlocutors; and Plato, in relation to the reader.

THE *GORGIAS*

Form

Plato's *Gorgias* is a dialogue, not a treatise, and it is important to ask at the outset why Plato chooses to write this way instead of simply telling us what he believes in some straightforward fashion. Is it his idea to make philosophy entertaining, to put a sugar coating on the dull pill of truth, or does this form have purposes of another kind? In particular, why do we have three interlocutors, of such different capacity and character, talking with Socrates on the same subject? This will mean that the same arguments are brought up all over again, in somewhat different terms and contexts, and that some arguments raised in early conversations are later dropped and never answered. Moreover, the topic of the dialogue never seems to stay fixed; now it is rhetoric, now pleasure, now what we mean by the shameful or the admirable, now whether it is important to be able to protect oneself against harm, and so on. Nor are the methods of argument all of a piece: sometimes Socrates engages in a logical refutation, sometimes he tells stories, sometimes he plays tricks, sometimes he makes speeches. What is worse, some of the arguments he makes are plainly specious, and others one suspects to be so, though Plato never tells us which ones he regards as defective. Why does this text have this apparently unphilosophical form? What does Plato achieve by using it that he otherwise could not? To put it in terms by now familiar to us, what relationship does Plato thus establish with his reader, and what does he teach us?

These questions obviously cannot be answered in a sentence or a paragraph; they should be taken instead as suggesting the sort of attention that the *Gorgias* will invite and reward. But it may be helpful to suggest now that the dialogue itself is meant to exemplify the kind of life that Socrates calls "dialectic." The form of the dialogue is not a primitive or bizarre method for setting forth a doctrine that Plato is too perverse or incompetent to say straight out; what it offers is an engagement in an activity, and this activity is its true subject. As we shall see, Socrates does occasionally say something to describe dialectic, but its clearest and truest definition is to be found not in what he says but in what he does.

We shall here be concerned with "rhetoric" and "dialectic" only as they are defined in this dialogue, not as they are treated by Plato or others elsewhere.[2] But it is worth observing that certain aspects of the process exemplified here are very close to what is usual in Plato's other Socratic dialogues and to Socrates' description of his mode of life in the *Apology*. There we are told that Socrates would typically seek out a person who claimed to know how to do something—here the teaching of rhetoric, elsewhere generalship or mathematics or teaching virtue—and ask his interlocutor his central questions: Who are you? What do you do? and What do you know? Since we all know how to do things that we cannot explain, things we have never thought about beyond saying "I am a banker" or "I am a surgeon," this line of questioning has the result of making conscious what before was not, the relation between self and culture. I am a football coach or a law professor, I say, and only then begin to realize, when for Socrates that is not a sufficient answer, that this identity is a cultural one, not necessary but chosen, and chosen by me without my wholly knowing or understanding it. In the ensuing conversation the interlocutor's account of himself and his motives is shown to make no sense even in its own terms; it is seen to be internally incoherent. The one who claims to know knows nothing after all. This is the *elenchus*, or refutation, of which Socrates repeatedly speaks, and it is the heart of dialectic. It results in a mortification or humiliation of a special kind, for one is mortified by the invocation not of new facts or ideas but of what one already knows or claims to know. One part of the self is appealed to against another part, and in the process a previously unknown self-contradiction is revealed.

The intellectual process by which this aspect of dialectic typically works is a movement from a point of disagreement between Socrates and his interlocutor to a more general proposition, which both accept; this is then shown, by reasoning sometimes sound, sometimes fallacious, to lead to conclusions opposite to those previously asserted by the interlocutor. In the process the language of the interlocutor is remade, converted into what are called paradoxes (that is, previously impossible or unimaginable statements that he must now accept or that he is at least incapable of rationally rejecting). The effect of all this is to disturb the relation between self and language, to break down the sense of natural connection and coherence between them. One comes suddenly to see both self and language as uncertain, as capable of being remade in relation to each other. The true aim of a dialogue that works this way, the *Gorgias* among others, is the reconstitution of self and language.

Language

To understand the ways in which Socrates works on his language and on the speakers whose attitudes are to some extent formed by that language—and the ways in which Plato works on his reader and *his* language—it is essential to have some knowledge of the central terms of the Greek language and culture and how they are related to one another. Indeed, the reader will find that many of the questions raised in this text are, in the first instance at least, really questions about the proper use of particular Greek words. They invite responses that are partly objective or empirical, reporting what Greek usage in fact is, and partly normative or persuasive, asserting how a word ought to be used. In either case, there is a sense in which some of the questions presented here can be asked only in Greek and answered only in Greek. Not surprisingly, the common English equivalents for the key terms—e.g., "good," "shameful," "noble"—are hopelessly inadequate as substitutes, in part because they are laden with moralistic overtones that are inappropriate to the Greek context. (What kind of person would ever say in English, for example, that he "pursues the good"? Yet in Greek that would be a commonplace, almost a tautology: one central meaning of "what is good" is "what one pursues or chooses," whether or not it is "morally good.") An English translation of this text thus tends to have an unreal and goody-goody quality, which makes one wonder how the questions the dialogue addresses could possibly interest a serious person. In Greek, by contrast, the argument is vital and threatening, gripping the mind through its very language. Indeed, the reason why, in the dialogues, people turn away from Socrates, and why, in the world, he was killed, is not that what he says is too vapid but that it is too real and threatening.

All of this presents obvious difficulties for the English-speaking reader. These cannot be entirely eliminated, but I will try to reduce them by providing some lexicographical information to begin with and, thereafter, by using certain Greek terms along with, or instead of, English substitutes.

THE MOST IMPORTANT Greek terms of value used in this dialogue are *agathon* ("good") and its opposite, *kakon* ("bad"), and *kalon* ("noble") and its opposite, *aischron* ("shameful").[3] These words are the most powerful terms of praise and blame in the Greek of the time, operating as terms of final conclusion in an argument: if it is *kakon* or *aischron*, no one could want it; if it is *agathon* or *kalon*, everyone will want it, for that is what the terms mean. Not surprisingly, then, they have a very wide range of use and association, not wholly reproducible in English even by lengthy disquisition, let alone by bland substitutions, such as the traditional ones given in parentheses above; and, as one would expect of such terms, within their ranges of meaning there are deep conflicts and contradictions, reflecting tensions basic to the culture as a whole. The *Gorgias* is in fact in large part about these words and others related to them: about what they should be taken to mean, how they should be defined or redefined; about the ways in which the contradictions they entail might be resolved; and about the patterns of meaning in which they should be arranged. The object of the dialogue is to construct a coherent language of value out of the naturally complex and inconsistent materials of the time and, in doing that, to define new possibilities for the life of the self and the life of the community.

A short account of the meaning of these central terms might go this way. The word *agathon* ("good") has one very powerful strain of meaning that has nothing to do with what we would call morally "good"; it is much closer to our ideas of "successful" or "first class" or "someone that counts" or "something that matters." As applied to a person, the term originally denoted the member of an aristocratic warrior class, and it commended qualities that that class regarded as essential virtues: bravery, martial prowess, skill at counsel, and the like. In this pattern of associations, *kalon* commends the conduct or condition of one who is *agathos*; its opposite is *aischron*. Thus victory is *kalon*, defeat *aischron*, in battle or in games; the powerful man is *agathos*, the weak man *kakos*. (We do have English uses of "good" that are like this use of *agathon*, such as "good at," "good for," "a good tackle," "a good shot," and so on.) When *agathon* in this sense is used to describe the object of striving, it means what men strive for in fact; and *kakon* accordingly means "what no one would choose." (In this sense Socrates' often repeated statement that no man willingly chooses the bad [the *kakon*] says nothing surprising but just what the terms imply.) When it is applied to objects or practices, *agathon* in this usage can often be equated with "useful" or "advantageous"; when it is applied to men, it means something like "successful." Similarly, *kakon* should be rendered not as "morally bad" but as "worthless" or "no good" or "harmful." *Kalon*, which characterizes the conduct of the *agathos* as viewed by others, implies (as its opposite *aischron* also does) a social world functioning as the source of approval or disapproval. "Noble" is empty to modern ears; perhaps "admirable" is the best we can do. *Aischron* is usually translated as "shameful," often a rather weak word in our world; "degrading" or "humiliating" may catch the sense of it better. It is important also to add that *kalon*, when applied to external features, means what we would call "beautiful," and *aischron* means "ugly."

These uses are far from modern experience. A few Americans, if they had access to the terms, would, I suppose, regard themselves as *agathos*, others as *kakos*, by birth; many more, as *agathos* by wealth, especially if they themselves had earned their money, or as *agathos* by virtue of the power they had acquired. This use of the word would have almost nothing in it of what we mean by "goodness"; it would not matter if the money had been earned in the candy business or the arms trade, or if the power had been acquired legally or through a corrupt political machine.[4] *Agathos* is a term of what we weakly call prestige.

97

There are other uses in Greek of the words *agathon*, *kakon*, *kalon*, and *aischron* that commend or decry what we would be more inclined to call moral virtues: lawfulness, mercy, a sense of community and equality, and the like, which can be summed up for our purposes, as Plato and Socrates do, under the headings of justice and temperance. The tension between these two kinds of usage (and it may oversimplify the difficulty to reduce them to two, as I have done) creates a problem deep in the language and the culture that it is a central purpose of the dialogue both to elaborate and to address.

Structure

The dialogue, you will remember, goes in outline something like this. When asked "who he is," as defined by what he does in the world, Gorgias says that he is a rhetorician and a teacher of rhetoric. In response to a series of questions put by Socrates, he defines rhetoric as the art of persuading others, especially those with power in the state, primarily about questions of justice and injustice (454b). Rhetoric is thus itself an enormous power, which can be used for good or ill. It works not by imparting knowledge about these things but by giving rise to desired opinions (455a). When Socrates asks whether the individual who is to practice this art must himself nonetheless know about the just and the unjust and the humiliating (*aischron*) and the admirable (*kalon*) and the advantageous and the good (*agathon*) and the worthless and the bad (*kakon*), which he is to talk about, Gorgias says that he must of course know these things. If a student comes to him who does not know them, Gorgias will teach him (460a).

Notice that Socrates does not now pursue the line of questioning obviously left open by Gorgias' response, i.e., what the nature of "justice" is and how it can be learned and taught; he simply lets him off the hook. This is because this dialogue is not about the nature of justice—for that, see the *Republic*—but about a prior question, the proper place and standing of talk about justice in the world. When Gorgias concedes the importance of the question, he concedes Socrates' essential point.[5]

Polus, eager to tangle with Socrates, now breaks in and rejects the concession Gorgias has just made. He says that Gorgias is simply ashamed (*aischunesthai*) to admit the truth, that the rhetorician need have no special knowledge of justice and injustice and the rest in order to practice the art of persuading about them (461b). Socrates welcomes his participation, at least so long as Polus agrees to engage in the process of refutation by question and answer and to refrain from making long speeches. He can either question or answer, as he chooses. Polus elects to do the questioning and, quickly revealing that he has no idea at all how to do it, ends up simply asking Socrates what kind of art he thinks rhetoric is. Socrates in response makes a brief speech, in which he says that rhetoric is not an art at all but merely a knack, which has as its object the production of pleasure—in fact it is merely a form of flattery,⁶ as cosmetics or cookery are (463b).⁷

Socrates is now asked an amusingly confused series of questions by Polus, at the heart of which is the assertion that it must be a great thing to be a rhetorician, for they have so much power in the city; they are practically dictators. Socrates responds to this by asserting a set of paradoxical propositions that Polus at first denies and then is forced to concede. The first of these is that the rhetorician and the dictator have the least power in the cities of which they seem to be master, "for they do virtually nothing that they want to do but only whatever they think best" (466e).⁸ (They can do whatever they like, that is, but they can be mistaken about whether it will advance what they really want.) In similar fashion Polus is led to concede that it is worse (more *kakon*) to do injustice than to suffer it and that, while the unjust man cannot be happy, he will be less wretched if he is punished than if he is not (479d–e).⁹

These statements are simply impossible; it cannot be "better," in the competitive sense of more "agathos," to suffer an injury—a diminution of autonomy and power—than to inflict one. Socrates compels them in his usual manner, first by eliciting acquiescence in certain propositions that the interlocutor cannot deny, then by showing that they lead to conclusions very different from what the interlocutor had imagined. In this conversation the key admission made by Polus is that, while it is worse (more *kakon*) to suffer injustice, it is more ugly and humiliating (more *aischron*) to do it. Socrates shows that this is not a possible set of positions, because what is more *aischron* must also be more *kakon*.¹⁰

At this point Callicles intervenes. He rejects this concession, saying that Polus, like Gorgias, is ashamed (*aischunesthai*) to admit what he really thinks, which is that it is obviously better to do than to suffer wrong, better to avoid punishment than to suffer it (482e). The defect in Socrates' refutation, he says, is that it confuses the categories of nature and convention: it is *kakon* by nature to suffer injustice, but to do injustice is *aischron* only by convention. If one looks to nature rather than convention, it is both more *kakon* and more *aischron* to suffer than to do injustice. That is the position that Polus was ashamed to admit. Just as Socrates earlier claimed that whatever is *aischron* is *kakon*, Callicles here reverses the equation: what is *kakon* is *aischron*. The conventions that establish the conventional sense of *aischron* used by Socrates and accepted by Polus, says Callicles, are the work of weak people who seek to protect themselves against their natural masters. Being inferior, they are happy enough to settle for a general equality. But nature itself declares that it is just both for the better (more *agathos*) to have more than the worse (the more *kakos*) and for the more powerful to have more than the less powerful. This is natural, as opposed to conventional, justice.

Callicles in this way rejects the very language of morality on which Socrates' refutation depended. He seeks to avoid the traps and limits of the language of his culture by standing outside it; in short, he claims the power to remake his language to accord with reality as he sees it.

His substantive position is a radical hedonism. According to what he calls natural justice and excellence, he who wants to live correctly should allow his desires to be as great as possible; he should not restrain them (*kolazein*) but serve them with his manliness and intelligence, satisfying each desire as it arises. This is of course impossible for most people, so they blame such a man, through shame (*aischunēi*) at their own weakness, and call licentiousness (*akolasia*) shameful and ugly and humiliating (*aischron*)(491e–492a). It is because of their own lack of manliness that they praise temperance and justice. Wantonness and licentiousness and liberty, if they are supported by force, are virtue and happiness.

When asked whether or not some pleasures are better than others—how high does the pleasure of scratching an itch rank with him, for example?(494c–e)—Callicles at first persists in refusing to acknowledge distinctions among them and asserts that the good and the pleasant are the same. But he is then made to admit, among other things, that the coward feels as much pleasure at the retreat of the enemy as the brave man, perhaps even more, and the foolish man is as capable of pleasure as the intelligent man (498a–c). Will Callicles therefore call the pleasures of such people good (*agathon*)? If all pleasures are equally good (*agathon*), he must do so. In consequence, the man called *kakos* because of his cowardice or stupidity becomes as *agathos* as the *agathos* man, an absolutely impossible position for Callicles, for whom the *agathos* man is, above all, manly, brave, and successful. But to admit that some pleasures are better than others is to accept a standard of judgment of exactly the sort he has been at pains to deny; and this in turn opens up the question by what art that standard is to be discovered and defined, which returns us to the subject of rhetoric and dialectic. Callicles thus begins as one who boldly claims to remake his language to accord with moral reality as he sees it, but he quickly finds that he cannot escape his commitment to its central terms after all. He retreats into a sullen pretense of acquiescence.

Now that Callicles will no longer engage in conversation with him, Socrates himself speaks at length in favor of orderliness within the self and in the world. The unrestrained (*akolastos*) man, such as Callicles admires, cannot be friend to man or god, for he is incapable of community (507e). As for his own alleged incapacity to protect himself against having injustice done to him, Socrates says that the art of not suffering wrong requires either (*a*) that one become an absolute dictator or (*b*) that one seek to ingratiate oneself in every way with those who do have power, praising and blaming the same things as they do and thereby becoming like them (510a–e). If those who have power are unjust, to protect oneself against suffering injustice will require that one become unjust oneself, which, as we have already seen, is the most *kakon* and *aischron* of things. One cannot, that is, protect oneself against the one injury without suffering the other, and greater, injury.

The alternative to such ingratiation, by which one becomes like the object of one's flattery, is to have the object not of pleasing the people who have political power but of making them as good as possible (most *agathos*). This is in fact the aim of Socrates and of dialectic, and it means that he is one of the few, if not the only one, who practices the true art of statesmanship (521d). This also means that, given the way the world is, Socrates could not put up much of a defense if someone used the law unjustly against him; but he does not think that this is humiliating or shameful (*aischron*), as it plainly would be if he were unable to protect himself against the far greater evil of saying or doing unjust things (522d). Socrates then tells a story of the afterlife, in which the person's soul is judged naked, just as it is, for what it is; and he says that this is the trial for which he wishes to prepare himself, not some proceeding brought against him by his enemies at Athens (526d). What is at stake in their conversation is nothing less than who one is and becomes.

He concludes by saying this:

> "Among the many arguments we have made, while the rest were being refuted [*elenchesthai*], this one alone stood firm: that one should avoid doing injustice more than suffering it and that, more than anything, it should be a man's object to be, not to seem, good [*agathos*], both in public and in private; and if one becomes bad [*kakos*] in some respect, one must be punished or corrected [*kolazesthai*]; and that the second good [*agathon*] after being just is to become so, and be corrected [*kolazesthai*] by paying the penalty;[11] and that one should shun all flattery of oneself or others, of the few or the many; and that rhetoric should always be used toward the end of justice, as should every other activity." [527b–c]

This is the way in which we should live and call upon others to live, "not [the way] that you trust and call upon me to share; for it is worth nothing, Callicles."

101

DIALECTIC

Throughout the dialogue Socrates has been at pains to define what he calls "dialectic" as a way of thinking and living and to oppose it to rhetoric. For example, he says at the beginning that he does not want to hear an oratorical display by Gorgias but wishes to engage in conversation with him. And when Gorgias makes great claims for the power of rhetoric, Socrates rather gently says that he would like to take issue with what Gorgias has said, for it does not seem consistent, but he also does not want to be offensive. He himself welcomes being refuted (*elenchesthai*) when he says something untrue, and welcomes refuting others when they say something untrue, and, if Gorgias is of the same mind, they can proceed; otherwise they should let it drop. It is only when Gorgias agrees to this procedure that Socrates begins his questioning.

Thus we discover that dialectic proceeds by question and answer and that its object is something called "refutation" or "correction." We then discover something more about it when Polus seeks to establish that a man can be both unjust and happy by citing the instance of Archelaus, the tyrant of Macedonia. Socrates first speaks to Polus not about the merits of his claim but about the method by which he is proceeding; he says that this sort of argument may be persuasive rhetorically, because most people would perhaps agree with it; but it is no demonstration whatever in dialectic, because he, Socrates, does not agree with it, and a dialectical refutation (*elenchos*) requires that one make the other agree with what one says (471e–472c). What matters between us is not the other witnesses who can be brought forward to support your view or mine but whether you can make me your witness or I can make you mine. For dialectic to exert its full force upon the individual mind, complete frankness is essential, a kind of shamelessness in saying what one really thinks. Thus Gorgias and Polus perhaps avoid the full force of Socrates' mind by agreeing with him too readily; and Socrates welcomes Callicles' bluntness of speech, for his candor may make possible a real engagement of mind with mind (487a).

As we have already seen, dialectic proceeds in part by exposing contradictions in one's thought, which are for Socrates contradictions in one's very self. He tells Callicles that he must either refute (*exelenchein*) what has been said about doing injustice being the worst of evils and the like

> "otherwise, Callicles himself will not agree with you,
> Callicles, but you will be in discord all your life; and yet
> I at least think it would be better that my lyre be out of
> tune and discordant, or that a chorus I might equip
> might be discordant, or that most men might disagree

with me and say the opposite of what I say, than that
I—just onc man— be discordant with myself and say
opposite things within myself"(482b).

Still, as I suggested above, the most important definition of dialectic is
not to be found in such statements as these but in the activities presented
in the text, those by which Socrates engages with his interlocutors and
Plato engages with his reader. What can be said of these?[12] What is the
life that is exemplified here, and how does the peculiar form of the dialogue work to express it? That is, if the dialogue does not function as a
coherent set of arguments, how does it function? What kind of attention
does it invite, and what kind of meaning does it yield?

Mind and Language: Dialectical Culture

I

We can start with the paragraph of the dialogue (above, p. 101) in
which Socrates sums up his position. Here we have a set of propositions
each one of which has been repeated over and over during the course of
the dialogue; upon them Socrates now says that, however erroneous his
other statements may have been, he confidently rests. He thus explicitly
offers these propositions as the central statement of the text as a whole.
But it is a rather strange statement, for all of the propositions collected
here, as their earlier reception in the dialogue has made plain, are what is
called, in Greek as well as in English, "paradoxical," that is, preposterous,
"out of place," what no one would ever say. How can it possibly be more
agathon (advantageous) and *kalon* (befitting to the powerful) and less
aischron (humiliating) and *kakon* (worthless) to suffer wrong than to do
it? It seems that the words cannot bear the meanings given them. If the
rest of the dialogue did not exist, that is, and these statements stood
alone, they would seem crazy or meaningless. They could certainly not
be taken seriously, for they arrange the materials of the culture in ways
that are, in the first instance at least, simply impossible.

But this very fact suggests a way of understanding an aim of the dialogue as a whole: it is to offer the reader a set of experiences that so
change his sense of things, including his sense of his language and himself, that when, at the end, these statements occur together as a kind of
summary of what has been said over and over in various ways in the rest
of the dialogue, they seem no longer paradoxical but natural and coherent and powerful and clear. In this rather literal sense it can be said
that the object of the dialogue is the making of a new language.

But what kind of language is this, and how is it put together? It is not, for the most part, an artificial or theoretical language, based on stipulative definitions that are then combined in propositions connected by the laws of logic. It is rather what might be called a natural or poetic language, in which terms have overlapping and inconsistent meanings, internal complexities and lacunae. In establishing this language, the dialogue, accordingly, does not proceed by a logical progression, from premise to conclusion, but in what might be called an associative fashion, with many repetitions of question, idea, and term, often leaving a subject only to return to it later, perhaps in a surprising way. It is full of play and paradox and has less the structure of formal argument, as we usually think of it, than that of a poem, drama, or musical composition. The recurrences of terms and statements are thus not really repetitions, after all, for they acquire new meaning from what else has happened, as a metaphor or image or melody can do: at the end they make sense in a new way. In showing us how it makes a language the dialogue shows us how it defines a life.

This view of the dialogue helps explain how Socrates can speak, in the quoted paragraph, so dismissively of the other statements he has made (when he suggests that they can perhaps be refuted): the reason is that the relationship between those statements and what he now says is not one of logical proof (if it were, the validity of his conclusions would depend absolutely on the validity of the earlier statements), but is both looser and more complex than that. For example, some of the "proofs" offered in the body of the text were plainly specious,[13] others we suspected to be so, and much of what was said was plainly motivated, in emphasis at least, by the nature of the social or dramatic moment.[14] Socrates is here saying that he knows all this and that it does not matter. Not that we could not go back to those things and straighten them out or at least arrive at a common view of them. But we cannot do everything at once, and the things he says now are the things that matter most and that we know most clearly. Socrates here also tells us that he does not put the same weight on everything he says, as he would have to do if the form of the discourse were that of mathematical or scientific proof; rather, he recognizes that we live in a world in which there are many things to say. Some of them are jokes; some of them seem right but we are not sure of that; some seem dubious; but on some of them one rests, and it is these that we are given in Socrates' paragraph of conclusion.

II

How is this language made? The most obvious method is overt definition of terms. Consider, for example, the definition of rhetoric that Socrates leads Gorgias to make at the very beginning. He starts with the question With what is the art of rhetoric concerned? With words (i.e., speech)? But so, in a way, are many other arts, such as medicine, which uses words for diseases and medicines. Is it concerned, then, with words abstracted from the material universe—with words alone, so to speak? But so is arithmetic. Gorgias then says that what rhetoric offers is the power to persuade (*peithein*). But rhetoric is not the only art of persuasion, Socrates responds; in fact, every art that has a subject persuades with respect to that subject, as medicine does. With respect to what subject does rhetoric persuade? Gorgias answers: With respect to what is just and unjust (449d–454b). And so on. This is a process of conceptual clarification that seems to be not threatening but helpful, a way of asking how we can accurately describe this part of our social and intellectual universe. And the fact that the definition is not stipulated but cooperatively arrived at means that it is not merely a clarification but an instruction in the processes of making things clear.

By contrast, in his own definition of rhetoric as flattery, Socrates does not draw distinctions his interlocutors already make (perhaps without knowing it) so much as offer a new set of distinctions for shared use, and he does this argumentatively, for he knows that the others will not see things this way. Socrates similarly creates a new system of meaning when, in his engagement with Polus, he draws a distinction (not present in ordinary Greek) between doing "whatever one thinks best" and doing "what one wants."

The verbal "proofs" by which Socrates first establishes his paradoxes, that to do injustice is more *kakon* than to suffer it and that to remain unpunished is more *kakon* for the wrongdoer than to be punished, are language-making of another kind: they overtly redefine the central value terms of the discourse, *kakon* and *aischron*, *agathon* and *kalon*. The same can be said of his proof to Callicles that the *agathon* and the pleasant must be different, which works by showing that the pleasant coexists and coterminates with its opposite—as the pleasure of drinking and the pain of thirst, do, for example—while the *agathon* does not (495d–497a).

But the effect of such proofs is peculiar. They produce acquiescence in the auditor but of an unsatisfactory kind; for it arises not from conviction of the truth of what has been said but from a sense that, at least for the moment, one cannot answer it. What is produced is not belief but a sense of helplessness or defeat, a sense that one has been manipulated by a mind more clever than one's own but not more sound. "I cannot answer, but I still don't think it is right." The interlocutor is left wishing he could respond, knowing that he cannot, and feeling frustrated and competitive. The effect of the "proof" is not to persuade but to disorient him, to break down for the moment his sense of security and competence in the command of his language, to place him, as it were, nowhere, for he has nothing to say—he is in a position, in fact, rather like that of Achilles in Book Nine—and all this stimulates in him a need for a new sense of order and meaning.[15] The reader, on his part, responds to these incompletely persuasive proofs in a similar way, to similar effect. He is frustrated by the fact that neither Plato nor Socrates ever tells him which proofs are valid, which not, and by Socrates' temporary dismissal of them all, at the end, when he rests on the central statements quoted above.

This frustration has a purpose: it places responsibility for making sense of the arguments on the reader, where it belongs. The unresolved question is left with him. And what does he do? He tries to test out the proofs, to decide which are fallacious and which valid.[16] In doing this he is himself engaging in the activity of "refutation," which is a central part of the "dialectic" that it is the aim of the text to teach; just as in his momentary identification with the confused and beaten interlocutor, he has experienced "being refuted," which is the other part. In such ways as this the text teaches its reader to think for himself.

There is another movement in the dialogue, a refutation that operates not by redefining terms but by returning to their accepted meanings. When Callicles is shown that his hedonism means that he must logically call the coward an *agathos* man, he recognizes that he cannot do that, he of all men, since the ethic he is trying to maintain is based on the traditional meaning of *agathos*, of which "brave" is a central component. He who has so boldly claimed the power to remake his language, in competition with Socrates, is at the end unable to escape its central terms.

The language of Socrates is at times overtly poetic rather than logical, for example in the fable by which he seeks to show Callicles that the orderly (*kosmios*) are more happy than the licentious (*akolastos*). Imagine two men, he says, each with a number of jars to be filled with wine, honey, or milk. The jars of the one are sound and full, and he wants nothing; the jars of the other are leaky, and he must constantly struggle to keep them full. Does this image not portray the difference between the life of one who wants nothing and the life of one who is constantly scurrying after pleasures? (493e–494a). This fable is not addressed to the intellectual part of Callicles but to the part of his mind that thinks and feels in images. It asks him to imagine what it would really be like, almost as if he were dreaming it, to be a leaky jar, constantly running out and being refilled, and an owner in frantic motion, constantly filling, and what, on the contrary, it would be like to be sound and full and at rest. As in a dream, the image of the self takes more than one form, here both jar and owner, and the story is about deep feelings within the self: anxiety and loss versus security and gain. Or think of Socrates' discussion of Archelaus. To ask a person to imagine himself to be another, and to see how he would like it (what might a modern equivalent be?) is very different from asking an abstract question. It invites a response of feeling and taste as well as of intellect. Likewise, the imagined trial in the afterlife should be read not as a religious statement—and especially not as an expression of a proto-Christianity—but as a way of conceiving of the self as an entity, naked and isolated. Notice that the social implications of these modes of discourse are different from the logical refutations; they are less competitive and combative. The logical proofs and refutations have a kind of forcefulness that the myths and stories and speeches lack; but their very form means that they can be refuted, as the more poetic parts cannot be, at least not in the same logical way.

III

The dialogue thus isolates and disorients the interlocutor (and the reader) by breaking down and reconstituting his language in ways that he cannot resist but does not wholly accept, and the language thus remade has a special kind of richness and power that derives from the associative way that it is put together in the text. Themes (such as the distinction between the "good" and the "pleasant," between an "art" and a branch of "flattery") recur in ways that at first surprise the reader but are then seen in a flash of understanding to be appropriate, and patterns of association, not wholly translatable into English, are gradually established in the text, such as the connection between the word for "punishment" in the conversation with Polus (*kolazesthai*) and the word for "licentious" in the conversation with Callicles (*a-kolastos*, un-punished).

One particularly important network of associations of this kind is built on the verb *aischunesthai* (to feel shame). This is the word used by Polus when he says that Gorgias was ashamed to admit that the good rhetorician did not need to know about justice; by Callicles when he says that Polus was ashamed to admit that it was more *aischron* as well as more *kakon* to suffer injustice than to do it; and by Socrates when he says that he would be ashamed not to have the power of preventing himself from doing wrong. It is connected etymologically with *aischron* and functionally with *elenchomai* and *elenchos*, the words for the kind of refutation that is achieved in dialectic, for they imply a kind of humiliating defeat. In the course of the dialogue the use of these terms is transformed so that *aischunesthai*, which originally meant to be ashamed before others, is internalized and comes to mean ashamed before oneself. And the kind of shame before others that does remain, the refutation, is seen as benign, not hostile.

This set of changes is deeply connected with the fundamental ethical premise of the dialogue, the central importance of motive or intention in determining the condition of the self. Thus the difference between rhetoric and dialectic is at heart not one of technique but of aim. It is for this reason that Socrates is satisfied when Gorgias says that the good rhetorician must know and be able to teach justice; for, once that aim is granted, everything else that Socrates cares about will follow.

In the course of the dialogue, *agathon* undergoes a somewhat similar shift from the external to the internal. At one point it is reduced by a kind of analytic definition to "what one chooses in fact"; but by the paragraph quoted above it has become "what one ought to choose or be," and here it is connected in new ways to the ideas of order and health and friendship and community and separated from pain and pleasure. And compare the discussion of the question that arises when Callicles concedes that some pleasures are good, others not. What is the standard of good to be? Socrates says that it takes an art to discern it and that all arts proceed by creating order and arrangement, not disorder and chaos; the good of the self and of the city will therefore be orderly (*kosmion*) in nature, not disorderly (*akosmion*) or unrestrained (*akolaston*) (503e–504e). It may be thought that this is an incomplete statement, for the question still remains, What kind of order shall it be?[17] But Socrates' concern has not been with that question but with even larger ones: whether orderliness and restraint are good things, whether temperance and justice are to be valued as *kalon* and *agathon*, and so on. For him the central question is at heart one of disposition or motivation: toward such things, or away from them? Likewise, the state from which Socrates seeks to preserve Callicles is one of division and discord within the self.

IV

In such ways as this the text offers its reader the experience of a mind dialectically reconstituting its language. The language so made is powerful, in a sense unanswerable, in large part because it does not seek to eliminate but accepts and clarifies the variabilities and complexities and inconsistencies of ordinary life and language. It is a language not merely of theory, for it has something of poetry in it too, of literature; and a language so made cannot be refuted by simply disproving one or another point. One must respond to it as a whole. Indeed, the only true refutation would be the creation of a better alternative. This is what Callicles attempts but fails to do.

It would be possible for us as readers simply to memorize the definitions, proofs, and propositions we find in this text and make them part of our own intellectual equipment. This would be one way of learning to speak the language that is reconstituted here. But this is not what the text invites, or not the most important thing. For while it is true that the quoted paragraph states propositions on which both the text and Socrates rest and that these are offered to us as important truths, merely to memorize that paragraph without making it in a deep sense one's own would be of little value. What the text really seeks to teach its reader is not how to speak this language but how to remake a language of his own. It does not teach a particular set of questions and dialectical responses, to be repeated on other occasions, but—what Polus shows to be much harder than he had imagined—how to ask questions of one's own. To do this, the reader must be a center of independent intellectual energy, a remaker of language and a composer of texts, and it is with helping him to become these things that this text is ultimately concerned.

How does the text seek to do this? It treats the reader rather as Socrates treats his interlocutors. It works on him in large part by isolating and disorienting him, by creating a conscious gap between self and language that makes the nature of both problematic in new ways. Like the interlocutor, the reader is broken out of his culture, out of the language and activities that define him; he is thus prevented from defining himself by simply repeating established forms of speech or conduct. He is forced to function on his own: to take and define positions of his own creation and to respond to those, valid and invalid, asserted by Socrates. It is in this way that the dialogue defines and makes meaningful its central subject, the nature of the self and of community. For nothing less than this is at stake in the choice between "rhetoric" and "dialectic"; and the apparently distinct subjects of the dialogue, the nature of rhetoric and dialectic and the nature of the happy and unhappy life, are really one. Rhetoric and dialectic are forms both of life and of statesmanship.

Self and Other: Dialectical Community

As we have seen, the social character of rhetoric is directly contrasted with that of dialectic at every point. The goal of rhetoric, for example, is the power to persuade (*peithein*) others, to reduce them to one's will. The goal of dialectic is the opposite of persuasion: it is to be refuted (*elenchesthai*), humiliated, corrected. This means that rhetoric naturally treats others as means to an end, while dialectic treats them as ends in themselves. Rhetoric persuades another not by refuting but by flattering him, by appealing to what pleases rather than to what is best for him; if successful, it therefore injures him. And it injures oneself as well, for the flatterer in the nature of things becomes like the object of his flattery. He praises what the other praises, blames what he blames; in the fullest sense he comes to speak the other's language. And unless such a one is a model of what one would be, one becomes what one would not be, in one's very self; and that is the worst, the most *kakon* and *aischron*, thing of all.

Dialectic is wholly different both in method and in object. It proceeds not by making lengthy statements or exhibitions but by questioning and answering, one to one. Its object is to engage each person at the deepest level, and for this it requires utter frankness of speech on each side, a kind of shamelessness in saying what one really thinks. One's concern is not with what people generally think, or anything of the kind, but only with what one thinks oneself and what the other thinks. This is not a competition to see who can reduce the other to his will; it is a process of mutual discovery and mutual refutation. One accepts refutation gladly, for it reduces the divisions and disharmonies within the self, which Socrates tells Callicles are so much worse than those in an orchestra or those between oneself and others. The object of it all is truth, and its method is friendship, the full recognition of the value of self and other in a universe of two. One can see why the language of sexuality seems natural to describe these two relations: dialectic is a recognition of self and other, rhetoric a reification and seduction.

But as the reader may have noticed, in the world presented in the text the ideal of dialectic is never realized, for Socrates' attempts to establish relations of this kind all end in failure. Gorgias concedes a central point but does so without understanding it. Polus is refuted but only in the limited sense that he is beaten and cannot go on; he has not been brought to the position of independent understanding that dialectic requires. (What can you imagine that he might do with this experience? Would he remember some of Socrates' propositions, some of his moves, and try to repeat them? Would he merely remain disturbed in his relation to his language and his teacher? Or not even that?) As for Callicles, having begun with total frankness as his great boast, at the end he simply refuses to talk with Socrates in any honest way and leaves him alone, without an interlocutor, making the speech in which he defends the way of life that may bring him death. The story of the *Gorgias* is in this sense the story of a failure of community, not its success.

This suggests that the central object of Plato's text is to create in the real world with its reader the kind of dialectical relationship that Socrates tries and fails to establish with others in the world of the text. And see how this textual community works: it has as its only object the education of the reader, making him (as Socrates says he tries to make the citizen) in the Socratic sense more *agathos*; and it works only by his free cooperation and engagement. Its proofs and paradoxes operate, as I have suggested, to loosen the moorings that connect the reader to his language and culture; they break down his language so that he can say neither what he used to say nor what Socrates invites him to say. He becomes a self outside his culture, faced with the fact of his own responsibility for making sense of what he hears, for becoming his own center of meaning and language. The reader is led to see that what is at stake when he decides how to speak and what to say—whether to do "rhetoric" or "dialectic"—is nothing less than "who he is" and what kind of community he will have with others.

There is a sense in which the text is more perfectly dialectical than Socrates attempts to be, for its interest in the welfare of another is more realistic and in that sense more complete and genuine. Whatever he says, Socrates cannot hope to establish a dialectical relation with Polus or Callicles, while Plato does seriously hope to establish such a community with his reader. The text is also a more perfect teacher. It offers its reader a set of experiences that teach him his responsibilities as a free person and give him some material with which to begin to discharge them. The ultimate value of the text, performed in the way it at once teaches and respects its reader, is the value of the individual person, whom it is its object to protect and improve. In this text Plato makes himself his reader's dialectical friend.

*   *   *

OUR READING OF THE *Gorgias* is among other things an example of what it can mean to do philosophy rather than poetry or history. In reading the *Iliad* we saw the poet reorganize the materials of his world in patterns and images of his own to make something new out of his preexisting cultural material, like a musician or an architect. The historian, as Thucydides shows, records the processes by which life is lived, successfully or unsuccessfully, and seeks to make sense of them. The philosopher—or at least this one—establishes a world of two within which language and life can be cooperatively rethought and remade.

But this is a world of only two. The ideal reader of this text becomes a philosopher, and what does he do then? What happens, for example, when he turns to the world of politics and trade, of war and poetry, and seeks to work within it? What kind of community does he have with others then? This question, as we know, became the central question of Plato's own life. His two main literary responses to it were the different versions of an ideal state that he sets forth in the *Republic* and the *Laws*, in both of which the philosopher's relation to others is that of ruler. His other response was his establishment of the Academy, a place permanently set aside for the continuation of his dialectical practices, apart from the world. The academy is still with us—we are part of it when we read this text—and it still does not know how to turn to the larger world and work within it.

Socrates teaches us something new about the relationship between self and language when he shows that language itself can be remade by the individual mind and that, when that happens, the self and world are remade too. One need not speak only what has been spoken, say only what the situation calls for—what any competent speaker of one's language would say—for one can remake one's language anew. But this can be done for good or for ill, as the performance of Callicles demonstrates, and how are we to evaluate what we do? By what methods, and subject to what standards and limits, ought we to proceed? In what place can we stand when we make such judgments? For Socrates the answers to these questions are to be determined, each time anew, by the two members of the dialectical community, engaged in mutual testing and refutation, to which all loyalties are given and for which Socrates claims an absolute liberty. Of course the Platonic premise (elsewhere expressed) is that, beyond language, the absolutes themselves exist, and it is toward these that we struggle: truth and beauty and justice and love, the Good itself. The criteria are ultimately eternal and need only to be discovered. But until they are discovered, this kind of absolutism produces a radical relativism in method, a world of two making sense only for each other. How is such a life to be lived, even on its own terms?

And what happens if we turn to the larger world and acknowledge our fidelities to the language that constitutes it, to the people who inhabit it? How are language and culture to be made and remade on that scale? From what position, by what methods, subject to what limits and criteria? Questions like these return us to the formal subject of the *Gorgias*, the nature of rhetorical life, and they suggest that something can be said on behalf of rhetoric by, say, the modern diplomat (the direct successor of the representatives of Corinth and Corcyra) or the modern lawyer. Such a one can claim to be one of those who maintains the culture—the language—by which the world is constituted and made real; in which materials for the definition of self and motive can be found; and without which nothing human can occur.[18] An inherited language, as the repository of our collective experience, may indeed have much to teach its users.

But this is to get ahead of ourselves. At present it is enough to say that the *Gorgias* leaves us with two lines of questioning, which we shall treat first separately, then together. The first can be called dialectical. Taking seriously Socrates' claims of the creative power and liberty and responsibility of the community of two, we shall examine a series of texts as responses to the question What kind of language should we speak? As Socrates shows us, this is also to ask Who should we each be, and what world, what community, should we have? These questions will be asked, as dialectic suggests they should, primarily of the world of two created between a text and its reader.

The texts with respect to which we shall pursue these questions will be English texts, for our own language is English, and any reconstitution of it will be English too. In observing the remaking of language in Greek, we have had the luxury of looking from a comfortable distance; the key terms taken apart and put together again were not those by which we structure our own experience. What happens when dialectic goes on in our language, in our minds? It is with questions such as these that we shall examine Swift's *Tale of a Tub*, Johnson's *Rambler* essays, and Jane Austen's *Emma*, examining the different kinds of language and community they constitute. From them we shall learn, among other things, that it is important to keep asking not only how we can remake our language but how we can be remade by it.

The second line of questioning might be called political or, if you will, rhetorical. However perfectly dialectical a community a speaker may establish with an auditor, or a writer with a reader, what can that community possibly have to do with the constitution or reconstitution of a larger community—say, that of the family or village or nation? Can one imagine a politics of dialectical friendship, for example? Of some other kind of friendship? It is questions of this sort that we shall bring to our reading of Jane Austen, Edmund Burke, and the legal materials of the final chapter.

5

Making the Reader
Make His Language

Swift's *A Tale of a Tub*

In turning from Plato's *Gorgias* to Swift's *A Tale of a Tub*, written at the end of the seventeenth century, we may seem to take an enormous leap, and of course in a strictly historical sense we do. But the idea is obviously not that the *Tale* comes right after the *Gorgias* in time but that it can profitably be placed beside it in our reading. My reason for thinking that it can is that the *Tale* is in important ways very similar to the *Gorgias*: in its conception of the relation between mind and language, in its sense of the individual's responsibility for the language that he speaks and for the person that he becomes in doing so, and in its aim to educate its reader by disturbing his sense of himself and his world. The *Tale* can indeed be taken as something of an example of what Socrates would call a dialectical text, written not in Greek but in our own language.

"Written for the Universal Improvement of Mankind"

We are told in the Author's "Apology" that the *Tale* is meant to be a satire on "*Corruptions in Learning and Religion.*" This means, in more modern terms, that it is about what we should call proper thinking and speaking and writing, and this of course includes as well proper attitudes both toward one's culture and toward other people.

It would perhaps be easy to assume that the "corruptions" Swift attacks have nothing to do with any contemporary matters and certainly nothing to do with the reader himself. The text attacks certain identifiable schools and tendencies of Swift's own time, we say—the fanatic Calvinist, the superstitious Catholic, the mechanist who believes that all thought can be reduced to manipulation of quantities, and so on—and what can that have to do with us? On this view the *Tale* could be viewed as a sort of virtuoso tiger shoot: the reader sits on the platform with Swift and studies, with admiration, the skill with which he picks off his foes. The reader's interest will be that of an observer, not a participant, and it is likely to be mainly technical, academic, or aesthetic in kind. And of course it is true that Swift's text was in part directed at certain individuals and tendencies in his own world. But to see this text as aimed exclusively at others is altogether too comfortable a view of the matter. The central concern of the *Tale* is in fact not with others but with the reader himself, including the modern reader; it is above all our corruptions that it intends to expose and correct. The *Tale* is thus deeply dialectical in character: it is concerned with the welfare of the reader and proceeds by a kind of perpetual refutation of him. Insofar as it is concerned with tendencies or attitudes in the culture more generally, these turn out to be far more contemporary than one might think at first. A proper reading of the *Tale* will lead to a new way of reading both one's own productions and the world one inhabits, its communities and languages.

How does the *Tale* attempt to do these things? It begins not by immersing the reader in a working rhetorical universe, as our other texts did, but, as befits a satire, by locating him in a crazed and impossible world in which he has to make his own way. Nothing seems to work right. The effect is to force upon the reader the task of working his own way out of the place the text defines for him, of making his own position against its perpetually deconstructive force. The text thus compels the reader who engages with it to become, in a new way, active and self-conscious in reconstituting his language. For Swift, as for us, this means that the reader also becomes more active in constituting himself and his world. The ultimate meaning of this text thus literally is the person the reader makes himself as he responds to it, as he becomes his own version of what I have called its "ideal reader."

SWIFT'S MAIN INTEREST is in the impossible forms of life and thought and language to which we are susceptible when our language decays into platitude and cliché or, even worse, when we allow our grandiosity to dissolve the connection between our language and the world. He gives us a series of diseased actors and voices and forces upon us the question: How can we avoid speaking like that, being like that? Or, to put the matter in more general and even more serious terms: How is it possible, in a world (like our own) so much made up of false speech and dead speech, for the mind in need of education to form itself and learn to talk? Such are Swift's questions, and it is not surprising to find that a ruling metaphor at work here is that of health and its opposite. The "*Corruptions*" that Swift attacks are for him literally diseases of the mind and heart, forms of insanity, and the state to which he wishes to help his reader is one of health.

The method of the text is a mixture of irony and parody. As a look at any page will demonstrate, it is full of distortions and deformations, sometimes of the most wild and grotesque kinds. Take the title, for example: is it meant to be cute, or childish, or allegorical, or what? And how are we to understand the subtitle, which declares that the book is "Written for the Universal Improvement of Mankind"? (On the reverse of the title page we see a list of other books by the same author, soon to be published, including such items as "*A General History of* Ears" and "*A modest Defence of the Proceedings of the* Rabble *in all Ages.*") The more one reads, the stranger it seems. The text in this way promises to be a series of jokes or "put-ons," and how are we to learn anything important from a text that works like that?

In one sense this is a simple question, which can be answered by saying that the very life of this text is its wildness and its irony, its exuberance and wit, and that it teaches by the experience of language and feeling that it offers. But to say what sort of experience this is, how it teaches us, and why we should take it seriously—how, for example, it differs in brilliance and seriousness and power from undergraduate humor—are matters of extraordinary difficulty. For one thing, the process of reading the kind of irony and parody present in this text cannot be reduced to a simple reversal by which one could say that Swift "always means the opposite of what he seems to say." As will shortly appear, there is much that Swift affirms, as well as much that he rejects. It will be our task to distinguish between them, and how can we possibly do that with any degree of confidence? And even if we are capable of reconstructing some "true meanings" from what seems to be the wild chaos of the text, there remains the puzzle: why did Swift not tell us these things plainly and directly? What experience can he offer his reader this way, through the very wildness of the text, that he could not if he spoke directly, and what is its value? Is there any way that this text, working in such negative ways, can be taken as affirmatively defining the civilization Swift admires, as establishing a working sense of how people ought to think and speak, as instructing us in our language? Or is it essentially destructive and empty? Does it ultimately define and affirm a set of values, a kind of culture—offering its reader a place to stand like Book Twenty-four of the *Iliad*, for example—and if so how? Or is Swift's wit a kind of universal acid, deeply destructive in nature, that can be turned against anything?

I SAID ABOVE that this text creates a set of puzzles for its reader and that its teaching lies in what it means to work on them. But suppose in the end they mean nothing at all, that the ideal reader constituted by this text has no character, no language of his own at all, that all coherence and meaning are proved impossible? Such is the fear the *Tale* stimulates in its reader, a fear of what it calls madness. Some have indeed read the text as realizing that fear, as ending nowhere.[1] For me, as I will hope to show, a coherent language can be made in response to this text, but only by a process of reading—in which it instructs us—that is so constructive and active in nature as to be almost a kind of writing.

As one may gather from what I have said, this is not a text easily summarized, for it has (for the most part) the structure neither of a narrative nor of a logical argument; it is, rather, a shifting series of distortions and confusions, each with its own effect. In what follows, we shall accordingly focus our attention in the main on particular passages and read them with some care.

The Author's "Apology"

An item entitled "An APOLOGY For the, &," immediately follows the list of titles reproduced above. Added in the fifth edition, it purports to defend the *Tale* against certain attacks published against it, but its more important purpose is to make the problem of reading this text a subject of the text itself. Swift does this by speaking in two impossibly inconsistent voices and thrusting the problem of making sense of them directly upon the reader. Some of what he says, for example, is impossibly megalomaniac: "*Therefore, since the Book seems calculated to live at least as long as our Language, and our Tast[e] admit no great Alterations . . .*"; and "*such Treatises as have been writ against this ensuing Discourse . . . are already sunk into waste Paper and Oblivion.*" But other statements seem perfectly sensible, e.g., that the author thought "*the numerous and gross Corruptions in Religion and Learning might furnish Matter for a Satyr, that would be useful and diverting.*" Swift addresses the tension between these two voices by making an explicit appeal to the reader, saying that he

> acknowledges there are several youthful Sallies, which
> from the Grave and the Wise may deserve a Rebuke. But
> he desires to be answerable no farther than he is guilty,
> and that his Faults may not be multiply'd by the igno-
> rant, the unnatural, and uncharitable Applications of
> those who have neither Candor to suppose good mean-
> ings, nor Palate to distinguish true Ones. After which,
> he will forfeit his Life, if any one Opinion can be fairly
> deduced from that Book, which is contrary to Religion
> or Morality.

The function of this passage (and of others like it) is to tell the reader that he will constantly have to ask himself, as he works through this text, how he is reading it. Are his understandings of it "fairly deduced"? Has he properly exercised those powers of perception and judgment here called "Palate" (or taste) and "candor"? The very use of these terms commits Swift to the topic they define, informing us that they will continue to be a subject of attention, explicit or implicit, and that they state, or point to, a set of values, as yet undefined, that the text will support.

With similar purpose Swift warns the reader that much of the text consists of "*Parodies, where the Author personates the Style and Manner of other Writers, whom he has a mind to expose*"; that "*there generally runs Irony through the Thread of the whole Book*"; that the text is imperfectly revised, being published from a "*surreptitious Copy*"; and that he has never seen the notes that appear at the bottom of the pages. In these ways Swift at once tells the reader that he will have to call on his own literary and social resources to make his way through this text (Who speaks this way? What does it mean?) and promises him that the text itself will help him learn the art required for reading it.

The Bookseller's "Dedication"

I

The *Tale* proper is preceded by several relatively short and nominally prefatory pieces—a bookseller's "Dedication," "The Bookseller to the Reader," the Author's "Epistle Dedicatory" to "Prince Posterity," and the Author's "Preface"—each of which is meant to complicate the reader's sense of the text and his relation to it and to sharpen his sense that he will have to make his own way through it.[2] Of these the bookseller's "Dedication" to "The Right Honourable JOHN *Lord* SOMMERS,"[3] is especially interesting, both as an instruction in the kind of reading that the rest of the *Tale* will require and as a kind of qualifying examination in the art.

One way to begin to look at the "Dedication" is to suggest that it is composed in part as a solution to an actual problem: how can Swift write a real dedication to a real person he actually admires without sounding trite or false? If he were simply to make a list of Lord Somers's good qualities and to say that the text was dedicated to him on account of them, nothing would distinguish this dedication from a hundred others. The problem is a little like the modern one of writing a letter of recommendation for a first-class candidate. How can I write what is good and remarkable about this candidate without my letter sounding like a fulsome form-letter ("truly extraordinary brilliance of mind")? How can I give the reader some reason to trust my judgment and my honesty? Perhaps an even closer parallel would be this. Imagine that you are invited to give a speech in appreciation of a public or private figure you actually admire. How can you do it without sounding like an idiot? ("Unparalleled devotion to public service"; "wonderful family man, loyal friend"; "great personal sacrifice"; "exemplar of American ideals," etc., etc.) It is not an adequate response to say that one will simply state in plain terms what one means, as if language were a simple intellectual instrument for naming qualities and expressing judgments.

For language is a social construct, made by people for all the purposes of social life, including the worst, and it is subject to corruption and abuse. When a speaker makes a "few remarks in appreciation," or a Memorial Day speech about sacrifice and ideals, or a Dedication to a Noble Lord, one expects to hear, once again, what one has heard so often. The language, like the occasion, has decayed into platitude and cliché; the words that at first seem right and appropriate have in this sense literally lost their meaning, and we cannot use them. It is the task of the writer on such an occasion to remake his language so that it and his judgments are sound and fresh and to demonstrate qualities of mind and character in which the auditor can have confidence. His task is at once ethical and intellectual: he must give himself both a character and a language. It is not easy.

In the "Dedication" Swift takes striking advantage of the very expectations that create his seemingly insuperable problem, for he sees that the trite forms of speech common in a dedication represent a special and readily accessible case of the general subject of the *Tale* as a whole, namely, "*Corruptions in Learning and Religion*," or, as we might say, abuses in thought and language and character. If he can find a way to write a dedication against the force of those expectations, and one that praises genuinely for just those virtues most commonly reduced to cliché, he will have both defined and corrected a corruption in the culture and will have done so in a way that prepares his reader for the even more serious matters that lie ahead.

The method he uses might be called ethical irony. He praises Lord Somers and his virtues not in his own voice (which is to be suspected of motives of flattery) but in the voice of the bookseller (we would say publisher), who frankly admits that his only interest in his trade is its profit. He has no interest in Lord Somers's actual virtues and in fact quite openly wishes that they were replaced by other qualities, more valuable for the purpose at hand. He expresses his disappointment in the dedication he had his "Poets" prepare for him in these words:

> I expected, indeed, to have heard of your Lordship's
> Bravery, at the Head of an Army; Of your undaunted
> Courage, in mounting a Breach, or scaling a Wall; Or, to
> have had your Pedigree trac'd in a Lineal Descent from

the House of *Austria*; Or, of your wonderful Talent at
Dress and Dancing; Or, your Profound Knowledge in
Algebra, Metaphysicks, and the Oriental Tongues. But
to ply the World with an old beaten Story of your Wit,
and Eloquence, and Learning, and Wisdom, and Justice, and Politeness, and Candor, and Evenness of Temper in all Scenes of Life; Of that great Discernment in
Discovering, and Readiness in Favouring deserving
Men; with forty other common Topicks: I confess, I
have neither Conscience, nor Countenance to do it.

That the bookseller, in what lawyers would call a declaration against interest, admits of himself what must be true of many like him makes
"credible" both his bored recital of Somers's virtues and his statement of
his authority for what he says: the "universal Report of Mankind."[4]

But this is "credibility" of an odd kind, and properly put in quotation
marks, because the bookseller is not a real person, whose statements are
to be believed or disbelieved, but a voice created and employed by Swift
(whose motives remain, from the circumstance of the dedication, as suspect as they ever were). It is only in the imagined world of the "Dedication" that the bookseller exists and only there that his voice is credible. In
the real world the issue is not whether the statements about Somers's virtues are to be believed or not but whether Swift has produced a dedication that will please his patron and instruct his reader; and this he most
certainly has. Indeed, the most remarkable aspect of the dedication is
that it is necessary to its success that Lord Somers understand and appre-
ciate what Swift has done; and to assume that he will is a compliment
whose elegance and sincerity are beyond doubt.

II

For Swift the problem of praising Somers for his virtue is a special case
of a larger problem: how to define and recommend the virtues themselves in ways that will break through the clichés of moralistic talk and
command attention and assent. One way he does this is surprising. In the
passage quoted above he gives us a list of central virtue-words, and one
would expect this to be the dullest and least effective statement of value
one could imagine. But in placing this list ("Wit, and Eloquence, and
Learning, and Wisdom, and Justice") not in the context of an adulatory
dedication or a sermon but in that of the bookseller's blunt talk, Swift establishes a tension between word and background that gives these terms
a revived clarity and life. By putting these words in such a speech, made
by such a person with such motives, Swift makes the reader feel for a

moment something of what we might think of as their original, if incomplete, force. The reader cannot reject them. It would be difficult, for
example, to imagine an actor reading that list of words and maintaining
to the end the tone of boredom and disgust that the context seems to demand. In the midst of all this irony and caricature these words function
for the moment as stable statements of value made in plain English. It is
a little as if he has made a bet with himself, or with his reader, that he can
include a string of terms like these in a dedication and make his reader
feel them to be alive and significant.

This passage thus affirms a set of traditional values and the plain
terms in which they are usually stated; but, beyond freeing them from
their usual trite associations and restoring something of what might be
called their natural sense, it does little to define them. We now know in a
general way where this text stands, and this knowledge will be of real
help when we get to the difficulties that lie ahead. But it is not in such a
list as this that the meaning of a text is given its most important definition; for that we must look to the experience of thought and feeling it
offers its reader.

What Swift achieves through the use of irony and caricature he could
not have achieved through the use of direct and simple speech, for this
kind of writing makes a special set of demands on the reader. To work his
way through it, he must call on a very wide range of social and linguistic
competences, making active much of his knowledge of language and of
men. He must constantly ask how to make sense of what he reads, and
when he succeeds—when he understands the joke and feels at home in
the text—he finds that he has affirmed the understandings by which the
text has become intelligible. Because humor involves the perception of
the incongruous, it also involves the implicit assertion of shared con-
gruities; otherwise it could not be understood. In this sense an important
object of the text is to teach its reader how to read it. Swift makes the
reader work, but he rewards him with the knowledge that he understands what he has read. So far at least, it has not been impossibly
difficult.

The Structure of the Tale

I

The main body of the text is constructed in alternating chapters. One
series tells a story, which, as the "Apology" informs us, is a satire on
abuses in religion; the other is a set of digressions said to be an attack on
abuses in learning. The narrative portion has a simple enough structure.
A father wrote a will in which he left his three sons no estate but a suit of

clothes apiece, which had two virtues: that *"with good wearing"* they would *"last you fresh and sound as long as you live,"* and that *"they will grow in the same proportion with your Bodies. . . ."*

> *"Here, let me see them on you before I die. So, very well,*
> *Pray Children, wear them clean, and brush them often.*
> *You will find in my Will* (here it is) *full Instructions in*
> *every particular concerning the Wearing and Manage-*
> *ment of your Coats; wherein you must be very exact, to*
> *avoid the Penalties I have appointed for every Trans-*
> *gression or Neglect, upon which your future Fortunes*
> *will entirely depend."*

The coats were rather plain, and the young men very fashionable; when it became the fashion to wear shoulder knots, for example, the brothers were tempted to do so too. But on this point "their Father's Will was very precise, and it was the main Precept in it, with the greatest Penalties annexed, not to add to, or diminish from their Coats, one Thread, without a positive Command in the Will." The sons engaged in various forms of specious interpretation that permitted them to attach first shoulder knots, then (as they came into fashion) gold lace, flame-colored satin, fringes and points, Indian figures in embroidery, and so on. Their interpretive devices included such things as the invention of oral tradition, the addition of a fictitious codicil, the skillful redefinition of terms ("Silver Fringe," in an explicit prohibition in the Will, is read as meaning *"Broom-stick"*); the use of maxims of interpretation (of which the most useful is *cum grano Salis*); and finally their decision "to lock up their Father's Will in a *Strong-Box*, brought out of *Greece* or *Italy*, (I have forgot which) and trouble themselves no farther to examine it, but only refer to its Authority whenever they thought fit." The first stage of the narrative concludes with the fraudulent acquisition of a great house by Peter, one of the sons, into which, as their superior, he invited his brothers.

This is of course the story of the development of Christianity prior to the Reformation, especially of the processes by which the authority of the Bible was gradually eroded, and it is easy enough to follow.[5]

But early Christianity has no monopoly on the processes by which the plain commands of authority are perverted, and this satire, which is apparently directed at particular *"Corruptions in Religion,"* is really much more general in its scope: it is a satire on abuses inflicted on the mind by desire. For the defects exhibited in these misreadings of the Will are not primarily defects of what we would call the intellect—indeed no intellect could support them, and that is part of the point—but defects of charac-ter. What we see at work here is man's insistent demand to get what he wants, brushing aside without a thought whatever might stand in his way and employing all his mental resources to have his wish. It is a picture of intellect subjugated to desire; a story of conflict of will with Will indeed.

II

Peter next adopted a very grand style of life, to support which he undertook a series of income-producing projects, including "a *Whispering-Office,* for the Publick Good," an "*Office of Ensurance,*" and his "famous Universal *Pickle.*" (These are, respectively, confession, indulgences, and holy water.) Even more ambitious projects were the purchase of "a Large Continent," theretofore unknown, which he sold in parcels "*again,* and *again,* and *again,* and *again*" (this is Purgatory), and his "Sovereign Remedy for the *Worms*" (penances), described as follows:

> The Patient was to eat nothing after Supper for three
> Nights: as soon as he went to Bed, he was carefully to
> lye on one Side, and when he grew weary, to turn upon
> the other: He must also duly confine his two Eyes to
> the same Object; and by no means break Wind at both
> Ends together, without manifest Occasion.

Peter lorded it over his brothers insufferably. In one important scene he serves them a loaf of bread, which he calls both meat and wine ("*Come Brothers,* said *Peter, fall to, and spare not; here is excellent good Mutton; or hold, now my Hand is in, I'll help you*"), and he abuses them when they object. (This passage of course ridicules the doctrine of transubstantiation.)

When the two others, now called Jack (Calvin) and Martin (Luther), had had as much of this as they could stand, they examined the Will, "by which they presently saw how grosly [*sic*] they had been abused: Their Father having left them equal Heirs," and resolved to return to its dictates. (This is of course the Reformation.) But in trying to return his coat to its original shape and form, Jack became a fanatic and tore off the lace, the shoulder knots, the lining, and so forth, with such zeal that he reduced his coat to rags and shreds. When he saw Martin proceed with more moderation, he was consumed with envy and rage, ran "mad with Spleen, and Spight, and Contradiction," and ended up the laughingstock of boys in the street.

While this story is being told, it is interrupted by another series of chapters that consists of an introduction (on "Oratorial Machines"), "A Digression concerning Criticks" (the true critic is a "*Discoverer and Col-*

lector of Writers Faults"), "A Digression in the Modern Kind," and "A Digression in Praise of Digressions," each of which is intended to be about abuses in "*learning*," as the *Tale* proper is about religion. These digressions are written in a much more difficult and brilliant way than the *Tale* itself (which seems easy enough to follow), and they involve the reader much more directly in intellectual and moral error. The reason for this is that instead of telling us a story about the follies of others, whose defects can be the object of shared ridicule, Swift in the digressions presents the reader directly with the problem of making sense of the effusions of a crazed modern writer, the putative "author" of the book. As we shall see in a moment, this is difficult in the extreme.

III

First, however, we may pause to ask how the *Tale* has thus far been working. It seems plain, to start with, that the center of value throughout the narrative has been the Will and the plain, direct, and modest language in which it is written. The deviations are from that norm; the corrections are movements back toward it. Swift has made the voice of the Father (in every sense) the center of his work. In telling the story of its misreading, he has also explicitly raised the general question of what proper reading is, including reading this very text. In addition, this is obviously an allegory, and, to understand it, it is necessary to understand the history to which it refers; in fact, much of the pleasure is in seeing how perfectly this narrative fits with the historical one. The digressions similarly require knowledge of the literature to which they allude. This means that to read the text fully one must bring to life what one knows—and one must learn more—both of ancient learning and of Christian history. And to do these things in the ways in which Swift's prose demands is to affirm both the religious and the secular parts of the inherited culture.[6] Finally, the digressions, by their very nature as abrupt shifts out of the story, express a kind of broken or chaotic sensibility, which stirs in the reader a sense of the value of the opposite—of wholeness and integration. (In their substance they are plainly meant to exemplify the modern pretensions that Swift deplores.) As I suggested above, the misreadings of the Will are caused not by what we would call intellectual defects but by defects of character, the overpowering of the mind by the human will, and we see in the careers of Peter and Jack that the disease is progressive and terminal. Martin, on the other hand, is meant to represent the recognition of imperfection, the moderate wish for realistic self-correction; this is a kind of health, which is the value that embraces all the others.[7]

But there is also a tension deep in the structure of this work, for this text not only affirms the value of plain talk and ordinary virtue but continuously and brilliantly performs an allegiance to wit, to the imagination, and to invention (and, in this last sense at least, to modernity). Is this tension ever addressed by the text, and, if so, how and with what result? Or is it just left open, in a display of essential incoherence?

"The Serene Peaceful State of Being a Fool among Knaves"

The view that the text is in fact incoherent receives some support when, after the seventh chapter, the structure of alternation breaks down. Here the "Digression in Praise of Digressions" is (naturally enough) followed not by a return to the *Tale* but by two other digressions, one on the "Learned *Aeolists*," who maintain the "Original Cause of all Things to be *Wind*" (that is, those, like Jack, who pretend to inspiration) [8] and one called "A Digression concerning the Original, the Use and Improvement of Madness in a Commonwealth." This is our next subject, and it proves not to be a digression at all but a place where the two lines of the work come together, united in the theme of madness and sanity.

"A Digression concerning the Original, the Use and
Improvement of Madness in a Commonwealth"

I

The Digression begins this way (speaking of the Aeolists):

> NOR shall it any ways detract from the just Reputation
> of this famous Sect, that its Rise and Institution are
> owing to such an Author as I have described *Jack* to be;
> A Person whose Intellectuals were overturned, and his
> Brain shaken out of its Natural Position; which we com-
> monly suppose to be a Distemper, and call by the Name
> of *Madness* or *Phrenzy*. For, if we take a Survey of the
> greatest Actions that have been performed in the World,
> under the influence of Single Men; which are, *The Es-*
> *tablishment of New Empires by Conquest: The Advance*
> *and Progress of New Schemes in Philosophy; and the*
> *contriving, as well as the propagating of New Religions:*
> We shall find the Authors of them all, to have been Per-
> sons, whose natural Reason hath admitted great Revo-
> lutions from their Dyet, their Education, the Prevalency
> of some certain Temper, together with the particular In-
> fluence of Air and Climate.

In seeking to explain why it matters not from whence the vapor comes but how and where it strikes the mind, and "upon what *Species* of Brain it ascends," and how it is that the same vapor can produce such different effects, as "*Alexander the Great, Jack of Leyden*, and Monsieur *Des Cartes*,"[9] the narrator says: "The present Argument is the most abstracted that ever I engaged in, it strains my Faculties to their highest Stretch; and I desire the Reader to attend with utmost Perpensity; For, I now proceed to unravel this knotty Point." Here is his explanation, in full:

    *   T H E R E is in Mankind a certain   *   *   *   *
    *   *   *   *   *   *   *   *   *   *   *

Hic multa   *   *   *   *   *   *   *   *   *
desiderantur. *   *   *   *   *   *   *   *   *
    *   *   *   *   *   *   *   *   *   *   *

    *   *   *   *   *   And this I take to be a clear
                          Solution of the Matter.

There now follows a famous passage of extraordinary difficulty and interest, which will repay the closest scrutiny:

> HAVING therefore so narrowly past thro' this intricate Difficulty, the Reader will, I am sure, agree with me in the Conclusion; that if the *Moderns* mean by *Madness*, only a Disturbance or Transposition of the Brain, by Force of certain *Vapours* issuing up from the lower Faculties; Then has this *Madness* been the Parent of all those mighty Revolutions, that have happened in *Empire*, in *Philosophy*, and in *Religion*. For, the Brain, in its natural Position and State of Serenity, disposeth its Owner to pass his Life in the common Forms, without any Thought of subduing Multitudes to his own *Power*, his *Reasons* or his *Visions*; and the more he shapes his Understanding by the Pattern of Human Learning, the less he is inclined to form Parties after his particular Notions; because that instructs him in his private Infirmities, as well as in the stubborn Ignorance of the People. But when a Man's Fancy gets *astride* on his Reason, when Imagination is at Cuffs with the Senses, and common Understanding, as well as common Sense, is Kickt out of Doors; the first Proselyte he makes, is Himself, and when that is once compass'd, the Difficulty is not so great in bringing over others; A strong Delusion always operating from *without*, as vigorously

as from *within*. For, Cant and Vision are to the Ear and
the Eye, the same that Tickling is to the Touch. Those
Entertainments and Pleasures we most value in Life,
are such as *Dupe* and play the Wag with the Senses.
For, if we take an Examination of what is generally understood by *Happiness*, as it has Respect, either to the
Understanding or the Senses, we shall find all its Properties and Adjuncts will herd under this short Definition: That, *it is a perpetual Possession of being well
Deceived*. And first, with Relation to the Mind or Understanding; 'tis manifest, what mighty Advantages Fiction
has over Truth; and the Reason is just at our Elbow;
because Imagination can build nobler Scenes, and produce more wonderful Revolutions than Fortune or Nature will be at Expence to furnish. Nor is Mankind so
much to blame in his Choice, thus determining him, if
we consider that the Debate meerly lies between *Things
past*, and *Things conceived*; and so the Question is only
this; Whether Things that have Place in the *Imagination*, may not as properly be said to *Exist*, as those that
are seated in the *Memory*; which may be justly held in
the Affirmative, and very much to the Advantage of the
former, since This is acknowledged to be the *Womb* of
Things, and the other allowed to be no more than the
Grave. Again, if we take this Definition of Happiness,
and examine it with Reference to the Senses, it will be
acknowledged wonderfully adapt. How fade and insipid
do all Objects accost us that are not convey'd in the Vehicle of *Delusion*? How shrunk is every Thing, as it appears in the Glass of Nature? So, that if it were not for
the Assistance of Artificial *Mediums*, false Lights, refracted Angles, Varnish, and Tinsel; there would be a
mighty Level in the Felicity and Enjoyments of Mortal
Men. If this were seriously considered by the World, as
I have a certain Reason to suspect it hardly will; Men
would no longer reckon among their high Points of Wisdom, the Art of exposing weak Sides, and publishing
Infirmities; an Employment in my Opinion, neither better nor worse than that of *Unmasking*, which I think,
has never been allowed fair Usage, either in the *World*
or the *Play-House*.

One way to work through this passage is to ask what sentiments and
attitudes it seems to invite us to adopt and to confirm. The fact that the

text is ironic is of course no bar to reading of this kind; for, as we saw in connection with the bookseller's dedication, to understand an irony is to share for the moment the premises and attitudes that make it comprehensible. An ironic text can of course have elements within it that are not undercut or rejected, like the bookseller's frankness, and we have seen that we can understand such things too.[10] As I suggested above, the text is in part meant to teach the reader the art of reading it, and by this stage we should be pretty comfortable in the assurance that we can do it. It has not been too hard, after all, to follow the absurd pretensions of Peter and Jack, their delusions of vanity and pride and selfishness, and we know where to stand when they are deflated: on the side of acknowledged limits, plain and honest talk, the principle of reality in the assessment of the self. All of this has been intelligible and presumably a source of pleasure as well. How about these two paragraphs, then?

To start at the beginning, we can ask what attitudes Swift asks us to take toward this proposition: "Then has this *Madness* been the Parent of all those Mighty Revolutions, that have happened in *Empire*, in *Philosophy*, and in *Religion*." The view of the Aeolist, that all things can be explained by a mechanical theory of vapors, is of course mad, but its conclusion, that the forms of ambition spoken of are also mad, happens to be true. In this sentence we acquiesce in a conclusion reached by a kind of insane reductionism and thus for a moment in the reductionism itself— even though it is insane, and insane for the very reason that the revolutions in empire, philosophy, and religion also are, namely, that it tries to reduce all things to its notions. We may feel our feet slip here, but we can catch ourselves; and in the next sentence Swift seems to give us firm ground to stand on: obviously we should side squarely with "pass[ing] one's] Life in the common Forms," shaping "[the] Understanding by the Pattern of Human Learning," and being instructed in one's "private Infirmities," and we should be against "subduing Multitudes to [one's] own *Power*, [one's] *Reasons* or [one's] *Visions*," forming "Parties after [one's] particular Notions," and so on. This sentence suggests just the set of attitudes that will satisfactorily correct the momentary imbalance or uncertainty of the preceding one. So far, so good.

The text goes on: "But when a Man's Fancy gets *astride* on his Reason, when Imagination is at Cuffs with the Senses, and common Understanding, as well as common Sense, is Kickt out of Doors . . ." When we read this, it seems plain enough that we are to side with common sense and common understanding and reason and against fancy and imagination, which lead to the sort of madness that the Aeolist exemplifies and admires and that Swift attacks. And the rest of the paragraph proceeds in a way that we can easily follow. The speaker praises these things: "Cant and Vision"; "Tickling"; such pleasures as "*Dupe* and play the Wag with the Senses"; a kind of happiness that consists in a "*perpetual Possession of being well Deceived*"; the "Advantages Fiction has over Truth"; the "*Imagination*" as compared with the "*Memory*"; and "*Delusion*" (including "false Lights, refracted Angles, Varnish, and Tinsel") as contrasted with the "Glass of Nature"; and he abhors "the Art of exposing weak Sides, and publishing Infirmities," which he says is neither more nor less than a species of "*Unmasking*." In reading this we naturally know to oppose what it praises and to accept what it attacks. (Perhaps one who remembers the "Digression on Criticks" will be uncomfortable to find himself allied with the "Art of exposing weak Sides"; and one who has felt himself fully engaged with the life of the *Tale* may be uncomfortable with the attack on "Imagination." But these discomforts, if they exist, will be very small—no larger than a man's hand.)

II

We then read the following, and what are we to make of it?

IN the Proportion that Credulity is a more peaceful Possession of the Mind, than Curiosity, so far preferable is that Wisdom, which converses about the Surface, to that pretended Philosophy which enters into the Depth of Things, and then comes gravely back with Informations and Discoveries, that in the inside they are good for nothing. The two Senses, to which all Objects first address themselves, are the Sight and the Touch; These never examine farther than the Colour, the Shape, the Size, and whatever other Qualities dwell, or are drawn by Art upon the Outward of Bodies; and then comes Reason officiously, with Tools for cutting, and opening, and mangling, and piercing, offering to demonstrate, that they are not of the same consistence quite thro'. Now, I take all this to be the last Degree of perverting Nature: one of whose Eternal Laws it is, to put her best Furniture forward. And therefore, in order to save the Charges of all such expensive Anatomy for the Time to come; I do here think fit to inform the Reader, that in such Conclusions as these, Reason is certainly in the Right; and that in most Corporeal Beings, which have fallen under my Cognizance, the *Outside* hath been infinitely preferable to the *In*: Whereof I have been farther convinced from some late Experiments. Last Week I saw a Woman *flay'd*, and you will hardly believe, how

much it altered her Person for the worse. Yesterday I
ordered the Carcass of a *Beau* to be stript in my Presence; when we were all amazed to find so many un-
suspected Faults under one Suit of Cloaths: Then I laid
open his *Brain*, his *Heart*, and his *Spleen*; But, I plainly
perceived at every Operation, that the farther we proceeded, we found the Defects encrease upon us in
Number and Bulk: from all which, I justly formed this
Conclusion to my self; That whatever Philosopher or
Projector can find out an Art to sodder and patch up the
Flaws and Imperfections of Nature, will deserve much
better of Mankind, and teach us a more useful Science,
than that so much in present Esteem, of widening and
exposing them (like him who held *Anatomy* to be the
ultimate End of *Physick.*) And he, whose Fortunes and
Dispositions have placed him in a convenient Station to
enjoy the Fruits of this noble Art; He that can with *Epi-
curus* content his Ideas with the *Films* and *Images* that
fly off upon his Senses from the *Superficies* of Things;
Such a Man truly wise, creams off Nature, leaving the
Sower and the Dregs, for Philosophy and Reason to lap
up. This is the sublime and refined Point of Felicity,
called, *the Possession of being well deceived*; The Serene Peaceful State of being a Fool among Knaves.

    In the first sentence of this paragraph we are given terms in which to
define the opposition the text has been working toward: "Credulity" versus "Curiosity." From what we have read, we know to reject the former—
which is associated with the "Peaceful" state of permanent delusion, tinsel, fancy, etc.—and to approve the latter. Thus, when the speaker admires the "Surface," we know we should admire the "Depth," and when
he praises a kind of life by "Sight and Touch" and rejects "Reason," which
comes "officiously, with Tools for cutting, and opening, and mangling,
and piercing, offering to demonstrate, that they are not of the same consistence quite thro'," we know what to think about that and about him.
    Then we read: "I do here think fit to inform the Reader, that in such
Conclusions as these, Reason is certainly in the Right; and that in most
Corporeal Beings, which have fallen under my Cognizance, the *Outside*
hath been infinitely preferable to the *In*: Whereof I have been farther
convinced from some late Experiments. Last Week I saw a Woman *flay'd*,
and you will hardly believe, how much it altered her Person for the
worse." We suddenly have a version of the "curious" side of things, to

which we have become committed, that is more horrible, more foolish, and more insane than anything the "credulous" voice has supported. We next hear the story of laying open the "Carcass of a *Beau*," in which "I plainly perceived at every Operation, that the farther we proceeded, we found the Defects encrease upon us in Number and Bulk: from all which, I justly formed this Conclusion to my self; That whatever Philosopher or Projector can find out an Art to sodder and patch up the Flaws and Imperfections of Nature, will deserve much better of Mankind, and teach us a more useful Science, than that so much in present Esteem, of widening and exposing them." Our guiding voice here turns from curiosity back to credulity, saying that the happiest man will be he who can "content his Ideas with the *Films* and *Images* that fly off upon his Senses from the *Superficies* of Things; Such a Man truly wise, creams off Nature, leaving the Sower [Sour] and the Dregs, for Philosophy and Reason to lap up. This is the sublime and refined Point of Felicity, called, *the Possession of being well deceived*; The Serene Peaceful State of being a Fool among Knaves."

III

Where does this leave us? Favoring the "credulous" or the "curious"? In reading this passage, we first rejected the voice that favors the "Surface" of things (and delusion and fancy and so forth) in favor of its opposite, the implied voice that prefers reason and depth and understanding; but then we find that to be impossible too. So, what now? Are we to swing back to the position we rejected and accept the "Serene Peaceful State" that the last sentence promises us?[11] If not that, what? And what has happened to the "common Forms" and the "Pattern of Human Learning" upon which we before depended? What has happened to *us*?

This is what has happened: in the course of these two paragraphs the relationship between the author and reader has changed in a dramatic and unforeseen way, so that the text works on us directly, almost like a kind of trick. For up to this point the text has offered a first-class instruction in reading, training our ear to recognize the pretentious and self-deluded when we see it in others or might see it in ourselves. The "abuses" corrected have been for the most part other people's, only hypothetically our own. But here the sole object of correction is the reader himself. The text works on us directly, through our perfectly natural desire for clarity and certainty, our wish for the sort of "serenity" and "peace" that comes from knowing what the text expects of us and complying with it.[12] We have been taught to read ironic texts, and we think we know how to read this passage; but when we do what we have been taught to do, we find ourselves ending up in an impossible position, in a universe that offers us no place to stand, nowhere to go. By leading us to this point and then leaving us there (the next paragraph begins: "BUT to return to *Madness*"), Swift makes us recognize that we cannot make our way through his text, or through the world, either by accepting what we are told or by converting it into its opposite. The experience of reading this passage is the experience of error, committed and corrected; we shall have to work our own way out of it.

The key to the passage (if one dare use such a phrase in speaking of Swift), is that the opposite of the false views presented here are also false. When we step on the ground we think is offered us, it gives way. This is a surprise, because it is the usual expectation of a reader of irony, at times reinforced in the *Tale* itself, that something like the opposite of what is said is what is "actually meant." Another way to put it is that whenever a writer uses a term of value, he normally commits himself to some version of it as a real value. For example, when one sees Swift speak of "*Candor*" and "*Tast*" and "fair deduction" in the Apology, one knows that he is making these topics the subject of real attention; they may exist in false forms, to be rejected, but it is implied that they exist in true forms as well. While this is in a sense true here as well (Swift values both truth and fiction), there is a sense in which it is not; for the true subject of the passage is not the things being contrasted but the way of making the contrast itself. When he says that "Imagination is at Cuffs with the Senses" and a "Man's Fancy gets *astride* on his Reason," what is wrong is not with Imagination or Sense or Fancy or Reason but with the relationship expressed between them: "at Cuffs." It would be just as bad if a man's Reason got "*astride*" on his Fancy. (That, as we shall shortly see, is the lesson of Gulliver's voyage to the Houyhnhnms.) Another way to put it is to say that the questions on which the passage is organized are false ones: credulous *vs.* curious, surface *vs.* depth, truth *vs.* fiction, memory *vs.* imagination, nature *vs.* art, and so on. These are questions with no right side, and, once we get going, it is easy to think of others like them: form *vs.* substance, liberty *vs.* restraint, reason *vs.* emotion, general *vs.* particular, etc.[13] In reading this passage, our instinct to oppose what we read, coming from such a person as this, is perfectly sound. Our mistake is to oppose the particular position taken (in favor of the credulous, say) rather than the way the question is perceived; and that mistake leads to our commission of the very error of mind exhibited by the voice we are rejecting.

It will obviously not do to say that what Swift favors is the "mean" between the "extremes," enacted in this passage, for these pairs do not admit such treatment. What, for example, could be the mean between truth and fiction, between memory and the imagination?[14] (And such a solution is far too mechanical to figure in this text except as an object of parody.) To ask such questions as these is to divide up the world, to divide up man himself, in an impossible way: an insane version of the "rational" mind at work.

And more than that: as the tendency to reduce the world to false questions moves outward from the self, it divides and destroys the integrity of the culture as well as that of the individual. For the terms that are here made the object of false choice, and others like them, properly function as the fundamental topics on which branches of culture can be based. Liberty *vs.* restraint, for example, is the central topic of the complex system of discourse we call the law; form *vs.* substance defines a tension close to the center of what we mean by art; and so on.[15] To force such a choice is to destroy the life that the opposition makes possible and to deny the difficult reality it expresses.

IV

The structure of this passage is in some respects similar to that of the last voyage in *Gulliver's Travels*. There one is first led to admire the benign rationality of the Houyhnhnms, cut off as they are from what seem to be the grosser aspects of human nature, until one realizes the full hideousness of the alternatives created by this split: a chaotic and constant warfare of unmediated feeling versus a tyranny of "reason." It is only the despised Yahoos, after all, who love their young; and in the principled and rational utopia of the Houyhnhnms Gulliver so far forgets his own nature as to speak with equanimity of a canoe covered with "the skins of Yahoos well stitched together"; of a sail made of "the skins of the same animal; but I made use of the youngest I could get, the older being too tough and thick"; and of caulking his canoe with "Yahoo's tallow." The defect in him, and in the Houhyhnhnms, is an absence of the sympathetic imagination,[16] the same defect that permits the speaker in the *Tale* to talk as he does of the flaying of a woman. (The kind of imagination missing here is at the center of what the *Iliad* has to teach us.) In the rational and "truthful" world of the Houyhnhnms there is no place for fiction, for which indeed they would presumably use the same circumlocution they do for the word "lie": "to say the thing that is not." A truthfulness that fails to distinguish between deceit and fiction cannot recommend itself either to the writer or to the reader of *Gulliver's Travels* or *A Tale of a Tub*.[17]

The reason why these two paragraphs are central to our experience of the whole work (and not merely pieces of a digression) is that they bring to the surface a problem of reading we have had, without wholly knowing it, since the beginning of the *Tale*. They force us to look back in a new way on everything we have done so far, like a hiker who, from an elevation, looks back on the trail he has been following and sees it with new eyes, new understanding, and a new set of questions.

The Meaning of the Tale

I said earlier that the center of value in this work is the Will and the plain and direct and moderate voice in which it is written, and there is a way in which that is of course true. But it is an incomplete statement if there ever was one, for it misses something obvious about our own experience of this text. How can we say of this book, of all the works ever made by man, that its central value is plain and direct speech? *A Tale of a Tub* is a masterpiece of imagination and invention, and much of its value for us must lie there. Swift offers us a created world with its own original life, and the reader feels it as pleasure. The frank bookseller; the sons, first decorating their coats outlandishly, then ripping them apart; the modern author, proving that the ass is a symbol of the critic by showing that critics (at least some of them) are gall-ridden cuckolds (Q.E.D.); mad Peter's banquet of bread, and so on—all this has a reality that lives wonderfully in the mind. Swift's great achievement is one not of plain prose but of the imagination.

Yet, in the reading of the *Tale* that we have done here, we found ourselves repeatedly taking the side not of "imagination" (which was presented as delusion or fancy or pretension) but of "truth"; and in doing that we then committed the error we commit again in the "Digression on Madness" when we reject "fiction" for "truth," "imagination" for "memory"—the error it is the purpose of these paragraphs to expose and correct. For example, part of the pleasure of the bookseller's "Dedication" is in the unmasking of the literary and social form we call a dedication, and we laugh at its hypocrisy and fraud; but this part of the text is in fact a real dedication, something we tend to forget. At Peter's banquet we see that the bread, for which Peter makes such absurd claims, is only bread; but (while his claims for it are indeed absurd) it is not true that it is "only bread"; for Swift it is the material of sacrament. From the claim that it is "only bread," indeed, the line is clear to saying: "Last Week, I saw a Woman *flay'd*, and you will hardly believe, how much it altered her Person for the worse." For to strip an event or an object of all context and circumstance in the interest of "plain truth" is to strip it of all meaning; to deny the value of the imagination is to destroy the capacity for sympathy and break down the system of shared meanings—the "fictions"—that constitute our culture. We start by reducing pretension to truth and end by reducing truth to a kind of falsity.

Our experience of this text thus teaches that the tension between the imagination and fancy and wit, on the one hand, and plain and direct speech on the other, which here is presented with such extraordinary fullness, cannot be resolved by a choice of one thing over the other but only by learning to live with both.[18] The imagination is as necessary to ward off the madness of pure rationality as reason is to ward off that of pure fantasy; either one alone, like "justice" or "expediency" in Thucydides, is a delusion that denies the truth. The false division of "truth" and "fiction" that characterizes this passage—and indeed the *Tale* as a whole and the Houhynhnm episode as well—is a form of disease, a division of the self and culture that amounts to a kind of madness. For to divide this way is to deform; it denies, by falsely resolving them, structural tensions that are central to human life and experience. Acceptance of them is essential to maturity and health.

But what can this "acceptance" mean in practice? How, for example, does the "Digression on Madness" instruct its reader to heal the false divisions and to put to work, in a single language, the pairs that it has placed in a false opposition? Swift's main answer is that this must be the work of the reader, upon whom this text places the responsibility for making his own sense of things, for making his own language. Swift knows that he cannot teach the proper use of language by collecting beautiful, witty, or intelligent statements for us to use, in imitation of him,[19] because language is not an instrument or machine to be perfected by an expert and used by the rest of us. It is an inheritance that must be made and remade, over and over, for good or ill, by all who use it. His interest is in the process by which self and culture are reconstituted by the active mind, and he wishes to reach the reader at a place below the surface of consciousness, at the place where his language is made. In this sense his conception of the relationship between self and language is Socratic, and the community he establishes with his reader is deeply dialectic. For he does not define for his reader a culture that he admires and wishes his reader to adopt; instead, he offers a text that requires the reader to put his resources of experience and invention to work in an activity of reading that is so constructive as to be almost a kind of writing. The reader must create his own language.

But Swift does not merely create a predicament from which the reader must extricate himself; he offers, in the processes by which his text can be made intelligible, an affirmation of the possibility of meaning. The reader of this text can create from it, as it were by a kind of triangulation, a stable place of the sort we found missing in Thucydides, a platform from which the world and one's life can be seen to make sense. This entails an affirmation of certain possibilities of the culture and a rejection of others. This text works in part as the *Iliad* does, by pulling its reader this way and that; but it works intellectually rather than sympathetically, moving the reader from what anyone would say to what no one could say and then back again, over and over. The dialectic of this text thus helps the reader make a place of his own, and—unlike the Socratic dialectic— it is a place within a culture, where the reader can continue to learn from what is around him. This text destroys the language of its ideal reader in the sense that it makes certain kinds of utterance impossible for him. But in doing this it forces him not so much into sheer invention as back upon what he knows, rendering active and conscious what had been passive and unrecognized. The reader is thus led to recognize tendencies within himself and to see what they mean. Words are made to lose their meaning so that they may be given meaning of a new and deeper kind.

Just as the *Tale* is dialectical in the responsibility it places upon the reader, it is ethical in its central concern with character. The way of reading it teaches consists largely in listening for a voice, then asking who speaks that way, then judging it. It thus constantly trains what could be called the ethical ear, for to read it at all one must constantly be assessing character as it is manifested in language. The defects that appear in the text as delusion, false questions, withdrawals from reality, unlimited ambitions, failures to connect, and the like are not merely intellectual or cognitive deficiencies but diseases of character, the only remedy for which is the kind of wholeness and health Swift seeks to stimulate in the reader. To read sensibly, to write sensibly, and to be sensible are, for Swift, intimately connected.

This kind of training of the ear is the greatest gift this text makes to its reader.[20] Anyone who reads the *Tale* well will be forever different, alert in new ways to faults and defects of the self as they exhibit themselves in speech or writing; for he will be trained to ask himself how this sentence or phrase would sound in the world of Swift's "author." One might sum it up by saying that in this text Swift creates a psychological and intellectual vacuum that it is the reader's task to fill with language of his own making; in doing this the reader cannot simply use the words and phrases and forms that he finds around him but must give them meanings of his own. When he does so, he will discover that he has affirmed the central truths and values of his culture, that he has learned the meaning, in a new way, of his inherited language. Swift's own part has been to train the reader's ear to recognize the sounds of health and madness in what he reads and in the language that he himself produces. In this way Swift offers his reader a set of experiences that remake his perceptions of himself, his language, and his world; he remakes his reader as a maker of language.

✳   ✳   ✳

SWIFT ADDS to our reading of Plato a sharpened sense that the gap between the individual and his culture may be a sign of a defect in the former, not the latter. One's sense of having discovered a truth that denies the teachings of the past is likely to be a delusion of grandiosity. Yet one cannot simply accept one's inherited forms and parrot the sentences one has been taught without sounding like, and being, a fool. The culture exists in forms both sound and diseased, and it is the task of every person to reconstitute what he has inherited, one way or the other. The responsibility is inescapable. And while one is trying to judge one's inherited and invented resources, one must at the same time constantly be judging oneself, looking for distortions of heart and mind. The true subject of the *Tale* is the folly and knavery, not of others, but of the reader himself. This adds a new level to the already difficult task of cultural judgment, for we must not only learn to judge the culture that has made us what we are (and where can we stand to do that?); we must judge our own judgment. How can this be done?

At this point Swift's training of the "ethical ear" can be seen to have a new and critical significance. In this world of uncertainty, what can in fact be most stable and secure is our educated sense of who it is that speaks. Our sense of character and relation is the ground on which criticism of culture and self can ultimately rest.

6

Teaching a Language of Morality

Johnson's *Rambler* Essays

In the series of essays he published as the *Rambler* (twice a week from 1750 to 1752), and in the rest of what can be called his moral writings—especially "The Vanity of Human Wishes" (1748) and *Rasselas* (1759)—it is Samuel Johnson's aim, as it was Swift's, to teach his reader how to make and to use a language of reason and value. But his method seems to be directly the opposite of Swift's: what Swift did through irony and parody, through distortions and deformations that forced the reader to call on his own experience and resources and to make active his knowledge of himself and his language, Johnson tries to do directly, in a prose overtly didactic. This is a literature of moral instruction.[1]

This means that in these essays Johnson defines explicitly, and not by ironic implication, a set of resources for the constitution of self and community, for giving direction to life and for claiming meaning for what happens within it. The language of Christian morality within which he works is, if any language deserves the term, a language of value, and Johnson demonstrates that it is a language of reason as well.

But what interest can we expect to have in a literature that is at once moral and didactic in this way? How can either its terms of value or its methods of reasoning recommend themselves to the modern reader, who may be unable to share the religious feeling that animates nearly everything that Johnson writes and to whom, especially at first, Johnson's moral vocabulary may seem hopelessly out of date? Many of the "moral and religious truths"[2] that Johnson seeks to inculcate will seem to the reader thoroughly familiar, mere commonplaces of our culture (and of an earlier time at that). What kind of textual community can be constituted in such a literature as this? What kind of life can it have for us? It may seem simply impossible that such overtly didactic writing as this can reach the mind where Swift reaches it, at the place where language and character are made. As readers of these essays, we will be mere instructees, it seems, receiving a set of directions to life and thought, not acting as participants in the discovery and constitution of language and community. The language will come straight from Johnson to us; it can never be our own, except as we learn to repeat it. How can it possibly be otherwise?

The actual experience of reading the *Rambler*s upsets or confounds such expectations as these. For Johnson is not interested solely in the truth of a set of moral propositions and the validity of the arguments supporting them (though for him the propositions he advances are true, and the arguments are persuasive); he is interested as well in the relationship between these propositions and the mind that utters and receives them, in the relationship between language and the self. His concern reaches beyond a set of more or less restatable truths to include the internal life by which they are apprehended for a moment, then lost, forgotten, or misunderstood; or perhaps renewed, clarified, and grasped—for how long?—firmly as principle. For him the true subject of moral writing is not just a set of statements but the experience of struggling first to attain and then to hold on to them; it is this experience that gives to abstract truths whatever life and meaning they can have, that establishes the condition of any moral discourse. It is not with truth abstracted from experience that Johnson is concerned but with truth enacted in it; for him, language is a part of life.

Johnson accordingly has a central interest in the place a particular statement holds in his own mind and experience as he utters it and in the place he can give it, by his writing, in the mind and experience of his reader; he is interested, that is, in what might be called its depth or weight or fullness, in the mind and in the text. For he knows, as we all do, that a particular statement can be what we call a truism (or cliché or platitude or received idea), stated in some automatic or unthinking way, or it can be a serious truth, deeply felt and understood, not repeated in imitation of others but in some sense made one's own. The question he constantly addresses, then, is this: What distinguishes the first kind of writing, and the kind of thought and life it expresses, from the second? What distinguishes—to use his terms—"commonplace" from "principle"?

This is an issue for him not only in moral discourse but in every kind of writing where the cliché is a danger. For example, in the series of *Idler* essays on "Dick Minim"[3] he shows this excellent critic propounding a set of critical truisms, all perfectly true, many expressing ideas held by Johnson himself, but all existing in the text merely as platitudes:

> When the theatres were shut, he [Minim] retired to
> Richmond with a few select writers, whose opinions he
> impressed upon his memory by unwearied diligence;
> and when he returned with other wits to the town, was

> able to tell, in very proper phrases, that the chief busi-
> ness of art is to copy nature; that a perfect writer is not
> to be expected, because genius decays as judgment in-
> creases; that the great art is the art of blotting, and that
> according to the rule of Horace every piece should be
> kept nine years. . . . His opinion was, that Shakespear,
> committing himself wholly to the impulse of nature,
> wanted that correctness which learning would have
> given him; and that Johnson [Ben Jonson], trusting to
> learning, did not sufficiently cast his eye on nature. He
> blamed the stanza of Spenser, and could not bear the
> hexameters of Sidney. Denham and Waller he held the
> first reformers of English numbers, and thought that if
> Waller could have obtained the strength of Denham, or
> Denham the sweetness of Waller, there had been
> nothing wanting to complete a poet.

One can imagine Dick Minim, upon being told that his views are trite and boring and that he is no critic, demanding: "Why not? What have I said that is wrong? What have you said that is better? What would you have me say?" There is, of course, a sense in which what he says is unexceptionable, but that is part of the problem. The trouble with his views is not that they are untrue but that they are not his own in any meaningful way; they are merely the received opinions of the age, platitudes and clichés lifted from the writings of others.[4]

But to say this would presumably not mean much to such a mind as his. The only full answer to Minim, and to the Minim in each of us, would have to lie in the performance of criticism itself, and it is accordingly to his own critical writings, especially to *The Lives of the English Poets*, that we should look for Johnson's response. For our present purposes it is enough to observe that what is true of the language of criticism is for Johnson true of the language of morality as well. Moral truths learned as precepts from authority are perhaps more quickly and completely reduced to platitude than any other kind of statement. Our own desire for comfort drives us to it; for to understand the teachings of our moral tradition as real truths would limit our freedom and reduce our self-importance. As Johnson sees it, we therefore find other ways to deal with them, such as merely repeating them, which empties them of meaning, much as a repeated metaphor gradually loses its life.

In his moral writing Johnson thus has two simultaneous concerns. One is to work out statements of what seem to be important truths about life (many, but not all, of which seem to be simple enough and close to what we have in some sense "always known"); the other is to see to it that what he says has the standing of what he calls "truth" or "principle" (as opposed to "commonplace"), both in his own life and writing and in the reader's experience of his work. When, for example, Johnson speaks of the "principles" with which "it is the duty of every man to furnish his mind," so that in a time of disaster he may be able "to act under it with decency and propriety" (No. 32), he is not talking about memorizing a set of maxims or aphorisms but attaining a ground of action by an alteration of sentiment and disposition, a change in the nature and structure of the self.[5] Johnson accordingly offers his reader more than a set of arguments and conclusions; he offers him the experience of a mind engaged in a constantly renewed struggle with its own resisting and delusive forces, putting itself in motion toward what is stable and true. The language in which Johnson does these things cannot be learned by rote or imitation; it must be remade, every time, as it is put to use by the active mind, and one purpose of this writing is to instruct the reader, by example, in the process by which that is done.

But how does Johnson actually do these things in practice? From what beginnings, and by what movements, does he carry us to his conclusions? By what process does he seek to ensure that what he says has the character of principle, not commonplace, as it is enacted in his text and as it is experienced in the mind of the reader? What kind of language does he make, and how does he do it? These are our questions.

Endpoints: From Commonplace to Principle

What I have called Johnson's didactic mode receives perhaps its clearest expression in the statements with which it is his frequent habit to conclude an essay. Here are four examples:

> False hopes and false terrors are equally to be
> avoided. Every man, who proposes to grow eminent
> by learning, should carry in his mind, at once, the dif-
> ficulty of excellence, and the force of industry; and
> remember that fame is not conferred but as the
> recompense of labour, and that labour, vigorously con-
> tinued, has not often failed of its reward. [No. 25]

> It seems to me reasonable to enjoy blessings with confi-
> dence as well as to resign them with submission, and
> to hope for the continuance of good which we possess
> without insolence or voluptuousness, as for the restitu-
> tion of that which we lose without despondency or
> murmurs.

The chief security against the fruitless anguish of impatience, must arise from frequent reflection on the wisdom and goodness of the God of nature, in whose hands are riches and poverty, honour and disgrace, pleasure and pain, and life and death. A settled conviction of the tendency of every thing to our good, and of the possibility of turning miseries into happiness, by receiving them rightly, will incline us to "bless the name of the Lord, whether he gives or takes away." [No. 32]

It is therefore to be steadily inculcated, that virtue is the highest proof of understanding, and the only solid basis of greatness; and that vice is the consequence of narrow thoughts, that it begins in mistake, and ends in ignominy. [No. 4]

Whoever commits a fraud is guilty not only of the particular injury to him whom he deceives, but of the diminution of that confidence which constitutes not only the ease but the existence of society. He that suffers by imposture has too often his virtue more impaired than his fortune. But as it is necessary not to invite robbery by supineness, so it is our duty not to suppress tenderness by suspicion; it is better to suffer wrong than to do it, and happier to be sometimes cheated than not to trust. [No. 79]

It is not hard to imagine that a reader who saw these and similar paragraphs of conclusion, as he leafed through a collection of the *Rambler* essays, might ask himself why he should bother to read them at all. He already knows that virtue is good, vice bad, that he should recognize both the rewards and the difficulties of labor, and so forth. Yet these paragraphs are not lapses from Johnson's high standard, or drawn from the less satisfactory essays, or otherwise to be explained away; they exhibit an important tendency of his mind to conclude with what looks like a statement of received ideas.

When one turns to the beginning of a *Rambler* essay, one observes what seems to be the same tendency, although here it is manifested in a somewhat different form. For again and again Johnson begins with a statement of what has been "often observed," or "generally agreed," or "universally believed," that is, with the commonplaces of moral life overtly defined as such. Here are four examples drawn from the early essays:

That man should never suffer his happiness to depend upon external circumstances, is one of the chief
precepts of the Stoical philosophy. [No. 6]

That every man should regulate his actions by his
own conscience, without any regard to the opinions of
the rest of the world, is one of the first precepts of moral
prudence. [No. 23]

There are some vices and errors, which, though often
fatal to those in whom they are found, have yet, by the
universal consent of mankind, been considered as entitled to some degree of respect, or have, at least, been
exempted from contemptuous infamy, and condemned
by the severest moralists with pity rather than detestation. [No. 25]

Among the many inconsistencies which folly produces, or infirmity suffers in the human mind, there
has often been observed a manifest and striking con-
trariety between the life of an author and his writings.
[No. 14]

If the reader compares this set of statements with the concluding
statements quoted earlier, he may notice, even the first time through,
that there is an important and repeated difference between the two sets of
passages. The statements of conclusion are much more firmly and directly stated, as positions taken and held. The statements with which the
essays begin are by contrast made problematic; they are distanced from
both Johnson and the reader by being attributed, for example, to "Stoical
philosophy" or by being themselves self-evidently dubious. (Who asks us,
for example, to "respect" vices, especially "fatal" ones?) Johnson thus begins with fragments of his inherited moral discourse as they lie around
him, unjudged and unmediated; they are pieces of the culture in which
he participates by virtue of his language and education, but what he
wishes us to think of them we do not yet know. The statements with
which the essays end are drawn from much the same discourse, but they
are clarified and solidified, cast as propositions on which Johnson and his
reader can confidently rest. This movement from a confused and problematic background to a clear statement is in form like the movement of
the *Gorgias*, but Johnson's conclusions are for the most part not innova-
tive or paradoxical, as Socrates' were, but restatements of what in some

sense is already familiar. They are reaffirmations rather than rejections of the traditional moral language.

Johnson's beginnings are thus a way of starting where the reader actually is, surrounded by truisms and clichés, in a condition of uncertainty or doubt, perhaps of essential thoughtlessness, from which he may be moved to a new position of clarity and truth. But the familiarity of the conclusions, when we get to them, shows us something important about the condition initially addressed in the reader and out of which Johnson himself seems to speak: we are in a perpetually recreated condition of error, subject to repeated fallings-off from what we have once partly known (and in some sense still know) into a seemingly unnecessary, almost willful, ignorance. The real starting point of these essays is thus the fact that we—both Johnson and his reader—do need to discover or to be told, again and again, the things that he discovers and tells us, for our knowledge of them is always imperfect and subject to constant erosion and loss.[6] This means that the process by which we have lost our grip on what we "know" (so that it comes as a familiar surprise to learn it again) is one subject of these essays—as it is of the *Iliad*—and it is their object to reverse it. What might be called the pressures toward thoughtlessness are in a sense enacted in the prose itself, for it is against them that Johnson moves as he carries us from such beginnings to such endings.

There is a seeming paradox in this version of the structure of the essays, for the "distanced" beginnings have a kind of life, arising from the very tensions and uncertainties that make them unsettled, that the closing statements, which in isolation often seem like lifeless platitudes, appear to lack. It is of course true that the beginnings have a special kind of life, the life of a difficulty or problem that invites further work. But the endings, in their context, have a kind of life too, of a different kind. Retrospective, not prospective, in character, it arises from the relationship between the ending and the text of which it is a part. It is their relationship with their context, with the movement that leads up to them, that gives these endings their meaning, their life, and their character as principle.

THE MOTIONS OF THE MIND

It is no accident that the *Rambler*s are a series of essays rather than a single composition, for Johnson wishes to affect his reader in ways that could not be achieved by a single chain of reasoning, however elaborate, or by a single set of arguments or reflections, but only by the repeated exposure, under continually varying conditions, to the motions of his mind at work. Reading through this set of more than two hundred essays is very much like coming to know a person in the real world. The moments of acquaintance are brief, in a sense ephemeral, all slightly different, all essentially the same, and the effect is cumulative and internally most complex. The experience of the work cannot, of course, be perfectly summarized, but some idea of the whole may be suggested by an examination of two or three essays that exhibit the tendencies of Johnson's mind with special clarity.

"Schemes of Future Felicity"

I

The second *Rambler*[7] begins with what seems to be a statement of Johnson's deepest theme, the subject of his recently composed *The Vanity of Human Wishes*. But by being placed, as is his custom, at some distance from himself and from the reader (it is "remarked" not by Johnson but by undesignated others), this statement is made an object of critical contemplation.

> That the mind of man is never satisfied with the objects immediately before it, but is always breaking away from the present moment, and losing itself in schemes of future felicity; and that we forget the proper use of the time now in our power, to provide for the enjoyment of that which, perhaps, may never be granted us, has been frequently remarked; and as this practice is a commodious subject of raillery to the gay, and of declamation to the serious, it has been ridiculed with all the pleasantry of wit, and exaggerated with all the amplifications of rhetoric.

The central proposition about the loss of the present in the future, of reality in hope, is stated perfectly directly, because it is for Johnson a real (though incomplete) truth. But he distances himself from it, at first quite gently, with the words "frequently remarked," and then more obviously, as the character of those remarks is made more plain, with the words "ridiculed" and "all the amplifications of rhetoric." * Johnson thus directs

---

* The sense of exaggeration is continued in the next sentence: "*Every* instance, by which its absurdity might appear *most* flagrant, has been *studiously* collected; it has been marked with *every* epithet of contempt, and *all* the tropes and figures have been called forth against it" (emphasis added).

the reader's attention to two distinct matters simultaneously: to the meaning of the proposition itself and to the meaning of the way in which it is stated.

In the next paragraph Johnson focuses on the second of these matters, and shows us what it means for a proposition to be reiterated not as a "principle" but as a "common topick." The motives that give rise to this kind of repetition of a maxim are plain: "Censure is willingly indulged, because it always implies some superiority," and "the pleasure of wantoning in common topicks is so tempting to a writer, that he cannot easily resign it: a train of sentiments generally received enables him to shine without labour, and to conquer without a conquest." It is indeed so easy and pleasant "to exemplify the uncertainty of the human state, to rouse mortals from their dream, and inform them of the silent celerity of time" that authors are often more willing "to transmit than examine so advantageous a principle."

In thus defining a thoughtless way of talking about the uncertainty of the human state, Johnson has defined a problem both for himself and for his reader: How will his own writing be different? He starts to answer this question by showing us something of what his kind of thought can do. He resists the truism by affirming what it opposes, human hope: "This quality of looking forward into futurity seems the unavoidable condition of a being, whose motions are gradual, and whose life is progressive." Hope in some form is a necessity of life, for a man must "intend first what he performs last; as, by continual advances from his first stage of existence, he is perpetually varying the horizon of his prospects, he must always discover new motives of action, new excitements of fear, and allurements of desire." "The natural flights of the human mind are not from pleasure to pleasure, but from hope to hope."

But just as this view is a correction of another, so is it, in turn, corrected, and recorrected, by Johnson's naturally resistive or argumentative mind. He first redefines the standing of a common topic, granting that, after all, "few maxims are widely received or long retained but for some conformity with truth and nature." This "caution against keeping our view too intent upon remote advantages is not without its propriety or usefulness, though it may have been recited with too much levity, or enforced with too little distinction." But this view is itself resisted: Johnson observes that there would be "few enterprises of great labour or hazard undertaken, if we had not the power of magnifying the advantages which we persuade ourselves to expect from them." The next step is still another correction: for it is often true that our hopes are as impossible as the imaginings of Don Quixote, and the "understanding of a man, naturally sanguine, may, indeed, be easily vitiated by the luxurious indulgence of hope."

Johnson has here moved himself to a position that is at once complex and qualified. He is neither for nor against "hope" in simple terms; he confines himself to saying that the "luxurious indulgence of hope" has its dangers, at least for a man "naturally sanguine." Even for such a one, he implies, rational hope is good and necessary, and, for those who are naturally timid or depressed, even an excessive hope may be more good than bad. To put this in terms familiar from our reading of Swift, we can say that Johnson starts with a false question of just the sort that Swift's persona loves to state: Are you for or against hope? Then, after complicating it beyond recognition, he arrives at last at a statement of principle that can bear some real weight. But it is also true that by then Johnson has run out of things to say. The mind that follows each statement with a countering statement has gone as far as it can; it has arrived at a silence not unlike that of a participant in a Socratic dialogue.[8] One kind of thinking has come to an end. What can Johnson do now?

II

His turn out of this position is characteristically upon himself and his present circumstances. "Perhaps no class of the human species requires more to be cautioned against this anticipation of happiness, than those that aspire to the name of authors." For one of "lively fancy" it is especially easy to move from a "hint" in the mind to "the press, and to the world, and, with a little encouragement from flattery, [to push] forward into future ages, and [to prognosticate] the honours to be paid him." Johnson's vision of the writer captivated with the idea of his own grandeur is a figure from the same universe as those who repeat maxims without understanding or examining them, and both are versions of Johnson himself, who is now writing about the hopes he actually has for the series of essays he has just begun. He makes this fact explicit: "while I am yet but lightly touched with the symptoms of the writer's malady" I will "endeavour to fortify myself against the infection, not without some weak hope, that my preservatives may extend their virtue to others, whose employment exposes them to the same danger."

And how will he "fortify" himself and teach us to do likewise? He turns to the "sage advice of Epictetus," to think of what is most "shocking and terrible" in order to "be preserved from too ardent wishes for seeming good, and from too much dejection in real evil." (The contemplation of real catastrophe, that is, will make one's actual sorrows seem less by comparison.) For a writer, Johnson says, with both truth and irony, the worst fate of all is neglect, "compared with which reproach, hatred, and opposition, are names of happiness"; yet this is a fate that "every man who dares to write has reason to fear." On the one hand, a writer may deserve ne-

147

glect, for "nature may not have qualified him much to enlarge or embellish knowledge, nor sent him forth entitled by indisputable superiority to regulate the conduct of the rest of mankind." (This is a way of teasing himself.) On the other hand, he may deserve recognition but not get it: "his merit may pass without notice, huddled in the variety of things, and thrown into the general miscellany of life." After all, he solicits the regard of a "multitude fluctuating in pleasures, or immersed in business," and most of his judges are precluded by passion or prejudice from approving anything new: "some are too indolent to read any thing, till its reputation is established; others too envious to promote that fame, which gives them pain by its increase." "What is new is opposed, because most are unwilling to be taught; and what is known is rejected, because it is not sufficiently considered, that men more frequently require to be reminded than informed. . . . [H]e that finds his way to reputation, through all these obstructions, must acknowledge that he is indebted to other causes beside his industry, his learning, or his wit."

WHEN JOHNSON turns the question on himself, we see that he addresses it first by an appropriate use of inherited learning, which gives him a serious topic—indeed, his own present concern—namely, neglect of the writer. Of neglect, there are two kinds, the deserved and the undeserved, both bad, and at the end he turns to an acknowledgement of providence that is close to a prayer. The movement of the whole essay is thus from a distanced examination of a maxim to a position of essential solitude where he recognizes both the futility of false expectations and the propriety of real hope and at once resigns himself to providence and commits himself to life. This is the kind of complexity of attitude or sentiment that can make a "principle" of what might have been a commonplace.

Thus the process by which the essay moves, as it criticizes and remakes its inherited moral discourse, is one of opposition and complication. Whatever is said is resisted in the name of some omitted fact or sentiment; the new statement is in its turn resisted, the dialectic always moving toward complication and correction. Perhaps the image of an unsteady vessel caught in a weltering sea, going too far in one direction, then too far in another, but gradually righting itself as its sails fill and it settles to its course, gives some idea of the movement of mind here. Or slipping on ice: just as Swift's prose could be said to offer the reader no steady footing, so that wherever he puts his foot it shoots out from beneath him, so Johnson could be said to show the reader how to keep his feet even there. The tendencies to slide are presented, as it were, in slow motion—which means that they can be felt, understood, and resisted—rather than in Swift's fantastically speeded-up universe, where one's footing is lost in an instant and, it sometimes seems, in two directions at once.

In writing of this journalistic kind, where the first draft is often the last, what we are offered is not a carefully planned experience but contact with a mind actually at work on its own difficulties.[9] The pressures toward error, the "slippings" with which Johnson is concerned, are not benign traps into which we are led by a superior strategist; they are Johnson's own, and this helps explain the extraordinary fact that in this literature of moral instruction we do not feel preached at or patronized in the least. It is not merely Johnson's talk about "our" weaknesses and temptations that achieves this result, for that device is available to the most pompous and patronizing sermonizer; it is Johnson's enactment of his own involvement in mistake, the reality and presence of his proclivities toward error and the nature of his efforts to resist them. We are not talked down to but are treated with respect and more, for we are offered a part of his internal life as it is actually lived.[10]

"To Carry in the Mind, at Once, the Difficulty of Excellence, and the Force of Industry."

I

An essay that is especially self-corrective is *Rambler* No. 25. I have already quoted its opening sentence, but I will repeat it here:

> There are some vices and errors, which, though often
> fatal to those in whom they are found, have yet, by the
> universal consent of mankind, been considered as
> entitled to some degree of respect, or have, at least,
> been exempted from contemptuous infamy, and con-
> demned by the severest moralists with pity rather than
> detestation.

This sentence seems almost out of control. What is this voice that asks us to grant "respect" to a vice? To a vice, moreover, that is "often fatal" to him in whom it is found? The phrase "the universal consent of mankind" contains hints of *A Tale of a Tub*, and we know from *Rambler* No. 2, which we have just finished examining, that such exaggeration can be an important sign of distancing in Johnson. But the course of the sentence toward incoherence is broken by a shift: "or have, at least, ..." His statement bends out of shape and threatens to break but does not quite do so, for Johnson returns at the end to the truth it contains, which he then seeks to develop. He gives the examples of "rashness and cowardice":

> two vices, of which, though they may be conceived
> equally distant from the middle point, where true forti-

tude is placed, and may equally injure any publick or
private interest, yet the one is never mentioned without
some kind of veneration, and the other always considered as a topick of unlimited and licentious censure, on
which all the virulence of reproach may be lawfully
exerted.

How are we to regard this train of thought? Is this a continuation of
the voice of the first sentence, misleading the reader in an accidental—or
perhaps a deliberately Swiftian—way? Or is this seriously meant by Samuel Johnson? The next sentences, elaborating what Swift would call a
mechanical metaphor, do little to reassure the doubtful:

It may be laid down as an axiom, that it is more easy
to take away superfluities than to supply defects; and,
therefore, he that is culpable, because he has passed
the middle point of virtue, is always accounted a fairer
object of hope, than he who fails by falling short. The
one has all that perfection requires, and more, but the
excess may be easily retrenched; the other wants the
qualities requisite to excellence, and who can tell how
he shall obtain them? We are certain that the horse may
be taught to keep pace with his fellows, whose fault is
that he leaves them behind. We know that a few strokes
of the axe will lop a cedar; but what arts of cultivation
can elevate a shrub?

This seems to lead to insupportable analogies and conclusions. Are we
to think that more is better than less in every human enterprise: treason,
arson, fraud? Johnson has been betrayed by his disposition to reach for
generalization, by his hunger for coherence, and by a false geometrical
image into an impossible position—one that belongs on the pages of
Swift. In the next paragraph he shows that he knows there is something
wrong, for he returns to what he knows is the main point, but with a
slight shift of image: "to walk with circumspection and steadiness in the
right path, at an equal distance between the extremes of error, ought to
be the constant endeavour of every reasonable being." He now returns to
what he has been saying, but with a different emphasis:

. . . [as] to most it will happen often, and to all sometimes, that there will be a deviation towards one side
or the other, we ought always to employ our vigilance,
with most attention, on that enemy from which there is

150

greatest danger, and to stray, if we must stray, towards
those parts from whence we may quickly and easily
return. . . .

Presumption will be easily corrected. Every experiment will teach caution, and miscarriages will hourly
shew, that attempts are not always rewarded with
success. . . .

It is the advantage of vehemence and activity, that
they are always hastening to their own reformation; because they incite us to try whether our expectations are
well grounded, and therefore detect the deceits which
they are apt to occasion. But timidity is a disease of the
mind more obstinate and fatal; for a man once persuaded, that any impediment is unsuperable, has given
it, with respect to himself, that strength and weight
which it had not before. He can scarcely strive with vig-
our and perseverance, when he has no hope of gaining
the victory; and since he never will try his strength, can
never discover the unreasonableness of his fears.

Johnson began with the Aristotelian image of a virtuous midpoint between two vices, but this was a mistake; for, as he now learns and reveals,
his own view of the world is in fact not geometric in that way or even so
much as is implied in the image of keeping or straying from the path of
righteousness. What he is really talking about, as this powerful passage
makes plain, are these major themes: first, that life is motion and that to
be idle or listless is to be, that much, without life; second, that it is experience, by which hope is disappointed and expectation frustrated, that
teaches us the nature of our condition and enables us to act and think
well. Without motion there is no experience, no education, no life.[11] The
movement of the essay is thus from a false expression, drawn from our
general stock of clichés, to a reconception of it in terms that are nearly in
accord with the truth as he means it. It is a movement of self-correction.

From this point (which could have been an ending) Johnson now turns
to literature, where people are often subject to a kind of "cowardice" that
keeps them from doing anything at all. This can arise either from a false
timidity or from a false confidence, which, because it is unrealistic, is certain to be destroyed. He concludes:

False hopes and false terrors are equally to be
avoided. Every man, who proposes to grow eminent by
learning, should carry in his mind, at once, the difficulty of excellence, and the force of industry; and re-

151

member that fame is not conferred but as the recompense of labour, and that labour, vigorously continued,
has not often failed of its reward.

After the experience of this essay, the last sentence reads very differently from the way it did when we first saw it. It has a meaning that is
in part performative, for Johnson's struggles with his own mistaken forms
of thought in this essay have demonstrated both the "difficulty of excellence" and the "force of industry" and have obtained, for him and for us, a
"reward." Looked at slightly differently, this sentence has a life that
springs from the simultaneous comprehension of opposing tendencies,
revealed in the stress now placed on its central terms, "at once." For these
reasons it offers a security on which he and we can rest.

The activities of mind by which these essays move thus comprise a
steady pressure to correct and complicate; a constant openness to new
facts or ideas; a repeated turning from system or theory to experience;
and a hunger for balance, for the capaciousness of mind that can retain at
once two opposing tendencies in their full force.[12]

II

Johnson's tendency to think by recognizing and including contraries is
at work not only within each of the essays but across them as well. One
essay will often respond to a conclusion reached in another, placing it in a
slightly different light. Thus Number 175, supporting a "prudent mis-
trust," is written with Number 79 in mind, where Johnson had concluded
with advice "not to suppress tenderness by suspicion." Similarly, Number
82 criticizes the collecting of antiquarian curiosities as useless and ridiculous; the next essay complicates this judgment, expressing a reluctance
to condemn any innocent activity, especially one that increases learning.
It changes the criticism to a statement of the danger that such a collector
may be operating below his own best level. Number 183, written against
envy, concludes with the statement that one may even enlist one's pride
against this vice, a judgment that would surprise the reader of Number
185, which inveighs in the strongest terms against pride, calling it the
force that impedes forgiveness, prevents peace, and destroys a true sense
of dignity and worth.[13] Many other examples of apparently incompatible
or inconsistent statements might be given.[14] It could not be otherwise in
such a series of essays as this, each of which begins afresh in the world of
ordinary language and moves in its own direction.

This is not a defect in Johnson's work but a consequence of its essential character: the conclusions reached are themselves subject to reexamination and complication, to a further process of thought; they are not

offered as building blocks of a theoretical system. His conclusions are in this sense open-ended or presumptive in character, structurally tentative. Not that a particular conclusion is not firm, but it must be understood for what it is, as inextricably part of a larger system of expression. It is firm only in the context that gives it life and meaning and renders it a principle rather than a commonplace.

This means that these essays cannot be read as Dick Minim would read them, reducing them to a respository of repeatable propositions. Since every principle is in some sense impermanent, subject to complication as it is placed in real or seeming conflict with other principles or facts, it cannot simply be remembered and repeated. It must be recreated by the reader, and it is the function of these essays to instruct us in the process by which this can be done.

THE LANGUAGE OF THE *RAMBLERS*

Definition

I

Part of the achievement of the *Rambler* essays is teaching of a different kind from the one we have been considering, for they contain arguments, distinctions, and definitions that continue to live in the mind, and that can become part of the reader's intellectual equipment for later use. That is, Johnson constructs a moral language not only by making the reader aware of the conditions of his life and thought, of the precariousness of his conclusions, of the uncertainty of everything—even the truth—as we experience it. He also offers lessons of an overt kind by drawing distinctions that we have missed but recognize immediately as proper and by defining terms in ways that will compel us to use them differently—by offering us, in short, a moral language superior to our own. (This is the side of Johnson that found expression in the *Dictionary*, where he also proceeds by generalization and clarification to remake a language for use by others.)

Consider, for example, the terms in which he distinguishes hypocrisy from affectation and defines the attitude appropriate to each. Hypocrisy, he tells us, is pretended virtue, while affectation is the "art of counterfeiting those qualities, which we might, with innocence and safety, be known to want [i.e., to lack]." To pretend devotion in order to perpetrate a fraud is hypocrisy; to boast of amorous conquests never made is affectation. "Contempt is the proper punishment of affectation, and detestation the just consequence of hypocrisy" (No. 20).[15]

These distinctions between "hypocrisy" and "affectation," between "detestation" and "contempt," give us the entire set of terms in a new way.[16] By placing the words in a working relationship with each other, a relationship the reader himself can employ, Johnson makes a language of value not by giving us what we might think of as conceptual definitions of his central terms (that is, by making statements of verbal equivalence) but by offering us definitions in use and operation. He defines a term by showing how it can be combined with others[17] and, in doing so, not only clarifies established meanings (for all the words) but makes possible the new expression of substantive truths. He is not building a conceptual scheme but teaching a language.

Compare the definitions and clarifications in the following passages:

> [*Sorrow:*] Sorrow is properly that state of the mind in which our desires are fixed upon the past, without looking forward to the future, an incessant wish that something were otherwise than it has been, a torment-ing or harassing want of some enjoyment or possession which we have lost, and which no endeavours can pos-sibly regain. [It is] perhaps the only affection of the breast that can be excepted [from the general remark that our passions] naturally hasten towards their own extinction by inciting and quickening the attainment of their objects. [No. 47]

> [*Resentment:*] Resentment is a union of sorrow with malignity . . . [No. 185]

> [*Envy:*] Envy is almost the only vice which is prac-ticable at all times, and in every place; the only passion which can never lie quiet for want of irritation. [No. 183]

> [*Pride and anger:*] Pride is undoubtedly the original of anger: but pride, like every other passion, if it once breaks loose from reason, counteracts its own purposes. A passionate man, upon the review of his day, will have very few gratifications to offer to his pride, when he has considered how his outrages were caused, why they were borne, and in what they are likely to end at last. [No. 11]

> [*Flattery:*] But flattery, if its operation be nearly ex-amined, will be found to owe its acceptance not to our

154

ignorance but knowledge of our failures, and to delight
us rather as it consoles our wants than displays our possessions. [No. 155]

[*Advice:*] Advice is offensive, not because it lays us
open to unexpected regret, or convicts us of any fault
which had escaped our notice, but because it shows us
that we are known to others as well as to ourselves.
[Ibid.]

[*Anxiety:*] Anxiety of this kind is nearly of the same
nature with jealousy in love, and suspicion in the general commerce of life; a temper which keeps the man
always in alarms, disposes him to judge of every thing
in a manner that least favours his own quiet, fills him
with perpetual stratagems of counteraction, wears him
out in schemes to obviate evils which never threatened
him, and at length, perhaps, contributes to the production of those mischiefs of which it had raised such
dreadful apprehensions. [No. 29]

II

The same view of language is at work in the *Dictionary*.[18] There Johnson does give verbal equivalents for the terms he defines, but he does not
stop with them. In his choice and arrangement of definitions, and especially in the quotations in which they are exemplified, he offers his readers understandings of a different kind. "Happiness," for example, is first
defined as "Felicity; state in which the desires are satisfied," but the initial quotation locates that term in a way that directs the mind toward the
moral and religious life:

"*Happiness* is that estate whereby we attain, so far as
possibly may be attained, the full possession of that
which simply for itself is to be desired, and containeth
in it after an eminent sort the contentation of our desires, the highest degree of all our perfection." (Hooker)

In giving the reader this quotation, Johnson invites him to ask what those
things are that ought to be "desired simply for themselves"; what his
"perfection" entails; and what limits on his hopes and expectations are
implied in the clause "so far as possibly may be attained." The next quotation (from Denham this time) relates happiness to "innocence" and "se-

curity"; the first is the proper object of every life, the second expresses the futile wish that the world were different: "Oh! *happiness* of sweet retir'd content, / To be at once secure and innocent." It is only after these definitions that the rest of the meanings of the term are given, including "good luck" and "fortuitous elegance."

Similarly, his first *Dictionary* definition of "idle" is a term of blame: "Lazy; averse from labour," and his quotation brings it home: "For shame, so much to do, and yet *idle*." Only after the central moral weight of the term has been established are the other definitions given: "Not busy; unactive; useless; worthless; and trifling."

III

Both the generalizing statements in the *Rambler* and the definitions in the *Dictionary* thus work not merely by a process of verbal substitution but as a series of performances of proper meaning, demonstrations of the ways a word can be used well. In speaking of definitions one is often tempted to use the metaphor "range of meaning," but in Johnson's work, at least, it is not the case, as the metaphor seems to imply, that the definitions establish the outer boundaries of a field or the termini of a spectrum within which any point is equally well represented by the word in question. The notion of a set of appropriate uses is also wrong if it is implied that the uses exemplified are exhaustive. For every use of a word, in literature and in life (everywhere except in a dictionary, perhaps), has other objects than the use of the word itself, and these objects can themselves be admired or condemned.[19] Johnson's *Dictionary* reflects this fact and continually makes implicit and explicit judgments about the objects of speech (which are of course the objects of life itself). It is words in action, made into literature by minds that he admires, serving ends that he approves, that Johnson offers us in the *Dictionary* and enacts in the *Rambler*. His interest is not simply in the ways words are in fact used, but in the ways they can be used well, with all that this may mean.

IN BOTH THE *Dictionary* and the *Rambler*, then, Johnson offers his reader improved resources for his own thought and expression, a new constitution of his language; but it remains true that these resources—even the definitions—cannot be used by repetition and imitation. They must be put to work by the reader himself, in his own way; he must become a speaker and maker of the language that he uses, creating something of his own out of the materials that Johnson (among others) has given him, improved for his use; and, as we have seen, it is one object of Johnson's work to teach him how to do this.

Integration

The language of the *Ramblers* has another quality, alluded to above, which for want of a better term I shall call its integrative character. By this I mean that this language combines into one things often spoken of as separate; it unites what we often divide. This occurs in two dimensions. First, this language cannot be broken down into the modern categories of fact, reason, and value; and second (largely as a consequence), it addresses the reader—indeed, for the moment it constitutes him—not merely as one who now observes, now ratiocinates, now feels or prefers, but as one who does all these at once and more, as one who works as a whole mind. The language is thus integrative, both of itself and of the reader. When, for example, Johnson tells us that "idleness never can secure tranquillity" (No. 134), he at once asserts a truth about life and language, expresses an attitude, and argues implicitly for a particular conclusion. When he says that "poverty may easily be endured, while associated with dignity and reputation, but will always be shunned and dreaded, when it is accompanied with ignominy and contempt" (No. 202), he gives us directions for the use of a set of words (as he did with "hypocrisy" and "affectation") that express a value, are rooted in social fact, and are also material for our thought.[20] To try to analyze such a sentence as this by breaking it down into statements of fact, value, and reason would be to dismember the prose and destroy its life and meaning. In writing of this kind, Johnson makes a language that integrates, that turns into one, kinds of speech and internal life that we have come to think of as separate or distinct; and in doing so, he calls on the reader to respond not merely with his intellect or feeling or capacities of observation but with all of these at once.

I

What I have called the integration of both language and the reader is in fact a major subject of *Rambler* 185. This essay does not begin with a commonplace, like the others we have read, but with what might be called a problem. The problem is stated, however, in an abstract, almost desiccated way. "No vitious dispositions of the mind more obstinately resist both the counsels of philosophy and the injunctions of religion, than those which are complicated with an opinion of dignity." Moving from the general issue to a particular example, Johnson then says that this is the reason why "scarcely any law of our Redeemer is more openly transgressed" than that "by which he commands his followers to forgive injuries." "Many who could have conquered their anger, are unable to combat pride."

In a series of paragraphs, he now sets forth a lengthy set of arguments in favor of forgiveness. He says that to insist on the right to take revenge is really to claim to be a judge in one's own cause, and to permit that would "destroy all the order of society"; that since "some must at last be contented to forgive," it is "surely eligible to forgive early"; that early forgiveness is easier, both because the sentiment of revenge is not yet habitual and because "it is easiest to forgive, while there is yet little to be forgiven"; and, finally, that "a wise man will make haste to forgive, because he knows the true value of time."

This chain of argument now runs out, leaving us to ask what it can mean. Since everyone already knows that he should forgive, any argument to that conclusion is superfluous; on the other hand, since we all fail to do what we know we should, any argument to that end, however logically persuasive, is in some sense pointless. So what can reasoning of this sort achieve?

In a characteristically self-reflective turn, Johnson makes the weakness of his argument his next subject, and, also characteristically, he locates the weakness not in the argument but in the self. He closes his chain of reasoning by saying that "whoever considers the weakness both of himself and others, will not long want persuasives to forgiveness." But to "consider our weaknesses" is precisely what we do not do. The implicit question then becomes, why not? What is there about *us* that makes this chain of reasoning, which is in some sense so strong, in practice so weak? "From this pacifick and harmless temper, thus propitious to others and ourselves, to domestick tranquility and to social happiness, no man is with-held but by pride, by the fear of being insulted by his adversary or despised by the world." The evident failure of the chain of reasoning to affect conduct has the effect of defining, in us as well as others, the force that resists it, what Johnson earlier called "dignity" and now calls "pride."

Pride becomes his next subject:

> It may be laid down as an unfailing and universal axiom, that, "all pride is abject and mean." It is always an ignorant, lazy, or cowardly acquiescence in a false appearance of excellence, and proceeds not from consciousness of our attainments, but insensibility of our wants.

This is argument of a new kind, purporting to reason not from premise to conclusion but by assertion and definition. Johnson addresses the mind to which the claims of "dignity" are powerful by using a string of terms no proud man would ever want used of himself ("ignorant," "lazy," "cowardly") in order to strip from resentment all connotations of dignity.

"Nothing can be great which is not right."[21] But that "pride which many who presume to boast of generous sentiments, allow to regulate their measures, has nothing nobler in view than the approbation of men." He who allows himself to be guided by considerations such as those "has little reason to congratulate himself upon the greatness of his mind; whenever he awakes to seriousness and reflection, he must become despicable in his own eyes." Pride is not a form of true dignity, after all, but radically incompatible with it.

In the way that is by now familiar, Johnson thus defines "pride" and "dignity" not only by distinguishing between them but by establishing an active relationship between each word and another term, "forgiveness." These three words are given meaning not in isolation from each other, as if they were separate means of conveying discrete information, but in connection with each other, as parts of the same language, parts of the same activity of thinking about life. When one thinks of forgiveness and its difficulties, if one has read this essay well, one will now think of pride and then of dignity; when one thinks of dignity, one will think of pride and then forgiveness. This is Johnson's method: one thing is defined in terms of another, and a life is created between them.

He closes in a different mode, a kind of prayer. It is almost as if he had forgotten until now the most central truth of all and had caught himself just in time:

> Of him that hopes to be forgiven it is indispensibly
> required, that he forgive. It is therefore superfluous to
> urge any other motive. On this great duty eternity is
> suspended, and to him that refuses to practise it, the
> throne of mercy is inaccessible, and the Saviour of the
> world has been born in vain.

As often in these essays, Johnson writes himself at the end into a kind of essential solitude, where he is alone with himself, addressing a distant God.

II

This essay is in part about a split between "reason" and "feeling," between the mind and heart, which it is intended, for the moment at least, to heal, perhaps most of all in the prayer of the closing sentences. In the first part of the essay we have seen that Johnson offers us a chain of reasoning in favor of forgiveness, which, as reasoning, is conclusive, unanswerable, and irrestible; but as a principle of action in the world it is weak, and felt to be weak, because it fails to recognize the resisting or opposing force of dignity or pride. In the second section he enlists against a self-destructive pride not only logic but dignity itself. In doing this he redefines not only pride but "reason": what is entitled to that name is not the chain of argument in the first part of the essay but the employment of all the resources of mind and feeling called for by the essay as a whole. It is our own experience of the intellectual force and emotional weakness of the arguments for forgiveness that compels us to recognize what it is, in ourselves and in others, that makes the argument ineffective. Our sense of discomfort, our need for an explanation, operates as a kind of definition; and when the topic explicitly shifts to pride, we already know something of the place it fills in life. Just as principles are not merely restatable ideas but deserve the name only when active in the formation of character and the determination of conduct, so for Johnson reason is not merely logical progression from premise to conclusion but a kind of thought that unites the mind and heart, an engagement of the self with nature and experience. It is the kind of thought, in short, toward which he repeatedly struggles in these essays.

I earlier said that the movement of these essays was from commonplace to principle; here I observe a movement from a kind of division of self and language to what I call integration, achieved in a moment of solitude or isolation. I hope it is clear that these are not two movements but one and the same; for his endings in solitude define the condition out of which a language of principle can be made. The movement typical of the essays is a constant struggle through layers of feeling, patterns and habits of thought, and impulses of resistance to a kind of central awareness from which, and only from which, truth and strength can flow. In writing this way, beginning with his own constantly recreated confusion and moving toward the kind of clarity that is achieved when contraries are comprehended in the mind at once, Johnson creates an extraordinary textual community with his reader. "Intimacy" would be too weak a word for describing it and perhaps too sentimental; for what Johnson ultimately exposes is the life of his essential being, stripped of accident and superfluity, where he is full of awe, dread, and hope; and we are too.

*　　　*　　　*

SWIFT OFFERS HIS READER an experience that remakes him as a maker of language, giving him a new ear for delusion in what he himself produces, but Johnson explicitly offers his reader a language. It is not a language ready-made, created by Johnson and to be used by the reader, for that would be to perpetuate life at the level that Johnson calls "commonplace" and I have called "cliché" or "truism." It is a language that must be made, again and again, out of the materials of everyday life, as a language of

160

principle. Thus Johnson's object is not to leave us with a wisdom that can be learned by imitation and repetition. His purpose is to teach us a method of contemplation and criticism, a kind of thought, by which we can remake our minds and lives by remaking our language and the culture it defines. Johnson knows that we cannot maintain any perception or sentiment permanently, unchanged. Our grasp will slip, and it must all begin again. What Johnson seeks to teach us is how to do it on our own: how to move out of our perpetually recreated condition of confusion, how to engage the mind and move it in the direction of truth.

Swift and Johnson can thus be said to demonstrate different ways in which a writer can be what we have called "dialectical" with his reader in English. In reading through the perpetual distortions of Swift's text the reader is forced to resort to what he actually knows of life and language and to exercise his own capacities for making sense of things. If he does not do this but acquiesces in the text, as if it were an easy ironic venture, he finds himself taking positions he cannot possibly mean to take and becomes inextricably involved in delusion. The text requires him to make conscious and available what he knows both as a speaker of ordinary language and as an actor in the ordinary world. As dialectic should, it works by refutation, in this case refutation of the reader's sense of self-importance and by the deformations of mind and language and action to which that leads. But, unlike Socratic dialectic, Swift's text is meant to restore to the individual the cultural education he is always in danger of losing (when he thinks, for example, that he can reduce the world "to his own notions" or that he enjoys a unique and divine inspiration). The text thus leaves its reader in a place of his own making. But it is a place within culture, for, if he is to read the text well, the reader must call on his own experience of what he actually knows and values and thinks.

The *Rambler*s are similar in object to the *Tale* but different in method. Instead of forcing the reader into a position of elementary distress from which he must extricate himself, as Swift and Socrates both do, Johnson shows the reader how he himself moves from a perpetually recreated condition of ignorance and distortion to a restoration of truth: to a clearer sense of himself, his world, and the conditions of life. This is of course refutational too, but it is in the first instance Johnson, not the reader, who is refuted, and the effect is to teach the reader a method of contemplation and self-correction that he can imitate. It is like—indeed for Johnson it is a species of—teaching the reader a method of prayer.

For both Swift and Johnson the mere platitude, the false question, and the mechanical metaphor are all forms of the emptiness and death from which it is their object to rescue themselves and their readers. This is to be done not by converting a defective inherited language into paradox, as Socrates did; instead, language is to be restored or reconstituted by the reader and the author. The culture in its best forms and parts is, for both Swift and Johnson, though in different ways, a resource, not an obstacle; and an important part of education involves learning what it has to teach. If you find yourself out of tune with your inherited language, they would say that it is likely to be you, not the language, that needs changing, that it is your own way of talking and thinking that is in error, not the possibilities of the culture.

Even more than Swift, Johnson brings his reader to a place within the culture; for it is specific parts of our cultural inheritance—its maxims, platitudes, and truisms—that Johnson seeks to revive in the reader's life. In the *Rambler* and the *Dictionary* alike, he shows us what words can mean by showing us what they have actually meant, in different contexts and combinations. These restored meanings are made momentarily available to his reader. The standard by which truth and the adequacy of language are measured is a simple one: correspondence with the substantive view of the world he holds, in which plain religious truth is paramount; and, at the level of the individual mind, an integration of the self that renders thought and experience coherent. In writing to his reader in such a way, Johnson gives new meaning to the conception of the writer as the reader's friend.

But the language and community of these texts is essentially private, not public. Are there what might be called political or social implications of this kind of writing? Could one, for example, imagine a community outside the text—say, in the family or the school or the city or the nation—that was like the community Johnson establishes with his reader: a community of persons each seeking to educate the self and the other, to restore the truth, to achieve an integration of mind and heart, of knowledge and will and action? Johnson's own political views were strongly Tory and traditionalist. He believed, among other things, in the value of social and economic rank, even though his own position was entirely self-made and he never enjoyed anything like economic comfort. His conservatism was possible partly because politics and money were to him not very important matters. When he discussed what mattered most, in essays such as these, he claimed for himself and his reader the dignity that is proper to a being engaged in its own correction, in reconstituting its language and world and life, and this is a radical assertion of independence, responsibility, and an essential equality. Johnson suggests no forms of political thought and action that reflect this conception of himself and his reader, but, as we shall see in later chapters, similar conceptions of the nature of human life and its possibilities will prove to have powerful political implications.

7

"Conversation, Rational and Playful"

The Language of Friendship in Jane Austen's *Emma*

In *Emma*, a novel of education and manners, Jane Austen might be said to combine the methods of Swift and Johnson described in the two preceding chapters. Like Swift's *Tale*, for example, *Emma* in some respects works directly on the reader, involving him or her immediately in distortion and misconception. To make one's way through it at all, one must be constantly active and discriminating; and since no one does it wholly right the first time through—or the second or the third—the text can be seen as a continual education in the activity of reading that it requires. But Austen also explicitly corrects her reader, much in the manner of Johnson, by clarifying and organizing what is mistaken and straightening things out at last. Again, like both Swift and Johnson, she believes that a proper relation with one's culture—or at least with the culture represented in this text by the ideal figure of Mr. Knightley (himself formed partly on the model of Johnson)—includes the activity of learning what it has to teach. Like Johnson, indeed, she can be said to make out of her inherited materials a moral language of extraordinary range, discrimination, and coherence and to teach her reader how to make it his own so that he may use it in his own life, as an instrument of perception and judgment.[1]

But in Jane Austen there is an emphasis largely missing in the other two writers, and this marks an important difference of concern and aim. She is interested not only in the way the individual reconstitutes his language and in those relationships between two persons in which education can proceed—between Emma and Mr. Knightley, in the world of the novel, and between Austen and her reader, in the text itself—but in the relation between the social worlds so established and the larger world: that of the family, the village, and perhaps, by implication, England itself. She brings our attention, that is, to the question I asked at the end of the last chapter: What connections can possibly be established between a community of two created in a text (or between two people in their actual lives in the world) and the larger social and political universe? This is also the question that the *Iliad*, as we read it, left unresolved when, at the end, it created an ideal relationship for which no future could be imagined. It is only on a small scale that Austen explicitly addresses this question: she moves from the relationship of two to the family and the village. But that step is an important one; and, as we shall see later on, in taking it Austen establishes terms and methods by which larger movements might occur.

WHERE EMMA BEGINS: DISTORTIONS OF LANGUAGE AND OF SELF

Language

We begin this text, as usual, with an immersion in the workings of a particular discourse, in this case the disturbed language in which Emma Woodhouse constitutes her self and her social world. The movement of the novel will be from the point so defined to a condition of health and knowledge, as Emma's initial habits of thought and feeling break down under stress and yield to new ones that are more nearly in accord with the facts of her condition and with her inherited language of social and moral life.

I

We are introduced to Emma's way of thinking in the way she is described in the opening sentence:

> Emma Woodhouse, handsome, clever, and rich, with
> a comfortable home and a happy disposition, seemed to
> unite some of the best blessings of existence; and had
> lived nearly twenty-one years in the world with very
> little to distress or vex her. [P. 5]

By its use of "seems" and "some" this sentence suggests at the very outset that there is a distance between Emma and the narrator—that we will be told things that Emma does not see or would not agree with—and this is our first clue that in reading this text we shall constantly have to ask ourselves whether what we see is Emma's distorted view or a stable reality, whether the values expressed and the language used are presented ironically or straight. Here, for example, we are led to ask: Are these "blessings" really the best blessings of existence after all, and did Emma really "unite" them? What are the other blessings, here implied but not actually named, and what does it mean that Emma is not said to have them? And how are we to regard the statement that she had lived twenty-one years with "very little to distress or vex her"? Is that a "blessing," as it may seem, or is it perhaps a disadvantage?[2]

We can already see that one object of this text—and in this it is rather like Swift's *Tale*—is to train the reader in judging the social and ethical significance of language. This exercise in reading continues as Emma's circumstances are presented in greater detail. We are told that she is the younger daughter of a "most affectionate, indulgent father," of whose house (partly because of her sister's marriage) she had been "mistress" from a "very early period." Her mother had died when she was very young, "and her place had been supplied by an excellent woman as governess, who had fallen little short of a mother in affection."

> Sixteen years had Miss Taylor been in Mr. Woodhouse's family, less as a governess than a friend, very fond of both daughters, but particularly of Emma. Between *them* it was more the intimacy of sisters. Even before Miss Taylor had ceased to hold the nominal office of governess, the mildness of her temper had hardly allowed her to impose any restraint; and the shadow of authority being now long passed away, they had been living together as friend and friend very mutually attached, and Emma doing just what she liked; highly esteeming Miss Taylor's judgement, but directed chiefly by her own. [P. 5]

The subject put before us here is friendship, especially its relation to "affection" and "fondness," on the one side, and "restraint" and "authority" on the other. The language that defines the attachment of "friend and friend" as "Emma doing just what she liked" and that links "affectionate" and "indulgent" as practical synonyms is meant to represent Emma's way of thinking, and a highly defective language it is.[3] Such utterances, like certain passages in Swift, would be impossible in the mouth of any speaker who really knew what he or she was saying; for we know that the term "friendship" is not properly the equivalent of "indulgence," since it also includes discipline, correction, and the speaking of unwelcome truths. But Emma does not know this, nor does the reader know it yet as fully as he will; for on a first reading it is easy to slide over these terms, nearly all of which are positives, and to accept the language almost as one's own.

When we first encounter Emma, she is indulging in a reverie in which she uses this language to speak to herself. The occasion is Miss Taylor's marriage, and Emma is experiencing "sorrow—a gentle sorrow." ("It was Miss Taylor's loss which first brought grief.") It is the evening of the wedding day, and Emma sits, we are told, in "mournful thought," the quality of which does much to tell us who she is. On the one hand, "the event had every promise of happiness for her friend," for "Mr. Weston was a man of unexceptionable character, easy fortune, suitable age and pleasant manners." On the other, "the want of Miss Taylor would be felt every hour of every day."

> [She was a] friend and companion such as few possessed, intelligent, well-informed, useful, gentle, knowing all the ways of the family, interested in all its concerns, and peculiarly interested in herself, in every pleasure, every scheme of her's;—one to whom she could speak every thought as it arose, and who had such an affection for her as could never find fault. [P. 6]

Emma looks sadly to a future without Miss Taylor, for though she "dearly love[s]" her valetudinarian and kindly father, he is without mind or judgment and can be no companion for her: "He could not meet her in conversation, rational or playful." Her sister lives too far away for frequent visiting, and Highbury, the large and populous village, "almost amounting to a town," to which Hartfield belongs, affords them "no equals."[4] She will be wholly without company of the kind she needs and is used to.

IN ETHICAL OR PSYCHOLOGICAL TERMS, what is most wrong with Emma's speech here is that it reveals a highly incomplete recognition of the claims of others and an undue sense of her own importance in the world. Looked at as a discourse—imagining that we are asked to speak this language and live on its terms—what is most wrong is that it has no internal opposition, no tension to give it life and to make meaning possible. The terms just run into one another, without contrast or definition: "affection" becomes "indulgence," which becomes "can never find fault." Without internal opposition, this language cannot be organized on a topic, such as What is true affection? True friendship? The proper relation between affection and discipline? What this language lacks is what Thucydides shows that talk about either justice or expediency must have: the contrasting other term that makes thought possible.

In its want of internal life this discourse is directly analogous both to the commonplace, which it is Johnson's aim to complicate into difficulty and meaning by the simultaneous comprehension of contrary tendencies, and to the false question which so repeatedly seduces the mind of Swift's narrator. Emma's reflections are indeed a little like a response to

the question, "Do you favor affection or discipline?" that plumps solidly
for the former. This is a discourse without poise or opposition; its function
is to be evasive, and it is thus a perfect medium for reverie or daydream.

II

Yet we soon learn that for Emma there is at least one other version of
friendship, and it deeply contrasts with the self-indulgence and sentimentality of the opening paragraphs. When her father, asleep in his chair
after dinner, awakes and makes it "necessary" for Emma "to be cheerful,"
her intoxicating reflections simply stop and are replaced by another mode
of being altogether (p. 7). She applies herself directly to maintaining his
spirits, and "spare[s] no exertion" on his behalf. When he complains to
her about the loss of "poor Miss Taylor" (much as she herself has just
been complaining to herself), Emma is capable of speaking rightly on the
subject, praising Mrs. Weston, stating her natural claims to "a house of
her own"—where she need not "bear all my odd humours"—and explaining that, having moved only half a mile away, she will still be an active
part of their daily lives. Here Emma proves capable of being a real friend,
both to Miss Taylor, whose true situation she recognizes, and to her father, whom she cheers and, in language admirably suited to his capacities, instructs.[5] This means that the Emma of the self-indulgent reverie is
not the only Emma, that she has another manner of being, with which
her self-regarding sentiments and language are inconsistent. If Emma
were nothing but a single defective voice, as, in their different ways, such
people as her father and Miss Bates are, one could expect no change, no
education. But she does have another side, another set of capacities for
thought and speech and life, and these can be called on to correct the
former. Her contrasting modes of being, however, are not yet in conscious
opposition.

III

Friendship is given still another meaning for us by Mr. Knightley, who
now walks in, for he is the one person who does not bend to Emma's
whims but seeks to correct them. Emma cannot convert him into the material of her fantasy life but must recognize him as a center of energy and
judgment of his own. Here he is characterized, in a rather understated
way, as a "sensible man," about thirty-seven or thirty-eight years old, an
old friend of the family, and the elder brother of John Knightley, who is
married to Emma's sister, Isabella.[6] He is said to have "a cheerful manner
which always did him good," and we get an immediate instance of it
when he says, of the wedding, "Being pretty well aware of what sort of joy

you must both be feeling, I have been in no hurry with my congratulations. But I hope it all went off tolerably well. How did you all behave? Who cried most?"

Later in the conversation, Mr. Knightley, speaking ostensibly to Mr. Woodhouse but actually to Emma, sums up what Emma ought to think and feel about Mrs. Weston's marriage:

> "It is impossible that Emma should not miss such a
> companion. . . . We should not like her so well as we
> do, sir, if we could suppose it. But she knows how much
> the marriage is to Miss Taylor's advantage; she knows
> how very acceptable it must be at Miss Taylor's time
> of life to be settled in a home of her own, and how im-
> portant to her to be secure of a comfortable provision,
> and therefore cannot allow herself to feel so much pain
> as pleasure. Every friend of Miss Taylor must be glad to
> have her so happily married." [P. 11]

Here we are told in firm and stable terms something of what true friendship in such a case entails: honest acknowledgement of one's own loss and participation in the friend's greater gain. This is a discourse built on a Johnsonian "but"—a word wholly impossible to the mind of the opening reverie. Indeed, the very movement of the chapter has been like one of Johnson's essays: we start in a kind of confusion, from which our author distances us a little, and work through to a clarification cast in direct and simple language. The difficulties of the stable position offered us by Mr. Knightley, like the difficulties of Johnson's closing statements, are not so much intellectual—everyone would know the precepts—as emotional: it is hard to give them active place in one's sentiments and affections, for to do so requires the recognition of uncomfortable facts—for Emma, acknowledgment of the claims of her friend. As readers, we experience a correction a little like the one Emma experiences here; for while we do not exactly share her incoherent language of friendship—the markers are too clear for that—we do experience, at least the first time through, a confusion that is here resolved into clarity.

MR. KNIGHTLEY'S FRIENDSHIP is thus established at the outset as that of a teacher. As the text makes explicit, he alone is a good enough friend to Emma to correct her: he is "one of the few people who could ever see faults in Emma Woodhouse, and the only one who ever told her of them" (p. 11). (As for her father, we learn that Emma cannot bear to have him "suspect such a circumstance as her not being thought perfect by everybody" [p. 11].) Throughout the text he will be her constant corrector, expressing approval and disapproval in many ways and on all sorts of occasions.[7] Emma indeed internalizes him, responding in her thoughts to criticisms she imagines he would make. ("Mr. Knightley, he is *not* a trifling, silly young man" [p. 212].)

Conversation

But Emma's friendship with Mr. Knightley has another dimension. This consists not in his instruction of her but in his conversations with her, and here she proves herself to be not only his friend but his equal.[8] Unlike her father, he is a companion; with him, that is, "conversation, rational and playful" (p. 7), is possible, and much of the life of the novel lies in the development of what these conversations mean. The novel will accordingly prove to be only in part a novel of correction, in which Emma's distorted ways of speaking and being are broken down by experience; it is also a novel of change through affirmative experience. It is the version of herself that Emma becomes in her conversations with Mr. Knightley that enables her to experience the final blow of his apparent loss as she does: to see it clearly and to face it honestly.

One conversation between Emma and Mr. Knightley occurs in the first chapter. Emma, responding to Mr. Knightley's correct and sententious remarks about what Emma, as a friend, must feel about Miss Taylor's marriage, shifts the subject slightly, claiming an additional pleasure that comes to her as the one who "made the match": "to have it take place, and be proved in the right, when so many people said Mr. Weston would never marry again, may comfort me for any thing" (pp. 11–12). Mr. Knightley shakes his head; her father—being opposed to all marriage, all change—responds with mild alarm. Emma goes on to claim that she loves to make a match—"it is the greatest amusement in the world." And she intends to keep it up, "not for myself, papa," but for other people. "After such success you know!"

In a markedly Johnsonian manner Mr. Knightley challenges her assertion: "I do not understand what you mean by 'success'. . . . Success supposes endeavour" (p. 12). He goes on: "Why do you talk of success? where is your merit?—what are you proud of?—you made a lucky guess; and *that* is all that can be said." It is Emma's response that is important. She does not simply accept her correction but teases him: "And have you never known the pleasure and triumph of a lucky guess?—I pity you." She touches him here at the point where life begins, at the sense of pleasure that knows nothing but itself.

> "I thought you cleverer—for depend upon it, a lucky
> guess is never merely luck. There is always some talent

in it. And as to my poor word 'success,' which you quarrel with, I do not know that I am so entirely without any claim to it. You have drawn two pretty pictures—but I think there may be a third—a something between the do-nothing and the do-all. If I had not promoted Mr. Weston's visits here, and given many little encouragements, and smoothed many little matters, it might not have come to any thing after all. I think you must know Hartfield enough to comprehend that." [P. 13]

On this point Mr. Knightley does give way or at least is silent; but he does not give way on the moral question, with respect to which he is still her instructor: "You are more likely to have done harm to yourself, than good to them, by interference."

Enacted in this conversation is a preexisting relationship of great and productive intimacy, in which Emma is in some respects wholly Mr. Knightley's equal or even his superior as a person and a mind. This means that for these two characters the movement will not be simply that of falling in love; they will also discover that they already do love and what that means. For us, as readers, the inconsistencies among Emma's linguistic and psychological habits—among the different sorts of "friendship" of which she is capable and the modes of being and acting they entail—demonstrate an incoherence of mind and language that provides a starting point for the work of the novel. In this way we are led, like Mr. Knightley (as he later confesses to Mrs. Weston), to "wonder what will become of her" (p. 40).

Psychology

The Emma to whom we have been introduced in this chapter is a real puzzle. She is at times grandiose, self-indulgent, and confused in her language of human relations, but in another state of imagination and feeling she is a realistic friend to her father and capable of conversing as an equal with Mr. Knightley. She seems split into two parts, of which at least one is disturbed.

But the self-division, however difficult for Emma to resolve, makes a certain psychological sense. The absence of her mother, the indulgence of her governess, and her father's dependence on her for comfort and amusement have led Emma to maintain much longer than is normal the grandest of ambitions: to lead forever a perfect life with her father, in an idyllic world—"mistress of her father's house" indeed. The idea that Emma is "perfect"—an essential part of her dream—has extensive support, and not only from her father. (It is sufficiently accepted to permit

Mr. Weston to resort to it when he tries to save the situation at Box Hill by a flattering piece of humor: "What two letters of the alphabet are there, that express perfection?" "Emm-a" [p. 371].) A perfect life of this kind is governed by certain absolutes, the most fixed of which is that the people in it shall never change but always be the same and always enjoy the same relations with oneself. It is right, then, that the action of the novel should begin with the first real challenge to the fantasy, the transformation of Miss Taylor at Hartfield into Mrs. Weston at Randalls, and that it should later turn on a far greater challenge, the threatened loss of Mr. Knightley.

It is essential to the maintenance of this perfect life that Emma remain unmarried, and the way she deals with that requirement is important. What she says to her protégée, Harriet Smith, is most revealing:

> "My being charming, Harriet, is not quite enough to induce me to marry; I must find other people charming—one other person at least. And I am not only, not going to be married, at present, but have very little intention of ever marrying at all."
>
> "Ah!—so you say; but I cannot believe it." . . .
>
> "I have none of the usual inducements of women to marry. Were I to fall in love, indeed, it would be a different thing! but I never have been in love; it is not my way, or my nature; and I do not think I ever shall. And, without love, I am sure I should be a fool to change such a situation as mine. Fortune I do not want; employment I do not want; consequence I do not want: I believe few married women are half as much mistress of their husband's house, as I am of Hartfield; and never, never could I expect to be so truly beloved and important; so always first and always right in any man's eyes as I am in my father's." . . .
>
> "But still, you will be an old maid! and that's so dreadful!"
>
> "Never mind, Harriet, I shall not be a poor old maid; and it is poverty only which makes celibacy contemptible to a generous public! A single woman, with a very narrow income, must be a ridiculous, disagreeable old maid! the proper sport of boys and girls; but a single woman, of good fortune, is always respectable, and may be as sensible and pleasant as anybody else." [Pp. 84–85]

This speech is remarkably explicit, as only pre-Freudian literature can be, about the nature of the fantasy that constitutes Emma's conception of felicity. And, in the way that people commonly have of uttering terrible truths without seeing them as such, Emma declares outright the price her fantasy exacts: that she never learn to love. The terms in which she talks here about the elements of a happy life are continuous with those of the first sentence of the book: fortune, employment, consequence, power, and being "beloved and important." Her sexual feelings and ambitions are expressed not in a language of love and marriage, in an imagined life of conversation with another, but in terms of a fantasy that measures felicity by class status and esteem, not by achievement of character and love. On this view, the only thing marriage could offer her is more of what she has; and what she has, she claims, is all she wants. Even the foolish Harriet Smith sees more clearly than Emma does what is really at stake: "But still, you will be an old maid! and that's so dreadful!" How dreadful, Emma has still to learn.

This view of Emma's psychology helps explain her interest in matchmaking. She has engaged her powerful feelings and imagination in trying to maintain a child's paradise, a timeless world in which she is a princess beyond compare. Since she cannot contemplate marriage or her own sexual feelings, she displaces these feelings, putting them to work in a kind of fantasy play with the lives of others.[9] At the end of the first chapter she has accordingly determined on making a match for Mr. Elton, the new vicar and the only eligible man in the neighborhood. "I think very well of Mr. Elton, and this is the only way I have of doing him service" (p. 13). (It is important for her to think so!)

THE ELTON FIASCO: WHAT CAN EMMA LEARN?

The first section of the novel tells the story of Emma's attempts to make Mr. Elton's match. She takes up as a companion and protégée one Harriet Smith, the "natural daughter of somebody," who attends the local boarding school. First she induces her to reject a highly eligible offer of marriage from Robert Martin, a sensible, kindly, and prosperous young farmer to whom Harriet has become attached. Then she fills her full of hopes of attracting the infinitely "superior" Mr. Elton, and she devises artifices to bring them together. But Mr. Elton, as the reader sees from the beginning, is an unctuous young man, not likely to throw himself away, and in fact he has aspirations toward Miss Woodhouse herself, in which she, without being aware of it, gives him encouragement. The denouement is a nighttime carriage ride in which Mr. Elton presses his case, asks for her hand, and is rebuffed by an Emma at once mortified and angry.

In the course of all this we see Emma at her most insufferable, and speaking an impossible language.[10] We are told, for example, that she decides to accept Harriet as a friend because Harriet is

> so far from pushing, shewing so proper and becoming
> a deference, seeming so pleasantly grateful for being
> admitted to Hartfield, and so artlessly impressed by the
> appearance of every thing in so superior a style to what
> she had been used to, that she must have good sense
> and deserve encouragement. [P. 23]

(What a definition of "good sense" that is!) In speaking with Mrs. Weston about this relationship, Mr. Knightley defines for us in explicit terms what is wrong: "I think [Harriet Smith] the very worst sort of companion that Emma could possibly have. She knows nothing herself, and looks upon Emma as knowing every thing. She is a flatterer in all her ways; and so much the worse, because undesigned. Her ignorance is hourly flattery" (p. 38). For Mr. Knightley, as for Socrates and Swift, true friendship is corrective and refutational, and to please by flattery is an act not of friendship but of its opposite; it is a species of "indulgence."

Emma's friendship with Harriet does have another, but hardly more constructive, aspect, for in a comically twisted version of the sort of relationship that Mr. Knightley has had with her, Emma intends to become Harriet's instructress: "She would form her opinions and her manners" (p. 24). After she has met Mr. Martin, for example, she pronounces upon his "entire want of gentility," and she then offers Harriet the following disquisition on manners:

> "In one respect, perhaps, Mr. Elton's manners are supe-
> rior to Mr. Knightley's or Mr. Weston's. They have more
> gentleness. They might be more safely held up as a
> pattern. There is an openness, a quickness, almost a
> bluntness in Mr. Weston, which every body likes in *him*
> because there is so much good humour with it—but
> that would not do to be copied. Neither would Mr.
> Knightley's downright, decided, commanding sort of
> manner—though it suits *him* very well; his figure and
> look, and situation in life seem to allow it; but if any
> young man were to set about copying him, he would
> not be sufferable. On the contrary, I think a young man

might be very safely recommended to take Mr. Elton as
a model." [P. 34]

In this speech Emma shows that she has learned enough from Mr.
Knightley to imitate his tone of voice, his capacity to draw accurate distinctions, his interest in manners and conduct, and his willingness to
give advice, but the feelings and the judgments are of course all wrong.
This is not an imitation but a perversion of Mr. Knightley's way of talking.[11] Emma sees manners as artificial modes of behavior to be adopted as
techniques of social success, and not, as Mr. Knightley does, as manifestations of character. For Mr. Knightley, that is, and for Jane Austen as
well, what is meant by manners is the application of the whole intelligence to the meaning of what one says and does, to the nature of the
relationships—the friendships—one establishes with others, and to the
character one makes for oneself in the process.[12] Emma's view of manners, by contrast, is of a piece with her conception of happiness in terms
of attributes and of superiority in terms of social position. One who followed either Emma's advice or her example here would be incapable of
the kind of friendship, the kind of conversation and manners, that this
text is intended to define and celebrate.

In persuading Harriet to adopt her conception of manners and in her
acquisitive and manipulative view of the relations between the sexes,
Emma does real damage: Harriet abandons a relationship based on genuine attraction in order to hope for an unattainable marriage with a cold
and selfish man, who, however "superior," has—as we are later told—
none of Mr. Martin's "true gentility." As Mr. Knightley puts it, when he
learns that Emma has persuaded Harriet to reject Mr. Martin: "You have
been no friend to Harriet Smith, Emma" (p. 63).[13]

In the course of the narrative Emma not only misreads Mr. Elton's
unctuous conduct (which we can plainly see is aimed at pleasing not
Harriet Smith but Emma Woodhouse) but behaves in ways that Elton not
unreasonably believes are designed to encourage him. Without consciously knowing it, Emma is playing not only with Harriet's life and feelings but with her own; for she is carrying on an insincere and unaware
courtship with the only eligible and attentive (however unsuitable) man
she knows. We see what she does not and are confirmed in our capacity
to read this world. We look forward with pleasure to the moment of clarification, when Mr. Elton—"spruce, black, and smiling" (p. 114)—presses
his suit, and we expect Emma's consequent mortification to be corrective.

Our expectation proves to be only partly right. It is true that after the
humiliating interview Emma has the capacity—the "common honesty"—
to reread both Mr. Elton's conduct and her own. This capacity to face at
least some of the truth, and to check her wishes by what she sees, is an

important strength; indeed, it is essential to Emma's growth, for without it her experience could teach her nothing.[14] But in this case the lesson she learns is most imperfect. While she is embarrassed by her mistakes in reading conduct, she is unbending in her self-approval for having persuaded Harriet not to accept Mr. Martin. "There I was quite right." Her experience has corrected her, that is, at the level of surface behavior but not at the deeper level of self and sexuality: she insists that her interference with the forces of attraction between man and woman was correct. Her matchmaking is not only a displacement of her own emotional and sexual feelings—"Were you, yourself, ever to marry, she is the very woman for you," Emma tells Mr. Knightley of Harriet—it is a perversion of it, an attempt to make class and status and social position rather than a person the object of attention and desire and love; and this perversion remains wholly uncorrected.

The problem the novel addresses is thus much more difficult than it may, at first, have appeared to be, for how can experience correct a fault of this kind? Emma cannot build on her own tender and sensible side, expressed in her relation with her father; for it is her attachment to that relation, and what it means—the perfection of existence—that bars her full participation in life. She seems locked in her attitudes, in a central place unreachable by experience. How then can she change?

EMMA'S CONVERSATIONAL LIFE

With Mr. Knightley

It is perhaps partly to answer this question that Jane Austen gives us, directly after the Elton disaster, another conversation between Emma and Mr. Knightley, in which Emma once again proves herself capable of being his good-humored equal. Here we are shown a different sort of possibility for change: not through correction of error but through the experience of being a better self in relation to another person. In this scene Emma and Mr. Knightley are discussing the impending arrival of Frank Churchill, Mr. Weston's son by his earlier marriage, whom neither of them has ever seen but about whom Emma has certain romantic ideas. He was raised by his wealthy aunt and uncle, whose name he has adopted; and though he has seen his father yearly in London, he has never visited him in Highbury, even upon his marriage to Miss Taylor. For this default in a man of twenty-three Mr. Knightley, evidently jealous but not aware of it, believes there is no excuse:

> "There is one thing, Emma, which a man can always
> do, if he chuses, and that is, his duty . . . . A man who

felt rightly would say at once, simply and resolutely, to
Mrs. Churchill—'Every sacrifice of mere pleasure you
will always find me ready to make to your convenience;
but I must go and see my father immediately. I know he
would be hurt by my failing in such a mark of respect to
him on the present occasion. I shall, therefore, set off
to-morrow.'—If he would say so to her at once, in the
tone of decision becoming a man, there would be no
opposition made to his going." [P. 146]

Emma's response is to make fun of Mr. Knightley: " 'No,' said Emma,
laughing; 'but perhaps there might be some made to his coming back
again. Such language for a young man entirely dependent, to use!—
Nobody but you, Mr. Knightley, would imagine it possible.'" Emma corrects Mr. Knightley's sense of language and manners by teasing of a
good-humored and familiar kind, which rests on clear and intimate
understandings:

"But you have not an idea of what is requisite in situations directly opposite to your own. Mr. Frank Churchill
to be making such a speech as that to the uncle and
aunt, who have brought him up, and are to provide for
him!—Standing up in the middle of the room, I suppose, and speaking as loud as he could!—How can you
imagine such conduct practicable?" [P. 147]

Here, for the moment, their roles are reversed, and Emma becomes Mr.
Knightley's corrector.[15] She calls on circumstance and experience to
show him how far he has strayed from his usual sense of manners and
decorum. What is more, she perseveres in her judgment and does so
without rancor, even when Mr. Knightley, moved as he is by his jealousy
to an uncharacteristic irritability of temper and a refusal to reconsider,
does not give in. In this conversation Emma uses her intelligence, her
wit, her sense of reality, and her will in an integrated way to a single
end.[16] This conversation establishes the possibility of a highly favorable
answer to our question, What will become of her?

With Frank Churchill

Quite another set of possibilities is suggested by Emma's extended flirtation with Frank Churchill, with whom she "makes a match" for herself
of just the artificial and self-obliterating kind she has just been promot-
ing for Harriet. On her side the relationship between them is a fantasy;

on his, it is wholly manipulative, for he is offering attentions to Emma only to hide his secret engagement to Jane Fairfax. His pretended court-ship of Emma herself is flattery, as Harriet's adoration was; but, unlike hers, it is of a designing kind.

In Emma his attentions produce language and feeling of an impossible sort. For example, when he goes to London—sixteen miles by horse—ostensibly to get his hair cut (actually to order a piano, to be anonymously delivered to Jane Fairfax), and then returns "without seeming at all ashamed of what he had done," Emma, eager to defend him, "thus moral-ize[s] to herself":

> "I do not know whether it ought to be so, but cer-tainly silly things do cease to be silly if they are done by sensible people in an impudent way. Wickedness is al-ways wickedness, but folly is not always folly.—It de-pends upon the character of those who handle it. Mr. Knightley, he is *not* a trifling, silly young man. If he were, he would have done this differently. He would ei-ther have gloried in the achievement, or been ashamed of it. There would have been either the ostentation of a coxcomb, or the evasions of a mind too weak to defend its own vanities.—No, I am perfectly sure that he is not trifling or silly." [P. 212]

This is a severe distortion of proper language and feeling, a perversion of the way Mr. Knightley has taught her to think about manners and lan-guage. (How can a "sensible" man act in an "impudent" way?) We have here a deformation of the self and language that belongs in the pages of Swift. But it is more than "mad"; it is dangerous. For what Emma finds herself praising and accepting, without knowing it, is a mind that is not "too weak" but strong enough to "defend its own vanities," that is, a char-acter firmly organized behind its selfishness. It is true that Churchill is not "trifling and silly"; he is much worse than that.

Conflict and Development

As the novel proceeds, we observe a continuing growth in Emma's re-lationship with Mr. Knightley and a resulting intensification of the split within her between the two ways of being that are called into life by the two men. The movement of the novel is not, as it may appear, one of sim-ple progress, either as Emma is gradually corrected by experience or as she gradually becomes more fully her better self in her relations with Mr. Knightley. Instead, the novel shows a developing and sharpening schism between her different possibilities for being and acting. In some respects, as her supposed corrections by experience occur, she becomes not better but worse, increasingly captivated by her powers of fantasy; and her growing intimacy and equality with Mr. Knightley are interrupted by panicky realizations of her very worst tendencies. These oscillations become more rapid and extreme as the novel proceeds to its climax at Box Hill.

I

As an example of the different versions of herself that are called into being in her relations with these two men, consider the different kinds of teasing in which she engages at the party at Mr. Cole's. Upon their arrival Emma teases Mr. Knightley playfully and affectionately, approving of his coming by carriage instead of walking; she says that this will make him less stiff than he usually is (p. 213).[17] Our participation in the intimacy of this teasing extends to the pleasurable sharing of Emma's fancy: we know quite well that she is wrong about the dependence of Mr. Knightley's demeanor upon his mode of transport, but we also know that her general point about his self-consciousness is correct, and we can feel, as he does, that she is teasing him for a trait that she loves.

This exchange is directly followed by quite another kind of teasing in her conversation with Frank Churchill. The tone here, distancing and hard, is set at the beginning, where, in response to her question "Why do you smile?" he fences "Nay, why do you?"; and it continues right to the end. He teasingly draws out Emma's speculations about the piano sent to Jane Fairfax, and in doing so he confirms the unrealistic tendencies expressed in her first reverie: Emma's fancy runs to the possibility of a disappointed and improper love between Jane and Mr. Dixon, the husband of her friend; Frank Churchill's interest in hiding the fact that the piano was his gift leads him to acquiesce. He teases Jane Fairfax too, by remarking to Emma (within Jane's hearing) that the piano must be an "offering of love." This statement perfectly characterizes this conversation, for it is true, and it satisfies Churchill's need to say what he feels; but it is true in a way entirely hidden from Emma, whom it in fact confirms in her error. The state of mind and feeling stimulated in Emma by her friendship with Frank Churchill is expressed in the language, devoid of anything like real feeling, in which she reflects upon the progress of the "match" she has been making for herself: "Emma continued to entertain no doubt of her being in love. Her ideas only varied as to the how much." With a truth she does not know, Emma declares, "I am quite enough in love. I should be sorry to be more" (pp. 264–65).[18]

As she earlier did with the possibilities represented by Mr. Elton,

Emma ultimately deals with her feelings toward Frank Churchill by displacing them. When he mentions Harriet's name in a letter to Mrs. Weston, Emma shifts her romancing imagination from her own life to that of her pretty and mindless alter ego and "makes a match" between Frank and Harriet, which of course proves to be another fiasco. Despite her determination not to interfere, Emma cannot help being encouraging when Harriet tells her that Mr. Elton has been replaced in her affections by one "so superior" (p. 341). (It would be bad enough if that one were in fact Frank Churchill, as Emma supposes; but, unknown to her, the man Harriet fancies is not Churchill but Mr. Knightley.)

II

As an example of the different way in which Mr. Knightley affects Emma's responses, consider their conversation at the ball, after he has rescued Harriet from the rudeness of Mr. Elton by dancing with her. Emma, we are told, has no opportunity of speaking to Mr. Knightley until after supper, when "her eyes invited him irresistibly to come to her and be thanked." This is a moment of shared feeling. Mr. Knightley says that the vulgar Eltons "aimed at wounding more than Harriet," and Emma admits that she had wanted Elton to marry Harriet, "and they cannot forgive me."

> He shook his head; but there was a smile of indulgence with it, and he only said,
> "I shall not scold you. I leave you to your own reflections."
> "Can you trust me with such flatterers?—Does my vain spirit ever tell me I am wrong?"
> "Not your vain spirit, but your serious spirit.—If one leads you wrong, I am sure the other tells you of it."
> [P. 330]

This expression of confidence in Emma has an immediate effect on her, bringing out her good sense and candor, much as Churchill's "Nay, why do you?" had an immediate effect of the opposite kind. Without embarrassment Emma now simply says, "I do own myself to have been completely mistaken in Mr. Elton." To which Mr. Knightley responds: "And, in return for your acknowledging so much, I will do you the justice to say that you would have chosen for him better than he has chosen for himself.—Harriet Smith has some first-rate qualities, which Mrs. Elton is totally without" (p. 331). In this moment of mutual acceptance and regard, the language they use is that of personal merit, wholly free of the language of class and status.[19]

They are now called to dance, and it is now natural for them to move, for the first time, into a new kind of intimacy. Their speeches should be read slowly:

> "I am ready," said Emma, "whenever I am wanted."
> "Whom are you going to dance with?" asked Mr. Knightley.
> She hesitated a moment, and then replied, "With you, if you will ask me."
> "Will you?" said he, offering his hand.
> "Indeed I will. You have shown that you can dance, and you know we are not really so much brother and sister as to make it at all improper."
> "Brother and sister! no, indeed." [P. 331]

III

But this is followed by a real breakdown of their relations. Emma's unrealistic fantasies about Jane Fairfax and Mr. Dixon are deliberately stimulated by Frank Churchill, who continues to play his complex game of pretending attentions to Emma while actually giving them to Jane Fairfax. The effect on Emma is a loss of self-possesion; she gets caught up in his forceful but incomprehensible behavior, his frantic and mirthless joking, in a way that she cannot control. The flirtation itself is a flattery, doubly irresistible because the side of her now being flattered, her fantasizing side, is the one that has formerly—in her relations with Mr. Knightley—been corrected. Instead of reproof she now meets with apparent admiration, as a person of superior discernment; and with Frank Churchill she now joins a kind of conspiratorial relationship. For example, while playing an alphabet game after dinner, Churchill gives Emma the letters that make up the word "Dixon," which is a great joke; he then proposes to make it even greater by offering the letters to Jane Fairfax, which he does, and Emma participates in the pleasure of seeing her blush (p. 349). (This is displaced sexuality indeed!)

It is after this event that Mr. Knightley, who has thus far believed that Churchill's attentions have been sincerely directed at Emma (and have in large measure been successful), tries to warn Emma that he has recently seen indications that Churchill may have "some inclination to trifle with Jane Fairfax." He begins by asking about the alphabet-game joke. Emma, who is "ashamed" of having imparted her suspicions to another, refuses to tell him. When he asks whether Churchill may have some interest in Jane Fairfax, Emma says, "You amuse me excessively. I am delighted to find that you can vouchsafe to let your imagination wander—but it will not do. . . . I will answer for the gentleman's indifference" (pp. 350–51). The confidence of this declaration silences Mr. Knightley and isolates Emma from him and from what he means.

MORTIFICATION AND RECOGNITION: EMMA'S VISION OF HER FUTURE

From this it is but a step to the party at Box Hill, where Churchill, frantic with feelings about Jane Fairfax (who has just broken with him), is unable to repress himself, and Emma, disconnected from Mr. Knightley and the side of herself that responds to him, shares his compulsive and self-centered gaiety to the point of saying something genuinely wounding to the defenseless and kind-hearted Miss Bates. This is the crisis that leads to her mortification and correction. But the process of correction is not as simple and direct as it may seem. It comes in several stages.

First, and not surprisingly, comes Mr. Knightley's reproof, perhaps the last he shall ever give: "Emma, I must once more speak to you as I have been used to do: a privilege rather endured than allowed, perhaps, but I must still use it. I cannot see you acting wrong, without a remonstrance. How could you be so unfeeling to Miss Bates?" (p. 374). He goes on, rejecting her attempts at palliation—"I dare say [Miss Bates] did not understand me"—until Emma is silent with mortification.

Once home, her first move is to summon thoughts of her father and of her own conduct in that relation: "As a daughter, she hoped, she was not without a heart" (p. 377). The next is a proposed reformation of conduct: she will pay attentions to the Bateses, and to Jane Fairfax, of a kind she has hitherto omitted. "If attention, in future, could do away the past, she might hope to be forgiven." But all of this has the quality of an observed performance, a kind of staginess: "In the warmth of true contrition, she would call upon [Miss Bates] the very next morning." We learn, if we need to, who her imagined observer is when we see her reflect, the next morning, that it was "not unlikely" that she "might see Mr. Knightley in her way; or, perhaps, he might come in while she were paying her visit. She had no objection. She would not be ashamed of the appearance of the penitence, so justly and truly hers" (pp. 377–78).

Perhaps to the reader's surprise, the correction afforded even by this mortifying experience thus promises, like the earlier ones, to be superficial and incomplete. Emma does direct her attention away from Frank Churchill back to Mr. Knightley and to his standards of value, but there is no fundamental change in perception and attitude. She attempts to continue as Miss Woodhouse, the center of attention, and to seek the approval of another. This is not growing up but moving back to an earlier phase of moral supervision. What is more surprising, and more deeply

181

threatening, is that Emma's repentance seems to be accepted as sufficient even by Mr. Knightley himself. When he learns of her visit, "he look[s] at her with a glow of regard" (p. 385). Clearly marked here is the possibility that Emma will go no farther, since Mr. Knightley has done all that he can. Anything more is up to her alone.

The next stage is Emma's attempt to establish relations with Jane Fairfax, making up for years of neglect. These are unsuccessful, for Jane will have nothing to do with her. Emma's response does her credit, for she can understand something of Jane Fairfax's motives, and "she had the consolation of knowing that her intentions were good, and of being able to say to herself, that could Mr. Knightley have been privy to all her attempts of assisting Jane Fairfax, could he even have seen into her heart, he would not, on this occasion, have found anything to reprove" (p. 391). But her progress is incomplete: although she does not feel it necessary to have the real Mr. Knightley know what she has done or to receive approval directly from him, it remains true that her sense of the rightness of her own conduct and feeling is expressed by imagining how he would judge them.

But all of this is only a preparation for a mortification of an altogether different kind. When Emma prepares to break to Harriet the news of Frank Churchill's engagement, Harriet reveals that it is not Churchill but Mr. Knightley whom she loves, and she says that she has grounds to believe that he returns her affection. When Emma is told this, "It darted through her, with the speed of an arrow, that Mr. Knightley must marry no one but herself!" (p. 408). It is the knowledge of her own desire for another, entailing the possibility of loss and refusal, that clears her mind: "Her own conduct, as well as her own heart, was before her in the same few minutes. She saw it all with a clearness which had never blessed her before." She sees not only how badly she has acted toward Harriet; she also sees that her own interests are in jeopardy and that she can act to protect them. She inquires into the nature of Harriet's hopes and finds them better founded than she could have dreamed. Her statement does justice to Harriet, to Mr. Knightley, and to herself: "Harriet, I will only venture to declare that Mr. Knightley is the last man in the world, who would intentionally give any woman the idea of his feeling for her more than he really does" (p. 411).

Owing partly to the prospect of losing him and partly to her own development, Emma can now for the first time regard Mr. Knightley as external to herself. This frees her in two ways: she can begin to function without him, recognizing her own autonomy as well as his, and she can make him the object of her own desire in a new way.

With the recognition of what she has heretofore hidden from herself—her own capacity and need for love—comes a recognition of something else: the impermanence of life, the effect of time, and the possibility of real disappointment. The acknowledgment of desire is a wish for change, and this necessarily destroys the fantasy of perfection. In a passage that marks her maturity, as her initial reverie marked her protracted infancy, Emma for the first time now views her future realistically. She now sees that with Mrs. Weston occupied with her child, Harriet at Donwell, and Mrs. Elton ruling in Highbury, she will lead a life, winter after winter, without society or companionship; she will indeed be, as Harriet once told her, "an old maid like Miss Bates." Her dream of "perfection," and her attempt to maintain forever the "blessings" of having first place in her father's home, disappear in an instant, and "the only source whence any thing like consolation or composure could be drawn, was in the resolution of her own better conduct, and the hope that, however inferior in spirit and gaiety might be the following and every future winter of her life to the past, it would yet find her more rational, more acquainted with herself, and leave her less to regret when it were gone" (p. 423).[20]

But this is not how it is to end, for she is to have Mr. Knightley after all. In the love scene in the garden at Highbury there are misunderstandings on both sides. Mr. Knightley believes that Emma loves Frank Churchill, and, when he discovers that she does not, he wishes to declare himself to her; but Emma, thinking that he means to speak of his love for Harriet, first stops him, then changes her mind.

> Emma could not bear to give him pain. He was wish-
> ing to confide in her—perhaps to consult her;—cost her
> what it would, she would listen . . . .
> "I stopped you ungraciously, just now, Mr. Knightley,
> and, I am afraid, gave you pain.—But if you have any
> wish to speak openly to me as a friend, or to ask my
> opinion of any thing that you may have in contempla-
> tion—as a friend, indeed, you may command me.—I
> will hear whatever you like. I will tell you exactly what
> I think." [P. 429]

Emma has now reached a stage of maturity at which she is able to treat Mr. Knightley, as he treated her, with disinterested concern for his welfare; she is thus ready to hear him, to respond to him, and to enjoy that "perfect happiness"—to which she in her way contributes as much as he in his—of which the last line of the novel speaks.

I SAID AT THE BEGINNING that this is a novel of education. It begins with Emma speaking an incoherent language, expressing a self at once split and disordered, and it moves through a series of mortifications and con-versations to a position of coherence and health, both in language and character. I say "language and character" as if they were one because, for Jane Austen, they are one; at least they are different aspects of the same unity. She has no notion of a self untouched by its conduct or of a mind or heart divorced from its expressions. It is in speech and behavior that character is at once expressed and determined. No sharp line separates the self from deed and word, and what a person says or does is a manifestation of character as directly continuous with the self as if it were made of the same tissue: the language is the mind.

That is why it is so serious that Emma talks as she does, at the beginning and elsewhere, in her infantile or fantasizing mode. Her speech is a definition of what she is, and she cannot change it without changing herself. This means that the kind of education she needs is not merely a matter of cognition—of receiving the right lessons—or of adapting her behavior to prescriptions. It is not enough to repeat truisms learned from others or to copy their conduct. This is made clear enough by her ridiculous attempts to imitate Mr. Knightley—for example, in her disquisition on manners to Harriet or in her defense of Frank Churchill's impudence. For Emma, success requires that she become the source of her own sentences and her own conduct, that she constitute her own center of principle and meaning, and this is what she is shown to achieve in her vision of her future.

How is this alteration accomplished? In a first reading of the novel it may seem as though the process of education is one of mortification—as though Emma's misjudgments lead her into circumstances that force upon her a painful knowledge about her own feelings and behavior—and this is no doubt part of it. But as we have seen, the lessons learned by mortification, even by the events at Box Hill, are very limited. It is only Emma's last "mortification"—the apparent loss of Mr. Knightley—that effects a substantial change in her, and much less than the others is this mortification a product of her own misjudgment. What changes her the most, in fact what prepares her to respond honestly to this blow when it comes, is not so much the series of embarrassments she inflicts on herself as the continued development of her relationship with Mr. Knightley. It is not the negative knowledge of what she is but the positive knowledge of what she can become—of what she has become in conversation and friendship with him—that enables her to recognize her love for him and thus to face something of what life without him would mean. Emma learns not so much from her errors as from her experience of becoming, in conversation with another, an improved version of herself. The movement of the novel is thus only partly the correction of error through experience; it is more deeply the development of self through friendship. It is this friendship that is the center of life and value in this world.

TEXTUAL FRIENDSHIP AND THE RECONSTITUTION OF CULTURE

Jane Austen's ideal of friendship is given meaning and definition not only in the relationship between Emma and Mr. Knightley but in the relationship that she as a writer establishes with her reader in this text. The textual community of *Emma* in fact directly parallels the imagined community between Emma and Mr. Knightley: it is educative in its concerns, it works by pleasure and conversation, and its central aim is to help the reader become an improved version of himself.

The analogy between Emma and the reader begins with the very act of reading, as we both try to observe things accurately and to understand what they mean. For as Emma must learn to "read" her world if she is to judge and act and speak well within it, we must learn to read the text well if we are to understand what happens to us as readers. Like her, we are constantly trying to locate ourselves with respect to what we are told, to figure out what to expect and how to respond; like her, we are always asking what things mean, and we ask that question of the same things she does. It is a question for both of us, for example, what it means that Mr. Elton praises the portrait of Harriet in just such a way or that Frank Churchill supports Emma's suspicions about the origins of the piano. For both of us, the process begins with questions of an obvious, even a somewhat crude, kind that are forced upon us (Whom does Mr. Elton pursue?), and from these we move by stages to questions of increasing refinement and significance.

Although we share her questions, we do not directly share Emma's experiences of error and correction.[21] Sometimes, as with Mr. Elton, we see clearly, and with immediate pleasure, how Emma is wrong, and the effect of later events is to confirm our capacities as readers. Elsewhere, as in connection with Frank Churchill, we do not see the truth clearly the first time through, but we know, as Emma does not, that something is wrong with the situation and with her. We do not share Emma's point of view, nor do we enjoy a position of secure omniscience; instead, we experience the events of the text with a partial and incomplete intelligence, different from that of any of its characters; it is almost as if we were ourselves actors within it. Our task, like Emma's, is to read our way into understanding.

A part of this reading, as of all reading, is re-reading. Emma does this through her memory, going back over what she has observed and the way she interpreted it, trying to understand her mistakes, and this is what we do too in our ordinary lives. But as readers of this text we can repeat the actual process of reading the text and so learn to see more and more clearly what at first we saw awkwardly and dimly or missed entirely. This is a text that must indeed be reread to be read at all, for an essential part of the experience it offers the reader is the correction of his earlier misreadings, by which it teaches him or her how to become the audience, the partner, that the text defines and requires.

In this sense the text engages its reader in a kind of conversation, like those between Emma and Mr. Knightley, in which at every clarification one feels recognized and rewarded with pleasure and knowledge. The reason the text offers its reader such continual freshness, such a sense of surprise and learning, is that one's sense of it, and of oneself, is always changing. At each discovery one finds oneself invited, as one who has *now* seen such-and-such a point, to ask how this clarification affects the rest of one's reading; this in turn leads to another set of questions and puzzles and clarifications; and so on. The experience is a little like taking a progressive series of tests, each one of which is intelligible only when you have passed its predecessor. It is in some sense the same paragraph one reads, but each time one both sees it differently and feels differently addressed. One hears Jane Austen's voice in new ways, asking new questions, making new comments, and in the process one moves into an increasingly confident and intimate understanding of the text and its author. It is this movement of mind into harmony with mind that is responsible for the sense, shared by so many readers of Jane Austen, that one has a secretly privileged and personal relationship with her, a special kind of friendship; this sense is, for one who has read her well, literally true.[22]

Another way to put this point is to say that this is an ethical literature that includes among its central concerns the character of the reader. It is one lesson of this novel that there is an important connection between friendship and what I have called reading, for it is only through speech and interpretation, through the manifestation and recognition of character in relation with others, that friendships can exist. One can be a good friend only if one utters what will not mislead and reads correctly what one is told. As we learn to read this text more completely and to respond to it more fully, we become better readers, not only of this text but of our world, and better speakers and actors too; in this sense it can be said that the ultimate object of this text is to teach us to become better friends. Just as it is Emma's experience of who she actually becomes in her conversations with Mr. Knightley that enables her to become a better version of herself, whether she is to live in isolation or in marriage, so it is the reader's experience of who he becomes in conversation with this text— his discovery of his own capacities for thought and feeling—that constitutes its ultimate value for him. This text teaches its reader to value himself, and in doing this it teaches him the seriousness of the questions: who he is, who he becomes.

These questions are given special force and intensity for Emma in her reflections at the central moment of her career, when she contemplates future winters endured without friend or conversation, in isolated solitude, where her only consolation can lie in her resolve to speak and act as she ought and to leave behind as little to regret as she can. In contrast to her first mournful imaginings (and to her more extravagant claims to Harriet when she told her she would never marry), Emma here recognizes the reality of her situation, including the effects of time and the necessity of change. Her fantasy of permanent perfection has gone, and she has entered the stream of human life and feeling, of hope and disappointment. She can even foresee her father's death. She now realizes that what awaits her, the princess of Highbury, is to be an old maid at last, as Harriet foresaw; she will no doubt be respectable enough, but she will lack the essential fulfillment that only marriage can offer man or woman. She still has the "blessings" described in the first sentence, but she has learned how little they are if she is to have nothing more.

With all these changes comes another, the recognition that the stable world of stable values, which provided the standard by which her defects could be defined and her correction motivated—upon which she has learned to found her life—is imaginary; or, more precisely, it is real only when it is actively created and recreated in conversation and community. Part of what has been brought home to her is that her social world is not fixed, as she originally thought, but fluid and uncertain. It has by now become apparent, for example, both that Emma's initial conception of her own social standing was considerably more grand than the facts warrant and that positions on this social scale are by their nature highly impermanent.[23] Mr. Weston's family, for example, has been "rising into gentry," while the Bateses have fallen into poverty; Miss Taylor by her marriage escapes a dependence, as a governess, that the elegant Jane Fairfax faces as a realistic threat; Harriet Smith's standing is uncertain throughout; and, by the end of the novel, the despicable Mrs. Elton has established herself as Emma's equal or perhaps, by virtue of her marriage, as her superior. And Emma's delicacy about her own superior position has been shown to be merely idiosyncratic; her alarms at being invited to the upstart Coles's are shared by no one at all.

But the instability of Emma's world is not merely a matter of rapid movement up and down the ladder of social status. It extends to all the values of personal and social life, which prove, against Emma's expectations and our own, to be highly variable and uncertain. We thought this was a social world with clear and established fundamentals, but we can now see that it is populated by discrete individuals who have very different conceptions of the world and of themselves. All of the persons in this book have their own ways of seeing and talking, and real conversation among them is very rare.[24] Think, for example, of the marvelous dialogue between Mr. Weston and the "good-hearted" Mrs. Elton, in which he talks only of his son, she only of Maple Grove (pp. 305–10), or of the argument between Mr. Knightley and Mrs. Weston over the wisdom of Emma's association with Harriet, where her resistance to his claims is impenetrable (pp. 36–41). And what conversation, beyond kind noises, could ever be possible with Miss Bates or Mr. Woodhouse? Or consider the far more serious matter of Frank Churchill, whom, after all, Emma might in other circumstances have married. His last letter of explanation and apology (pp. 436–43), which is apparently offered as a prelude to a pleasing and successful life, is a problem not so much because it is low on the scale of merit established by Emma and Mr. Knightley (and Jane Austen) as because it is simply not on it at all. There is almost no overlap in sympathy and perception, in language and feeling, between this letter and the way Emma and Mr. Knightley talk; almost no conversation is imaginable between either of them and the essentially foreign mind that wrote that letter. And Jane Fairfax, of whom that is not so true, counts herself happily in love with him.

What Emma perceives in her bleak view of future winters, then, is the essential subjectivity and relativity of this world—what we might call its modernity. Contrary to the surface impression, it turns out that in this world—even in this world, one is tempted to say—there is no stable culture, external to the self, on which one can simply rely. On this view morality and friendship take on a quite different significance for Emma—and for Jane Austen too. In Emma's life, we can now see, it has been only in conversation with Mr. Knightley, and to a lesser degree with her other friends, that her values have been defined, her self and identity established. And at the end she does not live, as she and we expected, in a world of shared and permanent understandings. (When she marries Mr. Knightley, for example, Mrs. Elton pities him and regards her as having made a surprising catch.) She is to live either in the deepest sense alone or, if she is lucky, with her friends. So far it has been on her relationship with Mr. Knightley that she has most been able to depend, but it now looks as if those conversations have come to an end and that she must face life alone. The veil has been torn from life, and we can see that Emma's training in morality, which to some eyes might earlier have seemed overly punctilious and restrictive, is not a limitation but a resource, and an essential one, for her continued existence. Her sense of who she is—how she speaks and acts—is important, more than important: it is everything, because it is all that she has.[25]

But Emma is not to be alone after all, for Mr. Knightley recognizes his love and need for her. And what has been said of Emma is true of him as well: he is, after all, not the voice of powerful tradition, supported by the universe, as may at first seem, but a man seeking what men seek. Like Emma, he needs another person with whom to create by conversation a world of shared meanings. In this context we can see that Emma's imagination (earlier she rightly called herself an "imaginist"), which in its diseased form gives rise to fantasies that keep her from seeing or imagining truly, is also an enormous strength, for it can be creative as well as delusive. Indeed, the powerful sense of a stable society with stable values that informs this text (which many readers wrongly see as Jane Austen's view of her own world) is in the world of the novel defined as the product of Emma's powerful imagination.[26] Emma has the force of mind and will, the insistence on meaning, that enable her to maintain the artifices by which life is given significance, the fictions that constitute the culture that she and Mr. Knightley have made out of the materials of their world. This means that she, with him, can create on the only scale on which it is possible, in conversation with another, the stable society and stable values that are absent from the world around her. She has the imaginative power to be a source of meaning and language, a true partner in conversation, equal to anyone.

Emma's language is still a way of creating a world and a self, just as it was in the opening reverie; but the world that she now creates is congruent with the essential conditions of her existence. Her language has become both a way of directly facing circumstances that cannot be changed (as in her vision of her future) and a way of making a better world upon them if the opportunity offers (as it does in her conversation with Mr. Knightley). The major stylistic quality of the language that she and Mr. Knightley use at the end—and in this it is rather like the language that closes the *Rambler* essays—is its simplicity and directness: "My Emma, does not everything serve to prove more and more the beauty of truth and sincerity in all our dealings with each other?" (p. 446). The tensions that give complication and life to such a statement as that are not explicit in the statement itself but contextual: it is from our experience of various kinds of falseness and insincerity in what has preceded that such a sentence gets its meaning. Emma ends as one who remakes her world and her language in constant conversation with another, but the terms in which she does so are the standard terms of her moral culture, clarified by experience and context. Her new world is an old world remade.

ALL THIS IS A WAY of talking about Jane Austen too; for Austen herself lives, and knows it, in the world of Emma's wintry vision, where she cannot rely on an externally established stable world of social structure and value but must create, in conversation with others—in her texts—a culture of her own. The culture from which Emma and the reader learn is not simply to be found in the world, as may at first appear, but is created by the author's active mind and imagination. Of course inherited materials are used (such as the *Rambler* essays), but they do not mean much until they are reconstituted by the individual mind. In this novel Jane Austen makes an ideal to which she assimilates her heroine, her reader, and herself.

KINDNESS

The central relationships in this novel, those between Emma and Mr. Knightley and between the author and the reader, are the conversational and educative friendships in which culture can be reconstituted and life given shape and meaning. But there is another kind of friendship presented here as well, and in its own way it is equally important. This friendship is based not on conversation but on kindness: kindness to Mr. Woodhouse, to Miss Bates, to Harriet; the kindness of Miss Bates herself. These two sorts of friendship work in different ways, of course; for conversation—like justice and compassion in Thucydides—presupposes equality, but kindness extends to all, including those with whom no conversation, as Jane Austen defines it, is possible. But while there is this difference, there is no inconsistency; for the kind of conversation that Jane Austen defines and celebrates here rests ultimately on the recognition of another person, and that is the central idea of kindness as well: imaginative sympathy with the experience and circumstances of another, respect for his claims and autonomy. Kindness and conversation alike proceed from a perception of common humanity. Austen's text in this way addresses a question omitted from Plato's *Gorgias*, from Swift's *Tale*, and for the most part from Johnson's *Rambler* essays: What kind of relation can one have with those who are not members of the dialectical community of two and who perhaps cannot become members of such a community? We learn that what should motivate those relations, and provide the standard by which they should be judged, is kindness.[27]

Emma shows at the beginning that she can recognize and respond to the circumstances of another when she treats her father as she does, and she exhibits similar qualities both in visiting the family stricken by illness and poverty and in the way she talks about them. But she lacks this sort of kindness in her other relations, in part because true kindness requires true observation and a true understanding of one's own condition, and at the beginning Emma's mind and heart are in these respects distorted. It is through the changes worked by conversation, as she becomes more completely the sort of partner she can be with Mr. Knightley, that Emma's deficiencies in kindness are corrected.

Emma thus trains its reader not only in conversation but in a certain sort of kindness. It does so partly in the way it teaches us to understand who Emma is, for the central error it corrects is not our failure to see the secret evil behind the plausible surface—as in Swift and in Austen's own *Pride and Prejudice*—but our failure to see the unobtrusive and easily missed good beneath an unappealing surface.[28] This is a training in sympathy and generosity as well as in accuracy of observation. Not that Emma is not truly awful in her conversations with Harriet, for she certainly is; but she is something else at the same time as well, something we do not see the first time through: she is capable of genuine kindness and, with her capacity for conversation and self-correction, it is this that makes possible the change she achieves at the end. The error of the reader that is corrected here is a bit like that of the parent of an adolescent child who is so exasperated by certain aspects of his child's speech and conduct that he simply fails to see strength and intelligence and balance and goodness that are right before his eyes. This is a deficiency in our capacity to observe that is just as destructive and unintelligent as the one more commonly corrected, the failure to see what is bad, and it is also a deficiency in our nature. This text seeks to correct both kinds of deficiency in its reader.

Emma is not thought to be a political novel. In fact it has frequently been criticized for what some see as its unquestioning acceptance of an unjust social order, and it is certainly true that Jane Austen is not concerned with political questions of the usual sort: the best arrangement of institutions, the proper structure of government, the choice of one social aim over another. But there is another sense in which it is deeply political, for it invites you to ask: If I become the ideal reader this text defines, the version of myself it calls into being, what will I do, what will I be, when I turn to my own larger world and act within it? (It would certainly be a perversion of this text to use it, as some do, as the occasion for a reverie of one's own, like Emma's, an escape to a happier time.) Of course Jane Austen's attention is not on forms of public thought and action but on certain prior matters, which can be summed up as conceptions of the self and the other. But she makes the question about the larger world unavoidable for one who reads her properly, and, in addition, she suggests two modes of activity by which it can be addressed: what I have called "kindness" and "conversation." Is it possible to have a larger community whose central value is kindness, its central method conversation? The very suggestion is the beginning of a response to the question the *Iliad* left with us, and left wholly open: How can we move from an ideally created world of two, in the text or in the world, to a larger world of social and political life and action? It is this possibility that we shall explore in the remaining chapters, in which we shall first examine Edmund Burke's *Reflections on the Revolution in France* and then think about the possibilities of American law and democracy.

8

Making a Public World

The Constitution of Language and Community in Burke's *Reflections*

Edmund Burke's *Reflections on the Revolution in France* is a political text in just the sense that Jane Austen's novels are not, for it is explicitly concerned with the ways in which community should be established and organized at the national level. Burke asks not how an individual ought to lead his life, alone or with others, but how the British ought to constitute themselves as a nation, giving themselves a proper character and a proper life. In contrast to the texts we have been reading since Thucydides—each of which has offered an essentially private or individual response to the question of how to live in a world in which self and language are subject to perpetual and reciprocal change—Burke offers us a response that is overtly public in character. In its politically constitutive purpose this text might indeed be compared with the speeches of Pericles or Cleon.

An essential part of the method of Burke's text, perhaps of all such texts, is to create the objects of its persuasion. Here the objects are the "British Constitution," which is held out as an ideal, and the "French Revolution," which is held out as its negative opposite and potential destroyer. These are of course not physical objects; they are what I have been calling languages or cultures, structured ways of thinking and talking and being by which value and character are defined and community is constituted. The aim of the text is, first, that its reader will come to talk the language of the British Constitution and thus become a member of the community that that language creates and, second, that he will reject the other possibilities—for the nation, for the reader, and for the author—represented by the "French Revolution."

When I say that the text creates the language it holds out for admiration and for use, I do not mean that it creates it out of nothing. Burke starts, as he must start, with the possibilities established by the ordinary language of his time as they actually exist: somewhat loose, potentially inconsistent, and reflecting a divided community. He starts in fact where his reader starts and then reconstitutes their common language, making a new version of it that promises a new organization of the world.

Consider, for example, this sentence, which sums up accurately enough much of what Burke says: "the British Constitution is founded upon property and religion." While this will of course make some kind of sense to the reader innocent of Burke, it can be fully understood only as part of the language constituted in this text, in which such terms as "religion" and "property" are given meanings of a new kind. What meanings Burke gives them, and how he does so, will be important parts of our subject; but I give nothing away if I say now that his methods—like Johnson's and Austen's—are what might be called literary rather than theoretical, for he gives meaning to his words by association and use and pattern rather than by stipulation and deduction. In this text Burke makes a language in which his inventions can become real, and he teaches it to his reader.

When I say that the "British Constitution" and the "French Revolution" are communities defined by languages, I mean nothing unfamiliar to the reader of this book, for it is by what we have been calling languages—shared conceptions of the world, shared manners and values, shared resources and expectations and procedures for speech and thought—that communities are in fact defined and constituted. Here the relevant community is the one that accepts Burke's offer to learn and to use his reconstituted language. In the first instance this will be a community between the individual reader and the text. But if this text succeeds, this community will also become a community among many readers of the text, who will adopt its terms and methods and use them to achieve their purposes in the world. This is, then, a political text, not merely in the sense that it is about politics, but in the sense that it is itself a part of the politics of its time: it is Burke's hope that what we have called a "textual community" will become an actual political community as well.

All this means something about the kind of persuasion Burke is seeking to achieve. It cannot be enough for him to secure the reader's intellectual assent to the truth of certain propositions, for he must have active belief, commitment, and participation. He wants his readers to see things in the world as he presents them in his text, to think and to feel about them as he does, and to form a community—strenuously opposed to the French Revolution, strenuously supporting the British Constitution—that is grounded, in part at least, on this text and speaking its language.[1] His object is to give the British Constitution he defines such an identity, and such a reality, that it can be the center of a real community, as clear in its sense of self as was the community, as Thucydides describes it, that lived on the island of Melos.

The ideal reader of the *Reflections* would thus not say at the end merely that he now "believed in" certain propositions for "certain reasons." He would see the world differently, would conceive of himself and his nation differently, would think, speak, and act differently. He would have mastered a language of fact, motive, and sentiment that would affect his conduct and his feeling forever. This text seeks to persuade its reader not to a set of propositions but to a language—a language of belief and of action. It means to offer him an education that will equip him differently for life.

FOR US THIS VIEW of the aims of Burke's text suggests a familiar set of questions. To start with, what is the nature of the textual community that Burke actually establishes with his reader? It is plain from what I have already said that he is trying to persuade us of something, and it does not take much exposure to his prose to see that he is not exactly eager to reconsider his own position or to have it subjected to what Plato called "refutation." Burke does not seem to offer us puzzles to work out or to want to share with us the processes by which he has moved from commonplace to principle, as Swift and Johnson did; nor does he establish a pattern of deepening understanding and intimacy, as Jane Austen did. What is our function in reading this, then? Are we just to swallow what we are told? What makes things even worse is Burke's frequent exaggeration or overstatement, his tendency to portray people and events in such caricatured form that they cannot in any ordinary sense be true. There is a kind of violence of mind here, in the face of which we may well ask: Who are we to this text and in its life?

Second, what is the nature of the political community that Burke describes and means to recommend? We quickly learn that he means to celebrate a constitution that is based on an inherited aristocracy, an established church, and an electoral franchise that not only is limited to a very small class of people but is distributed unequally even among them. Our own political instincts rebel, for here we are closer in spirit to the French Revolution Burke attacks than to the British Constitution he supports. How can we possibly respond to the politics of this text other than by rejection?

Finally, what is the relation between the textual and political communities? Is it possible to move directly from one to the other, as I suggest Burke wishes us to do, and, if so, on what terms? One can see how Jane Austen can enact in her text the ideal of friendship that she portrays in her novel, which she also means to recommend as a possibility in life. But how can there possibly be such a continuity between Burke's textual community, which is between two, and his public constitution, which is among thousands or millions? One would like to say that it is in the "con-

194

stitution" established by this text that the "British Constitution" Burke celebrates is to be found, that the most important expression of the values that his essay is "about" is their enactment or performance in the community this text establishes with his reader. But is such continuity possible between the public and the private, between the individual and the general? If so, is it possible only because both are based on some unattractive and authoritarian principle of obedience or submission, or is it conceivable that such continuity can exist between two communities we can admire—between friendship and the nation? A composition—a constitution, a language—that united such things would be remarkable indeed. Even to suggest the possibility is to wonder whether one could imagine, and make real, a political life that was a species of friendship.

THE TEXT CREATES A WORLD: CONSTITUTIONAL CONVERSATION

If we take what I have said as a rough statement of Burke's aims, it is hard to see how he can proceed. It obviously will not do for him simply to outline his theory of government and then seek to show that it is superior to some other theory; for that would tend toward the wrong kind of persuasion—the merely intellectual—and would mistake the object of his persuasion, which is not a theory but a way of life. (For Burke, what is most wrong about the French Revolution is what he calls its theoretical character, which he sees as intimately associated with its pride, its blindness, and its irrationality.) The other obvious method would be through narrative, by telling a story in which he created characters, gave them speeches and deeds, and constructed a series of connected events, all moving from one point to another—say, from felicity to disaster. But this will not work either, since for Burke—unlike Thucydides—a constitution is not an object to be observed and judged but a community to be joined. In fact, Burke uses neither of these methods, or, more accurately, he employs both of them and many others, putting them to work in a text that has a structure and a character of its own. In its own way it is as original in form, and as difficult to classify and summarize, as Swift's *Tale*.

The Epistolary Form

Burke begins by casting his essay in the form of a letter to an (unnamed) "very young gentleman at Paris"[2] who has asked him for his views on the French Revolution under the misapprehension that, as a supporter of "liberty," Burke will naturally support it. This misapprehension is based partly on the young man's misunderstanding of the activities of two English clubs, the Constitutional Society and the Revolution Society.

195

Burke's choice of the epistolary form has important consequences. For one thing, it provides him with a modest justification for writing at all. Instead of declaring his views from a podium of his own, as if they were automatically of interest to the world, he can seem to be merely responding to a request for them. Indeed, he begins not as a propounder of views at all but as a corrector of misimpressions. And the young and naive foreigner is a perfect surrogate for Burke's true audience, the Englishman tempted by the rhetoric of revolution; for Burke can correct the foreigner's mistakes by representing his own view as "what every Englishman knows" and in this way address his true audience without ever accusing it of the errors he corrects.

But most of all it means that this essay can begin as a private letter from one man to another—from an Englishman to a Frenchman—and grow by a natural process, much of which we observe, into a great public declaration. This movement within the text is significant because it mirrors Burke's fundamental claim about the British Constitution, that it unites the public and the private: in this world one can turn without a break from a private letter to public business. To put it slightly differently, Burke, in beginning as he does, claims not only that there is a place in the British Constitution for the individual voice, for the individual auditor, for the individual everything, but that—on certain conditions to be elaborated below—there is no topic or public matter upon which the individual voice may *not* be heard. Burke's British Constitution has its beginnings, and comes to life, in actual conversations, between actual people, of just the kind exemplified here.

Burke himself says that the epistolary form also makes it possible for him "to throw out [his] thoughts, and express [his] feelings, just as they arise in [his] mind, with very little attention to formal method" (p. 92).[3] The significance of this is not that it permits him to be lazy or offhand, as his sentence almost seems to suggest, but that it enables him to write a composition that is ordered in a certain way: not theoretically, as a set of abstract propositions about the nature of government, but organically, as a set of interconnected themes and attitudes and images, emerging now in one context, now in another. For this essay is not organized into sections, each designed to establish a distinct point, but is associative and repetitive in structure, and its effects are contextual and cumulative. Burke's literary style (like the British Constitution itself) is in fact intended to unite in a kind of poetry the particular and the universal, the individual and the general, the private and the public. No place can be torn without tearing the whole, and every part belongs with every other part. To read the essay at all, one must resist the impulse to turn it into theory,[4] and this itself is an important part of its teaching.

196

Burke's text accordingly works in part by creating an imagined world, with imagined characters and events, with respect to which the reader is invited to locate himself in particular ways. But this created world of fused particularity and generality is meant to be real as well as imagined: real in the past, with the authority of history, as the best representation of what has occurred, and real in the future, with the authority of rhetoric and politics, as a world that people will, if the text succeeds, choose for their own.

Owning and Representing

It is appropriate that Burke begins his letter, and the constitution of his world, with a matter not of mere theory or mere fact but of political and social reality: the definition of the character of the two clubs, the Constitutional Society and the Revolution Society, whose publications have led at least one young Frenchman to believe that they speak for the British nation in support of the French Revolution and that Burke, as a friend of liberty, will naturally support them. In describing these clubs, Burke diminishes them. Of the Constitutional Society he says, "I never heard a man of common judgment, or the least degree of information" speak favorably of it. Of the Revolution Society he has never heard, but he finds "upon inquiry" that it is a "club of dissenters [who] have long had the custom of hearing a sermon in one of their churches" on the anniversary of the English Revolution, and "afterwards they [spend] the day cheerfully, as other clubs do, at the tavern" (p. 87). Whatever they may claim, Burke tells the young man, in England these clubs are of no account.

In diminishing them, Burke disowns them and invites the reader to do likewise. This is a performance of an activity central to the text as a whole, the double activity of "owning" and "disowning"; for it is Burke's central object that the reader shall "own" the British Constitution and "disown" the French Revolution as he defines them, and it is no accident that "property" is a key term in his discourse.

This focus on owning and disowning means that Burke's subject is not the public world alone or the individual alone but the relationship between them. We are immediately presented with another important version of this relationship in the claims of the two clubs to "represent" the nation. The Constitutional Society, in particular, has presented itself to the French Assembly as the representative of the British people and has been received by them in that character. Burke says he would never perform such an act, for "I should think it at least improper and irregular, for me to open a formal public correspondence with the actual government of a foreign nation, without the express authority of the government un-

197

der which I live" (p. 88). If the Society had presented an "argument," it would have mattered little from whom it came, but "this is only a vote and resolution" (p. 89).

> It stands solely on authority; and in this case it is the mere authority of individuals, few of whom appear. Their signatures ought, in my opinion, to have been annexed to their instrument. The world would then have the means of knowing how many they are; who they are; and of what value their opinions may be, from their personal abilities, from their knowledge, their experience, or their lead and authority in this state. [P. 89]

Burke's view that the instrument should have been "signed" is a way of saying that it should have been "owned"—in this case, perhaps, "owned up to"—by the individuals behind it. This, like the epistolary form of his own essay, underlines Burke's insistence that behind the forms of social organization our world consists of individual persons. He will repeatedly remind us that it is always individuals who act and suffer and that the benefits of government are to be measured as benefits to people, not as abstract or theoretical rights.

But, since Burke's own text is itself a kind of representation, how can he attack the "representative" claims of the Constitutional Society? Can the two kinds of representation be distinguished? It is true that Burke says, at the beginning, that he writes "neither for nor from any description of men" and that "my errors, if any, are my own. My reputation alone is to answer for them" (p. 85). And, at the end, he reasserts the personal character of what he has written: "I have told you candidly my sentiments. I think they are not likely to alter yours. I do not know that they ought" (p. 376). But in between he is constantly declaring the views of the people of Great Britain to the young Frenchman, speaking for a whole nation perhaps more completely than any man has ever done. We may well ask, by what authority does he do this?

His answer lies in his talk about "argument." Unlike the bald declarations of the Constitutional Society, his text makes no claim to an authority to speak for others beyond the authority it can actually earn from them by the force of its appeals. It can be owned—or disowned—by any of the subjects in the kingdom, and without their assent it can have no life or force.

This not only distinguishes Burke's way of representing the nation from that of the Constitutional Society, it defines by performance the process of representation that lies at the heart of the actual British Constitution as Burke conceives it. For him, representation in Parliament does not work by the simple delegation of authority from the people to their representative, as we might imagine; instead, it has, like Burke's own text, an essentially rhetorical and ethical character. The right to represent must be earned over and over again; it has no clear limits; and it is not subject to direction by the constituency. In Burke's view it is in fact one of the great merits of the British Constitution that each member is not chosen by a roughly equal number of constituents; for, if this were the case, each member might fall into the habit of thinking that he represented only his own constituents, against the rest of the nation, and that he would best represent them by simply acting on their preferences or on what Burke calls their "will." As it is, each member of Parliament is understood to represent the nation as a whole and to represent not its temporary will but its largest interests (p. 303). It is in the action of the individual mind seeking to persuade others that the community has not only its life but its origins both of change and of conservation. This kind of representation is an essentially rhetorical activity of which this text can be regarded as an exemplification.

THE TEXT CREATES A LANGUAGE: "THE BRITISH CONSTITUTION"

Burke insists throughout the *Reflections* that the language in which he works will be real English, with all its richness and complexity of associations, its tensions and ambiguities—its correspondences with the society and culture of which it is in some sense the central part—rather than a language of theory. Burke's insistence on using a language of feeling and action and judgment—what he would call a language of the mind, not merely of the abstract intellectual faculty—is essential to his achievement as a whole, since for him, as for us, there is an intimate and necessary connection between the organization of language and the organization of community—between "text" and "constitution"—and between both of these and the organization of the individual mind.

This is why, for Burke, the way he speaks in his writing, and the way he invites his reader to speak, is so important. He wishes to offer his reader a language, running from the self to the world of nature, in which the community he sees and values can be constituted and maintained, even defended. To be adequate to these purposes, his language must be many things, the first of which is comprehensive, capable of addressing a question as a whole, as it really is, and of putting together everything that bears upon it.

Combination

In a famous early passage of the *Reflections*, Burke makes language his explicit subject and tells us how we ought to think and talk about "liberty": not in isolation or abstraction but in combination with everything with which it is naturally connected.

> I flatter myself that I love a manly, moral, regulated
> liberty as well as any gentleman of that society, be he
> who he will. . . . But I cannot stand forward, and give
> praise or blame to any thing which relates to human
> actions, and human concerns, on a simple view of the
> object, as it stands stripped of every relation, in all the
> nakedness and solitude of metaphysical abstraction.
> Circumstances (which with some gentlemen pass for
> nothing) give in reality to every political principle its
> distinguishing colour, and discriminating effect. The
> circumstances are what render every civil and political
> scheme beneficial or noxious to mankind. Abstractedly
> speaking, government, as well as liberty, is good; yet
> could I, in common sense, ten years ago, have felici-
> tated France on her enjoyment of a government (for she
> then had a government) without enquiry what the na-
> ture of that government was, or how it was adminis-
> tered? Can I now congratulate the same nation upon its
> freedom? . . .
> When I see the spirit of liberty in action, I see a
> strong principle at work; and this, for a while, is all I
> can possibly know of it. . . . I must be tolerably sure,
> before I venture publicly to congratulate men upon a
> blessing, that they have really received one I
> should therefore suspend my congratulations on the
> new liberty of France, until I was informed how it had
> been combined with government; with public force;
> with the discipline and obedience of armies; with the
> collection of an effective and well-distributed revenue;
> with morality and religion; with the solidity of property;
> with peace and order: with civil and social manners. All
> these (in their way) are good things too; and, without
> them, liberty is not a benefit whilst it lasts, and is not
> likely to continue long. The effect of liberty to individu-
> als is, that they may do what they please: We ought to

see what it will please them to do, before we risque congratulations, which may be soon turned into complaints. [Pp. 89–91]

Burke's message here is combination. A discourse rooted in a single
value will always be too simple to be true, he tells us, and to think about
liberty at all one must therefore think at the same time about all the
things with which it is connected, practically and morally. Thus he refuses to use "liberty" as a single unqualified term of praise or blame. Its
actual meaning—its meaning for the happiness of mankind—lies not in
the fact of liberty itself but in its "circumstances," in its "use," in the
"principles, tempers, and dispositions" of those who exercise it—gram-
matically speaking, in its terms of qualification and combination. Burke
loves not "liberty" itself but "manly, moral, regulated liberty." This teaching is familiar to the reader of *Emma*, who has learned that "some of the
best blessings of existence" are worth very little unless they are combined in the right way with other blessings, and to the reader of Johnson's
Rambler, who has been shown that the essence of moral thought is the
simultaneous comprehension of contrary tendencies in the mind. The
real task is not the isolated definition of values but their combination,
their composition into a whole.[5] This sort of thought is genuinely difficult; but, Burke tells us, it has been the English willingness to face such
difficulties that has enabled them, over time, "to unite into a consistent
whole the various anomalies and contending principles that are found in
the minds and affairs of men. From hence arises, not an excellence
in simplicity, but one far superior, an excellence in composition" (pp.
281–82).

The "French" method is, by contrast, to employ a theoretical, single-
value discourse, and this leads first to a detachment from reality and ultimately—by stages demonstrated in the long second half of the *Reflections*—to chaos and disintegration. The French avoid difficulties that the
English embrace,[6] and the result of this method is disaster: "every thing
seems out of nature in this strange chaos of levity and ferocity" (p. 92).
Where the English method corresponds with the conditions of the world
and achieves an essential harmony with it, the French method produces
a kind of deformity, a creation that is so clearly "out of nature" that perhaps only the Virgilian word *monstrum* can express the sense of violation
Burke intends.[7]

The alternatives Burke thus defines are these: a difficult and comprehensive language of combination and composition, which offers a way of
putting things together into a whole, a way of constituting a culture and a
community; and an easy language of theory and abstraction, which offers

a way of taking things apart, a way of undoing order, which leads at last to chaos. The French process is dissolution; the British process—enacted for us in the composition of this text—is constitution.

Distinction

It is necessary to combine, but it is also necessary to distinguish. Our language must draw the distinctions that are required by the circumstances. But, Burke tells us, the language of the British supporters of revolution—here exemplified by Doctor Price—perpetuates confusion of the most fundamental kind. They have even confused the English Revolution of 1688 (and the Constitution based upon it, which Burke of course wholeheartedly supports) with the French Revolution of 1789, whose true English antecedent is not the Revolution of 1688 but the regicide rebellion of 1649. In insisting on this distinction between two kinds of revolution—which becomes the central polarity of his text—Burke separates into two what others wrongly see as one. "[W]e should separate what they confound" (p. 100). In this way he creates a historical and rhetorical world that is both more complex than that of his opponents and based on clearer and more accurate distinctions.[8]

This will be Burke's method throughout: to insist on distinctions that create a language at once of greater difficulty than the language his opponents use and having greater correspondence with the world than theirs. Consider, for example, his response to Dr. Price's assertion that "his majesty 'is almost the *only* lawful king in the world, because the *only* one who owes his crown to the *choice of his people*'" (p. 96) (emphasis in original). Dr. Price's language impliedly asserts that a people have either "chosen its king" or have not, and he lumps together all forms of government other than "choice" as illegitimate usurpation. Burke meets this by asserting a third possibility: the king of England holds his crown neither by choice nor by usurpation but by law, the principle of which is inheritance. He is "king by a fixed rule of succession, according to the laws of his country" (p. 98).

Burke complicates this distinction by drawing still others, all relating to the idea of "choice." It would be possible to say, for example, "that some of the king's predecessors have been called to the throne by some sort of choice; and therefore he owes his crown to the choice of his people" (p. 98). But that would be to use "choice" in a meaningless way, for how would that "idea of election differ from our idea of inheritance?" (p. 98).

It is also true that "there was at the Revolution [of 1688], in the person of King William, a small and a temporary deviation from the strict order of a regular hereditary succession; but it is against all genuine principles of jurisprudence to draw a principle from a law made in a special case, and regarding an individual person" (p. 101). In fact, the proper way to understand this event is to see that at the very moment when it was most possible to reject the principle of succession the nation chose to reaffirm it. To read the event otherwise would be to fail to distinguish the temporary exception from the permanent rule and to misunderstand the kind of choice that was actually made.

What is more, "choice" presupposes freedom, and the people of the nation were then not actually free to do what they pleased, except in the sense in which they were "free" to "abolish their monarchy and every other part of their constitution"—free, that is, as a matter of fact or power, not as a matter of social or moral reality.

> [T]hey did not think such bold changes within their commission. It is indeed difficult, perhaps impossible, to give limits to the mere *abstract* competence of the supreme power, such as was exercised by parliament at that time; but the limits of a *moral* competence, subjecting, even in powers more indisputably sovereign, occasional will to permanent reason, and to the steady maxims of faith, justice, and fixed fundamental policy, are perfectly intelligible, and perfectly binding upon those who exercise any authority, under any name, or under any title, in the state. [P. 104]

Indeed, if this were not true, "competence and power would soon be confounded, and no law be left but the will of a prevailing force" (p. 105).

By this method of complication—really a kind of legal education—Burke so alters our ideas of "choice" and "freedom" as to make Dr. Price's perhaps initially appealing slogans seem literally meaningless. And as the text proceeds he continues this process, repeatedly insisting on distinctions that the language of revolution obscures and making it increasingly impossible for the reader to imagine himself using the language Burke thus breaks down. For example:

> —The revolutionaries (Burke says) talk about King James as having been a "usurper," but in fact he was not a usurper, but a "bad king with a good title" (p. 108).

> —The revolutionaries speak as though the doctrine of inheritance by which the crown is held is simply a limitation on the rights of the people, but in fact inheritance is also the ground on which these rights are

themselves made real and secure. The very principle by which the king holds his crown also secures to the people their liberties and properties and rights, against him and against each other (p. 111).

—The revolutionaries speak as if those who support the right of the king to his crown are advocates of the divine right of kings. But the right of the king is not "divine" or merely "legal" but actual and—though Burke does not here use the term—constitutional (p. 111).

—The revolutionaries speak as though the people must have either a right to "cashier" their governors for "misconduct" or no right whatever to remove them. But there is no right to remove one's king on the basis of mere misconduct—"no government could stand a moment if it could be blown down with anything so loose and indefinite as an opinion of 'misconduct.'" On the other hand, this is not to say that a king cannot be deposed. Of course he can, as James was; not for misconduct but for the gravest of disloyalties to the state; not as a matter of "choice" but of necessity (pp. 112–13).

—The revolutionaries speak of kings as the servants of their people and hence as dismissible by them at will. There is one sense in which kings are servants, "because their power has no other rational end than that of the general advantage; but it is not true that they are, in the ordinary sense (by our constitution, at least) anything like servants; the essence of whose situation is to obey the commands of some other, and to be removeable at pleasure" (p. 115).

—The revolutionaries fail to see that their talk of "cashiering kings" belongs to a discourse different from that of law and constitution in which we have been engaged, for it "can rarely, if ever, be performed without force," and it then "becomes a case of war, and not of constitution . . . an extraordinary question of state," and one that is "wholly out of the law" (p. 116).

In such ways Burke shows that he distinguishes, as some do not, between himself and the two political clubs; between the English and the

French revolutions; between "misconduct" and "necessity"; between "right" and "divine right"; between "servant" in one sense and "servant" in another; between "election" or "choice" and "inheritance"; between rule and exception; between "abstract" and "moral" competence and between "law" and "force"; between the "liberty" a person or a nation enjoys and the "use" to which they put it.

Burke thus makes the propositions of his opponents increasingly impossible for the reader to accept or to use; they become literally unsayable. And it is the language itself that Burke undermines, far more than the assumptions of fact or value that lie behind it or the chains of logic by which the propositions are connected. He shows that the sentences on which his opponents rely simply cannot do the work we require of a language in which we constitute our common life.

Metaphor

But to insist that one accurately make the distinctions appropriate to one's natural and social circumstances is to make increasingly difficult Burke's original requirement, that one combine all elements into a single composition. How is that to be done? How is one to constitute a language and a community that will form a coherent whole? Burke's answer is (not surprisingly) to turn to a language of generality. But his is not a language of general theory in the usual sense; it is a language of metaphor, in which the entire culture is viewed as a kind of inherited property:

> You will observe, that from Magna Charta to the Declaration of Right, it has been the uniform policy of our constitution to claim and assert our liberties, as an *entailed inheritance* derived to us from our forefathers, and to be transmitted to our posterity; as an estate specially belonging to the people of this kingdom without any reference whatever to any other more general or prior right. By this means our constitution preserves an unity in so great a diversity of its parts. We have an inheritable crown; an inheritable peerage; and an house of commons and a people inheriting privileges, franchises, and liberties, from a long line of ancestors.
>
> This policy appears to me to be the result of profound reflection; or rather the happy effect of following nature, which is wisdom without reflection, and above it. A spirit of innovation is generally the result of a selfish temper and confined views. People will not look forward to posterity, who never look backward to their ancestors. Besides, the people of England well know, that the idea

of inheritance furnishes a sure principle of conservation, and a sure principle of transmission; without at all
excluding a principle of improvement. It leaves acquisition free; but it secures what it acquires. Whatever advantages are obtained by a state proceeding on these
maxims, are locked fast as in a sort of family settlement; grasped as in a kind of mortmain for ever. By a
constitutional policy, working after the pattern of nature, we receive, we hold, we transmit our government
and our privileges, in the same manner in which we
enjoy and transmit our property and our lives. The institutions of policy, the goods of fortune, the gifts of Providence, are handed down, to us and from us, in the
same course and order. Our political system is placed in
a just correspondence and symmetry with the order of
the world, and with the mode of existence decreed to a
permanent body composed of transitory parts; wherein,
by the disposition of a stupendous wisdom, mould-
ing together the great mysterious incorporation of the
human race, the whole, at one time, is never old, or
middle-aged, or young, but in a condition of unchange-
able constancy, moves on through the varied tenour of
perpetual decay, fall, renovation, and progression. Thus,
by preserving the method of nature in the conduct of
the state, in what we improve we are never wholly new;
in what we retain we are never wholly obsolete. By ad-
hering in this manner and on those principles to our
forefathers, we are guided not by the superstition of
antiquarians, but by the spirit of philosophic analogy. In
this choice of inheritance we have given to our frame of
polity the image of a relation in blood; binding up the
constitution of our country with our dearest domestic
ties; adopting our fundamental laws into the bosom of
our family affections; keeping inseparable, and cherish-
ing with the warmth of all their combined and mutually
reflected charities, our state, our hearths, our sepul-
chres, and our altars. [Pp. 119–20]

In this important passage Burke claims that what are often thought of
as separate and distinct sides of life can be talked of in common terms,
and given a common relation, when they are understood in the language
of inheritance. For Burke community is founded on sentiment, and he
here asserts that a man can have much the same sentiments about his

family, his house, his church, and his government. These sentiments in each case include gratitude to the ancestors who gave shape and meaning to the world one has inherited, obligation to those who will come after, and a sense of humility at the mystery of the process of cultural and domestic creation and transmission in which one is engaged.[9] As he later puts it, "We begin our public affections in our families" (p. 315); and it is a measure of the unnatural chaos into which France has fallen that "nothing is left which engages the affections on the part of the commonwealth" (p. 172). When the world is constituted and understood in the British way, Burke tells us, our "liberty"—the subject of the earlier paragraph—becomes a "noble freedom" (p. 121).

As he later tells us, the idea of inheritance also gives rise to an ethic, that of the trustee; for under this view each of us is only a life-tenant in his property, subject to deep obligation to both the past and the future:

> But one of the first and most leading principles on
> which the commonwealth and the laws are consecrated,
> is lest the temporary possessors and life-renters in it,
> unmindful of what they have received from their ances-
> tors, or of what is due to their posterity, should act as if
> they were the entire masters; that they should not think
> it amongst their rights to cut off the entail, or commit
> waste on the inheritance, by destroying at their plea-
> sure the whole original fabric of their society; hazarding
> to leave to those who come after them, a ruin instead of
> an habitation—and teaching these successors as little
> to respect their contrivances, as they had themselves re-
> spected the institutions of their forefathers. By this un-
> principled facility of changing the state as often, and as
> much, and in as many ways as there are floating fancies
> or fashions, the whole chain and continuity of the com-
> monwealth would be broken. No one generation could
> link with the other. Men would become little better than
> the flies of a summer. [Pp. 192–93]

In this way, as Burke elsewhere says, the institution of property "tends . . . to the perpetuation of society itself" (p. 140). The natural feelings for one's children lead the parent to improve and conserve, and this of course has benefits that reach far beyond the family. Property thus "makes our weakness subservient to our virtue, it grafts benevolence even upon avarice" (p. 140). The feelings that lead a man to plant a forest that cannot be harvested for three generations, or to spend his capital to improve his irrigation in ways that cannot be recovered in crops for decades, or to make his property beautiful ("To make us love our country, our country ought to be lovely" [p. 172]) are "natural" in two ways: they naturally arise in the heart of a parent, and they lead to the improvement of the natural world. Thus the correspondence with the world of nature of which Burke speaks is not a mystical idea but an actual reality. The England of which Burke speaks is a garden—not a garden created by the will of man and imposed on nature but a garden tended by duty and by love. It is the great strength of the British Constitution that it can draw on such feelings as these and refine and complicate them; as Burke conceives it, the Constitution thus creates a public culture based on sentiments of veneration and trust, as a result of which nature itself, the land of England, which is its wealth, is improved and made beautiful.

IN THIS WAY Burke offers us a language that is at once extraordinarily simple, in its essential imagery and method, and remarkably complex, for it is naturally connected with ways of speaking about the most complicated social and ethical realities. In terms that remind one of Coleridge's definition of beauty, we can say of Burke's language what he says of the British Constitution itself, that it achieves a remarkable "unity" amidst enormous "diversity." The central characteristic of this language, like the language of Samuel Johnson but on a larger scale, is its integrative force: it is a language that unites fact, value, and reason; thought and emotion; the family and the crown; the social and the natural worlds; ethical motives and material results. It has an integrative force not only in the political and social world but in the reader himself, for Burke addresses him not merely as a fellow subject or as a political philosopher but as a parent, child, farmer, landlord, church member, tenant, voter, and so on—as *all* the things that he is. And the integration of the reader is internal as well as external, for Burke speaks not merely to his intellectual side, or to his emotional side, but to him as whole mind and person, ready to think, to feel, and to act.

As Samuel Johnson turned cliché into principle by a process of complication, insisting on correspondence with the conditions of the world, so Burke offers his reader a language that similarly defeats cliché by complication, distinction, and composition. This is meant to be a language of generality to which the reader may turn from any of the activities of life in order to claim a meaning for what he does and to connect it with the rest of life; it is truly a constitutional language. This text thus creates a central place or platform from which the world can be viewed as a whole, as Book 24 of the *Iliad* does. But unlike that poem this text is a part of the world it criticizes; indeed, it is intended to become the basis for its change and preservation.

The Constitutional Process

In the world presented by Burke, human life is not static but active, and its essential enterprise is the cultural activity of maintaining, improving, and transmitting our inheritance: our land, our church, our government, our language, and our culture. But exactly how are these things to be done? How is one to make the language of the British Constitution one's own so that one may use it to describe and judge events in the world, to make appeals to others, and so on? How is one to participate in the cultural and constitutional processes by which this language, and the rest of one's world, are to be maintained and improved?

Reciprocity

These questions are made both more difficult and more important by Burke's central perception that the relation between self and culture is not instrumental but reciprocal. In his view we are in large measure constituted by the very culture it is our task to maintain and improve. Therefore, the kind of "ownership" that this text seeks to establish in its reader is not the mere claiming of title or the assertion of a right to possession, as of an object; rather, it is an engagement in a process by which both the individual and the culture are continually remade. This is true not only of the "ownership" of the constitutional language itself but of "ownerships" far more specific in kind. The holder of clerical or political office, the landowner or employer, for example, "owns" far more than an asset; he is possessed of a set of duties and opportunities for action in relation to others, in the proper discharge of which both he himself and his culture will be formed and defined.

This sense of reciprocity is implicit in Burke's own aim in this text; for it is his object to affect his culture by affecting his readers, to work changes in individuals that will lead to changes in the community. These changes, to mean anything, must in turn result in changes in people's individual lives, in their perceptions and sentiments and thoughts, in their actual character. To put it in explicitly political terms, the mystery of public life is that the government receives its character in part from the people, the people in part from the government, and the art of politics is understanding and managing this reciprocal process.

As an example of the reciprocal relation between self and culture, consider Burke's account of the first national legislature in France. He begins by restating the calamitous consequences of what has happened in France:

> [The French have rebelled] against a mild and lawful
> monarch, with more fury, outrage, and insult, than ever
> any people has been known to rise against the most ille-
> gal usurper, or the most sanguinary tyrant. Their re-
> sistance was made to concession; their revolt was from
> protection; their blow was aimed at an hand holding out
> graces, favours, and immunities.
>
> This was unnatural. The rest is in order. They have
> found their punishment in their success. Laws over-
> turned; tribunals subverted; industry without vigour;
> commerce expiring; the revenue unpaid, yet the people
> impoverished; a church pillaged, and a state not re-
> lieved; civil and military anarchy made the constitution
> of the kingdom. [P. 126]

The French decisions that produced these consequences were not "necessary," Burke tells us, but an "unforced choice, this fond election of evil"
(p. 127). In saying this he implicitly asks, Why has the National Assembly
behaved this way?

He finds his explanation in the character of its members, who were for
the most part lawyers of the least distinguished sort. Who could expect
anything great from men "who are habitually meddling, daring, subtle,
active, of litigious dispositions and unquiet minds"? Was it to be expected, for example, "that they would attend to the stability of property,
whose existence had always depended upon whatever rendered property
questionable, ambiguous, and insecure?" (p. 131). The rest of the Assembly—the lower clergy, doctors, speculators—are for the most part no better, and what has happened to France is simply the natural consequence
of putting "the supreme authority" in the "hands of men not taught habitually to respect themselves" (p. 130).

In this way Burke locates the cause of destruction not in the structure
of government but in the characters of men, not in the "constitution" of
the assembly—though it is "exceptionable enough"—but in what he
calls "the materials of which in a great measure it is composed, which is
of ten thousand times greater consequence than all the formalities in the
world" (p. 127). But the character of these men has in turn been formed,
as Burke here makes plain, by their education, their circumstances, and
their habits of life.[10] Burke thus does not see the cause of events—of
structure, of circumstance—simply in men's characters, nor does he see
human character as simply determined by externals. He imagines instead a reciprocal relationship between self and culture, which can work
to good ends or bad. When it works well, as it does under his "British Constitution," we find good men in positions of authority, capable of conserv-

ing what is best in what they have inherited and of reforming whatever is defective; such men maintain and improve a constitution that tends to produce, and place in authority, other men of similar ability and virtue, and so on (p. 132). When it works badly, as it does in "France," deterioration of culture leads to deterioration of character, and vice versa, in a constantly accelerating movement of dissolution. This is what Burke means when he says, "Man [is] . . . in a great degree a creature of his own making" (p. 189).

In a passage that will remind the reader of Thucydides on the effects of civil war, Burke describes the deterioration of language caused by the French Revolution:

> In these meetings of all sorts, every counsel, in pro-
> portion as it is daring, and violent, and perfidious, is
> taken for the mark of superior genius. Humanity and
> compassion are ridiculed as the fruits of superstition
> and ignorance. Tenderness to individuals is considered
> as treason to the public. Liberty is always to be esti-
> mated perfect as property is rendered insecure. [Pp.
> 160–61][11]

What kind of character should one expect to be formed by an education such as that?

Rights

But Burke has still not explained why these men were chosen for the assembly. For his explanation, he fixes on a general attitude or value among the French, namely, their doctrinaire insistence on attempting to "equalize" men: "you think you are combating prejudice, but you are at war with nature" (p. 138). This is for Burke one of the "false rights of man" established by the French: false because impossible—some will be uppermost, whatever we claim—and impossible because totally abstract.

The "French" method of talking about rights and duties is to posit a world of atomized individuals, to imagine ideal relations among them, and then to declare that these ideal relations exist, or will exist, as if all that were required to make them real were a simple act of will or power. The "British" method, by contrast, is to regard the constitution not as a set of theoretical political relations but, in the first instance at least, as the relations that in fact exist both among individuals and between individuals and their government and culture. In talking about rights, Burke thus begins with the actual conditions of life, in which all people are parts of cultures, families, and nations and all people start as dependent on others

211

and then grow slowly into their lives in the world, for well or ill; at the best, they are *educated* for it. They will have tasks and families of their own, motives and cares, political and economic relations, all intertwined and in all of this they are at once being formed by their world and forming it. The true rights of Englishmen are thus to be found not in declarations but in facts: in the moral and material "advantages" of their common life, including their wise "restraints" (pp. 149, 151). Our constitution is what we are, not a set of rights we wish we had. To proceed abstractly—which for many people is to be most rational—is for Burke to proceed irrationally and destructively.

Prejudices

But how is one to proceed "nonabstractly," as it were? Burke's most important response is his own performance in this text, in his reconstitution of his language and his world; but he is explicit on this question too, and he tells us that the answer is to look not to what the French call "rights" or theories but rather to what he calls "prejudices."[12] By this he means the inner condition corresponding to the existence of rights—like the rights of Englishmen—that are real, not merely theoretical: the deepest commitments of self to community.

> You see, Sir, that in this enlightened age I am bold enough to confess, that we are men of untaught feelings; that instead of casting away all our old prejudices, we cherish them to a very considerable degree, and, to take more shame to ourselves, we cherish them because they are prejudices; and the longer they have lasted, and the more generally they have prevailed, the more we cherish them. We are afraid to put men to live and trade each on his own private stock of reason; because we suspect that this stock in each man is small, and that the individuals would do better to avail themselves of the general bank and capital of nations, and of ages. Many of our men of speculation, instead of exploding general prejudices, employ their sagacity to discover the latent wisdom which prevails in them. If they find what they seek, and they seldom fail, they think it more wise to continue the prejudice, with the reason involved, than to cast away the coat of prejudice, and to leave nothing but the naked reason; because prejudice, with its reason, has a motive to give action to that reason, and an affection which will give it permanence.

> Prejudice is of ready application in the emergency; it
> previously engages the mind in a steady course of wis-
> dom and virtue, and does not leave the man hesitating
> in the moment of decision, sceptical, puzzled, and unre-
> solved. Prejudice renders a man's virtue his habit; and
> not a series of unconnected acts. Through just preju-
> dice, his duty becomes a part of his nature. [P. 183]

For Burke "prejudice" is thus a term of integration; it unites reason, motive, and affection, the self and the community, one's best instincts and one's habits, one's character and one's conduct. From all of this—the reciprocal interaction of self and culture, the necessarily specific character of meaningful talk about "rights," the establishment of character in the form of "prejudices"—Burke's central explicit political thesis arises and is made meaningful: that in modifying our arrangements, or in acting within them, we should proceed with constant reference to what we actually have, to what we actually are, lest, in our eagerness to see our ideas and theories made real, we destroy the organization of life that alone can give reality to what we value.[13]

We thus learn that the "English" have prejudices—the feelings that arise naturally in men who have been formed by a coherent culture that is itself consistent with the nature of the world—and that the "French" do not, for they operate either on the basis of theory or by the chaotic and unformed impulses of passion. But what kind of prejudices do the English have? What is the British Constitution that is supported by such sentiments?

Religion: The Language of Sacrament

Burke tells us: "We are resolved to keep an established church, an established monarchy, an established aristocracy, and an established democracy, each in the degree it exists, and in no greater. I shall shew you presently how much of each of these we possess" (p. 188).

Of these constitutional prejudices, the first, in favor of the establishment of religion, is Burke's most important, and it is also the most difficult for the modern American to comprehend, since our own prejudices run so strongly the other way. But for Burke the established church is the cornerstone of the British Constitution: "We know, and what is better we feel inwardly, that religion is the basis of civil society, and the source of all good and of all comfort" (p. 186). For the "English people" the establishment of their church is "not . . . convenient, but . . . essential," and in their minds the ideas of "church and state are . . . inseparable" (p. 198).

How does Burke define the connection between church and state that he celebrates? For him the establishment of religion is nothing less than the "consecration of government." It civilizes and ennobles power by teaching those in positions of authority to "have high and worthy notions of their function and destination." Religion teaches them that their "hope should be full of immortality; that they should not look to the paltry pelf of the moment, nor to the temporary and transient praise of the vulgar, but to a solid, permanent existence, in the permanent part of their nature, and to a permanent fame and glory, in the example they leave as a rich inheritance to the world" (p. 189). Religion is one source of the central idea that "all persons possessing any portion of power . . . act in trust," and it is by religion that they know that "they are to account for their conduct in that trust to the one great master, author and founder of society" (p. 190).

In a democracy in particular, religion will help to impress it on the people that no more than the will of kings can the "will" of the people be the "standard of right and wrong." They may exact from their servants and officers "an entire devotion to their interest, which is their right," but, so long as religion has force, never "an abject submisssion to their occasional will; extinguishing thereby, in all those who serve them, all moral principle, all sense of dignity, all use of judgment, and all consistency of character" (p. 191).

For Burke the establishment of religion incorporates into the constitution itself a way in which the community can talk about right and wrong, better and worse, under a permanent standard of justice and humanity. It is the church that maintains a language of character and conduct, of goodness and propriety—of religious manners and prejudices—by which the actions of men in power can be defined, checked, and encouraged; it is a central language of motive and meaning. The church provides, as it were, the second voice that is essential to any conversation if it is to engage fundamentals. In this way the political community of the British Constitution is also a religious community.

If the church is to do these things—instruct the powerful, control them, and set them an example of charity and goodness—it must have power and authority of its own. It cannot be dependent on the crown or on any other person or class. It must have its own rights and its own property.

Burke has thus connected religion and property in two rather practical ways: by founding religion on property and by uniting the religious and legal ideas of trust. This is a performance of the integration of life that his constitution promises us, and in the following passage he carries this process further, restating the position of his inheritance passage (quoted above, pp. 205–6) in new terms:

214

Society is indeed a contract. Subordinate contracts
for objects of mere occasional interest may be dissolved
at pleasure—but the state ought not to be considered as
nothing better than a partnership agreement in a trade
of pepper and coffee, callico or tobacco, or some other
such low concern, to be taken up for a little temporary
interest, and to be dissolved by the fancy of the parties.
It is to be looked on with other reverence; because it is
not a partnership in things subservient only to the gross
animal existence of a temporary and perishable nature.
It is a partnership in all science; a partnership in all art;
a partnership in every virtue, and in all perfection. As
the ends of such a partnership cannot be obtained in
many generations, it becomes a partnership not only between those who are living, but between those who are
living, those who are dead, and those who are to be
born. Each contract of each particular state is but a
clause in the great primaeval contract of eternal society,
linking the lower with the higher natures, connecting
the visible and invisible world, according to a fixed compact sanctioned by the inviolable oath which holds all
physical and all moral natures, each in their appointed
place. [Pp. 194–95]

In this paragraph Burke completes the fusion of his languages into
one. He has already defined "property" by connecting it with liberty, with
the rights of man, with the transmission of knowledge and wisdom from
one generation to the next, with the sentiments of benevolence that lead
a man to preserve and improve what he has, with the ethic of trust that
naturally arises out of inherited property, and with the loyalties and affections that run from the private home to the legislature and to the crown of
the kingdom. Here it is expanded to include commerce, contract, and partnership and becomes an image of connection itself: among men, among
generations, between man and nature, and between man and God.

Religion has been seen as the standard of judgment, external to the
self, that may lead a man or government to act rightly; as inspiring a
sense of humility, gratitude, and obligation; as establishing an ethic of
trust in those who hold power; as creating the community of people and
of interest that can make a nation; as the final source of meaning in life.
When the two ideas of property and religion are united, as they are here,
there is an extraordinary merger of languages into one, a new constitution of language and thought. Not only religion and property but art and

science and virtue and commerce, the family and the crown—all parts of life—are merged into a coherent whole. In the central claim of the paragraph, that the "contract" is part of a larger contract, "connecting the visible and invisible world," the community itself becomes a sacrament; in the language of the Book of Common Prayer, to which Burke alludes, it is the "outward and visible sign of an inward and spiritual grace."

In this sense Burke's own text is religious, too; for it seeks to define a way of talking by which the ordinary enterprises of life, from farming to elections to commerce, can be understood, organized, and guided; that is, it aims to make a discourse, above or beyond that of ordinary speech, to which one may turn for the attitudes and standards by which the reciprocal processes of constitution and reconstitution may be governed. Without such a discourse, without such a "religious constitution," men would be subject to internal and external processes of change over which they had no control. They would be little more than the "flies of a summer." [14]

France

Having spoken of the church, Burke abandons his plan to speak of the other parts of the British Constitution and turns his attention, instead, to France. In the remaining portion of his text he tells the story of its dissolution. His basic premise remains the interconnectedness of life. He has just shown us how everything can be combined into a "British Constitution" of life and health and growth; now he shows us how, in a "French Revolution," disorder can spread throughout the social organism in an irresistible course of dissolution.

He begins with the French parallel to the establishment of religion he has just been celebrating: the confiscation of church lands, ostensibly to pay the public debt. In the language that Burke has by now established, this confiscation—the direct opposite of establishment—is at once a sacrilege, a destruction of the constitution, and wild irrationality; it is a social *monstrum* by which the French destroy their own community, without justice and to no gain. It is a crime against education and charity, against learning, against dignity, and against the poor. He then speaks of the central institutions of the state. The National Assembly is founded on an impossible attempt to equalize votes by using inconsistent bases (territory, population, and wealth); this system destroys the representation of the country as a whole, replacing it with a competition among the districts. The king has been degraded; everything is still done in his name, but he has no powers to act or to veto, to reward or to punish. Judges are elected; they are men without learning and ignorant of the law. The army is without discipline, for its soldiers have learned the lessons of the revolutionaries and expect to elect their officers and to govern themselves. Finally,

216

the financial system is bankrupt, based, as it is, on the double crimes of confiscation and compulsory paper currency. Thus are destroyed the church, the nobility, the courts, the parliaments, the laws, the religion, the army, the agriculture, the commerce, the wealth, and the happiness of France.

Making and Remaking Language

Burke's purpose in the *Reflections* is not to communicate ideas that are already perfectly statable in existing languages but to make a language in which new ideas and new sentiments can be expressed, a new constitution established, in the text and in the world: a language he wishes his reader first to learn and then to own and use. It is essential to his purpose that this language be literary in character, not "theoretical." In reading this text, one cannot extract a word from its context, give it a stipulative meaning, and then place it in a statement of abstract theory without doing violence to Burke's text and mind and to our experience of both. Each word is attached by a dozen strings to other words (as we quickly see when we try to isolate one for analysis), and each of these, in turn, is similarly connected with other words. Moreover, every one of these combinations has its own weight of association and tradition behind it. Thus, as I earlier suggested, "property" and "religion" are as inextricably linked in Burke's language as they are (in his view) in the world, and that world is itself, in part, the creation of his text.

As another example of the way Burke gives meaning to his words by use and association, consider the definition of "toleration" achieved in the following passage:

> We hear these new teachers continually boasting of
> their spirit of toleration. That those persons should tol-
> erate all opinions, who think none to be of estimation, is
> a matter of small merit. Equal neglect is not impartial
> kindness. The species of benevolence, which arises
> from contempt, is no true charity. There are in England
> abundance of men who tolerate in the true spirit of tol-
> eration. They think the dogmas of religion, though in
> different degrees, are all of moment; that amongst them
> there is, as amongst all things of value, a just ground of
> preference. They favour, therefore, and they tolerate.
> They tolerate, not because they despise opinions, but
> because they respect justice. [Pp. 258–59]

This definition of "toleration" is not substitutive in character, assert-ing, as a dictionary often does, an equivalence between one word and some other word or words, but performative. Like Johnson's definitions, it works by using the key word in combination with other important words in sentences that establish contrast, connection, and hierarchy, and this makes all of these words available in a new way. To say that toleration is not a species of contempt but of justice is to define not one but all three terms, especially when it is observed that "justice" is at work on both sides of the equation: the preference is "just," as is the toleration. This is a complex and important achievement. And this passage and its key word "toleration" acquire additional significance from other passages in the text as a whole: from, for example, the early paragraph on liberty (above, pp. 200–201), or the passage in which Burke mocks Dr. Price's "curious zeal," "not for the propagation of his own opinions, but of any opinions . . . . Let the noble teachers but dissent, it is no matter from whom or from what" (p. 95). In such ways Burke's text exemplifies in its language the same "excellence in composition" that the "British Constitution" he intends to define and celebrate exemplifies in the political world. His definition of "toleration" becomes a part of the definition of an idea even more complex, even less restateable: that of the British Constitution itself.[15]

The form of the text is literary, too. It does not have the linear structure appropriate to abstract intellectual argument. Instead, it is circular or spiraling in shape. The reader finds himself returning again and again to the same questions, but on each new encounter he finds them transformed by the text that defines them. This text moves not by proof and demonstration, from proposition to proposition, but through a process of repetition and transformation, and the language thus made becomes more complete and more familiar. This means that the reader is not asked to move from one general proposition to another, checking fact against fact, logic against logic; instead, he is immersed in a world like the real world, in which judgments of fact and reason and value are continuous and where the questions that are asked are not merely general and not merely particular but both at once, as questions of statesmanship and citizenship always are. Burke starts where life starts, with the world as it is, and he speaks a language of description and feeling and judgment, a language for movement and life within the world he creates. To make one's way in the world this text creates, one must learn its language. That is how it teaches.[16]

In such ways as these Burke in this text offers his reader a "British Constitution" that is at once a version of the world that is England and a way of maintaining and improving it, since for him "constitution" has the force not only of a noun but of a verb: it is a structure of relations that includes the method of its own change, an activity in which we all engage. And since this activity is necessarily individual in character, the

"British Constitution" of which Burke writes, and which he wishes to improve and to perpetuate, is in its deepest form internal (as well as external) to the reader; it is a way of making and remaking identity and community through language.

TEXTUAL AND POLITICAL COMMUNITY IN THE *Reflections*

At the beginning of this chapter I suggested that Burke, like Jane Austen, is interested in the establishment of community but on an altogether different scale. Her interest is in various forms of individual friendship; Burke's is in the constitution of a nation. He wishes his text to contribute to the formation of a political community among people who will "own" the British Constitution that he defines and exemplifies and will "disown" the French Revolution, not only in their reading of his text but in their lives. We are now in a position to pursue directly the questions we raised at the outset and have since been addressing only obliquely: What kind of community does this text actually establish with its reader? What kind of community does it seek to establish in the world? And what is the relationship between these two communities? In particular, to what degree can either be called a community of friendship?

WITH RESPECT TO the textual community, we can judge the *Reflections* by the standards established by our earlier reading. Does Burke's text, for example—like Swift's—recognize the independence of the reader as a source of meaning and language and address him as one who must make his own sense of things? Does it—like Johnson's—teach him the motions of the mind by which language and self can be reconstituted, so that he may work and live at the level of principle, not at the level of commonplace? Does it—like Jane Austen's—engage him in a community of reciprocal and responsive action, of conversational friendship? Is this text, like a Platonic dialogue, "dialectical" and mutually educative in its relationship with its reader, or is it "rhetorical" and manipulative? Finally, to return to perhaps the deepest of our definitions of friendship, can we say that it recognizes, as Homer teaches us to do, the common humanity of all people? No text could do all of these things, or do them equally well, but these questions suggest some ways of judging the community Burke establishes with his reader. One may well wonder whether a text as stridently persuasive in purpose as this can possibly meet these tests of friendship.

As for the "British Constitution" that Burke defines and recommends, exactly the same questions can be asked of it. Does this Constitution recognize the citizen's independence of mind and language, his freedom as a source of meaning and action? Does it offer him an education and a context by virtue of which his thought and life may have the coherence and depth of principle, not commonplace? Does it establish with him a reciprocal community, to which he can contribute in ways beyond prediction? Does it engage him dialectically instead of seeking to manipulate him rhetorically? Does it recognize the common humanity of all people? The reader may well think that a constitution as fundamentally antidemocratic as Burke's cannot possibly meet the suggested standards.

There is also the question of continuity. What is the relationship between the textual community Burke creates and the political community he seeks to form? Can we say, for example, that the clearest and deepest definition of the British Constitution he means to recommend is its enactment in the relationship he establishes with his reader? Some such congruence between the two communities is essential if the reader is to turn, as Burke seems to intend, from the text to the world without a break, if he is to use in life the language Burke offers him in the text. But how can there be such a continuity when the *textual* community is between two while the *public* constitution comprises millions? If there is no such continuity, what is the relationship between the two worlds that Burke defines?

In this connection it may be helpful to think once again of the work of Plato. The central value of the *Gorgias* is the dialectical relationship achieved in different ways in Socrates' relationship with his interlocutors and in Plato's relationship with us, the readers of his text. But to generalize from the textual or individual community to the political world was a step Plato could not take. The ideal states described in the *Republic* and presented in the *Laws* are polities of radical inequality in which some men act wisely for the benefit of others. The intense and necessarily equal friendship of dialectic has no political parallel, at least not beyond a certain class. Is the same thing true of Burke? Or is there a kind of continuity between his textual and political communities that Plato did not seem to imagine as a possibility?

We shall address these questions, but it is important, first, to note the significance of the fact that they can be asked at all. That the questions we have been asking of Johnson and Austen can also be asked of Burke, and asked in virtually identical form of both the textual and the political communities he establishes, means that the literary questions we have from the beginning been asking of our texts can now be seen to be political questions as well. This is so in part because the literature we have been studying is a literature of friendship and because the central value of friendship—the recognition of others and the establishment of educative and reciprocal relations—can be stated as the central values of law and government too. The language of liberty and property, for example, can be seen as a language by which the self is recognized, defined, and given a basis for action; law can be regarded as a way of creating a world in which reason and action are possible; and the activities of self-government can be both participatory and reciprocal. If all this is so, our concerns with language, self, and the world, with text and culture—with "law" and "literature"—can be seen as one, and they point us toward a politics of friendship.

The Textual Community

Our question can be put in a familiar Platonic way: the *Reflections* is at its heart a rhetorical text, of which the design is to persuade. How then can its relation with us be one of friendship?

I

In thinking about this, we must first see that in this text there is no problem with insincerity of the sort that characterizes certain forms of rhetoric, such as the adman's pitch or the claims of the propagandist, in which the speaker advances every plausible reason, whether he believes it or not, to support a conclusion he has reached on other grounds. Burke is offering us the fullest possible statement of what he actually thinks and feels and why he really thinks it is in the interest of others to think and feel in the same way. Indeed, it is the very sincerity of some of his passages—the apostrophe to Marie Antoinette, say, or his description of the members of the National Assembly as acting like crazed and drunken players at a carnival[17]—that is the source of their embarrassment for us. The difficulty is not that Burke is insincere but that in his sincerity he offers us, as though it were real, a false or sentimental caricature we can accept only as a cartoon. There is no question of ulterior manipulation here or of acting to injure.

Moreover, in important respects this text actually is dialectical in character or at least refutational, for it breaks down an impossible language of slogans, making it impossible for the careful reader ever to talk that way again. In this it is rather like Swift's *Tale*, which breaks down the reader's disposition to cliché, and like Johnson's essays, which are a constant lesson in complication and difficulty. The language that Burke does want his reader to adopt is no mere set of propositions or collection of maxims or slogans[18] but a language in the fullest sense, which the reader must make his own if he is to use it at all. And to address one's reader as a learner and maker of language is necessarily to recognize his independence, his liberty, and his potentiality as a source of meaning.

Also, as we have seen, Burke repeatedly insists on addressing the reader not merely in his intellectual or affective or literary or political aspect but in all his aspects at once, as a whole person, capable of putting all his resources to work together; and this insistence by its nature works as a kind of education. The text addresses simultaneously the reader's intellect and feelings, his sense of history and his imagination; it speaks to him as a parent and educator; as one who has a profession and a religion, a home and a country; as one who can perceive differences in tone and manner; as one who lives in time, from infancy to old age and death; as one who belongs to a family whose members are constantly changing. It addresses the reader as knowing all that he knows about himself and his world. All this helps the reader attain a version of himself in which all his resources are for the moment at work together. This will happen, of course, only if the reader himself feels the multiple appeals and acknowledges their force and value; but, once this has happened, it will be hard, perhaps impossible, for him to accept any language that fails to meet its standards, that asks him to forget what he knows of the world, himself, and his language.

A complementary point is that Burke's text resists conversion into theory. To try to reduce it to a theoretical scheme, to a philosophy with an ordinary conceptual and schematic structure, is to destroy its life. The frustration of the reader's attempts to do that educates him in the fundamental conditions of political life and language. In both of these ways, then—in its definition of its audience and of its own voice—this text offers its reader an engagement that acknowledges and enhances his autonomy. In doing this, it offers him the particular kind of friendship that consists in helping another become more fully what he is.

II

But it remains true that Burke's aim in this text is to persuade his reader to his view of the world, to his sentiments and his language, and these are not held out for criticism or refutation. Our function is to join him in the cooperative enterprise he has defined but to do so on his terms. Burke may genuinely believe that it is best for us to do this, but what if we do not? Such a reader is conceived as a kind of enemy: if you are not with this text, you are against it. Reinforcing this impression is the violence of feeling that Burke directs against his enemies, caricaturing them to destruction, a violence the reader must himself feel as a threat, and a repugnant one. For us, all of this presents an especially acute problem, since the position to which Burke wishes so vehemently to direct us seems to be one we cannot imagine adopting: we are asked to admire the inherited privileges and the restricted franchise of the British Constitution.

The Political Community

How can one possibly claim that the political community this text is intended to establish—which accepts, among other things, inherited inequalities among men, restriction of the suffrage to men of property, and extreme inequality in representation—is a community of friendship? To use the test suggested by the *Iliad*, it seems difficult to claim that Burke's "British Constitution" recognizes the common humanity of all people. Listen to this:

> Good order is the foundation of all good things. To be enabled to acquire [i.e., for the society to build up wealth and capital], the people, without being servile, must be tractable and obedient. The magistrate must have his reverence, the laws their authority. The body of the people must not find the principles of natural subordination by art rooted out of their minds. They must respect that property of which they cannot partake. They must labour to obtain what by labour can be obtained; and when they find, as they commonly do, the success disproportioned to the endeavour, they must be taught their consolation in the final proportions of eternal justice. Of this consolation, whoever deprives them, deadens their industry, and strikes at the root of all acquisition as of conservation. [P. 372]

The modern American will naturally be inclined to reject such politics out of hand as being directly at odds with our most basic commitments to equality and democracy. One can hear the self-congratulatory tones arising in oneself. But such a response, however natural or inevitable for us, is not an adequate or a complete response. A closer reading will show, I think, that Burke's text itself provides an important way of understanding our response by placing it in a larger context.

I

We can start with our feeling of moral superiority. Our pride in our commitment to equality needs to be reminded, among other things, that suffrage was far from universal in the early United States even among men—even among men of European descent—and that one large part of the nation was held in chattel slavery by another. Even today it is hard to see what the rhetoric of equality means in practice: equality in income? wealth? education? health? Certainly none of these. We do not in fact believe in the equal distribution of social goods. So in what equality do we believe? A chance to run an equal race, but with staggeringly unequal handicaps? On the basis of our conduct, not our professions, it may seem that what we actually mean by equality—apart from the prohibition of certain odious forms of affirmative discrimination—is the equal right to participate in the process of self-government, which rests on the equal right to vote.

These are indeed rights that Burke's Constitution denies to many of its members, but it is not entirely clear what the actual effect of our equality or his inequality may be. If we use the test of the acknowledgment of the common humanity of man, for example, Burke would insist that it is in fact the signal excellence of the British Constitution that it establishes a true sense of "common-ness," or community, among men, even among generations of men. The British Constitution enriches what it means to be a human being, for it meets the deepest need of man, which is for a coherent culture. The French Revolution, by contrast, reduces man to the status of an isolated creature, without community; for it destroys the culture that alone makes meaning and value possible. Burke's British Constitution offers his fellow subject (what his text offers its reader) a way of defining a world of meaning, and a place for oneself within it, that adequately responds to what one knows of the world and knows of oneself. It creates a vocabulary for thought and speech and action of a kind that is simply impossible in a cultural vacuum such as that of "France." One can be a lawyer, for example, or a judge, or a litigant, one can complain about injustice, or resent it, or write a poem or play about it, only where there is an established language of law and justice. One can in a meaningful sense be a proprietor of land, or of liberty, or of other rights of man only where one's holding is secure. One can act with meaning only where meanings exist. The British Constitution not only recognizes the liberty of the subject; it enhances it into a "noble freedom" by giving it a set of useful and valuable objects and by establishing a field in which action can be meaningful, dignified, and truly powerful.

Burke's British Constitution recognizes the individual's liberty in another way, for it absolutely depends on his responsible and active exercise of that liberty. The Constitution is not, after all, self-executing; it requires the energies of individual men stimulated to act within its terms. It continually needs—what it also makes possible—intelligent and wise performance of the central cultural activity exemplified by this text: conservation, improvement, and transmission. What this Constitution asks of its members, this text of its reader, is not acquiescence but participation—and always of an individual kind.

If by the phrase "the common humanity of man" is meant sympathy for the needs and sufferings of others, Burke stands, if possible, on even firmer ground; for his Constitution contributes to the material welfare and security of society, the French Revolution to its poverty and imperilment.

Burke's insistence on thinking of a constitution in practical rather than theoretical terms (see, e.g., pp. 152–55) leads us to ask what it can mean for the "French," or for Americans, to declare allegiance to the "rights of man" if the rights are not both real and effective and combined with the other things a person needs from his community. The Soviet Union has a Bill of Rights that on paper looks very little different from our own; the difference is not in the rights declared but in the *actual* constitution, the community of understandings and expectations of which they are a part. What is more, even where rights are effectively established, it is foolish to talk, as perhaps we often do, as if the proper bundle of legal rights automatically produces a happy community—as if Sweden must be more fortunate than Portugal—for in fact, of course, prosperity and felicity, public happiness and even liberty itself are much more complex than that. One would not judge universities on such a ground; we would not, for example, declare one to be better than another simply because it had more complete faculty democracy or student democracy, even if one strongly believed in democratic university government. Nor would one presume to judge any other human organization in such a way: a law firm, a business, a medical partnership, a family, a school, a church, or a union. Why then so judge a nation? Not that the legal structure in any of these cases is irrelevant—far from it—but it is not everything; and to talk as if it were is to reduce man to his political aspect, to his "rights," in a silly and unreal way. It is not enough simply to say that all of us now have the vote while only some Englishmen had it then; one must ask, what do those facts mean?[19]

II

In response to that question, one might say something like this. For us the vote is essential to our sense of participation in our government, of belonging to our world. It is the mark of full citizenship, the key to the identification of the self with the public culture that is necessary to the formation of a community for which people will work and sacrifice, even fight and die. It is the basis of our sense that each of us is actually represented in our government. It is deeply related to our great talent for self-government in every part of life—in condominium associations, block groups, water districts, betterment associations, and so forth. For us the vote is tied to our idea that each person is equal under the law, entitled to equal justice and equal liberty. We should never give it up.

But we should also reflect that the vote alone may not always, in every context, have all these beneficial consequences, which depend very much on the nature of the community as a whole, on what Burke would call the constitution of the nation. In another place or time, one might feel that one's vote was too tiny to have any real meaning, or that none of the available choices of candidates or policies reflected one's views or character, or that the whole process was ineffective. Think, for example, of the meaning of the vote in certain newly emerging nations, or in such countries as Italy today, or among those in our own population who have the vote but not the sense of equal participation it is meant to entail. Conversely, it is imaginable, or ought to be, that one could have a sense of common identity and action, of belonging and participating, indeed of representation, without universal suffrage or the vote at all. Think of life in our own army in World War II, for example, or in modern China, as described by some, or perhaps in the British Constitution of which Burke speaks.[20]

THE SOMEWHAT self-congratulatory American response to this text proves to be the expression of a simple impulse to act on a simple value. As it works itself out over time, this impulse can become an insistence on that value at all costs, in which case it will lead to a position inevitably detached from the complications and realities of life; it will become what Burke would call a revolutionary impulse leading to dissolution. Or it can be combined with other considerations, chastened by reality as it were, and become part of a complex social and psychological constitution. It is one purpose of Burke's text to address such basic impulses and, educating them by complication, to convert them into principles on which rational action can be based. For the modern reader of Burke is not asked by this text to give up his claim for the central importance of the vote or his use of the language of equality but to see these things for what they are: the "prejudices" or deep commitments that lie at the heart of our own constitution.

III

To become full members of the audience Burke wishes to create in this text, it is essential, then, for us to recognize our own prejudices for what they are and to value them appropriately. Burke is not telling us, or any of his non-English readers, to have a House of Lords, an established church, a reduced suffrage, or any other particular thing on the grounds that it is by nature essential to any government worthy of the name or superior to any alternative. His aim is a more general one: to affect the attitudes and understandings with which we proceed when we seek to alter our form of government, indeed, whenever we administer the forms we have. And his first object is to bring us to see that behind all the theoretical talk of government and legitimacy, behind the systems and projects, behind even the forms of government itself, there is a culture, a living organization of mankind, upon which all the talk of system and mechanism depends, both for its intelligibility and for its effects, and without which there would be nothing but the chaos of Paris or of Corcyra. In whatever we do we must respect the reality of that culture. It is what we are in fact. In all its complexity and interconnectedness it is our substantive and actual constitution. This is the constitution we threaten or promise to change when we adopt a new structure of government; we ought therefore to proceed with great caution and humility, recognizing that we can understand only a little of what we are and of what we seek to change. It is literally irrational—unreasoning—to proceed like the French reformers, who construct a theoretical government in a hypothetical world and talk as if it could be made real by a simple act of will or power.

In all of this, Burke addresses a universal audience, for he speaks to any people who are engaged in the process of self-constitution (and that is all people), and he tells them above all to respect what they are. We can have no quarrel with this, or so I say, because Burke here is so close to our own best principles and practices that he can in a sense speak for us as well as to us; and he does so rightfully, for he has in fact contributed much to the attitudes that define us.[21]

IV

When we turn from constitution as activity to constitution as structure, we find, as I suggest above, that Burke's position is unacceptable on the most fundamental grounds. But even here he has much to teach us, for it is the nature of his text, as I have just tried to demonstrate, both to activate our prejudices and to engage us in a process by which they are clarified, complicated, and disciplined. This means, to return to our earlier question, that there is an additional sense in which this text is a friend to its reader, even to the reader who disagrees with it profoundly; for it helps him become more fully what he actually is, as an individual and as a member of his culture, and this is an act of friendship and recognition. And it is not only the modern American in whom Burke may activate prejudices contrary to his own (which he might cheerfully enough allow) but the contemporary Englishman, to whom Burke would (if he could) prohibit them. For the Englishman who sees himself and his world as differently constituted from the way Burke represents them may obey the primary command of the text, to function out of what you are, in ways that are inconsistent with its more specific claims. In this way the text may be a friend, though a conflicted and imperfect one, against its own surface intention.

Even the violence and extravagance of the writing do not destroy this point but in a way confirm it. The forces of hatred, caricature, and destruction that Burke exemplifies are forces of nature of the kind that it is the function of a "constitution" to organize and put to work in a productive way; the function of "dissolution" is to loose them upon the world to produce a kind of chaos. Burke's own violence is a demonstration of the importance, the necessity, of the kind of constitution he exemplifies and recommends. It is from his caricatures and exaggeration, his love of his own hatred, for example, that the reader must understand what he means when he says that "restraints" may properly be included among one's "rights" (p. 151). In an important sense the "French Revolution" Burke so violently opposes is in fact most clearly located not in his description of it but in the very violence of his opposition to it. On this view the true "British Constitution" celebrated here is not the way of life he defends with such violence but the composition that contains both the principle of order and the principle of disorder to such a marked degree. And, for Burke himself, something like this was actually true of the real British Constitution, within which he worked as a reforming politician; it provided the context in which his violent and destructive impulses (as well as his more constructive ones) could work to the good of the community, not to its harm. It is not surprising, then, that Burke defends this context with such absolute force—he could not contemplate even the tiniest electoral reform—for perhaps he felt that without it he would be overwhelmed by the forces of dissolution.

V

After all this has been said, it remains true that the way of talking that this text seeks to establish and celebrate, the British Constitution itself, is founded on inequality of an essential sort, which we could never accept. It is not so much an inequality between writer and reader or among readers of the text but between the rulers and the ruled. For it is perhaps true that any person who can read this text and chooses to join the community it defines is by its terms entitled to full participation in the culture and the constitution as it defines these things. But those who do not or cannot do so are left out. Burke makes a valiant attempt to show that even they are treated justly; but by our standards his attempt fails, and for the same reason that the similar attempts of the Athenians at Melos also failed: a fundamental equality is essential to what we mean by justice. And even within the community of the text itself Burke in some ways seeks to dominate rather than to liberate his reader.

But to say that this text is radically flawed in these ways should not obscure its truly remarkable achievement: it has given us a new idea of what a constitution is, what an individual is, and what kind of relation can exist between the individual and his world. The center of Burke's achievement is to see that culture and the self exist in a reciprocal relation, subject to perpetual reconstitution; that the processes by which such reconstitution occurs are both personal and social, taking place within the self and in conversation with another; that to be rational in any sense they must proceed on the basis of what we actually are, not on theoretical preferences based on abstract considerations; that the language in which they occur must be what I have called literary—merging fact, value, and reason, fusing the particular and the general, uniting thought and emotion, logic and image—rather than theoretical or conceptual; and that to understand these processes, and to subject them to conscious and intelligent regulation, we must find or make a place that is at once within the culture and outside it, a place from which we can observe and criticize what we do. To make such a place is the aim of his text; in a different way, it is the aim of my own. It is as though the *Iliad* ended differently: not with the removal of the poet and the reader from one world into another world, of the poet's making, but with the reconstitution of the first world itself, on terms that reflect what is discovered in the second.

*　　　*　　　*

FOR BURKE, civilization is a kind of art, for it involves, as he repeatedly says, the "composition" or "constitution" of a world out of preexisting "materials"; but it is an art of a remarkable kind, for the composition affects, as we have seen, both the human and physical materials of which it is made. The culture shapes the man, who shapes the culture; love of family and respect for nature convert England into a landscape at once prosperous and beautiful, while the French "gardener" reduces "everything to an exact level" (p. 285) and produces poverty. Homer taught us that the complete reality of a human event is what it means from the contrasting points of view of the participants, the victor and the vanquished. Burke adds a dimension of time: for the full meaning of an event, one must see it also from the point of view of those who are gone and those yet to come. At each stage the central idea is that of completeness: the constitution is not the theory, the abstraction, but the complete way of life; the individual is not to be spoken of, or spoken to, as a merely political or merely intellectual or merely emotional creature but as a complete person, knowing all that he knows, doing all that he does; and the relationship between the communal culture and the individual character is to be reciprocal and beneficial across the whole range of human experience. The activity of "constitution" is conversational and imaginative and difficult and creative, a kind of cultural art; it takes place within the individual, in his relations with others—in his friendships—and in his relation to his culture. It is the aim of Burke's text to engage its readers deeply in this activity in all its forms.

But is all of this, for the modern reader, only to define an impossible hope, to revive a lost dream of an organic and coherent world, a culture that unites art and friendship? That is the question that carries us to our own Constitution and our own laws and to the possibilities for life and action that they define.

9

Constituting a Culture of Argument

The Possibilities of American Law

Moved in part by what Burke would call our prejudices, and perhaps also as a way of subjecting those prejudices to examination, we now turn to a different kind of attempt to create a national community: the constitution of our own nation. In separating from Great Britain and setting up their own government, Americans claimed the freedom and the power to remake their world. That claim was of course not absolute, and a constant question at the time was how much of the old to change, how much to save. Nevertheless, what was proposed, and perhaps achieved, in America was nothing less than the self-conscious reconstitution of language and community to achieve new possibilities for life. The attempt is like Burke's in its scope but very different in its method; for it was a collective, not an individual attempt, and it sought to establish what he disclaims: a system of legal authority.

In this chapter we shall bring our familiar questions, and our experience of what they have meant in other contexts—our way of reading—to three texts: The Declaration of Independence, the Constitution of the United States, and Chief Justice Marshall's opinion in *McCulloch v. Maryland*. Of each we shall ask what kind of community and culture it seeks to establish and how it does so. We shall then consider what it can mean for an individual to participate as an actor in this legal culture.

THE DECLARATION OF INDEPENDENCE: AN UNSTABLE CONSTITUTION

We begin with the first sentence of the familiar document headed "The unanimous Declaration of the thirteen united States of America":

> When in the Course of human events, it becomes
> necessary for one people to dissolve the political bands

> which have connected them with another, and to as-
> sume among the powers of the earth, the separate and
> equal station to which the Laws of Nature and of Na-
> ture's God entitle them, a decent respect to the opinions
> of mankind requires that they should declare the causes
> which impel them to the separation.

What is perhaps most striking about this sentence is its voice. It is not a person's voice, not even that of a committee, but the "unanimous" voice of "thirteen united States" and of their "people." It addresses a universal audience—nothing less than "mankind" itself, located neither in space nor in time—and the voice is universal too, for it purports to know about the "Course of human events" (all human events?) and to be able to discern what "becomes necessary" as a result of changing circumstances. This voice operates on eighteenth-century assumptions about the universal character of human nature and experience. As Samuel Johnson expressed it, "We are all prompted by the same motives, all deceived by the same fallacies."[1]

This voice functions so securely on the plane of generality and is so totally removed, it seems, from the passions and difficulties of particular realities that it can speak with a remarkable mildness. As Stuart Tave has remarked, the "diction is as little violent as it can be. Dissolve the bands—not burst asunder the hoops of steel."[2] No throwing off the chains of tyranny, no shattering the manacles of slavery, but a reassuring statement of simple fact. The implicit claim that the "separation" was not chosen but made "necessary," "impelled" by certain "causes"—as the Declaration itself is not chosen but "required"—seems to lower the temperature of the sentence nearly to zero. This voice is not justifying a choice proudly made. It simply "declares" that certain "causes" have produced certain effects, and it does so with no more passionate motive than a "decent respect to the opinions of mankind."

Of its reader the text seems to ask very little. Our function is, apparently, simply to learn what the "causes" of the separation are and then, on that basis, to maintain a good "opinion" of the authors and those for whom they speak. Not that our "opinions" are unimportant to the voice speaking here, for it seeks the favorable judgment of posterity—the children of the nation of which this voice is the founding father.[3] But even the approval this text seeks is mild. Nothing could be more high-minded and genteel.

In fact, of course, the audience is not and cannot be a distant and undifferentiated "mankind," for whoever reads the Declaration will be English or American or French as well as a member of the human species; but this mild and civilized tone has an important rhetorical effect for each of these particular audiences. To the foreigner it operates as a claim of maturity and as a submission to the conventions of the international community. To the Englishman it is a performance of reasonableness that undermines the view of the American as an uncivilized fanatic. To the American royalist, it makes a switch of sides more possible; to the American patriot it offers something with which to reassure his critics; and to the undecided American—perhaps its most important audience—it is an appeal to join a community that is serene and reasonable and secure in its sense of self and place. Nothing to fear, says this voice: we are gentlemen of manners and reason. Even those predisposed against it will read on. For all audiences, the effect is reassurance. This is a declaration not of independence, it seems, but of dependence.

There is a sense in which these implications of tone are deeply misleading, as further examination of even the first sentence will show. Before we get to its main clause, which we have been discussing, there is a long subordinate clause. Under ordinary principles of composition it would be natural to treat this as of secondary importance. The reader slides through it, waiting for the emphasis of the subject and verb of the main clause; but when he gets there, he finds, without quite knowing how, that he has acquiesced in an astonishing set of propositions—in fact the central propositions that the Declaration is intended to establish: that America is "one people" (whatever that might mean); that "necessity" can justify a unilateral separation; and that, once separated, this people is "entitled"—by law, by nature, and by God—to an equal station among nations. In the cadence of this language—"the Laws of Nature and of Nature's God"—there is a hint of the fervor to which the text will later carry us, but it is instantly checked by the very next words: "a decent respect." The Declaration thus assumes in its subordinate clause the very heart of its case—that we are a nation and that all nations are created equal—and so does any reader who makes it as far as the main clause without a rebellion of his own. Despite the implications of its title, this document does not frankly address the questions central to its case but instead assumes them away.

Or so it seems at the end of the first sentence. The next paragraph upsets these expectations by explicitly affirming, and thus bringing to the center of attention, the central tenets on which the text and its authors claim to rest:

> We hold these truths to be self-evident, that all men
> are created equal, that they are endowed by their Crea-
> tor with certain unalienable Rights, that among these
> are Life, Liberty and the pursuit of Happiness. That to
> secure these rights, Governments are instituted among

Men, deriving their just powers from the consent of the governed,—That whenever any Form of Government becomes destructive of these ends, it is the Right of the People to alter or to abolish it, and to institute new Government, laying its foundation on such principles and organizing its powers in such form, as to them shall seem most likely to effect their Safety and Happiness. Prudence, indeed, will dictate that Governments long established should not be changed for light and transient causes; and accordingly all experience hath shewn, that mankind are more disposed to suffer, while evils are sufferable, than to right themselves by abolishing the forms to which they are accustomed. But when a long train of abuses and usurpations, pursuing invariably the same Object evinces a design to reduce them under absolute Despotism, it is their right, it is their duty, to throw off such Government, and to provide new Guards for their future security.

This paragraph seems an odd way to "declare causes" (which is what the first sentence has promised us), for it is neither a description nor an explanation but a statement of abstract principles of political theory. There is also a somewhat puzzling shift in tone, marked by the direct entry into the text of the voice that had earlier seemed so far removed: "We hold these truths to be self-evident." Who is this "we" and what does this change of voice mean? And what of the "truths" themselves? Are these the principles that justify the earlier assumptions, which are now held out for examination and criticism? Are they reassuring, as the tone has thus far been? Are they proud statements of radical politics? or what?

They are many things, perhaps all of the above; but what is most significant about this paragraph is a movement within it, in which I think lies much of the force and character of the Declaration itself, a movement from reassurance to threat. The first class of "self-evident truths" is perhaps not so very disturbing to the conservative American or English reader, at least in this context and coming from such a Congress. To say that "all men are created equal" is to state an impossible and harmless ideal and one to which the Americans cannot have been committed in any very extreme form. Not to mention slavery, no one at the time seems to have argued seriously for universal manhood suffrage, and property qualifications were an accepted part of life. And to declare rights to "Life" and "Liberty"—especially if liberty is defined as a civil status regulated by law—is to say nothing that Burke would have disapproved of, at least for Englishmen; and there is a sense in which the "pursuit of Happiness" is a far less threatening ending to the clause than the Lockean "property," to which it is perhaps an allusion.[4] In any event, statements cast at such a level of generality often do not lead to much in practical terms, and the reader may thus be inclined to discount them.

But by the end of the paragraph it has been asserted that they lead to very much indeed, and much that does not by any process of reasoning follow from them. For example, to say that certain things are one's "unalienable Rights" is not the equivalent of saying that it is the chief aim of government "to secure" them; and to say that, in turn, is not to say or imply that governments derive their legitimacy from the "consent of the governed"; and that proposition, even if accepted, does not entail the next, which is that "consent" may be withdrawn when the government is—or seems to be—"destructive of these ends"; and this in turn is not to say what follows next, that the people may then properly form such a government "as to them may seem most likely" to lead to their safety and happiness. At each transition there is a slide from the less to the more revolutionary, a slide not justified or explained by what has preceded but expressive of the disposition, the mind and feeling, of the author. It is the kind of slide, in fact, that it is one purpose of Swift's *Tale* to teach his reader to catch, in himself or in another.

This paragraph is not a chain of reasoning, as its form may suggest, nor is it a frank statement of a coherent set of complementary principles; it is a movement from one state of consciousness to another, a movement large with threat and passion. What is more (as we saw also in the first sentence), the form and tone to some degree conceal this movement. The reader may be willing to grant "self-evident" status to the first proposition, for example, but not to the last. Imagine, for example, how the paragraph would read if the order of the statements were reversed.

Now comes a momentary check, a seeming retreat to different grounds: "Prudence, indeed, will dictate. . . ." But this turns out not to be an expression of caution or self-doubt, as it seems, but a kind of circular proof of the rightness of rebellion itself: since "mankind are disposed to suffer" evils as long as they are tolerable, the very fact that mankind will no longer suffer them shows that the evils have become intolerable. What seems to start off as an invocation of the ethic of prudence thus becomes an argument for the rightness of rebellion whenever it occurs, and the circular character of the argument repudiates reason and demonstrates exactly the sort of unbending and rebellious resolve the tone has thus far been at pains to deny.

At the end of this sentence the right of revolution is reiterated, but with a significant intensification of diction. No longer is it the people's "right" to act; it is their "duty." No longer do they "dissolve the bands"; they "throw off such Government," and the occasion for doing so is not when government is "destructive of these ends" but "when a long train of abuses and usurpations, pursuing invariably the same Object evinces a design to reduce them under absolute Despotism." The document no longer states a general principle of action; it declares war.

In the next three sentences the form of the paragraph as a whole becomes clear:

> Such has been the patient sufferance of these Colonies;
> and such is now the necessity which constrains them to
> alter their former Systems of Government. The history
> of the present King of Great Britain is a history of re-
> peated injuries and usurpations, all having in direct ob-
> ject the establishment of an absolute Tyranny over
> these States. To prove this, let Facts be submitted to a
> candid world.

We now see that the sentence that declared the "duty" of the people "to throw off such Government" is to be the governing rule of the document, setting forth the conditions justifying rebellion; the next two sentences— about the sufferance of the colonies and the tyrannical ambitions of the king—assert the real existence of those conditions, which the third tells us it will be the function of the rest of the document "to prove" by submitting the "Facts" to a "candid world." The text in this way states what lawyers call a cause of action against the king, justifying the rebellion. We now discover that what the first sentence meant by a "declaration of causes" was not an explanation but an indictment.[5]

In what follows, the voice is no longer that of mild and dispassionate eighteenth-century reason, speaking universal truths to a universal audience in a universal language, but the fervid and hating voice, speaking in terms of final conclusion, of one who indicts a criminal. In stating the particulars of the case against the king with lawyerly completeness, this text defines him in unqualified and violent terms as a monster of humanity, an enemy of every American. Here are just two counts (out of dozens):

> He has plundered our seas, ravaged our Coasts,
> burnt our towns, and destroyed the lives of our people.
> He is at this time transporting large Armies of for-
> eign Mercenaries to compleat the works of death, deso-
> lation and tyranny, already begun with circumstances of
> Cruelty & perfidy scarcely paralleled in the most barba-
> rous ages, and totally unworthy the Head of a civilized
> nation.

How is one to respond to such a monster, who has behaved and is behaving in such ways toward one's own people? One must destroy him. The role of the reader of this text is not, after all, to modify his "opinions" about the rebellion but to join it; the "action" of which this document ultimately declares (or creates) the "causes" is not a legal action but a military one.

It is thus one achievement of the Declaration to carry the reader, without his quite knowing how it happens, from the reassuring reasonableness and mildness of the opening sentences to the white-hot violence of this call to battle. In the process the ideal reader will be moved from one state of consciousness to another, becoming, in the text and in his life, a kind of firebrand for liberty. At its heart the document is not reassuring or reasonable but incendiary.*

AT THE END of the long series of indicting clauses there is a marked shift in tone from attack to defense: "Nor have We been wanting in attentions to our Brittish brethren." What is the function of the paragraph that begins this way, and why does it occupy this place of prominence? The paragraph continues:

> We have warned them from time to time of attempts by
> their legislature to extend an unwarrantable jurisdiction
> over us. We have reminded them of the circumstances
> of our emigration and settlement here. We have ap-
> pealed to their native justice and magnanimity, and we
> have conjured them by the ties of our common kindred
> to disavow these usurpations, which, would inevitably
> interrupt our connections and correspondence. They
> too have been deaf to the voice of justice and of con-
> sanguinity. We must, therefore, acquiesce in the neces-
> sity, which denounces our Separation, and hold them,
> as we hold the rest of mankind, Enemies in War, in
> Peace Friends.

---

*The very form of the indictment leads the reader—even the reader who prudently reserves judgment on the merits of the charges—to acquiesce in the Declaration's central proposition, that the Americans are one people; for in describing the injuries, the text necessarily implies an identity in the injured. In a sense, indeed, it is the king who makes us one. Notice, also, that the charges of bad government by the king define by negation a conception of good government, and this constitutes a promise: we shall give ourselves the opposite of these things.

This paragraph is like the first one in the character it creates for its speaker. No longer the voice of accusation and war, this is the voice of one who acknowledges his ties to his "brethren" and engages in a complex set of social activities to maintain them: warning, reminding, appealing, and "conjuring by the ties of common kindred." This is not the voice of destruction but construction. It is not we but they who are less than wholly human, "deaf" to the "voice of justice and of consanguinity."

The final paragraph shifts the tone again. The text, no longer engaged in argument and appeal, announces that it is time to act:

> WE, THEREFORE, the Representatives of the UNITED
> STATES OF AMERICA, in General Congress, Assembled,
> appealing to the Supreme Judge of the world for the
> rectitude of our intentions, do, in the Name, and by Au-
> thority of the good People of these Colonies, solemnly
> publish and declare, That these United Colonies are,
> and of Right ought to be FREE and INDEPENDENT
> STATES; that they are Absolved from all Allegiance to
> the British Crown, and that all political connection be-
> tween them and the State of Great Britain, is and ought
> to be totally dissolved; and that as Free and Indepen-
> dent States, they have full Power to levy War, conclude
> Peace, contract Alliances, establish Commerce, and to
> do all other Acts and Things which Independent States
> may of right do.

This paragraph contains the act of declaration that the title announces, and in one sense it would be complete without anything that has preceded it. But it announces a dependence on its prior argument in the word "therefore," which incorporates, by reference, the preceding declaration, not of independence, but of "causes." This sentence thus draws a kind of inner force or resolution from the words of the indictment section and from its tone.

At the very end, the voice of the Declaration becomes wholly personal. No longer that of eighteenth-century reason or that of indictment or explanation, it is the voice of the individual heroic patriot, joining with other men of wealth and honor in a community of soldiers. "And for the support of this Declaration, with a firm reliance on the protection of divine Providence, we mutually pledge to each other our Lives, our Fortunes and our sacred Honor." The community the reader is asked by this text to join is a community of identical heroes. The "one people" the Declaration seeks to create is not a diverse people, different in talents and interests, in mode of life, in character and manners—not a nation as Burke has taught us to conceive it. It is a single whole, a single person, as it were, with a single set of sentiments and determinations, a people united by a fictional merger behind the single aim of the national war. "We" are blended into a single "one"; the stated ideal of equality among people becomes an ideal of a very different sort, of merger into a common identity.

IT SHOULD NOW BE apparent why I speak of the "unstable constitution" of this text. It has proved to be not a statement of the fundamental truths on which the nation is founded, nor does it establish a functioning social and rhetorical world, with parts and relations, roles and procedures, offering a basis on which to found a collective life more complex than that of national self-defense. Rather, it is meant to work a change of feeling in the reader: to move him from his ordinary state of consciousness, in which his ordinary senses of value and civilization operate, into a willingness to pledge his all in a battle to save the country it has defined as his. It creates in its ideal reader a resolve based on a sense of common identity, on the justice of the cause, and on necessity, and it does this enormously well. One can imagine that a soldier—in the Revolutionary War, perhaps even in a later one—wondering what he is doing as he freezes at night in a rainy orchard behind a wall, might remember it and feel restored. The Declaration is in fact not an intellectual but an inspirational text, and that is how it has ever after been used. Its effects are repetitive and cumulative; the reader is moved not once and for all but again and again into the state of feeling it defines. It reminds us of our own motives by recreating them.

There is of course a sense in which the great "truths" of the Declaration are important truths for us, statements of what Burke would call our "prejudices." Lincoln, for example, made the Declaration's statement of equality the central principle of the Union he was seeking to defend and reconstitute, and the Civil War amendments might be taken as giving this principle its formal constitutional standing.[6] But considered at the moment of their composition, these truths are slogans of simplicity that must derive their real meaning from later experience. To constitute a community that is able to do more than fight to assert its existence, that can flourish over time, must be the work of other times and other instruments.

Of the nature of those instruments there is in fact a hint in the declaring clause itself, when the "one people" of the Declaration is resolved not only into heroic individuals but into "Free and Independent States." What relation can possibly exist between the "one people" of colonial America—the people that "declare the causes" and claim "separate and equal station among the nations of the earth"—and these separate states, no one of which contains more than a small portion of that people? And what relation can exist between the "people" in that sense and the individual human beings, once their roles as heroes have come to an end? What relation can exist among these states? These are questions to which the Constitution is addressed.

The Constitution of the United States: Stable but Inert

It is the purpose of the instrument known as the "Constitution of the United States of America" to do what the Declaration neither attempted nor achieved: to establish and organize a national community not merely at a transcendent moment of crisis but in its ordinary existence and over time. It is not a battle-cry but a charter for collective life—for the life we have earned when the Declaration has done its work—and our questions accordingly are: What kind of life does it make possible? What roles does it establish? What relations does it define among them? What opportunities for speech and thought does it create? This Constitution means to establish the conditions on which, and many of the materials with which, life will actually be led by a people no longer claiming to be united in a splendid moment of common sentiment but now engaged in, and divided by, their ordinary activities and moved by their ordinary motives. How does it attempt to do these things? How well does it succeed?

The Preamble: A United, Active, and Constituted "WE"

We begin with the Preamble,[7] where the text, perhaps surprisingly, does purport to speak in a single voice for the people as a whole: "WE THE PEOPLE of the United States . . . do ordain and establish this Constitution for the United States of America." This is a claim to speak for an entire and united nation and to do so directly and personally, not in the third person or by merely delegated authority. (Think how differently the sentence would read if it said: "WE THE UNITED STATES OF AMERICA," or "THE PEOPLE of the United States," or "WE, the Representatives of the People of the United States.") The instrument thus appears to issue from a single imaginary author, consisting of all the people of the United States, including the reader, merged into a single identity in this act of self-constitution. "The People" are at once the author and the audience of this instrument.

The Preamble makes additional claims for "The People" who are its author and its audience. The diction tells us, for example, that they are engaged in an act that is sacred as well as secular in character and authority, for we know that ministers are "ordained" and that churches as well as constitutions are "established." The people are given further definition by the long subordinate clause placed between the subject and the verbs, which marks them as purposive and energetic. "WE" do this, the sentence says, "in Order to form a more perfect Union, establish Justice, insure domestic Tranquility, provide for the common defence, promote the general Welfare, and secure the Blessings of Liberty to ourselves and our posterity." This clause is not necessary to the sentence, which would make exactly the same performative claims without it; but it adds a great deal: it defines its author not as a people at rest, acquiescing in what is, but as a people moving toward what should be, shaping their lives by intention, action, and hope. And the better things that define their hope are not marginal improvements in life but the essence of collective happiness: union, justice, tranquillity, defense, welfare, and all the "Blessings of Liberty." Indeed the series of verbs marks this people as almost excessively active, full of all the energy and eagerness of youth, for the "WE" that is the subject of this sentence does not merely identify these things— justice, union, and the rest—as desiderata, to be obtained if possible; it intends to "form," "establish," "insure," "provide for," "promote," and "secure" them.

This sentence creates a sense of perfect unity of a kind that can be maintained only in an emergency or for a moment. In time, differences and oppositions and conflicts will surely force themselves upon us. To pretend a unity we cannot achieve is to make a constitution that is unstable at its center.

Accordingly, in the body of the Constitution this "one people" is immediately divided up into parts: the separate states, the branches of the federal government, the individual persons who fill various offices, and the citizens (who are protected against ex post facto laws, are guaranteed the writ of habeas corpus, and so on). The only respect in which the Constitution makes the claim that its people are "one" is in the establishment of the Constitution itself; once that is done, they are free to engage in the ordinary competitions of trade and politics, to pursue their conflicting interests, to form clubs and factions, and to seek and exercise power, so long as they do all this on the conditions, and, where relevant, in the ways, that the Constitution establishes.

The Two Voices of Authority and of Silence: Separating Powers and Establishing a Trust

In the body of the Constitution the voice changes. What we hear now is the self-certain voice of authority, brooking no opposition:

ARTICLE I

SECTION 1. All legislative Powers herein granted shall be vested in a Congress of the United States, which shall consist of a Senate and House of Representatives.

241

This tone continues: "The House of Representatives shall be composed of Members chosen every second Year"; "No person shall be a Representative who shall not have attained to the Age of twenty five Years"; and so on. Such imperatives of course characterize not just the beginning but the entire text, and they are not confined to matters of principle but extend to those of detail: "The Congress shall assemble at least once in every Year, and such Meeting shall be on the first Monday in December, unless they shall by Law appoint a different Day"; "Each House shall keep a Journal of its Proceedings, and from time to time publish the same"; "Neither House, during the Session of Congress, shall, without the Consent of the other, adjourn for more than three days"; and so on.

Authority is claimed to tell each branch of the government what its powers are and, subject to the power of amendment, to do so with finality. This claim to control even the elected representatives of the people is extraordinary, and the voice that makes it is a voice of nearly superhuman authority. It admits no qualification and no modification except on its own terms.

But there is also a sense in which the voice of this document can be said to be extraordinarily modest. While it enumerates the legislative "Powers," for example, it does nothing to define how they shall be exercised. These are the subjects on which you may act, it says. How you act or refrain from acting, and why, are matters wholly outside the jurisdiction of this instrument. By thus speaking with authority on some matters and remaining wholly silent on others, this document itself performs a separation of powers of exactly the sort it wishes to establish in the world. The legislature, the executive, and the judiciary are in this respect given the Constitution itself as a model for their emulation.

Consider, for example, the statement of the powers of Congress in Article I:

> SECTION 8. The Congress shall have Power To lay and collect Taxes, Duties, Imposts and Excises, to pay the Debts and provide for the common Defence and general Welfare of the United States; but all Duties, Imposts and Excises shall be uniform throughout the United States;
>
> To borrow Money on the credit of the United States;
>
> To regulate Commerce with foreign Nations, and among the several States, and with the Indian Tribes;
>
> To establish a uniform Rule of Naturalization, and uniform Laws on the subject of Bankruptcies throughout the United States;

To coin Money, regulate the Value thereof, and of foreign Coin, and fix the Standard of Weights and Measures;

To provide for the Punishment of counterfeiting the Securities and current Coin of the United States;

To establish Post Offices and post Roads;

To promote the Progress of Science and useful Arts, by securing for limited Times to Authors and Inventors the exclusive Right to their respective Writings and Discoveries;

To constitute Tribunals inferior to the supreme Court;

To define and punish Piracies and Felonies committed on the high Seas, and Offences against the Law of Nations;

To declare War, grant Letters of Marque and Reprisal, and make Rules concerning Captures on Land and Water;

To raise and support Armies, but no Appropriation of Money to that Use shall be for a longer Term than two Years;

To provide and maintain a Navy;

To make Rules for the Government and Regulation of the land and naval Forces;

To provide for calling forth the Militia to execute the Laws of the Union, suppress Insurrections and repel Invasions; . . . .—And

To make all Laws which shall be necessary and proper for carrying into Execution the foregoing Powers, and all other Powers vested by this Constitution in the Government of the United States, or in any Department or Officer thereof.

There is little in this list of powers that could serve as a statement of the values by which the legislature is to be guided in exercising them. The "common defence and general Welfare" are no doubt good things, and it is required that taxation be "uniform." "Commerce" is presumably a good thing, but nothing is said of the ways in which it is to be "regulated." There should apparently be laws on naturalization and bankruptcy, but the only value asserted is that such laws should be "uniform." Coining money, punishing counterfeiters, establishing a post office, punishing piracies, declaring war, and raising armies are not so much good or bad as necessities of national life. The copyright and patent provision has a more aspirational quality, perhaps, since it speaks of the "Progress of Science and useful Arts"; but what is to be regarded as useful and how progress is to be measured are matters on which the instrument itself is wholly silent.

In these respects the rhetorical character of the Constitution is much like that of a trust, of the sort frequently employed in estate plans or in the establishment of charitable institutions. Such an instrument will typically define with finality and in detail the property that belongs to the trust, the beneficiaries of the trust, how long it should run, and so forth. But in its other directions to the trustee it will normally be very general; he will be able to do with the property whatever seems appropriate, given the purposes set forth in the instrument, so long as he acts reasonably and in the best interests of the beneficiaries. The same reason explains the choice of this form for both the trust and the Constitution, namely, that it is impossible to foresee the future and one therefore cannot with any degree of confidence set down specific and complete directions ahead of time. If one were to try, it might well lead to exactly the wrong results. In both cases, what one does instead, not out of a foolish optimism about human nature but out of necessity, is to repose great confidence in the good will and competence of another while subjecting him to the discipline of a general law.

It is the character of the Constitution, then, to speak two ways at once: in declarations of absolute authority and in equally absolute silences. In this way it at once performs a separation of powers[8] and establishes a trust, placing complete confidence in others to do what should be done—a fact large with significance, as we shall see, for the activity of construction by which the Constitution will be given actuality and meaning.

Our Rhetorical Constitution: Its Speakers, Places, Occasions, and Topics

Even with regard to the matters on which it speaks with apparently imperious authority—about each House keeping a journal, for example—the Constitution must in fact rely on others to see that its commands are obeyed, for it is not a self-executing document. If the Senate keeps no journal, for example, the omnipotent author of this Constitution will not step down from the sky and force it to do so. And suppose that Congress passes a statute outside its enumerated powers? Who is to say to them nay?

My point here is a simple one. Despite its tone, and despite the way we often talk about it, the Constitution has no force except to the extent that it is invoked and used by individual Americans pursuing actual goals. Until used it is inert. Alone it can do nothing. There have been many grand but ineffectual "Declarations of Independence" in the world, each as confident in tone as our own, and there have been many elegant and cohcrent "constitutions"—like the French Constitution described by Burke—which in the event came to nothing. What matters is always what place, if any, such an instrument will have in the lives of those it is intended to regulate. Think, for example, of the way a treaty or a contract works in practice. One item of negotiation between the parties always is how the instrument is to be read: with what degree of respect or reverence, whether strictly or loosely, whether with an eye to its specific provisions or its general aims, whether as binding or merely hortatory, and so on.

But to say that a treaty does not bind its partners with hoops of steel or that a Constitution does not, like a dynamo, create something called "power" and distribute it, like steam or electricity, to the various parts of the machine of government is not to say that such instruments achieve nothing. What they actually do is alter the rhetorical conditions of life for those in whose name they are promulgated and those to whom they speak. In a way that the representatives of Corcyra and Corinth would instantly understand, the very existence of such a text as this makes available certain kinds of claim and appeal, certain kinds of movement and action, that would otherwise be impossible. "You are our ally"; "the treaty requires it"; "the Constitution prohibits it." At its most successful, an instrument like this can be said to establish the fundamental terms of new kinds of conversation; for it creates a set of speakers, defines the occasions for and topics of their speech, and is itself a text that may be referred to as authoritative. ("We must keep a Journal in this House, for the Constitution requires it.") The Constitution works by creating the occasions and warrants for making a certain set of claims, and in this respect it is like the other constitutions we are always making in our own lives, in the form of contracts and agreements, block-betterment associations, and so on.

What I mean by the creation of speakers is simple enough. For some purposes, and in some ways, an actual human being, no different in appearance from any other, will make a claim to be "the President of the United States" as that term is defined in this document. The instrument provides a way of validating or invalidating that claim, and it provides the speaker, and others, with materials of argument on the question whether the particular speech is appropriate or inappropriate for him, in form or substance. The case is similar with the judiciary and with Congress: the instrument provides a way of testing the claims of individuals to speak in the roles it creates and on the occasions it establishes. In many instances it also defines the topics of argument appropriate to various rhetorical circumstances, telling the speaker, and others, what kinds of speech are authorized or appropriate for him. One way to read the enumerated powers of the Congress, for example, is as a list of the topics on which they may deliberate and act. Similarly, the "cases arising under" language of Article III both points to the matters on which judges may, as judges, think, speak, and act and suggests the manner and methods by which they should do so. This text is thus addressed not to one ideal reader but to a set of readers, each defined by his role (including the role of one who invokes its language to control the conduct of others). Each of them will spend much of his life interpreting the instrument that creates his role and his world. This Constitution—like other such instruments—is thus in a literal sense a rhetorical constitution: it constitutes a rhetorical community, working by rhetorical processes that it has established but can no longer control. It establishes a new conversation on a permanent basis.

In this context the provision about the legislative "journal" takes on a new significance, for this requirement offers the possibility, in practice not much pursued, of developing a coherent and growing body of discourse, internal to each House, by which a set of understandings could be established about the kind of conversation that is appropriate on each of the topics set forth in Section 8. Not only that, but such a discourse could establish how these topics are themselves to be understood. Likewise, the language of Article II, which empowers the President to "require the Opinion, in writing, of the principal Officer in each of the executive Departments, upon any Subject relating to the Duties of their respective Offices," provides another opportunity, in the event largely but not entirely missed,[9] for gradually developing a body of discourse within the executive branch that would define the executive departments and the methods by which they proceed. There is, in addition, at least one occasion for conversation between the branches; this is established by the provision requiring the President to state his objections to any statute that he vetoes, and Congress is to give special prominence to these objections by recording them in its journals. Out of this practice a kind of nonjudicial constitutional law could have emerged. A similar opportunity, similarly wasted, is established by the provisions that permit the President to exercise certain of his powers only with the advice and consent of the Senate.[10]

Another opportunity for developing constitutional discourse is created by the establishment of the "judicial Power" that "shall extend to all Cases, in Law and Equity, arising under this Constitution, the Laws of the United States, and Treaties made, or which shall be made, under their Authority." But this language does not make it clear that this is a proper place for considering the relations among the branches or, indeed, that it is a particularly favored place for the development of constitutional language at all. In fact, the restriction of the power to "cases arising" seems to cut the other way; for, unlike the President and the Congress, the Supreme Court is not given a power to act on its own. It must wait until it is asked, by others, to act.

On this view it is one of the striking peculiarities of our history that our constitutional discourse has been most fully developed by the courts. Because it suggests some reasons why that is so and because it shows one way the power has been exercised, we shall now examine a particularly important opinion written by Chief Justice Marshall.

THE RECONSTITUTION OF CULTURE AND COMMUNITY BY THE JUDICIARY: *McCULLOCH v. MARYLAND*

The Constitution is by its very nature lifeless and inert unless it is put to work in the world by the citizens who live under it. Their cooperation is required for the achievement of any of its purposes. It is not too much to say, in fact, that the establishment of a certain kind of cooperation, a certain kind of community, is its central purpose. But how can this instrument be put to work? We can perhaps learn something about the process of constitutional conversation by examining one instance of it. We begin with a difficult question of constitutional meaning that arose early in our national existence and remained for many years a source of deep political division between the commercial and urban Federalists, on the one hand, and the agrarian and states'-rights Republicans, on the other: Has Congress the constitutional power to establish a national bank?

The question first arose, as such questions commonly do, in a nonjudicial context. When the Bank was first proposed, in 1791, President Washington asked Hamilton and Jefferson, as the secretaries, respectively, of the Treasury and State departments, for their views on its constitutionality. They divided, with Hamilton strongly for, Jefferson almost as strongly against. Jefferson's position was that the creation of a Bank was not within the powers of Congress enumerated in Article I nor within the two general provisions of that article, namely, "To lay . . . Taxes . . . , to provide for . . . the general Welfare of the United States," and "To make all Laws which shall be necessary and proper for carrying into Execution the foregoing Powers." Hamilton's view was that the enumerated powers necessarily entailed the existence of certain implied powers and that the creation of the Bank was fairly among them. (Madison, then a member of the House of Representatives, opposed the passage of the original legislation on the grounds that Congress had no power to create a corporation.) The political result was that the Bank was established but was limited to a twenty-year life.[11]

When the Bank's charter came up for renewal in 1811, it was defeated, owing partly to Republican ascendancy in national government and partly to the Bank's increasing unpopularity, especially with its competitors, the state banks. But the dissolution of the Bank led to considerable national inconvenience during the War of 1812 and to general economic distress and confusion thereafter. By 1816 even Madison was convinced, especially by the need for a uniform currency, and he at last acquiesced in the establishment of the Second Bank of the United States. It is the constitutionality of the legislation establishing this Bank that is at issue in *McCulloch v. Maryland.*

It is important to see that, although this question had been discussed intensely for over twenty-five years, the conversation about it had been for the most part formless and inconclusive in character, rather like a conversation among people in ordinary life. While much was said on both sides, the status of particular arguments or reasons was unclear; there was talk, and there was voting, but the connection between the two activities was not explicit. No one purported to sum up all that could be said and then to resolve the question.

Facts and Background

When the question came before it, how should the Supreme Court have decided it? The reader may say that he or she does not know enough to begin to respond, but we do know that the language of the Constitution neither expressly permits nor expressly prohibits the Bank. We have also seen an outline of the competing views, and there are some other facts, as follows.

The Bank of the United States was a private commercial bank, chartered by the United States and given the usual powers of lending money, discounting promissory notes, issuing notes of its own, and so forth. The United States held one-fifth of the shares in the Bank; the rest were held by private persons, including many Englishmen. The operations of the Bank were not subject to direction by the government, but it was bound to lend the government a certain amount of money on demand and to transfer government funds as directed by the Secretary of the Treasury. Its notes were declared to be receivable for debts due the government. In such ways the Bank provided a facility by which national funds could both be deposited with security and be put to work in the economy as a whole; it functioned as a source of credit, thought to be the more secure by the inclusion of private wealth; and it made possible a uniform national currency.

The *McCulloch* case arose in Maryland, which, like other states, had issued charters to state banks, which were being deprived by the Bank of the United States of a portion of the business that would otherwise have been theirs. Maryland accordingly passed a statute taxing the operations of all banks not chartered by her. The Bank of the United States did not pay the tax. Maryland sued successfully in her own courts for a penalty for issuing notes without payment of the tax, naming the cashier of the Bank, one McCulloch, as defendant. He sought review in the Supreme Court of the judgment against him.

Chief Justice Marshall, speaking for the Supreme Court, decided both that the establishment of the Bank was within the powers of Congress and that Maryland was prohibited from taxing its operations. This combination of holdings presents, as you might imagine, a serious rhetorical difficulty. To hold that the Bank was constitutional, Marshall had to find that the national government (which was conceded by all to be a government of limited and enumerated powers) had a power that was not expressly included in the list of its powers stated in the Constitution. To hold the state tax invalid, he had to find that the State of Maryland, which was acknowledged by all to be a government of general powers, unaffected by its membership in the national union except by the terms of that union (such, indeed, is the rule of the Tenth Amendment), was prohibited from exercising a power—that of taxation—that was universally agreed to belong to every sovereign. Marshall's task was to persuade the reader of his opinion of the rightness of these results, which seem contrary to the plain meaning and background of the Constitution.

But his task had a far larger dimension. Whenever a court or other body claims to have the power claimed here, of determining the constitutionality of a piece of congressional legislation or a law passed by a state legislature, there is always, at least by implication, a question whether it has the power it claims. It does not help to say that Marshall had claimed this power for the Court sixteen years before, in *Marbury v. Madison* (1803), for the authority of that case could still be called into question; or, more likely, it could be interpreted as applying only to a narrow set of circumstances.[12] In the years since *Marbury* no federal legislation had been declared unconstitutional; in fact, none was until the *Dred Scott* case in 1857. To make matters still worse, Marshall was a Federalist judge in Republican times, a member of a party that had been without national power since his appointment, and, as a judge, he held a lifetime position under a democratic constitution that placed its ultimate source of authority in "WE THE PEOPLE." Why should he and his Court, of all "people," have the final say on such constitutional questions as those presented here?

In *McCulloch*, Marshall must therefore persuade his reader both that his conclusions are correct and that he and his colleagues should have the ultimate authority to decide these questions of national importance.[13] How did he attempt to do these things?

The Opinion

I

We can begin with Marshall's opening sentences, in which he defines both the nature of the case before him and his own task in deciding it:

> In the case now to be determined, the defendant,* a
> sovereign State, denies the obligation of a law enacted
> by the legislature of the Union, and the plaintiff, on his
> part, contests the validity of an act which has been
> passed by the legislature of that State. The constitution
> of our country, in its most interesting and vital parts, is
> to be considered; the conflicting powers of the govern-
> ment of the Union and of its members, as marked in
> that constitution, are to be discussed; and an opinion
> given, which may essentially influence the great opera-
> tions of the government. No tribunal can approach such
> a question without a deep sense of its importance, and
> of the awful responsibility involved in its decision. But it
> must be decided peacefully, or remain a source of hos-
> tile legislation, perhaps of hostility of a still more serious
> nature; and if it is to be so decided, by this tribunal
> alone can the decision be made. On the Supreme Court
> of the United States has the constitution of our country
> devolved this important duty.

It is Marshall's object in this paragraph not to persuade us that his views on the merits of the case are correct (that will come later) but to begin to establish the propriety, indeed the necessity, of his having the authority to decide it at all. We are thus told that a "sovereign State" and the "legislature of the Union" are in active opposition—one "denies," the other "contests"—and that is enough to make us as citizens accept the

---

*By "defendant" Marshall means the "defendant in error," i.e., the party now defending the judgment reached below, not the "defendant" in the original proceeding, who was, of course, McCulloch, not Maryland.

need for a peaceful and persuasive resolution of the dispute. As Marshall says, the obvious alternative is hostility of one kind or another and hostility in any form threatens the nation as a whole. If the judiciary does not speak, things will apparently be left as they are, in a state of irreconcilable conflict; if it does speak, we may have peace and order.

Marshall has told us nothing about the substantive issue that divides these sovereign powers. That has two effects: since we do not know what the question is, we cannot imagine the two parties working out a negotiated resolution on their own, for we cannot even guess how their claims and concessions might proceed, and this makes their opposition seem implacable. The parties are in this way represented as involved in a conflict from which they are helpless to extricate themselves without judicial action. Second, without some idea of the substantive question we cannot imagine resolving it ourselves—we cannot even bring our instincts and prejudices to bear upon it—and this makes us feel all the more strongly that we need what Marshall will offer us, the judicial opinion that will reason its way to a persuasive judgment.

Marshall's claim in fact extends far beyond the particular case, indeed beyond the life of any particular Supreme Court justice. It becomes a claim for the judiciary itself. In these early opinions the Court is beginning to make an authoritative culture of argument, a body of law of which no one can foresee the end, and it all rests on the reader's confidence in judicial reasoning of just the sort Marshall is about to demonstrate. The most powerful "reason" Marshall offers for our acquiescence in his claim of authority for the Court is his demonstration that, in exercising it, the Court can offer the nation what no other branch can: the development, over time, of a self-reflective, self-corrective body of discourse that will bind its audience together by engaging them in a common language and a common set of practices. It is a claim to constitute a community and a culture. To those disposed to resist, Marshall implicitly says: if you agree that we should have the powers we claim to exercise, the nation will continue to have the benefit of the culture, the life, that we alone can provide. If you silence us, this is what you lose. The best thing about us is the kind of opinion we are about to offer you.[14]

Marshall thus daringly promises us an achievement of an extraordinary kind. How will he attempt to make good on it?

II

Having stated the question, whether Congress has the power to incorporate the Bank, Marshall's first step is, perhaps surprisingly, to tell us, not what he thinks, but what others have thought:

It has been truly said, that this can scarcely be considered as an open question, entirely unprejudiced by
the former proceedings of the nation respecting it. The
principle now contested was introduced at a very early
period of our history, has been recognized by many successive legislatures, and has been acted upon by the judicial department, in cases of peculiar delicacy, as a law
of undoubted obligation.

It will not be denied, that a bold and daring usurpation might be resisted, after an acquiescence still longer
and more complete than this. But it is conceived that a
doubtful question, one on which human reason may
pause, and the human judgment be suspended, in the
decision of which the great principles of liberty are not
concerned, but the respective powers of those who are
equally the representatives of the people, are to be ad-
justed; if not put at rest by the practice of the government, ought to receive a considerable impression from
that practice.

Marshall defines himself here not as a decider of impossible questions,
impossibly open, but as a reader of a common past, respectful of his inheritance as it has been made by others. No confident expositor of the
powers of his own reason, Marshall here admits that this is a question
upon which "human reason"—including his own—"may pause, and the
human judgment be suspended." For his sources of authority he looks
out of himself and to the world, especially that part of the world that is
"representative of the people."

In the next paragraph he explains why this history is especially worthy
of respect: the Bank bill "did not steal upon an unsuspecting legislature,
and pass unobserved," for in "fair and open field of debate" and "in the
executive cabinet" it was "resisted . . . with as much persevering talent
as any measure has ever experienced." It became law because it was
"supported by arguments which convinced minds as pure and as intelligent as this country can boast." Its dissolution in 1811 caused "embarrassments" that "convinced those who were most prejudiced against
the measure of its necessity." Marshall, we learn, is prepared not only
to examine history but to evaluate it; the fact that he happens to find
this particular tradition entitled to special respect does not diminish his
claim to determine what part of our inheritance is to be respected, and
what is not.

Why is this tradition, in Marshall's view, entitled to such respect? For
him the central merit of this history is the fact that it has been informed

both by argument of the highest kind and by the lessons of experience. The actors who have made this history are defined as a people engaged in a collective enterprise of self-government, and the twin instruments of this process are argument and experience: it is these that have "convinced" powerful minds among those negatively disposed. Notice that this "experience" takes its final form not out there in the world but here in the opinion, where it is recreated as the ground of decision. Marshall is not merely the observer of collective experience, then, or even its evaluator. He gives it definition, form, and meaning; in a literal sense, he constitutes it. His control over the "argument" half of the method of self-government he is celebrating is even more plain, for argument is the essential method of the law. The conception of self-government on which Marshall—with such seeming modesty—thus bases his respect for tradition in fact turns out to receive its final expression and fullest performance in Marshall's own judicial opinion. Of this form the servant of the Constitution is the authorized master.

III

When Marshall turns, as he next does, to his own view of the substantive issue, he begins in a puzzling way: with a disquisition on the highly abstract question, whether the Constitution is properly considered as "emanating from the people" or as the act of "sovereign and independent States." He concludes that the former is correct but draws no conclusion from it. Instead, he shifts to different but equally general topics. He says that the "government is acknowledged by all to be one of enumerated powers" but that the "question respecting the extent of the powers actually granted, is perpetually arising, and will probably continue to arise, as long as our system shall exist." He then addresses the question of what should happen when the "conflicting powers of the general and State governments" are "in opposition," and he concludes—as who could not?—that the national power must be supreme.

> If any one proposition could command the universal assent of mankind, we might expect it would be this— that the government of the Union, though limited in its powers, is supreme within its sphere of action. This would seem to result necessarily from its nature. It is the government of all; its powers are delegated by all; it represents all, and acts for all. . . .

Here we begin to see the point of Marshall's earlier disquisition on the nature of the national government: its origin in "the people" is one source of its supremacy. And what makes the Constitution supreme, namely, that it was an act of "all the people," is here implicitly said to favor its liberal or generous interpretation. But this sovereign, the people, intended to place limitations on its central government, and it intended these limitations as seriously as it intended its grants of power. How, then, can Marshall properly construe the grant of federal powers to include "implied" powers along with the enumerated ones?

Marshall's most famous paragraph is addressed to that question. He begins by stating frankly the case against him, observing that "among the enumerated powers, we do not find that of establishing a bank or creating a corporation." But, he quickly adds, "there is no phrase in the instrument which . . . excludes incidental or implied powers." Whether a "particular power" has been "delegated to the one government, or prohibited to the other" thus depends on "a fair construction of the whole instrument." But this statement establishes at most the textual possibility of implied or incidental powers. It leaves standing the implicit question, suggested above: Why shouldn't the limitations on the powers granted be read just as energetically as the grants themselves? Why, that is, does a "fair construction" by implication tend to expand the powers rather than limit them? Marshall's answer depends on his characterization of the very nature of a constitution:

> A constitution, to contain an accurate detail of all the subdivisions of which its great powers will admit, and of all the means by which they may be carried into execution, would partake of the prolixity of a legal code, and could scarcely be embraced by the human mind. It would probably never be understood by the public. Its nature, therefore, requires, that only its great outlines should be marked, its important objects designated, and the minor ingredients which compose those objects be deduced from the nature of the objects themselves. That this idea was entertained by the framers of the American constitution, is not only to be inferred from the nature of the instrument, but from the language. Why else were some of the limitations, found in the ninth section of the 1st article, introduced? It is also, in some degree, warranted by their having omitted to use any restrictive term which might prevent its receiving a fair and just interpretation. In considering this question, then, we must never forget, that it is *a constitution* we are expounding.

We can now see that everything that Marshall has said so far has been intended to reduce the embarrassment presented by the following obvious argument: "The United States is a government of enumerated powers; the power to create a bank is not among them; therefore, it is in excess of them and invalid." Marshall's effort has been to establish the conditions on which he could claim that such a reading, which would perhaps be appropriate to a "legal code" or to an interstate agreement, is inappropriate to a "constitution," which by its nature requires not mere explication but what he calls "expounding."

What is there about the Constitution that leads to these consequences? Part of the answer, as Marshall suggests in the paragraph just quoted, is the fact that any attempt to reduce all the powers to explicit statement would be impossibly complicated. But there is another line of argument, never made explicit by Marshall, and it is even more fundamental. It rests on the very material we have had difficulty in explaining, namely, the passages addressed to the question whether the Constitution is the act of the people or of the states. For who are these "people," and where are they now? In Marshall's rhetorical universe, the "people" are defined by their one great collective act of self-constitution. They existed once in time only, when the Constitution was made, and have since resolved themselves into their constituent units and groupings—as states, officials, individuals, and factions. The "people" thus no longer exist among us, and never can again. They have left behind them this instrument, the Constitution, which is technically amendable but was meant in its essentials to endure forever. Unlike the legislatures, unlike the states (had the Constitution been regarded as a compact among them), the "people" are not here to correct what we do, and the instrument was composed with the knowledge that they would not be. This is why it contains no technical rules telling us how it should be construed, or, as lawyers say, what "construction" it should be given. And this is also why it would be impossible for it to address every contingency in detail. The "people" of whom Marshall speaks existed only in their act of constitution, in a kind of momentary incarnation; everything achieved by the Constitution had to be achieved at one time; it could not be developed in stages or by gradual adjustment to experience. The people thus left behind them a testamentary trust that has something of the character of a sacred text. It is an instrument that requires the special kind of reading Marshall will give it.

This view of the Constitution establishes not only Marshall's point about the way in which the grant of powers should be read but his own position as the authoritative reader of it. As the expositor of the text that expresses the will of "the People," our only sovereign, Marshall claims to be the only instrument through which their will can be done. Far from holding a lifetime appointment against the rules of democracy, an appointment justified, if at all, by his technical competence as a member of a learned profession—as knowing about "fee tail" and "advowson" and "surrebutters" and the like—Marshall implicitly says that his position is, of all positions, the one most perfectly justified by the central principle of our democracy, for he alone expounds the instrument that is the single act of "all the people." He is indeed the voice of the people. His role is like that of a priest as well as that of a trustee, and he is entitled to this position by his excellence at the activity he calls "expounding."[15]

IV

But what is this special kind of reading, and why is Marshall himself, or the Court in general, uniquely qualified to do it, and do it well? How can Marshall meet certain obvious criticisms—for example, that, on the evidence of his opinion in *McCulloch*, "expounding" is a method of reading the Constitution that has the extraordinary merit (worthy of recommendation in Swift's *Tale of a Tub*) of finding in it what simply is not there?

From what he has already shown us we know something of this art. For example, we know that he will proceed at least in part on the authority of history, as he did in his first paragraph on the constitutionality of the Bank, and that he will not merely refer to or report on that history but evaluate it and reconstitute it in his own writing. He says that the reason the historical acceptance of the Bank is entitled to weight is that it reflects a general concurrence of judgment among the various branches of government, a concurrence arrived at over a considerable period of time; it thus comes close to expressing the views of "the People," the mythic authors of the Constitution, as those views are given definition through representative institutions. Marshall is in effect saying to his audience: this is not what I think but what "you, the People" already think.

Other aspects of Marshall's opinion work in much the same way. For example, an aspect of "expounding" that cannot have escaped the reader is Marshall's magisterial tone. He repeatedly declares with finality what can and cannot be said: "It has been truly said . . ."; "it will not be denied . . ."; "no political dreamer was ever wild enough to think . . ."; "if any one proposition could command the universal assent of mankind . . . ," and so on. Such sentences as these establish, almost as axioms, the propositions on which argument can be based. Their general character permits a kind of reasoning from premise to conclusion that can at least pretend to the form and force of reason of the most compelling kind: Euclidean deduction. From the great axioms are deduced corollaries, which it remains only to apply.[16] This is another way in which Marshall claims to rest on an authority that is both external to himself and the substantial equivalent of "the People"; for the assumption of such reasoning is that it is of such universal validity that all people must agree with it. As for the substance of his magisterial pronouncements, a somewhat similar claim is made for them: since no authority is cited for them but self-evidence, they must indeed be—or seem to be—self-evident commonplaces of the culture, and, as such, have the authority of the people themselves. In practice, of course, they are often question-begging. No reader of the following passage, for example, would deny that the government ought to have "ample means" for executing the "powers" granted it; but whether a national Bank is properly among them is a different matter entirely:

Although, among the enumerated powers of government, we do not find the word "bank" or "incorporation," we find the great powers to lay and collect taxes; to borrow money; to regulate commerce; to declare and conduct a war; and to raise and support armies and navies. The sword and the purse, all the external relations, and no inconsiderable portion of the industry of the nation, are entrusted to its government. It can never be pretended that these vast powers draw after them others of inferior importance, merely because they are inferior. Such an idea can never be advanced. But it may with great reason be contended, that a government, entrusted with such ample powers, on the due execution of which the happiness and prosperity of the nation so vitally depends, must also be entrusted with ample means for their execution. The power being given, it is the interest of the nation to facilitate its execution. It can never be their interest, and cannot be presumed to have been their intention, to clog and embarrass its execution by withholding the most appropriate means. Throughout this vast republic, from the St. Croix to the Gulph of Mexico, from the Atlantic to the Pacific, revenue is to be collected and expended, armies are to be marched and supported. The exigencies of the nation may require that the treasure raised in the north should be transported to the south, *that* raised in the east conveyed to the west, or that this order should be reversed. Is that construction of the constitution to be preferred which would render these operations difficult, hazardous, and expensive? Can we adopt that construction, (unless the words imperiously require it,) which

257

would impute to the framers of that instrument, when
granting these powers for the public good, the intention
of impeding their exercise by withholding a choice of
means?

Marshall is here working in what might be called his poetic mode, by
which he creates in words an imagined object of such a character as to
compel a certain attitude in us.[17] Here, for example, he defines the national government as a kind of public persona of heroic proportions, immense in strength and stature—a sort of Paul Bunyan among governments. What can be or ought to be denied a government such as this? It
seems as though nothing should, as nothing could, stand in the way of so
much size and force. Such a passage is not argumentative in the usual
sense at all; it is a way of creating the object of argument in such a way as
to make argument itself unnecessary.

The implications of this characterization of course go much too far,
since it reflects no recognition of the people's interest in limiting this government in favor of others or in favor of themselves. What will the limits
be? In the paragraph just quoted, Marshall deals with this question by
drawing a distinction (on which his whole opinion will depend) between
governmental "powers," which are enumerated and limited, and "means,"
which are not. He does not present this distinction in an explicit or theoretical manner, as a political scientist or logician might; instead, he introduces it at the end of a sentence, cast in ordinary English, and only
then does its importance emerge. His reader is thus led to perceive the
familiarity of the distinction, indeed its necessity, before he perceives its
significance.

Marshall seeks to give meaning to this distinction by putting it to work
in his refutation of Maryland's argument that the government has no
power to create a corporation. Marshall's answer is of course to define the
power to create corporations as a "means" available to the national government, not a "power" by implication denied it. He does this by appealing to a collective experience so universally characterized that, like the
"history" treated at the outset, it has something like the authority of a
declaration by "the People," whose understandings are reflected in it:

> The power of creating a corporation . . . is never the
> end for which other powers are exercised, but a means
> by which other objects are accomplished. No contribu-
> tions are made to charity for the sake of an incorpora-
> tion, but a corporation is created to administer the
> charity; no seminary of learning is instituted in order
> to be incorporated, but the corporate character is con-

ferred to subserve the purposes of education. No city
was ever built with the sole object of being incorporated, but is incorporated as affording the best means of
being well governed. The power of creating a corporation is never used for its own sake, but for the purpose of
effecting something else.[18]

In interpreting the clause providing that Congress shall have the
power "to make all laws which shall be necessary and proper for carrying
into execution the foregoing Powers," Marshall proceeds by making yet
another appeal to collective experience—to the ways in which the word
"necessary" is used in ordinary speech:

If reference be had to its use, in the common affairs
of the world, or in approved authors, we find that it frequently imports no more than that one thing is convenient, or useful, or essential to another. To employ the
means necessary to an end, is generally understood as
employing any means calculated to produce the end,
and not as being confined to those single means, without which the end would be entirely unattainable. Such
is the character of human language, that no word conveys to the mind, in all situations, one single definite
idea; and nothing is more common than to use words in
a figurative sense. Almost all compositions contain
words, which, taken in their rigorous sense, would convey a meaning different from that which is obviously
intended. It is essential to just construction, that many
words which import something excessive, should be
understood in a more mitigated sense—in that sense
which common usage justifies. The word "necessary" is
of this description. It has not a fixed character peculiar
to itself. It admits of all degrees of comparison; and is
often connected with other words, which increase or diminish the impression the mind receives of the urgency
it imports. A thing may be necessary, very necessary,
absolutely or indispensably necessary. To no mind would
the same idea be conveyed, by these several phrases.
This comment on the word is well illustrated, by the
passage cited at the bar, from the 10th section of the 1st
article of the constitution. It is, we think, impossible to
compare the sentence which prohibits a State from laying "imposts, or duties on imports or exports, except

what may be *absolutely* necessary for executing its in-
spection laws," with that which authorizes Congress "to
make all laws which shall be necessary and proper for
carrying into execution" the powers of the general government, without feeling a conviction that the convention understood itself to change materially the meaning
of the word "necessary," by prefixing the word "absolutely." This word, then, like others, is used in various
senses; and, in its construction, the subject, the context, the intention of the person using them, are all to
be taken into view.

In this paragraph Marshall establishes far more than the proposition
that the word "necessary" has a wide range of possible meanings. He defines the language of the Constitution, and hence the language of this
opinion and of the law generally, as continuous with ordinary language
and capable of the same richness, complexity, and variation—indeed, of
the same capacity for inconsistency. This is why he tucks in only at the
end the point that most modern lawyers would consider his most persuasive, that the use of the words "absolutely necessary" elsewhere in the
Constitution demonstrates beyond doubt that there is a scale of "necessity" in the language it uses.[19] His essential point goes beyond the establishment of a scale of meanings; it is that the language that he construes,
and the language he claims the right to use, have "such a character . . .
that no word conveys to the mind, in all situations, one single definite
idea." Since the language of the Constitution has this character (in our
terms it is "literary," not "theoretical"), the activity of interpreting it cannot be limited to looking to see what is there or to an obedience to plain
commands; it becomes instead a literary and constructive art, a way of
making sense *of* living speech *in* living speech.

Marshall in this way calls on an authority that is not exactly higher
than the text of the Constitution but prior to it: the language of which it is
made. That language has been established by its "use" in the "common
affairs of the world, or in approved authors"; it has its origins and life in
"the People" themselves, including the present reader, who must accept
and be willing to speak the language as Marshall reconstructs it. What
Marshall claims at last is that the Constitution is not to be regarded as
establishing a separate sphere of life or language; it must be seen as an
integral part of the culture of which it is made and which it, in turn, reconstitutes. This is indeed why it must be regarded not as a mere legal
instrument, resting on some abstract authority, but as a true *constitution*: of language, of community, and of culture.

V

Of the second part of the opinion, invalidating the Maryland tax, it is enough to say that Marshall meets Maryland's claim, that the tax ought to be permitted unless it is imposed abusively, by creating a rhetorical world in which there is implacable opposition and hostility between state and federal governments. See how he portrays the states in this passage, for example:

> If the States may tax one instrument, employed by
> the government in the execution of its powers, they
> may tax any and every other instrument. They may tax
> the mail; they may tax the mint; they may tax patent
> rights; they may tax the papers of the custom-house;
> they may tax judicial process; they may tax all the means
> employed by the government, to an excess which would
> defeat all the ends of government . . . .
> . . . This is not all. If the controlling power of the
> States be established; if their supremacy as to taxation
> be acknowledged; what is to restrain their exercising this
> control in any shape they may please to give it? Their
> sovereignty is not confined to taxation. That is not the
> only mode in which it might be displayed. The question
> is, in truth, a question of supremacy; and if the right of
> the States to tax the means employed by the general
> government be conceded, the declaration that the con-
> stitution, and the laws made in pursuance thereof, shall
> be the supreme law of the land, is empty and unmean-
> ing declamation.

The question between such antagonists as these is not one of confidence, as Maryland claims, but of "supremacy." If one is not master, the other will be.[20]

In defining the parties as implacably hostile to each other, as unre-strained by a sense of culture or community, Marshall provides support not only for his conclusion in the case at hand, that the Maryland tax is invalid, but, even more importantly for the argument he has implicitly been making since the opening paragraph, in support of his authority to expound the Constitution in the first place. Nothing could make more clear than this hostility both the necessity of a prompt and authoritative decision and the incapacity of the parties to reach it on their own. It dem-onstrates, as he has been assuming, that "the People," whose united act

261

the Constitution was, are no longer among us, or not in their original form, but have fallen from that moment of grace into the ordinary condition of man, that of hostility and competition, and have left behind them only this single instrument, expressive of their will. The governments cannot do it; the people cannot do it; only the Court can do it, for only the Court can claim to read the authoritative document—to expound it—in the pure and disinterested way it requires. Judges of course make choices, but, unlike the other two branches, the Court speaks as though it had no will of its own, and was entitled to none, but was always obedient to the authority of others: the authority of the text, of reason itself, and of "the People." [21] What is more, only the Court has available to it the resource of the judicial opinion, the form in which judges not only commit themselves to reasoned public judgment on the question before them but submit their preferences both to established authority and to the precedential force of their own prior decisions. (However the justices exercise their actual freedom to choose in a particular case, their present judgment will restrict their freedom in later cases.) The judiciary is uniquely qualified for the position of national arbiter of constitutional disputes.

VI

The mythic origins of the Constitution not only place the power of exposition naturally in the hands of the Court, they inform us as to the spirit and manner in which that power should be exercised. The original source of authority being forever gone, the instrument must be expounded as a kind of sacred and testamentary trust, with a recognition that it is not subject to revision by its Author and hence with an eye to purpose and structure and value, not to particular terms and details.

In thus claiming the authority to "expound" the instrument of national constitution, Marshall makes the largest of claims for himself and for the judiciary. But in the way he discharges this authority he is careful to define and to respect sources of authority external to his own will, especially those that approximate as closely as possible the views of "the People." Hence his appeal to the past national judgment on the constitutionality of the Bank; to our experience of distress upon its dissolution; to the ways in which corporations have in fact been used not as "ends" but as "means"; to the range of meanings that properly belong to the word "necessary" in ordinary English; to ordinary language itself; to the common understandings that are naturally invoked by arguments of *reductio ad absurdum*; and to the "propositions too plain to be denied," which he repeatedly asserts as universal starting places. The law that Marshall makes is thus constitutive much in the manner of the common law, which determines what the law should be in large measure by what it is, i.e., by the customs and expectations that in fact mark the community and the culture: what we are is our law. This means that even when Marshall speaks in his most magisterial tones there is still a sense in which he speaks with the voice of "the People." [22]

In all of this, Marshall's opinion has a double voice rather like that of the Constitution itself: on some matters it declares itself with authority; on others it is silent, for these are of necessity left to others. It is perhaps partly this quality that explains why Marshall's opinion seems to be less an interpretation of the Constitution than an amendment to it, the overruling of which is unimaginable; for it is written in a similar combination of voices and is in this way continuous with the original text. Like the Constitution itself, Marshall performs the separation of powers that is essential to his official existence. At the end, despite its magisterial tone, this opinion turns to the reader it has instructed in its methods and says to him: it is now time for you to remake our language, to constitute and reconstitute our community and culture anew, as I have done; you must build on what I have made.

There is thus one other external authority to whom Marshall appeals, and that is the reader himself. For only if the reader accepts the external authorities to which Marshall appeals will these authorities have the standing of acts of "the People." It is ultimately on the reader's assent that the success of the opinion depends. Like Burke's British Constitution, the Constitution that Marshall expounds must have an internal as well as an external existence, a whole life in the reader's own mind and capacities. Thus the reader becomes for a moment the framer, the expositor, and the critic of the Constitution; he is to look back to its origins and forward to its construction in the unknown future.

It is thus to his readers that Marshall offers the most, for he offers to them—to us, that is—a future. If we acquiesce in his opinion, it defines a future for us in which we can engage in activities of the sort Marshall exemplifies and continue to do so long after he has left the scene. He addresses us as rhetoricians, like himself, who will be enabled by what he has done to continue the process of constitution and reconstitution of culture that he has begun.

THE POSSIBILITIES OF AMERICAN LAW: MAKING THE IDEAL REAL

But what kind of future does the Supreme Court actually offer us in *McCulloch* and similar cases? What possibilities for life does it suggest or establish? Here our focus is not so much on the conclusions *McCulloch* reaches as on the kind of thing it is and the process it is part of: the nature of the form we know as the judicial opinion and the practices of judicial law-making by which the Supreme Court has established itself as a central institution for the self-conscious and authoritative reconstitution of our language, culture, and community.

The Conversational Process of The Law

The most prominent feature of the judicial opinion is that it is not an isolated exercise of power but part of a continuing and collective process of conversation and judgment. The conversation of which it is a part is not a political conversation of the usual sort, proceeding as such conversations ordinarily do—by a kind of jostling and compromise, focusing mainly on the problem of the immediate present—but a highly formal one, in which authoritative conclusions are reached after explicit argument. These decisions in their turn become the material of future arguments leading to future decisions, and so on in a continuing process of opening and closure, argument and judgment, of which no one can claim to foresee the end.

This is a way of saying that judicial opinions incorporate within their world both the past (to which the court looks for its authority) and the future (to which it speaks as an authority). The opinion reaches its judgment by elaborating what has gone before—in *McCulloch* mainly the language of the Constitution and the experience supporting the necessity of the Bank—but is itself left open to elaboration by others. This process establishes connections across time of the sort that Burke celebrates, but these judicial connections are not merely attitudinal but systematic and reliable. The judicial process at once acknowledges the necessity of cultural change and creates a method for effecting it.

I

The way a court works is deeply affected by the kind of question it addresses. A court normally avoids deciding hypothetical questions; it waits, inactive, until a case is brought before it, which it is asked by others to decide. Under our Constitution, indeed, the federal judicial power is limited to "cases arising" under certain circumstances, and the Supreme Court has elaborated a complex body of law defining those terms of limitation. It requires, for example, that a dispute be brought by parties with genuinely adverse interests and that it be neither premature (hence imperfectly focused) nor stale. It is only when these conditions have been met that the Court has claimed the power to determine the constitutionality of acts of the national and federal legislatures. The Court's claim to decide a constitutional question of this kind to a large degree rests on the fact that it is better situated to decide it than the legislature that passed the statute would have been. Suppose, for example, that Congress passed a statute and then immediately sought from a federal court an advisory opinion on its constitutionality. What claim could the court properly make that it had the power to do what it was asked? It could claim some legal expertise, no doubt, but legislatures do not lack that; some sense of the world and its demands, but surely no more than the legislature; some degree of removal from the contemporary political process, but the timing of the judgment sought would tend to blur that distinction, for judges are not immune to public opinion, and, in a case like this one, the judge, like the legislator, would mainly see the present need, since that is what would be before him. But the situation would be quite different when time had passed and a conflict had actually arisen, in the ordinary course of life, which one party cared enough about to bring before the court, the other to resist, and when the particular statute had been seen in operation with other bodies of law and with other expectations and demands rooted in other patterns of need and desire, arising in other times. Now the judge could make another kind of claim altogether: that he occupies a position for making a constitutional judgment that is inherently superior to that of the legislature passing the statute and superior also to what his own position would have been had he granted an advisory opinion.[23]

Cases are often not neatly packaged in the categories established by legislative or judicial rules but exhibit surprising configurations of their own, bringing to the surface hitherto unseen tensions and contradictions in our social life and culture. The legal case is always a narrative; and a narrative, as we saw in the *Iliad*, can always be a way of testing the presuppositions of the culture, forcing to the bright center of the mind difficulties we wish to push back into the twilight. This means that the case is always an invitation to the reconstitution of the language in the light of new circumstances and new intractabilities.

II

The fact that the case is always a narrative means something from the point of view of the litigant in particular. For him the case is, at its heart, an occasion and a method in which he can tell his story and have it heard. He has the right to a jury, to ensure that he will have an audience that will understand his story and speak his language.[24] The presence of a jury requires that the entire story, on both sides, be told in ordinary language and made intelligible to the ordinary person. This is a promise to the citizen that the law will ultimately speak to him, and for him, in the language that he speaks, not in a technical or special jargon. This, in the terms that Marshall has taught us, is a continuing acknowledgment of the supremacy of "the People" who are for us the ultimate source of law and authority. It is our law, and it must make sense to us. In addition, by its very structure the legal hearing achieves, at least for the moment, a performed equality among the speakers; this, as we learned from Thucydides, is the essential premise of the social practice of argument, as it is of compassion, gratitude, and indeed of all the social and political activities of free people.[25] Here equality is not only the condition of the legal process but its product—perhaps, indeed, its finest product: equality under law.

The judicial process not only recognizes the individual but compels him to recognize others. For the litigant, the lawyer, and the observer alike, the central ethical and social meaning of the practice of the adversary hearing is its perpetual lesson that there is always another side to the story, that yours is not the only point of view.[26] For the actors as for the judges, the juxtaposition of the two incompatible stories makes us ask in what language the story should be told again and a judgment reached; it compels what George Eliot, in describing the function of art, has called an "extension of [our] sympathies" into an "attention to what is apart from [our]selves," which, as she says, is the "raw material" of moral life.[27]

The law can thus be seen as a discipline in the acknowledgment of limits, in the recognition of others, and in the necessity of cooperation. It is a method of individual and collective self-education, a way in which we teach ourselves, over and over again, how little we can foresee, how much we depend on others, and how important to us are the practices we have inherited from the past. It is a way of creating a world in part by imagining what can be said on the other side. In these ways it is a lesson in humility.

III

But it is more even than this: it is the constitution of a world by the distribution of authority within it; it establishes the terms on which its actors may talk in conflict or cooperation among themselves. The law establishes roles and relations and voices, positions from which and audiences to which one may speak, and it gives us as speakers the materials and methods of a discourse. It is a way of creating a rhetorical community over time.[28] It is this discourse, working in the social context of its own creation, this language in the fullest sense of the term, that *is* the law. It makes us members of a common world.

This is not a language of social policy and political philosophy, though there are of course some (often rather exaggerated) continuities between these realms of discourse; for in the law questions are never addressed abstractly, and statements are never made to the air. Every legal speech is made from a defined position, to a defined audience, in a defined language. The law always assumes a speaker and audience located in the context it defines. This is how it makes a world and makes it real.

The legal text, for example—whether constitution, trust, statute, or contract—always requires that one who claims a meaning for it answer the question, "Who are you when you speak as you do?" What you wish to say, what you can say, and how what you do say will be understood will all vary dramatically with your answer, which might be, for example: "I am the manager of the condominium established in this agreement, and I say . . ."; "I am the tenant under this lease, and I say . . ."; "I am a Justice of the United States Supreme Court, given authority to decide certain cases of which I assert this is one, and I say . . . ." [29] Similarly, the lawyer or judge presented with a question about the meaning of a contract, statute, or judicial opinion or about the wisdom of a particular course of action—the commercial development of certain natural resources, for example, or cross-city busing to desegregate schools—will as a matter of second nature ask himself not only about the merits of the substantive question but who it is in our system that ought to have the authority to decide that question and under what procedures. The law creates a world by distributing authority within it. To speak as if all questions could be reduced to matters of substantive policy determined by what "we" think best would destroy the constituted "we" that is the great achievement of the law and substitute for it a community divided into two parts: a "we" that talks about and determines the policy and those others whose lives are to be affected by it.

The law is best regarded not so much as a set of rules and doctrines or as a bureaucratic system or as an instrument for social control but as a culture, for the most part a culture of argument. It is a way of making a world with a life and a value of its own. The conversation that it creates is at once its method and its point, and its object is to give to the world it creates the kind of intelligibility that results from the simultaneous recognition of contrasting positions. This recognition is necessary to the rational definition and pursuit even of the most selfish ends. Without it, neither reason nor ambition can have form or meaning.

IV

The fact that the conversation of the law is largely argumentative has important consequences of its own. Legal argument exposes in clarified and self-conscious form—in slow motion, as it were—the processes of agreement and disagreement—of persuasion—by which this part of our culture, and our culture more generally, are defined and transformed. For in legal argument the state of the discourse itself—how we should think and talk—is a constant subject of conscious attention and debate. This means that the contours of the culture are pushed to their limits and marked with extraordinary distinctness. As the argument proceeds, each speaker tests the limits of his language, subjecting its every term and procedure to all the strain that it can take—that we can take—in order to make things come out his way. And since he must always operate within strict limits imposed by time and the interest of his audience, he is constantly forced to discriminate among the arguments he might make, putting forward what seems best, holding back what is weak or unimportant, and so on. As the materials of the legal culture are tested in this manner, against each other and against the conditions of the world—as they are put to work—they are defined and reorganized in especially clear and reliable ways. This makes it possible to think clearly about their transformation.

Consider this point in the life of the modern lawyer. When he writes a brief or makes an argument, in court or in a negotiation, he offers us his best performance of the state of his art, as does the lawyer who opposes him. Between them they provide a momentary definition of the resources and limits of their legal culture. When the lawyers have done all they can and their capacities for argument are spent, we see where we are in a new way, a way that the unused materials of argument, lying about without order, arrangement, or force—mere sets of cases, rules, and commonplaces—would never allow. Each lawyer has made every proposal for change he thinks possible and has had to accept what he cannot change. In argument of this kind the speakers are forced to perform an allegiance to their common language, to the ways of talking that make the dispute intelligible and the community possible. One of the functions of a culture of argument, the law among others, is to provide a rhetorical coherence to public life by compelling those who disagree about one thing to express their actual or pretended agreement about everything else. Argument functions by agreement, and by agreement under stress, and is thus constitutive of the changing culture that even the opponents share. In compelling this kind of agreement, the law makes disagreement at once intelligible, limited, and amenable to resolution.

Legal argument by its nature contrasts one way of talking with another, one version of a narrative with another, and in this way gives its users (and their community) the benefits of contrast and tension. The lawyer speaks from and to various parts of the self, in various modes, and is always subject to the double duty of making sense both in ordinary English and in the specialized language of the law. It is in fact the inconsistencies among the lawyer's ways of talking that gives him the purchase necessary to propose, and to resist, changes in his discourse.

Argument of the legal kind thus defines a place that is part of a larger world yet distanced from it, at once representative and critical. It is a place something like the place that Achilles occupies in Book 9, but here the actors have something to say about their language and can propose changes in it. Legal argument is an organized and systematic process of conversation by which our words get and change their meaning.

The Life the Law Offers the Judge and the Lawyer

If a judge is to respond to the demands and possibilities presented by a legal case as I have outlined it, he or she will have to speak in an extraordinarily rich and complex way, not in a voice that is merely bureaucratic and official. To be true to the actual difficulties of a real legal case, an opinion must be full of the kind of life that comes from a set of acknowledged tensions: between the two versions of the story before the court; between the stories so told and the language of legal conclusion; between the demand that like cases be treated alike and the recognition that cases never are "alike"; between the fidelities owed to the past and the future and those owed to the present; between an awareness that the case is a particular dispute between individual persons and a sense that it is typical as well; and so on. That the judge's voice is an individual voice, speaking to individuals—to the parties and their lawyers, to future parties and lawyers and judges—is a performance and validation of our claim to be a government by "the People," for it is always one of us speaking to another one of us. And because legal cases arise in new configurations, full of surprise, both argument and judgment require more than a mechanical comparison of case with case; one must always be prepared to make active all that one knows. In the complexity and formality of his speech, its metaphoric character and its openness to uncertainty, in its tension between the general and the particular, the judge must indeed be something of a poet. He must speak as one who has something to learn.

I earlier suggested that it was a mark of the excellence of Samuel Johnson's moral thought, and of its truth, that in it he struggled toward the comprehension of contraries, and one can regard the law as an institution established on that very principle. For the legal process of adversary thought and argument tests each position by its opposite, each truth by an opposite truth.[30] In the law, as in Johnson and Austen, we find that "principles" are not merely generalities to be applied to particular cases but complex and disciplined attitudes of the mind and self, educated positions from which difficulty (in Burke's sense) can be acknowledged and addressed.[31]

Honesty requires the judge to acknowledge that his own acts of choosing cannot be wholly explained or justified. The good judge thus speaks in a double voice, as one who has brought to bear as well as he can the sources of authority external to himself, and as one who makes a choice for which he is responsible. An opinion is not merely an organized defense of his decision, the "best case" for the result reached, but an articulation of what he really thinks the case should mean, including an expression of his doubts. The best judge, like Socrates, exposes himself to refutation. The most important achievement of judicial writing, indeed, is ethical and intellectual: the manifestation in performance of a serious, responsible, and open mind, faithful to the sources of authority external to the self even while contributing to their transformation. Excellence measured in this way is far more important than excellence measured by our agreement with the votes a judge happens to cast, for by definition many of the cases that he decides will be hard ones, with much to say on both sides, and our own positions are themselves always subject to change. His most significant legacy by far is his definition of his own role and the institution of which he is a part.

From a lawyer's point of view, the future offered by *McCulloch* and similar cases is a life of argument in which he puts together cases out of the materials of the world, addressing the tensions between ordinary language and legal language and among various strains within legal discourse, and then offers to the judge, or to the jury, an ideal version of the case for their consideration and persuasion. The task of the lawyer is not simply to persuade, using whatever cultural devices lie at hand, but to persuade a judge or jury that one result or another is the best way to act in the cultural situation defined by these facts or this evidence and by this set of statutes and opinions and understandings. This suggests the beginnings of a response to Plato's *Gorgias*, for the lawyer is not committed simply to power through persuasion but to persuasion of a special kind that perpetually recreates an ideal version of his inheritance. The lawyer does become like the object of his persuasion, as Plato said the rhetorician would; but under our conventions—and the same could be said of those by which Corcyra and Corinth addressed Athens—the lawyer's audience is always ideal as well as real: he speaks to the judge or jury not as they are defined by their individual interests, passions, and biases but as they are defined by their role, which is to do justice. He thus speaks to, and becomes like, his own view of the best judge or juror he can imagine, and this is one form of the best version of himself.[32]

The Ideal Reader in Literature and in Law

There are ways in which the kind of reading and speaking that lies at the heart of the law is both like and unlike the somewhat more "literary" activities we have been examining in this book. I have repeatedly suggested, for example, that reading involves a dialectic between the ideal version of oneself that a particular text seeks to call into being and the rest of what one is. As we work through a text, we are thus always asking who the "ideal reader" of this text is and whether we wish to become such a one, even for a moment. Engagement with a literary text is in this way structurally tentative. (Our reading of Burke is an example of a dialectical process that ends in a qualified acceptance.) The reading of a legal text, by contrast, cannot be tentative in exactly this way, for in its own terms the legal text is authoritative. Whether you like it or not, as the reader of a statute, contract, trust, or judicial opinion you are in the first instance its servant, seeking to make real what it directs. But its authority is not unquestioned. When the text is once understood, it is checked, not only against other parts of the reader's being—other standards and sentiments and wishes—but against other parts of the literature of the law. How does this text, so read, fit within the larger legal culture? We look to the statute to see if the regulation is valid, to the Constitution to see if the statute is valid, to other opinions to see how the implications of this one fit with them, and so on.

There are other apparent differences between reading legal and other texts. For example, a legal text speaks directly to its reader, as other texts do, but the textual community it establishes with the individual reader is always a way of making another community as well, a community among its readers. In this sense, law is structurally ulterior in character, for it is always meant to affect what you say and do in relation to others. As we have seen, it is literally and deliberately constitutive: it creates roles and relations and places and occasions on which one may speak; it gives to the parties a set of things that they may say, and it prohibits them from saying other things. It makes a real social world in a way that a work of literature does not. It is also obviously true that individual works in the literature of the law seldom achieve greatness on any scale, let alone the greatness established by the *Iliad* or the plays of Shakespeare. And the canon of authoritative legal texts that must be read and dealt with is perhaps somewhat less subject to individual selection than is the canon of literary texts. If the law is to be great, it is more obviously the case than with literature that we must make it so.

Yet these points should not be overstated. Literary critics may sometimes feel that they are trapped by an authoritative canon of texts that is no less rigid than the lawyers' canon. There is a sense in which no text is great except as it is made so by readers who perceive its possibilities. And literary texts, like legal texts, are also in the first instance authoritative and seek both to establish community and to affect behavior. The differences are largely in emphasis and in the degree of explicitness with which these things are done.

Accordingly, the "ideal reader" remains a useful idea in reading law, at least as a way of defining the possibilities for this aspect of our lives. Instead of asking what a statute, opinion, or constitutional provision "means," as if we expected a one-sentence response, we can ask what it means in a different way: How would the ideal reader contemplated by this document, indeed, constituted by it, understand its bearing in the present circumstances? This requires an understanding of the text in its cultural and political context, in light of the accepted meanings of words

271

and with an understanding of the major purposes of the text, of its types and examples. It thus requires one to become an expert reader of the culture itself. Once a particular text is understood in this way, it must be joined with other texts and with the rest of the culture to make what we call a field or body of law. The lawyer becomes the ideal reader not only of one text but of a collection of texts in the very selection of which he or she participates.

To say that the culture is read not only to interpret but to check the text means that the lawyer is engaged in a continuous argument the terms of which are always changing as he works out the relation between the particular document and its larger world. The lawyer's work thus contributes to a process of collective or cultural education that is in structure analogous to that experienced by the single reader of a literary text.

Is the ideal reader of the law different every time, as the ideal reader of literature is? If so, how can we square that fact with our view of the rule of law? It follows from what I have said that the ideal reader of a legal text cannot be the same every time, partly because of differences among people (or differences among different stages in the development of one person) and partly because of shifts in the cultural context in which the words will have to work. But while ideal readers cannot be identical, any more than your *Iliad* and mine can be identical, in this case, as in the other, there can be either coherence and consistency among readers or the opposite of these things. The goal is not identity but something like what Wittgenstein calls a family resemblance. In law as in literature, I cannot state the meaning of a text in some other form and insist on that as the full equivalent of the original statement, for the meaning is in the original statement and nowhere else. But this is not to say that solid judgments cannot be made about the meaning of particular texts or that meaning is subjective and indeterminate, the mere function of our political or literary preferences.

It has been the genius of our law to recognize these things and to profit from them. It is not a defect but a merit of our system that judges are acknowledged to have discretion, that legal questions are seen as open and difficult, that juries can decide within a wide range. To pretend that all cases, all questions, can fit within some preexisting categorical scheme would be to pretend the impossible and to hide unjustified judgments behind a fiction. It is the aim of our law not to obliterate individual judicial judgments in favor of a scheme but to structure and discipline them, to render them public and accountable. This is true of the lawyer as well as the judge, and the client knows it; he does not pay for skill in determining mechanical consequences but for highly complex individual judgments. Reading is always writing, and it is always done by an individual mind. The reconstitution of our legal culture and its language must always be done, if it is to be done at all, by individual minds, and that means with individual differences. These differences, when properly publicized and disciplined, are not to be lamented but celebrated.

THE LAW IS A SET of social and intellectual practices that have their own reality, force, and significance. It provides a place that is at once part of the larger culture and apart from it, a place in which we can think about a problematic story by retelling it in various ways and can ask in a new and self-conscious way what it is to mean. Law works by a process of argument that places one version of events against another and creates a tension between them (and between the endings appropriate to each); in doing so it makes our choice of language conscious rather than habitual and creates a moment at which controlled change of language and culture becomes possible. The rhetorical structure of the law makes a place for each party and defines a relation between them by establishing the ways they may talk; in doing this it suggests a conception of justice as equality, for a person may find himself in any of these roles.[33] The method of criticism most appropriate to the law as such is concerned less with the wisdom of a particular policy choice or the rightness of a particular rule or result than with the character that a court, legislature, or other legal speaker gives himself and his institution, the place it defines for others, and the relation it establishes between them. The law is less a branch of the social sciences than of the humanities in that it seeks not to be a closed system but an open one. It learns from the past and seeks new terms for the expression of motives, new forms for the establishment of relations; it is a method of learning and teaching; and its central concern is with the kind of relations that we establish with our inherited culture and with each other when we speak its language.

To conceive of the law as a rhetorical and social system, a way in which we use an inherited language to talk to each other and to maintain a community, suggests in a new way that the heart of law is what we always knew it was: the open hearing in which one point of view, one construction of language and reality, is tested against another. The multiplicity of readings that the law permits is not its weakness but its strength, for it is this that makes room for different voices and gives a purchase by which culture may be modified in response to the demands of circumstance. It is a method at once for recognizing others, for acknowledging ignorance, and for achieving cultural change.

*　　　*　　　*

THIS ACCOUNT OF THE LAW is of course not a description of the way every lawyer and judge in fact goes to work or how he conceives of himself, nor is it meant to justify the actual operation and effect of our legal system, let alone our economic system, both of which in fact suffer from disgraceful injustices. Rather, I mean to suggest a set of possibilities implicit in the institution and its practices, to define the kind of aim that the lawyer can have for himself. And these possibilities and aims are remarkable. The "case arising" can be seen as a place for cultural definition, testing, and change; as a way of assuring continued congruence between our languages of justice and expediency; as a means for complicating clichés and first attitudes into deeper understanding and for extending imaginative sympathy to those differently situated from ourselves; and, finally, as a way of making a place of coherence in a process of cultural change. Even more: the case establishes an essential equality between people, making this value real; and it proceeds by a method of argument and conversation that both recognizes the individual's view of his own situation and complicates that view by forcing him to recognize the claims of another. It is like dialectic in that it is refutational, and it is a kind of friendship in its insistence on the reality and validity of others. It proceeds by a conversation in which each speaker is invited to present an ideal version of himself, speaking to an ideal audience.

Such is the promise of our early law. In this book I have not traced its subsequent history to see how far we have realized or destroyed our possibilities. But I hope that I have set forth grounds on which we can observe and judge what we have made of the chances we once gave ourselves.

10

An Afterword

In this book I have sought to draw the reader's attention, and my own, to certain aspects of our common life and to hold it there. My object has been to make more fully accessible to thought the ways in which we constitute ourselves and our relations with other people when we use, and in using recreate, the language that makes us what we are. I have done this partly as a way of learning more about the meaning of certain texts; but, as we have seen, it is also true that these texts have much to teach us about the more general matters I have mentioned.

The texts read here have been drawn from a wide diversity of generic types: poetry, history, philosophy, fiction, and law and the less easily classifiable texts by Swift, Johnson, and Burke. But we have read each of these texts in much the same way, pursuing the same questions, drawing analogies and connections between the texts, and so on. This has in part been a way of defining our subject not as poetry or philosophy or law or any of the others but as the general activity of which each of these is a species, namely, the cultural and ethical activity of making meaning in relation to others. By moving from one form to another I have tried to suggest that they can all be seen as one thing, not many, and to suggest a common way in which they can be read, understood, and learned from. By uniting in this way the forms of expression read in this book I mean to claim that there is a deep identity not only among them but among the topics with which they are centrally concerned: beauty and truth and justice.

The way of reading exemplified here is not an analytic technique that objectifies what it studies, nor is it a new conceptual system; rather, it is a way of responding to and thinking about the expressions of another mind. It has certain similarities with other ways of reading—with the attention to detail that characterizes the New Criticism, the respect paid to the text that is the hallmark of classical studies, and the reconstructive and participatory method of the law—but as a whole I believe it is different from any of them. It has been my purpose to record not merely a method or a set of terms but an activity of mind expressed in what I call a language. Such a language can be learned only by immersion in its processes. One understands it not when one can translate its terms into other equivalences but when one can do it oneself—when, in Wittgenstein's phrase, one knows how to go on—as I hope the reader has begun to do with the language at work in this text. The key words of analysis and criticism that I have been using accordingly acquire their meaning not from explicit definition but from the reader's experience of their use. While this book is not scientific in the usual sense, there is thus a sense in which it is nonetheless empirical, for it rests wholly on the reader's verification of its value in his or her own experience. It is an invitation to an activity that must prove itself in the reader's own terms.

What follows here is a sort of recapitulation: a concluding account of this activity and a summary of what it has meant to engage with these texts in this way.

Reciprocity and Uncertainty

My aim has been to focus on the complex fact that whenever we speak or write we define ourselves and another and a relation between us, and we do so in words that are necessarily made by others and modified by our use of them. When, for example, Achilles struggles with the limits of his inherited language—the only language he has—and tries to find a way to speak and act that does justice to his situation, we ask not only whether he will succeed in making meaning as he wishes but also what kind of character he will give himself in doing so and what kind of relations he will establish with others. Think also of the ways Emma defines herself as a person and a "friend" in her conversations with Harriet and Mr. Knightley; of what is said by Socrates to be at stake in the difference between dialectical friendship and rhetorical flattery as ways of relating to other people and to one's common language; of the variety of ways in which Odysseus, Phoenix, and Ajax define themselves and their relation to Achilles in their speeches to him and create a reality to which he can respond.

These processes of ethical and cultural creation are especially difficult to think about or talk about because self and culture are reciprocal, mutually formed and mutually forming over time. We are in part the products of our language, but each time we speak we remake it. This reciprocity is so deeply embedded in our experience that it is hard to recognize it. As we grow up in the world, our experience is formed by the language in which it is presented and talked about, and this language becomes so much a part of the mind as to seem a part of nature. One is perpetually telling one's story to oneself and others, trying to shape things so that the next step fits with what has gone before, ceaselessly claiming significance for one's experience and actions, and the question always is, in what language can (or must) one do these things? What are the implications—the adequacies and inadequacies—of our common ways of describing the world, of constituting relations, of feeling injury, of acting socially, and of aspiring to what is not yet? The language marks the mind, and one will normally see that one's language is contingent, not necessary, only if one experiences a basic cultural dislocation: the sense that words have lost their meaning.

This is what happens to Achilles, whose clear sense of social place and aim dissolves, leaving him no language in which to describe himself or his wishes, no social context in which to act; to Socrates' interlocutors and to the reader of the *Gorgias*, whose acceptance of the traditional language of Greek value is disturbed or broken down; to whatever reader of Burke's *Reflections* is at the beginning favorably disposed toward the slogans of Dr. Price, which are by that text rendered impossible; to the Athenians and Melians, who find they have nothing satisfactory to say to each other, even though both sides apparently want a conversation to proceed; and so on.

As these examples make plain, it is not always clear how to regard such a change in the relation between self and culture. It can manifest a diseased detachment from reality, as it does for Swift's persona, or a slide toward essential meaninglessness, as it does for the actors in Thucydides' *History*; or it can be a critical stage in a process of development toward maturity and independence, as it is for Socrates and, in another way, for Achilles. The culture has its limits, and rebellion against them may be a good thing; it has dead forms—seen, for example, in the clichés, the empty rationality, the sentimentality of Swift's persona—which must be shaken off; yet the rebellion may also be infantile or grandiose or foolish, itself a disease, and there is no easy way to tell which is the case. As Johnson, Swift, and Austen in their different ways teach us, each of us has much to learn from our language, even those parts that, when misunderstood, seem empty or trite. At its best, the process of life will be a dialectic between self and culture, checking one against the other and vice versa. But how can such a process be coherent when there is no stable self, no stable culture, to rely on? How can we trust what we see, what we feel, what we value? How can we judge and improve ourselves and our productions?

The uncertain reciprocity I describe is often felt to be intolerable, for it seems to entail an essential and universal relativism, extending even to our own character and consciousness. When the resources of a certain kind of thinking run out, a common response is to give up in despair; the disconcerting discovery that the conceptual and logical apparatus of quasi-scientific rationality will not do for the understanding of life or literature or law leads to the announcement that we live in an incoherent and elemental flux in which no reasoning, no meaning, is possible. But to say that there is no meaning or knowledge of one kind is not to deny the possibility of other kinds, and in our actual lives we show that we know how to read and speak, to live with language, texts, and each other, and to do so with considerable confidence. But to do this we must accept the conditions on which we live. When we discover that we have in this world no earth or rock to stand or walk upon but only shifting sea and sky and wind, the mature response is not to lament the loss of fixity but to learn to sail.

The Reconstitution of Language and Community

But how is "sailing" of this kind to be done? How is the essential reciprocity and instability of character and culture to be managed from the inside, the only way it can be done? How can we properly determine what we say, who we are, what relations we have with others, and what world of meaning we create?

These are the questions we have been pursuing from the beginning of this book, examining responses within the imagined world of these texts—the responses made by Achilles, say, or by Emma—and the responses the writers of these texts have performed in writing the texts. It has been my object not to propose some programmatic solution to such questions (that would richly deserve a place on the pages of Swift) but to define a way of thinking about them.

I

The first step, implicit in what has already been said, is to expand our conception of what we mean by reading and writing to include every effort to claim meaning or establish relations in language. The issues raised in this book are present not only in formal and literary speech but in speech and writing of every kind, whenever one tells a story and claims a meaning for it or otherwise acts with language in one's world. The second is to focus attention on the language and culture the writer has inherited and the kind of relationship he or she establishes with it. Then we examine the relation between the writer and the reader, that is, the relationship created by the text itself (what I call the textual community) and ask what connection exists between that textual community and the larger culture that supplies the materials with which it is formed. For while the text is necessarily made out of the resources found within the culture—its words, expectations, values, and conventions—it can nonetheless, as we have seen, be deeply critical of those materials and that culture. It may even propose a new world.

Chapter 10. An Afterword

In directing our attention to the language with which the actor or writer must work, we regard a particular system of discourse—that of the heroic Achaean world, for example, or of eighteenth-century English moral thought—as a system to be lived with, as if it were all we had, and ask what resources for life and action it offers, what restraints it imposes. What are its resources, its limits? Like law students, we try to imagine and reconstruct a life lived on terms different from our own: with its own ways of characterizing natural and social worlds, its own terms of value and motive, its own senses of reason. Our next question is what the actor does with these materials. How does he or she address their limits, employ their resources, and reconstitute them in his or her performance? Think, for example, of Socrates' redefinition of the central Greek terms of value, *agathos* and *kalos*; of the way "reason" is defined by Johnson as the engagement of the whole mind with the conditions of its existence, or by Swift, who demonstrates the utter irrationality of what is commonly called "reason" when it is separated from the rest of the self; or of the kind of connection between the individual and his larger world made possible by the language of Emma or Burke or John Marshall. What contribution, we ask, does each particular text make to the maintenance of its own resources, to a recognition of its own past, and to the establishment of a future for its author and its readers?

Our concern has thus been with the ways in which words—and languages—acquire and hold and lose their meanings, with the methods by which culture is maintained, criticized, and transformed. We are especially concerned with the central terms by which a social world is constituted and its values defined, the essential terms of praise or blame, of admiration and contempt, by which we define ourselves, our motives, and our relations with others—the terms by which we organize our lives. Think, for example, of the meanings that have been given by our texts to such terms as liberty, property, and religion; *agathos* and *kalos*; patience, pride, and forgiveness; toleration; credulity and curiosity; truth and fiction; justice and expediency. "Does not everything, my dear Emma, combine to teach us the beauty of truth and sincerity in all our dealings with each other?"

Our interest has naturally extended to the social and literary forms in which language is made and remade. We have looked at the kinds of conversations that work well and badly, for example, of which Plato's dialectic and rhetoric can be taken as clear examples; at the ways in which poetry, law, and history alike define a world and act upon it; at corruptions of language and mind, such as those exhibited by Diodotus, by Swift's persona, and by Emma Woodhouse; at the differences between false questions and real ones, between clichés and real principles, and at the differences also between purely conceptual languages, which address only the intellect, and the more poetic or literary languages that address

279

the reader as a complete and functioning intelligence; at the ways in which all power is a species of persuasion; at the difference between the mind that is controlled by its language and learns by imitation and the mind that assumes and discharges the responsibilities of a mature speaker in its world; and at the ways in which writing is a way of making a self and remaking a culture.

The written "text" has a unique place in the history of culture, for it reduces to permanence a process that is otherwise ephemeral and renders public, through the multiplication of readings, what is in the first instance essentially private. Unlike any other conversation, it has an unlimited number of anonymous but necessarily individual partners, located in an unlimited set of cultural contexts. It offers its reader an experience of cultural reconstitution that can be repeated in the imagination at any place or time. In this sense it is a part of the culture that transcends its own immediate location in space, time, and social context, as Thucydides knew well when he described his text as a "possession for all time." Since the text—whether it is an argument, a poem, or a work of history or philosophy—is always a reconstitution of the culture, it is necessarily *about* the culture, whether it idealizes it, ironically repudiates it, or elaborates its incoherences. The text is not a closed system but an artifact made by one mind and offered to another; it recreates the materials of the world for use in the world.

II

Our second concern cuts right across the first. It has to do with the community that every text establishes between its writer and its reader. While a writer is reconstituting his culture as he puts its resources to work in his composition, he is at the same time establishing a relationship with his reader, the person to whom he speaks. This community is different from the culture enacted in the real or imaginary world reported in the text and different from the culture in which the author lived; it is a community of his creation between himself and his reader. When we study the "culture of argument" enacted in the *Iliad* or Thucydides' *History*, for example, we reconstruct from the text the terms and conventions of argument that characterize the world represented in it, respectively the imaginary world of the heroic age and the historical world of fifth-century Greece; when we study the "textual community" created by Homer or Thucydides, we examine the social universe created by the text, between the author and the reader. This relationship has its terms and conventions, its characters and its methods, just as the culture of argument has. In the texts we have read, the author offers the reader an experience of feeling and thought with a shape and meaning of its own,

280

and this experience enacts the values and attitudes the author wishes us to share.

The textual community is partly created through the materials of the culture, and it always takes the process of reconstitution as part of its subject. That is, the writer addresses the reader, in part, as someone who shares his problem as a member of the same culture, and he is always asking and answering this question: What does it mean to be situated as we are? What can we say? What can we do?

This is what Homer does in the *Iliad*, where he addresses the problem of the relationship between the individual and his culture in two contexts: as it exists for the imagined actors in his poem, especially for Achilles; and as it exists for the poet who must speak this language in composing his poem. Out of the inherited materials of the heroic language he creates a textual community with the reader that is different from, and critical of, the heroic culture of which he writes, even though it is that culture that furnishes the materials of his composition, the very language of his text. The ultimate standard of judgment he establishes is not a new conceptual scheme or a new vocabulary but the person he leads the reader in fact to become, below the level of language, as he responds to this text. This poem makes something new in the reader, something that is not directly expressible in its language or contemplated by its culture. Partly for this reason, Homer's criticism achieves an astonishing level of generalization; for it is not only the heroic culture that he criticizes but any culture made by man.

In such ways as this, and for good or ill, the writer always makes a community with another in his text, and this community has a life and character of its own. To attend to this fact is to raise all the questions that such relations present: the nature of friendship, justice, and generosity, the way that the self and its interests are defined in relation to others, and what it means to try to form a social world that is better for both.

I have regarded the communities defined in these texts as forms of friendship. One thinks, for example, of Homer's stimulation of the reader's sympathy for others, his demonstration that we will forget what we know; of Plato's performance of dialectical friendship; of Swift's disciplined insistence that his reader recognize his own autonomy and responsibility; of Johnson's sharing with his reader the processes of mind by which he works his way back from perpetually recreated error to complex and stable perceptions of his circumstances; of Jane Austen's creation of an experience of progressive and educative intimacy with another mind; of Burke's attempt to constitute a political world by creating a discourse that the reader may use for the organization of his own life, from its most private to its public aspects; of the American legal materials, which are based on a conception of the citizen as equal reader, equal speaker. In these ways friendship has become the standard by which the reader of this book has been invited to judge textual communities and, indeed, other communities as well. A large part of the meaning of a text, a community, or a culture lies in the ways in which it invites its reader to become active in engaging with it. Does a particular text break its reader into parts and invite him to forget what he knows about his life and himself, or does it speak to him as a whole, reminding him of what it is his nature to forget? Does it recognize the equality and autonomy of its reader and seek to educate him, perhaps through the kinds of refutation or humiliation familiar to us from Plato, Swift, Johnson, and Austen, or does it seek to flatter or manipulate him?

In such ways as this the literary question—Who is the ideal reader of this text?—becomes a political question as well, and these texts, even the nonpolitical ones, have taught us much about the way that political communities, like textual communities, should be judged. Not that any of the political communities talked about achieves the ideal suggested, a world of conversational and refutational friendship, a world of equal speakers with each other. But they do establish points on a line that can be extrapolated into the future,* a conception of a public world toward which we may hope to work.

In a world of flux, where self and culture are in a process of continuous and reciprocal change, the ground of judgment on which we can best rely is the ground we make with each other when we talk. Our sense of character and relation is in the end the firmest foundation of value and basis of criticism. I do not mean a merely instinctive "feel," but a sensibility that requires education—education of the kind that each of these writers has in his or her way offered us. The sense of character and relation can be an ethical standard even for the pluralist, who wishes to acknowledge both the limits of his own mind and the force of his own culture upon it, yet wishes not to jettison his judgment in a sea of relativism. Consider, for example, what can be meant by "character and relation" in the law. For me the really important question to ask about a court that decides a difficult case is not whether it reached the result I happen to

---

*Do I mean the selection and arrangement of texts in this book to reflect the progress of the human race? In a sense, of course not; there has been no progress since the *Iliad* and never will be. But I do think Swift and Johnson and Austen are right to see more merit in their inherited language of morality and community than Plato could see in his, and I think, too, that the self-conscious constitution-making of the eighteenth century, especially in America, represented a new stage in the possibilities for collective life.

prefer but whether it established an appropriate character for itself and an appropriate set of relations with its own intellectual inheritance and the people in the case. The central idea of justice, on this view, is a matter not of rules, distributions, or correctives but a matter of relations. With respect to official invasions of privacy, for example, the central question is not "how far they went" but out of what relation between the citizen and the state the officials were functioning: what it *meant* that they did what they did. The essential idea of equality before the law is an equality of speakers, not an equality of distribution or results (though the former kind of equality has consequences for the latter). This is the idea at work in the culture of argument we saw in Thucydides; and if the speakers in those debates could have seen their equality as a product of their language rather than as a condition of its validity, they might have made an invention that would have saved their world.

It is often said that the major tension in modern political life is between the demands of equality and the demands of liberty, but the kind of equality of which I now speak is in fact deeply tied to liberty; it is really another feature of the same conception of the person. As Sartre said, in the work from which one of the epigraphs to this book was drawn, liberty and equality are simultaneously affirmed in the act of writing. Aristotle is right when he says that justice in its most general definition is the chief of the virtues, comprehending all the others; and he was perhaps more right than he knew when he said, in a sentence also used as an epigraph to this book, that "justice and friendship are about the same things and occur in the same relations."

Literary and Social Art

One way to sum up my views is to say that I regard all speaking and writing, and reading too, as a cultural and ethical activity that is itself a kind of literary and social art, a way of doing one thing with something else. This art is the activity by which the individual makes out of common materials a new version of what he has inherited, a reconstitution of his language and culture. This is of necessity a social and ethical process, for the writer or speaker always acts in the relationship of two that is implied in the act of expression; and a question that must then always be addressed is who these two are as individuals, as a community, and as a culture. This view brings together into the same field of action and comprehension matters often thought of as quite distinct, perhaps as unconnectable: ideas of culture and community, of beauty and justice; the processes of politics and friendship; the public and the private; the self and the world.

In speaking of reconstitution, I do not mean that the writer invents a wholly new and idiosyncratic way of talking but that he finds ways to give new meaning, and sometimes new form, to the terms, structures, and methods of the language he has inherited. He makes a "new language" but not out of nothing; he makes it out of an old language, reconstituting its terms of description and feeling, of fact and value, into new patterns of significance, new movements of the mind. I say that he makes his language out of something else, but not in the sense that a carver simply makes a figure out of wood; he works, rather, the way a musical composer makes his music, not only out of notes, tones, timbres, and rhythms—the physical material of his art—but out of the music that precedes what he writes, that is, out of musical expectations and understandings. Thus, he makes music at once out of sounds and out of music itself. Similarly, the lawyer or judge makes a case partly out of the trouble in the world—the injury, disagreement, or hatred that gave rise to the case—and partly out of the law itself, the preexisting expectations as to the proper way to speak about and resolve a case of this sort. In doing these things the artist also makes a community with another, which has both a life of its own and a relationship to the reconstituted culture. At its best this community is about the process of reconstitution, and it addresses, and seeks to educate, the reader as one who will engage in that activity on his own, as a fellow author. The constitutions and reconstitutions we have studied are accordingly internal as well as external, and they embody an activity that extends, by the reader's choice, into his own future.

∗   ∗   ∗

THIS IS WHAT I MEAN when I say that this book is meant to work out and exemplify a way of reading that is a way of being and acting in the world. My aim has been to offer the reader a place from which, and a language with which, he can engage, if he wishes, in his own version of the kind of reading exemplified here when, in his future life, he turns to these and other texts. The kind of reading I mean is not merely a method of interpretation or analysis but an active engagement with a book that is itself a form of the cultural and ethical activity that is our subject. By speaking of a place from which the reader can work, I express the hope that this book has offered the reader a set of experiences that can serve as the material of allusion and reference, a ground on which to stand in looking at other texts, including those of his or her own production.

The way of reading exemplified here is thus a way of attending at once to our language; to the ways we reconstitute it when we speak; to the relations with others that we create when we do so; to the relation between that community of two and the larger culture; and to the selves we constitute as we write and read. This book is itself a reconstitution of culture, for in it I have chosen certain texts and arranged them in a certain order and have made, I hope, something new out of my own inherited materials. It is meant to have a shape and life of its own and to work, partly by incorporation and juxtaposition, not only to say something to its reader but to engage him in an activity. It is meant to speak to him below the level of explicit forms, at the place where language is made, and its object is to affect the ways in which he will see, think, and respond to the world.

I do not hope or expect that the reader will from now on do just what I do with these texts or with others; but if this book has done its work, and the reader his, he should now have a sense of reading in a new and different way. To apply my own criteria to this text, its truest meaning is in its relationship with its reader: who it asks you to become in reading it, and what assistance it gives you in deciding how to respond to that invitation.

Bibliographies and Notes

Preface

Note

1. For an elaboration of this view, see my book *The Legal Imagination: Studies in the Nature of Legal Thought and Expression* (Boston: Little, Brown, 1973), 757–806.

Chapter One: A Way of Reading

Bibliography and Background

While I hope that my book is intelligible without secondary explanation, it may be helpful to some of my readers if I say something more about its intellectual origins and present context.

For me the beginning of reading is close attention to what actually happens in the language of the text itself, and my way of paying attention derives in part from the "New Criticism" in which I was trained. "New Criticism" is now often dismissed as outmoded and naïve, partly because of its purported assumption that each text was to be read as if it existed alone in the universe, without historical, cultural, or biographical context, and partly because of its supposedly reduced vocabulary of irony, paradox, metaphor, and organic design. But this is a caricature. The best critics of that time were guilty of neither of those vices, and those who were can be best understood if it is remembered what they were resisting: a tradition that reduced literature to something else, to a stage in a career or to a series of sources and influences. The achievement of the critical movement that is thought to have begun with Eliot was to draw

attention to the complexity and richness of the experience that a text offered its reader and to locate its central meaning there: in the process of
reading it made possible and in the education, in reading and in life, that
it offered.

To refer to my own experience, a great teacher like Reuben Brower
would say that his aim was to read with his students in "slow motion," to
unpack in detail and hence bring to understanding the process of reading
itself. (For a fuller statement and exemplification of his method, see
Reuben Arthur Brower, *The Fields of Light: An Experiment in Critical
Reading* [Oxford: Oxford University Press, 1951], especially chapter one.)
Of course one cannot understand the experience of a text unless one understands the language (and that includes the cultural situation) of its
author. It is significant in this connection that Brower's most important
book was *Alexander Pope: The Poetry of Allusion* (Oxford: Clarendon
Press, 1959), which was a study of the relations that this poet established
with the classical world and with his own immediate culture.

To focus on the experience of reading necessarily involves the critic in
a struggle of expression and understanding, for how is that experience to
be spoken of? One's attempt is always imperfect because all attempts to
reduce experience to language are imperfect. The best reading thus includes a retelling, one reader's version, which can be checked by other
readers against their own. This was a commonplace of the "New Criticism," and I see that it is also presented as a discovery of poststructuralist
hermeneutics today (see Joel Weinsheimer, "'London' and the Fundamental Problem of Hermeneutics," *Critical Inquiry* 9 [1982]: 303–22).
Such a method calls the reader's attention constantly to the relations between the writer and his language and between the reader and *his* language—relations it is my object in this book to examine in considerable
detail.

Another assumption of "New Criticism" and of criticism much earlier
than that, going back through Arnold and Johnson to Sidney and, beyond
him, to Longinus and Aristotle, is that the activity of reading ought to be
part of a larger activity of self-education; that the reader, whoever he or
she may be, has something important to learn from a writer like Homer or
Thucydides; and that the object of this process of education is not merely
cognition—the acquisition of information and ideas—but a true education of one's own sensibility and character. It will make the reader more
nearly what he or she ought to be. This view, despised as it is by some, is
my own, and this book, which is at its heart a report of my own search for
such an education, is directed to a reader similarly engaged.

Even while talking about it I have continued to put "New Criticism" in
quotation marks, for I have great doubts about the value of talking about
schools or theories of criticism in objectifying terms. Much of what is

wrong about modern critical discourse seems to me its assumption, probably borrowed from social science, that one's basic positions can be stated, in a single sentence or two, as a set of propositions that one supports, which can then be subjected to argument in defense and attack. (Is literary meaning to be found [a] in the text, [b] in the author, [c] in the reader, or [d] in the community of readers? Pick one of the above, then fight to defend it.) I think that such a method results in debates on questions that are false in the sense that they state alternatives neither of which can in any interesting way be true. Consider, for example, the contemporary theory (associated especially with Stanley Fish) that meaning is the product of the community of readers, who can make whatever poem they wish out of a Shakespearean sonnet, who can choose to make Jane Austen's beastly Mr. Collins the center of value in *Pride and Prejudice*, who can make a poem out of words they find scribbled on the blackboard, and so forth. (See, e.g., Stanley Fish, *Is There a Text in This Class? The Authority of Interpretive Communities* [Cambridge, Mass.: Harvard University Press, 1980], 323–24, 347–48.) In a trivial sense this is true, for we "can" of course do all these things, and there is no way to force a person who adopts a bizarre view to agree with you, as there may be in science or mathematics. But to make that kind of claim for the freedom of the critical community is to destroy the resource of a valuable distinction: between communities who properly regard themselves as free to do whatever they wish with whatever is their own—in setting up a business, for example, or establishing a college, or planning a clambake—and those who regard themselves as bound by external fidelities or authorities, for example, by the meaning of corporate documents or university statutes, or by the customs regulating a ritual observance, or by the meaning of a literary text.

Reading is simply not reducible to propositions of a simple theoretical kind, nor is argument of a theoretical sort very useful to us as readers. Reading is an activity of the whole mind, and I most fully understand your conception of reading when I know how you read, not just conceptually—so that I can repeat what you say about reading—but practically, in the sense that I have got the hang of what you do and can do my own version of it myself. Such is the conception of reading on which this book is built. In this opening chapter I do talk generally about the process, but the most important statement about the kind of reading I engage in and wish to recommend to the reader is not here but in the readings themselves. It is in the actual work, not in further degrees of explicit conceptual elaboration, that my key terms—language, reader, community, constitution, and so forth—will acquire their content.

IN ITS FOCUS on the experience of the reader this book can be placed in the tradition inelegantly known as "reader response" criticism (see, e.g.,

Wolfgang Iser, *The Implied Reader: Patterns of Communication in Prose Fiction from Bunyan to Beckett* [Baltimore: Johns Hopkins University Press, 1974].) But the view that reading literature is to be understood as a complex and interactive experience taking place over time is not original with the "reader response" critics, the "New Critics," or with anyone else. As I have said, my own sense of writing as a reconstitution of culture undoubtedly owes much to the teaching and writing of Reuben A. Brower. In directing attention to the kind of community that a text establishes with its reader, I have also been influenced by Wayne Booth (see especially " 'The Way I Loved George Eliot': Friendship with Books as a Neglected Critical Metaphor," *Kenyon Review* n.s. 2 [1980]: 4–27), and in some respects I am rather close to Stanley Fish's fine book, *Surprised by Sin: The Reader in "Paradise Lost"* (London: Macmillan, 1967). In this book Fish sees Milton as teaching his reader about sin by creating situations in which he does sin, in the life of his imagination, and is corrected. The major difference between his way of reading and my own is that I am less concerned to explain how the text works from a position outside of it, as if it were addressed to others, than I am to engage with it myself and to reflect the result of that engagement in my own writing. In this sense my reading is personal as well as professional. For me one model of criticism of this kind, in which the critic learns the language of his writer and shows what that means, is Stuart M. Tave's *Some Words of Jane Austen* (Chicago: University of Chicago Press, 1973). Also, as I remark in the text, another tradition of reading is reflected in this book: the kind of reconstructive and participatory reading that forms the heart of a legal education.

This book's title may also suggest that it bears affinities to the modern movement known as deconstructionism. My earlier book, *The Legal Imagination: Studies in the Nature of Legal Thought and Expression* (Boston: Little, Brown, 1973), can in fact be read as a kind of forced deconstruction of legal language against the resistance of the reader, undertaken to confront him with a part of the truth of his situation in the world. But there I ultimately present the law as a way out, as a method of constructing a world, a self, and a life; similarly, here, the emphasis is less on the fluid conditions of life and language than on the constructive responses to them achieved in the great texts examined here. As I read Thucydides, for example, he brings himself and his reader to face an ultimate disintegration of language, community, and self, and he performs one kind of response to that predicament through the very act of reconstituting that experience; Plato performs another response in the communal remaking of language and self of the kind that takes place in dialectical philosophy. Swift, Johnson, and Austen engage in similar constructive processes in communities that gradually expand beyond two; and in reading Burke and the other political writers, we examine attempts to reconstitute a world at the level of the nation and beyond. Unlike most de-constructionists, moreover, as my text makes plain, I believe in the accessibility of the text to the mind of the reader and in the possibility of a coherent and shared reading of it. Thus I hope that the reader will see that the title of this book does not express a postmodern despair but, rather, implies a kind of optimism. Of course words lose their meaning. That is what they have always done and will always do. What matters, in the face of this fact, is to understand the reconstitutions of language, character, and community that people have nonetheless managed to achieve in the texts they have made with each other and with us. My focus on the character a speaker gives himself and the community he establishes with others—on the ethics and politics of discourse—has, of course, very old roots. Plato's *Gorgias*, discussed in chapter four, is explicitly about such questions. But there are modern exemplars as well, perhaps at the moment most notably in the work of Jürgen Habermas, especially his *Communication and the Evolution of Society*, trans. Thomas McCarthy (Boston: Beacon Press, 1979); but see also Jean-Paul Sartre, *Qu'est-ce que la littérature?* (Paris: Gallimard, 1948; Eng. trans. by Bernard Frechtman, *What Is Literature?* [New York: Harper & Row, 1965]). For a fuller explicit statement of my views on legal and literary interpretation, see my article "Law as Language: Reading Law and Reading Literature," *Texas Law Review* 60 (1982): 415–45.

I wish to identify certain other books, many close in spirit to this one, that have been enough a part of my life to affect what I say and do here and to acknowledge my debt to them. These books would certainly include Arthur W. H. Adkins, *Merit and Responsibility: A Study in Greek Values* (Oxford: Clarendon Press, 1960); Owen Barfield, *Poetic Diction: A Study in Meaning*, 2d ed. (London: Faber & Faber, 1952); Wayne C. Booth, *A Rhetoric of Irony* (Chicago: University of Chicago Press, 1974); K. J. Dover, *Greek Popular Morality in the Time of Plato and Aristotle* (Berkeley: University of California Press, 1974); M. I. Finley, *The Ancestral Constitution: An Inaugural Lecture* (London: Cambridge University Press, 1971); Johan Huizinga, *Homo Ludens: A Study of the Play-Element in Culture* (Boston: Beacon Press, 1955); George A. Kennedy, *The Art of Persuasion in Greece* (Princeton: Princeton University Press, 1963); Hugh Kenner, *The Counterfeiters: An Historical Comedy* (Bloomington: Indiana University Press, 1968); L. C. Knights, *Public Voices: Literature and Politics, with Special Reference to the Seventeenth Century* (Totawa, N.J.: Rowman & Littlefield, 1972); J. G. A. Pocock, *The Ancient Constitution and the Feudal Law: A Study of English Historical Thought in the Seventeenth Century* (Cambridge, Eng.: At the University Press, 1967); James M. Redfield, *Nature and Culture in the "Iliad": The Tragedy of Hector* (Chicago: University of Chicago Press, 1975); Ian Robinson, *The Survival of English: Essays in Criticism of Language* (Cambridge, Eng.: At the University Press, 1973); Jean-Paul Sartre, *What Is Literature?*, trans. Bernard Frechtman (New York: Philosophical Library, 1949); E. P. Thompson, *Whigs and Hunters: The Origin of the Black Act* (London: Allen Lane, 1975); Raymond Williams, *Culture and Society, 1780–1950* (London: Chatto & Windus, 1958); and Gordon S. Wood, *The Creation of the American Republic 1776–1787* (Chapel Hill: University of North Carolina Press, 1969).

My conception of language as a kind of social action rather than a system of referential tags derives, of course, from Wittgenstein and is no doubt affected by J. L. Austin's *How to Do Things with Words* (Cambridge, Mass.: Harvard University Press, 1962) and John R. Searle's *Speech Acts: An Essay in the Philosophy of Language* (London: Cambridge University Press, 1969). Finally, my interest in constitutive discourse has been directly and indirectly influenced by Kenneth Burke, especially by his *A Grammar of Motives* (Engelwood Cliffs, N.J.: Prentice-Hall, 1945).

Notes

1. Thucydides, *History of the Peloponnesian War*, 3. 82.

2. On the complex and related meanings of "culture" and "cultivate," see Raymond Williams, *Culture and Society, 1780–1950* (London: Chatto & Windus, 1958) 61–63.

3. For a fuller account of this process, see my article "The Study of Law as an Intellectual Activity," *Journal of Legal Education* 32 (1982): 1–10.

4. For a theory of cultural judgment in some respects close to my own, see Gertrude Jaeger and Philip Selznick, "A Normative Theory of Culture," *American Sociology Review* 29 (1964): 653–69. On ideological criticism and the problem of transcendence in general, see Raymond Geuss, *The Idea of a Critical Theory: Habermas and the Frankfort School* (Cambridge, Eng.: At the University Press, 1981); in the ancient Athenian context, see S. C. Humphreys, *Anthropology and the Greeks*, (London: Routledge & Kegan Paul, 1978) 209–41.

5. On these points see William Empson, *The Structure of Complex Words* (London: Chatto & Windus, 1951), and Owen Barfield, *Poetic Diction: A Study in Meaning*, 2d ed. (London: Faber & Faber, 1952). For the best current account of the origins of the modern trichotomy of fact, value, and reason, see Alasdair MacIntyre, *After Virtue: A Study in Moral Theory* (London: Gerald Duckworth & Co., 1981). See also Donald McCloskey, "The Rhetoric of Economics," *Journal of Economic Litera-*

ture 21 (1983): 481–516, and Roger Scruton, *The Aesthetics of Architecture* (Princeton: Princeton University Press, 1979).

CHAPTER TWO: THE *Iliad*

Bibliography and Background

General Works

The best contemporary accounts in English of the *Iliad*, and of the Homeric poems generally, are these: Geoffrey S. Kirk, *The Songs of Homer* (Cambridge, Eng.: At the University Press, 1962) (also available in shorter paperback form as *Homer and the Epic* [Cambridge, Eng.: At the University Press, 1965]; Albert B. Lord, *The Singer of Tales* (Cambridge, Mass.: Harvard University Press, 1960); Eric T. Owen, *The Story of the "Iliad"* (New York: Oxford University Press, 1947); James M. Redfield, *Nature and Culture in the "Iliad": The Tragedy of Hector* (Chicago: University of Chicago Press, 1975); Cedric H. Whitman, *Homer and the Heroic Tradition* (Cambridge, Mass.: Harvard University Press, 1958). See also the excellent Alan J. B. Wace and Frank H. Stubbings, eds., *A Companion to Homer* (London: Macmillan, 1962).

The Epic Language and the Composition of the *Iliad*

Our understanding of the formulaic nature of Greek epic language derives from the work of Milman Parry, beginning with *L'Epithète traditionelle dans Homère* (Paris: Société d'éditions Les Belles Lettres, 1928). His collected papers have been published under the title *The Making of Homeric Verse: The Collected Papers of Milman Parry*, ed. Adam Parry (Oxford: Clarendon Press, 1971). For summaries, see Kirk, *Homer and the Epic*, 1–19, and C. M. Bowra, "Style," in Wace and Stubbings, *A Companion to Homer*; see also Michael N. Nagler, *Spontaneity and Tradition: A Study in the Oral Art of Homer* (Berkeley: University of California Press, 1974); Eric A. Havelock, *The Greek Concept of Justice* (Cambridge, Mass.: Harvard University Press, 1978), chap. 6; and on oral poetry in general, Ruth Finnegan, *Oral Poetry: Its Nature, Significance, and Social Context* (Cambridge, Eng.: At the University Press, 1977).

On what it is like to make poetry in such a language, consider the following: "The young singer must learn enough of these formulas to sing a song. He learns them by repeated use of them in singing, by repeatedly facing the need to express the idea in song and by repeatedly satisfying that need, until the resulting formula which he has heard from others

becomes a part of his poetic thought. He must have enough of these formulas to facilitate composition. He is like a child learning words, or anyone learning a language without a school method; except that the language here being learned is the special language of poetry" (Lord, *The
Singer of Tales*, 22). Lord is here speaking of Yugoslav bards, who also
compose in a formulaic language, but he means the observation to apply
to Homer as well. See also ibid., p. 36, and Nagler, *Spontaneity*, whose
view it is that the singer learns not so much particular phrases as the
patterns underlying them. But all agree that it is a language that he
learns. For an account of the morphology and syntax of the language of
Greek epic, see Leonard R. Palmer, *The Greek Language* (Atlantic High-
lands, N.J.: Humanities Press, 1980), 83–101.

The Iliadic Culture

For the principal contemporary account of the values of the Homeric
culture, see Arthur W. H. Adkins, *Merit and Responsibility: A Study in
Greek Values* (Oxford: Clarendon Press, 1960), chaps. 1–3. A. A. Long
responds to Adkins in "Morals and Values in Homer," *Journal of Hellenic
Studies* 90 (1970): 121–39, to which Adkins responds in turn in the fol-
lowing volume of the same journal. A rather different view of the heroic
culture was taken by Werner Jaeger in *Paideia*, 2d Eng. ed., trans. G.
Highet, 3 vols. (New York: Oxford University Press, 1945), vol. 1, chaps.
1–3. A comprehensive study of Homeric culture is M. I. Finley's *The
World of Odysseus*, rev. ed. (New York: Viking Press, 1965); see also Paul
Friedrich, "Sanity and the Myth of Honor: The Problem of Achilles,"
Ethos 5 (1977): 281–305, and Eric R. Dodds, *The Greeks and the Irra-
tional* (Berkeley: University of California Press, 1951), chap. 2.

All of these people think that the "values" of the poems are more
clear, and less open to debate, than I do. M. I. Finley says, for example,
"The heroic code was complete and unambiguous" (*The World of Odysseus*, 121).

I should also say that it is by no means obvious that inferences about
any actual society may be drawn from the world created in the Homeric
poems. This is not a picture of an actual world but of an ideal one. See,
e.g., George M. Calhoun, "Polity and Society," in Wace and Stubbings, *A
Companion to Homer*, 431–62. Professor Eric Havelock is so resistant to
the idea that the world of the *Iliad* is real that he thinks its heroic or Mycenaean elements are a "disguise" or "fantasy," a way of representing the
poet's own culture (Havelock, *The Greek Concept of Justice*, chap. 4). For
present purposes we need not concern ourselves with this problem, for it
is the world made in the text, not a real world, that I wish to analyze. For
further views on the relation between the Mycenaean and Homeric civi-

lizations, see Whitman, *Homer and the Heroic Tradition*, 125; Raphael Sealey, *A History of the Greek City States* (Berkeley: University of California Press, 1976), 15.

Both the remarkable completeness of the definition of the heroic world and the poet's capacity to criticize it may in part be explained by the chronological remoteness of the poet from the historical origins of the heroic world. Perhaps the poetic tradition on which the *Iliad* builds began within a heroic society, which it expressed simply and uncritically; but, centuries later, the poet must have been speaking to an audience quite remote in knowledge and feeling from that heroic world, and the traditional language must gradually have been reconstituted to tell its audience more and more about the heroic world it celebrated. It was at this point that Homer was able to write a poem that both defined the heroic culture with completeness and made it an object of contemplation.

Interpretations of Book Nine

The events of Book Nine have been read in a great many different ways, some consistent with the account I give of it, some very different. C. M. Bowra (*Tradition and Design in the "Iliad"* [Oxford: Clarendon Press, 1930], 195–97) and E. T. Owen (*The Story of the "Iliad,"* 102–3) see Achilles' rejection of Agamemnon's offer as a sin or a tragic wrong. Samuel Eliot Bassett (*The Poetry of Homer* [Berkeley: University of California Press, 1938] 195–201) thinks that, because no apology accompanies the gifts, Achilles' rejection is an expression of his "lofty ideal of honor." Adam Parry ("The Language of Achilles," *Transactions of the American Philological Association* 87 [1956]: 1 and 6–7) and William Sale ("Achilles and Heroic Values," *Arion* 2 [1963]: 86) see Achilles' rejection of the gifts as a rejection of all heroic values. The rejection is confused and inarticulate because Achilles is confined by the formulaic language he must speak and the values it is designed to express. David Claus ("*Aidōs* in the Language of Achilles," *Transactions of the American Philological Association* 105 [1975]: 13–28) believes that Achilles' rejection is not incompatible with heroic values but is an expression of them, for an essential characteristic of heroic action is its gratuitousness; but cf. M. D. Reeve, "The Language of Achilles," *Classical Quarterly* 23 (1973): 193–95: "Far from renouncing heroic ideals he is putting an absurdly high value on his honor." See also Paul Friedrich and James Redfield, "Speech as Personality Symbol: The Case of Achilles," *Language* 54 (1978): 263; cf. Whitman, *Homer and the Heroic Tradition*, 193, and Redfield, *Nature and Culture in the "Iliad,"* 16. On the speech of Phoenix, see J. Rosner, "The Speech of Phoenix: *Iliad* 9. 434–605," *Phoenix* 30 (1976): 314–27.

Chapter Two

Notes

1. Homer's original audience was of course made up of hearers rather than readers of a text, but I think it better here to use the perhaps somewhat anachronistic word "reader" to designate the one who is engaged with this work.

2. Of course the plastic arts can have some referential and ideational content. A Madonna is not just any mother, and the Crucifixion has a meaning of its own. But statues and paintings do not explain themselves. When the artist is through, there is silence. That is the quality I wish to catch. Compare John H. Finley, Jr., *Four Stages of Greek Thought* (Stanford: Stanford University Press, 1966), 3, where he describes the heroic world as characterized by an "outgazing bent of mind that sees things exactly, each for itself, and seems innocent of the idea that thought discerps and colors reality." For a wonderful comparison of visual and literary art, using Homer as the central text, see Gotthold E. Lessing, *Laocoon*, trans. the Rt. Hon. Sir Robert Phillimore (London: Macmillan, 1874). For another attempt to express the way the Homeric world is presented, see Erich Auerbach, *Mimesis: The Representation of Reality in Western Literature*, trans. Willard R. Trask (Princeton: Princeton University Press, 1953), chap. 1 ("Odysseus' Scar").

3. Such I think is the meaning here of *apereisia*, which has a surface meaning of "boundless."

4. On the forms and meanings of prayers and related acts, see A. W. H. Adkins, "*Euchomai, Euchōlē*, and *Euchos* in Homer," *Classical Quarterly* n.s. 19 (1969): 20–33. Here, the imperative is not peremptory. It expresses the intensity of the speaker's desire, and this presumes an intimacy of relation with the audience. Hence, "intimate, intense" in the text.

5. Why does Agamemnon reject the ransom? In a sense this is unexplained and unexplainable; but it may be taken as manifesting an insecurity about his position that he resists an attempt by another to affect his conduct and fails to see that it also increases his honor.

6. It is true that a parallel can be drawn with the scene in Book Seven in which Antenor suggests that the Trojans end the war by giving back Helen and all her possessions. Paris, responding to him, agrees to give back the possessions but refuses to give back Helen. This is the offer that is made, without further Trojan objection, and rejected by the Achaeans. From this one might infer that Paris has the absolute right to determine what should be done with Helen and therefore that the same could be said of any warrior of sufficient rank. But one could also read this passage not as Trojan acquiescence in the assertion of an unquestionable right but as a negotiated compromise. Paris not only makes a claim, he makes a concession; and Priam's acceptance of it, which stops the conversation, could well be taken as a decision not to push the matter further.

The implications of our modern question "has he the right" are inappropriate to this world, for this is a rhetoric that functions not by the definition of rights and the allocation of competences but in more particular ways. Compare the following: "In sum, the 'justice' of the *Iliad* is a procedure, not a principle or any set of principles. It is arrived at by a process of negotiation between contending parties carried out rhetorically" (Eric A. Havelock, *The Greek Concept of Justice: From Its Shadow in Homer to Its Substance in Plato* [Cambridge, Mass.: Harvard University Press, 1978], 137. I would agree with everything in Havelock's statement except the quotation marks around the word justice.)

7. It is true that in his suggested compromise (1. 281) Nestor asserts that Agamemnon is greater because he rules over more men. (M. I. Finley accepts this statement as authoritative. See his *The World of Odysseus* rev. ed. [New York: Viking Press, 1965], 76.) But I think this should be taken as a proposal, offered as part of a compromise, rather than as a declaration. And in any event it does not really explain the relations between Agamemnon and the other warriors. The expedition has as its goal the restoration of Helen to Menelaus, and Menelaus has apparently conferred a special standing on his older brother (see 10. 102–27). Is this the source of whatever special position Agamemnon has? Part of the tradition of the Trojan War is the exchanging of oaths before departing, and these too could be taken as establishing the terms of the relationship. But since this poem tells a story of life in an imaginary world, there seems to me little point in going beyond it to some other world, imagined or real, in an attempt to answer questions that the text does not invite. We can take it, I think, that we know all we need to know about Agamemnon's standing: that it is special and that it becomes, in Book One, highly problematic.

8. The assembly, that is, may be taken as giving a sort of juridical standing to facts generally known, as our own jury verdicts sometimes do. We may "know the facts" as well before the proceeding as after it, but the verdict has legally established them. (It does this, of course, even where we doubt the facts, before and after: the verdict means not only that we may, but that we must, take them as established.) The fact that Hera prompts Achilles to call the assembly may be taken as a direction from the poet to the reader to read the act as constructive rather than competitive.

9. Nestor's speech is read rather differently by Hugh Lloyd-Jones, who sees it not as creative but simply as seeking to persuade each man "to accord to the other his proper *timē* [honor]" (Lloyd-Jones, *The Justice of Zeus* [Berkeley: University of California Press, 1971], 13; cf. M. I. Finley, *The World of Odysseus*, 122–23).

10. Achilles is incompletely aware of this fact. His own conception of what will happen gets no farther than wanting a "longing" for him to

come upon the Achaeans, wanting Agamemnon to "tear your heart, raging that you did no honor to the best of the Achaeans" (1. 243–44). It is not Achilles but Thetis who sees that if he does not go home but stays nearby, if his withdrawal is only partial, his honor can be restored to him when Agamemnon is forced to beg for his return (1. 505–10). (It is true that when Athena stops Achilles from killing Agamemnon she promises him gifts "three times over" if he desists [1. 213]. But she does not explain how the gifts will come.)

11. Simone Weil, "*L'Iliade* ou le poème de la force," *Cahiers du Sud* (December 1940–January 1941) (first published under the pseudonym Emile Novis): "L'extraordinaire équité qui inspire l'*Iliade* a peut-être des exemples inconnus de nous, mais n'a pas eu d'imitateurs. C'est à peine si l'on sent que le poète est Grec et non Troyen." I here use Mary McCarthy's translation, which appeared in *Politics* 2 (November 1945): 321–31, reprinted as "The *Iliad*, or The Poem of Force," Pendle Hill Pamphlet no. 91 (Lebanon, Pa., 1956). For a different view of Homer's impartiality, see Johannes Th. Kakrides, *Homer Revisited* (Lund: Gleerup, 1971), chap. 2.

12. Weil, "*L'Iliade*," 30–31.

13. Cf. the observation of the rhetor Dio of Prusa, as reproduced in Werner Jaeger, *Paideia: The Ideals of Greek Culture*, trans. Gilbert Highet, 3 vols. 2d ed., (New York: Oxford University Press, 1945), 1:42: "'Homer,' [Dio] says, 'praised almost everything—animals and plants, water and earth, weapons and horses. He passed over nothing without somehow honouring and glorifying it. Even the one man whom he abused, Thersites, he called a *clear-voiced speaker*.'"

14. In his *Preface to Shakespeare* (1765): "[Shakespeare] . . . has perhaps excelled all but Homer in securing the first purpose of a writer, by exciting restless and unquenchable curiosity, and compelling him that reads his work to read it through."

15. Adam Parry, "The Language of Achilles," *Transactions of the American Philological Association* 87 (1956): 1–7.

16. See Paul Friedrich and James Redfield, "Speech as a Personality Symbol: The Case of Achilles," *Language* 54 (1978): 263, 267.

17. See Cedric H. Whitman, *Homer and the Heroic Tradition* (Cambridge, Mass.: Harvard University Press, 1958), chap. 6, for another view of the ways that formula and image combine.

18. See Samuel Eliot Bassett, *The Poetry of Homer* (Berkeley: University of California Press, 1938), chap. 6, and David H. Porter, "Violent Juxtaposition in the Similes of the *Iliad*," *Classical Journal* 68 (1972): 11–21. See also Carroll Moulton, "Similes in the *Iliad*," *Hermes* 102 (1974): 381–97.

19. From his otherwise verbatim report of Agamemnon's speech offering the gifts, Odysseus diplomatically omits the last two lines: "And let

him then yield to me, since I am the more kingly and am born the elder" (9. 160–61). Of course Achilles does not know of these remarks, which would wholly undo the act of submission that the embassy is intended to perform. Their inclusion here shows that, while Agamemnon is willing to do what is necessary to bring Achilles back, the problem between them is still unsolved. This gives the offer of gifts the familiar quality of doubleness: it is uncertain whether it is truly an act of submission or is an attempt to reduce the other to a kind of obedience, to persuade him. But this ambiguity inheres in every such performance of persuasion in this world, including Chryses' ritual appeal; Agamemnon's remark makes explicit the doubleness of meaning the performance naturally has.

20. Book Ten is widely recognized as having been composed after the rest of the *Iliad*, but the cinematic quality that marks it is present in the later books as well.

21. See, e.g., what Achilles says at 11. 607–9 and 16. 49–100.

22. By a subtle and surprising shift of emphasis from the earlier books, the contrast between the world of war (to which all men are doomed) and the world of the gods now operates less as an appeal away from war than as a sort of justification of it. To be sure, there is still the sense that the gods live in a world without peril, and this defines the life of man as one of sorrow. The constitutional struggle between Zeus and Poseidon, for example, directly parallels that between Agamemnon and Achilles and functions as a comedic version of what is all too costly in actual life. And the seduction of Zeus by Hera invokes a world of softness and sexuality and magic very different from the world of war. But another element now appears in the lives of the gods as well: a helpless caring for the people who will die. The lives of the gods have a peculiar pathos that human lives do not; for while they themselves need not die, they must face death at second hand and must do so without the opportunity to respond to that necessity in a heroic way. Life is given to those who must die of a kind no immortal can ever know; the experience of the gods is essentially derivative. The effect is to make human death seem somewhat less terrible, and this defines in a new and acceptable way the warfare to which Achilles sends Patroclus. See C. M. Bowra, *Homer* (New York: Scribner's, 1972), 111–12, and Bassett, *Poetry of Homer*, 223.

23. "Homer regularly externalizes a spiritual or mental state in the form of an image or a god. In the present case, he has externalized the humane side of Achilles in Patroclus" (Whitman, *Heroic Tradition*, 199). In his speech to Glaucus, Sarpedon roots the heroic life in an acceptance of the inevitability of death (12. 310–28). Achilles can accept and respond to this necessary fact because he has experienced it in the death of Patroclus.

24. The isolation and idealism of the final books is expressed in the

increasing surrealism of the narrative: horses talk, rivers fight, the funerals and games are rituals, almost dances, of reconciliation, and the last book is full of the blessing of the gods, protecting Priam with their charms. The funeral games, for example, can be regarded as an enactment of the major themes of conflict and jealousy upon which the *Iliad* is built, but here the struggles are harmless and the disputes are reconciled. There are prizes for everyone, even for Nestor, who does not compete; and a consolation prize goes to the best horseman, even though he does not finish the race. Achilles, of all people, is a peacemaker. The world in which Antilochus demands his rightful prize yet yields to the opposition of Menelaus, who then grants him the prize after all, is a stage on the way to Book Twenty-four.

25. For somewhat different views of the ending of this poem, see James M. Redfield, *Nature and Culture in the "Iliad": The Tragedy of Hector* (Chicago: University of Chicago Press, 1975), 24, 219, and 228 n. 27, and A. W. H. Adkins, review of *The Greek Concept of Justice* by E. Havelock, *Classical Philology* 75 (1980): 262–63.

CHAPTER THREE: THUCYDIDES' *History*

Bibliography and Background

Thucydides' Text

The Peloponnesian War lasted from 431 B.C. to 404 B.C. When it began, Athens and Sparta were at the height of their powers; at its end the Athenian Empire had been destroyed. Thucydides tells us that when the war first broke out he thought that it would be of extraordinary significance, and so he began to write his account of it directly. He was himself made an Athenian general, but after losing a battle in 424 B.C. he was sent into exile, from which he did not return until the end of the war. He never completed his text, which breaks off its story in 411 B.C. It is apparent that the *History* was written at least in part contemporaneously with the events it describes and in part from first-hand observation; but some statements show that Thucydides knew how the war ended, so that at least those must have been written after 404 B.C., and, obviously, his opportunities for observation were altered by his exile. There is thus a substantial question about the composition of this text. Some scholars believe that its unity is such that it must have been written in a single sustained act of composition near the end of the war, though with the use of notes made earlier; others think that the *History* was composed over time, under varying conceptions of the course and meaning of its events.

These questions are controversial and unresolved. For contrasting views compare John H. Finley, Jr., "The Unity of Thucydides' History," *Harvard Studies in Classical Philology*, suppl. vol. 1 (Cambridge, Mass., 1940), 255–98, and John H. Finley, Jr., *Thucydides* (Cambridge, Mass.: Harvard University Press, 1942) 76–80, with A. Andrewes, "Thucydides on the Causes of the War," *Classical Quarterly* n.s. 9 (1959): 223–27. See also A. W. Gomme, "Thucydides and Fourth-Century Political Thought," in *More Essays in Greek History and Literature* (Oxford: Basil Blackwell, 1962), 122–24. In this chapter I will not be concerned with the question of composition but will take the text as it is presented to us and ask what it means. I do not mean to deny that the text has strong discontinuities or that these can be traced, in some measure at least, to different stages and conceptions of its composition. But to say that is not to say all, for I think that these discontinuities have a significance beyond their etiology. It would be a mistake, for example, to explain them away as manifesting the incomplete or unsatisfactory nature of the text, for in my view, as I say in the text, they are essential to its structure and meaning.

The standard commentary is A. W. Gomme, A. Andrewes, and K. J. Dover, *A Historical Commentary on Thucydides*, 5 vols. (Oxford: Clarendon Press, 1945–81). It contains an exhaustive treatment of the composition question (5:361–444).

The Athenian Empire

On the nature of the Athenian Empire, see Russell Meiggs, *The Athenian Empire* (Oxford: Clarendon Press, 1972); Donald W. Bradeen, "The Popularity of the Athenian Empire," *Historia* 9 (1960): 257–69; and G. E. M. de Ste. Croix, "The Character of the Athenian Empire," *Historia* 3 (1954): 1–41.

The Mytilenean Debate

The view of the Mytilenean debate presented in the text is not a common one. Finley, for example, says, of Cleon's attack on the reopening of debate, that "it offers a startling contrast to Pericles' praise of free debate in the Funeral Oration . . . . Cleon attacks not only debate but the whole faith in reason and education that underlies it." The claim of justice he advances is "specious" and the "rejection of pity and decency . . . a departure from the famous sentence of the Funeral Oration, 'We get our friends by doing, not receiving, good'" (2. 40. 4). His words "signify the brutality of mood to which the war was giving rise." As for Diodotus, "his speech betrays the terse and logical elegance which was the fruit of sophistic training, and his ideas are also conspicuously enlightened." While he advocated what was to Thucydides' mind "both the wiser and the more humane course," he uses "far the more cynical arguments," and this fact is a "bitter commentary on the mood of the day . . . . [T]he advocate of simple decency had no other course than to talk in terms of calculation" (John H. Finley, Jr., *Thucydides*, 172–77). A. Andrewes, "The Mytilene Debate: Thucydides 3. 36–49," *Phoenix* 16 (1962): 64, 84–85, concludes that "Thucydides in effect makes two charges against [Cleon], that his imperial policy of repression was brutal and unintelligent, and that he diminished the rational element in Athenian debate." For Gomme, this pair of speeches was a testing of ideas, part of the practice of Thucydides' generation by which "every belief, every faith, every argument was turned inside out for criticism and analysis" (Gomme, *A Historical Commentary on Thucydides*, 2: 301). For Felix Martin Wasserman ("Post-Periclean Democracy in Action: The Mytilenean Debate," *Transactions of the American Philological Association* 87 [1956]: 37), Diodotus proposes a policy of "enlightened self-interest" of which Thucydides approves. A complex (but to me not wholly intelligible) analysis of these two speeches is given in Louis Bodin, "Diodote contre Cléon: Quelques aperçus sur la dialectique de Thucydide," *Revue des études anciennes* 42 (1940): 36–52, the main point of which is to trace out an extraordinary number of verbal and structural resemblances in the two speeches. The method of Bodin is applied to Thucydides generally by J. de Romilly, *Histoire et Raison chez Thucydide* (Paris: Société d'édition Les Belles Lettres, 1956), and Virginia J. Hunter, *Thucydides: The Artful Reporter* (Toronto: Hakkert, 1973).

In *"Ta Deonta Eipein:* Cleon and Diodotus," *Bulletin of the Institute of Classical Studies* 12 (1965): 70–82, R. P. Winnington-Ingram argues that there is an inconsistency between Cleon's positions that Mytilene is by nature an enemy and that Athens should be outraged at her committing an injustice toward her. But in my view the kind of injustice of which Cleon speaks, unlike that of the rhetorical world of treaty and alliance and gratitude, is not dependent on equality or consensual relations; it is simply injury itself, which his kind of justice seeks to avenge. On this view it is not inconsistent but natural to punish an enemy for his injustice.

The Melian Dialogue

It is not clear what Athens' motives for taking Melos actually are. Was it fear of appearing weak, as they claim? That reasoning has something of a circular character, as I suggest in the text. But if this is not why the Athenians wish to take Melos, what is the reason? This has been the subject of much discussion; see, e.g., Meiggs, *The Athenian Empire*, 321,

385–89; A. Andrewes, "The Melian Dialogue and Perikles' Last Speech," *Proceedings of the Cambridge Philological Society* n.s. 6 (1960): 1–10; W. P. Wallace, "Thucydides," *Phoenix* 18 (1964): 251–61. In my view Thucydides leaves it unexplained and, in doing so, demonstrates the unrestrained and unreasoning character of Athenian ambition.

Finley says that the Melian adventure was exactly the sort of mistake against which Pericles had warned (John H. Finley, Jr., *Three Essays on Thucydides* [Cambridge, Mass.: Harvard University Press, 1967], 38), but it is not at all clear to me that Pericles' view of the empire was a coherent one or that it would have prevented this adventure. It is true that Pericles says that the Athenians should not seek to expand their empire, but he qualifies this by saying "during the present war" (1. 144); and in his last speech he speaks of the empire of the Athenians as extending not merely over her allies but over half the world, the sea. He also acknowledges in this speech that it is simply not safe to let the empire go, even if Athens wanted to (2. 62–63); he looks forward, indeed, to the time when Athenian power shall have decayed (2. 64). This does not amount to a coherent view of Athens and her empire of a kind that would have forbidden the Melian conquest, nor does it furnish materials for a different way of thinking and talking about it.

As for the Athenian argument, it would be possible to read it (as Gomme believes the Athenian address at Sparta should be read; see note 16) as designed to achieve the opposite of its surface message, in this case the resistance rather than the capitulation of the Melians. The grounds for this reading would be that the Athenians make no argument they could expect the Melians to accept but in fact insist on what is impossible. (For an elaboration of the reasons why the Melians cannot accept the Athenian terms, see Arthur W. H. Adkins, *Merit and Responsibility: A Study in Greek Values* [Oxford: Clarendon Press, 1960], 222, 234–35.) The trouble with that reading is that it is hard to see what the Athenian motive for doing this would be. I think the argument is better read as a performance of the limits of Athens' self-created situation; in other words, this is all she *can* say.

But *is* it all she can say? Meiggs says that Athens could have argued that "the Melian oligarchs were suppressing the common people and that the champions of democracy had come to liberate Melos. They might have claimed that Melos was enjoying all the benefits derived from an Athenian thalassocracy without contributing to the cost" (*The Athenian Empire*, 389). But the former argument could have been made only to the people as a whole, which was precluded by the oligarchs themselves; and I do not see how the second argument could meaningfully have been made out of the materials available to the Athenians.

It is important to note that while the Athenians say that talk about justice can have no place in this negotiation, they do not take the positions of Thrasymachus in Plato's *Republic* or of Callicles in the *Gorgias*, that talk about justice is always meaningless or that might is the only right. On this, see, e.g., Gomme, Andrewes, and Dover, *A Historical Commentary on Thucydides*, 4:164.

The Speeches

In talking about the speeches, Thucydides seems to state two opposing ideas: that he recorded the speeches as accurately as he could and that they represent to some extent his own view of what should have been said (1. 22). Some of the speeches, perhaps most obviously the Melian dialogue, seem quite unrealistic, others much less so. And because the patterns formed by the speeches are pronounced and complex, it is hard not to see Thucydides' hand at work in their selection and arrangement. On the question of composition, Gomme's view is that they are for the most part accurate records of what was said (*Essays in Greek History and Literature* [Oxford: Basil Blackwell, 1937], 156–89; *A Historical Commentary on Thucydides*, 142–48). Finley's view is that the speeches expound "what Thucydides thought would have seemed to him the factors in a given situation, had he stood in the place of his speakers" (*Thucydides*, 96). Andrewes concludes that some are accurate, others not; the Corcyrean debates and the speeches given at Sparta "might be near authentic record"; at the other end of the scale, reflecting a different time of composition and different criteria of accuracy, are the Melian Dialogue and Pericles' great last speech (2. 60–64). With respect to most of the other speeches, however, "no hard and fast line can be drawn" (Andrewes, "The Mytilene Debate," 64, 70–71). J. de Romilly thinks the speeches are simply the work of Thucydides and not accurate reports at all (*Histoire et Raison chez Thucydide*, 299–303).

Thucydides himself makes a distinction between the way he presents the speeches and the way he presents the rest of his narrative. This distinction ought not to be exaggerated, for to some extent Thucydides is saying that he is equally interested in accuracy with respect to both the speeches and the facts but that accuracy must of necessity mean something different in the two contexts. And he does say that he kept as closely as possible to the general sense of what was actually said. But, when one takes all the speeches into account, it is hard to claim that anything like the same methods of reporting are actually employed for them as for the rest of the narrative. It has frequently been observed, for example, that the speeches are very much abbreviated, rather than full, reports of what was said; that they are generally written in the same, and characteristically Thucydidean, style; that they are responsive to each other in plainly artificial ways (as Cleon's speech is a version of Pericles' earlier speech on the empire); and that they are selected and ordered in patterns of significance that are Thucydides' own.

A line of partial reconciliation is that Thucydides' aim was less to record exactly what was said on a particular occasion than to reproduce the state of the discourse as it existed at different points in time. He could accurately do that—state what the occasion "called for"—without actually hearing and recording the speeches, through his own expertise in the discourse, just as a modern lawyer can tell you what the main arguments in a particular case are likely to be for both sides. On this view, the speeches we have read are not meant to be full arguments, individuated by the particular practitioner, but summary statements of the main lines of argument that any competent speaker would make in each situation. They are like argument headings from a typical brief. The fact that the style is Thucydides' own is irrelevant here, for his interest is substantive and his aim is conciseness.

I believe that this is an accurate view of Thucydides' aims and methods in the speeches we have discussed, but it applies much less comfortably to some of the other speeches, such as those by Alcibiades and Pericles, which are perhaps meant to be expressive of particular minds. And in any event this view does not deny, but merely seeks to explain, what Thucydides himself says, that the speeches are constructed by him in a way that the rest of the narrative is not.

The continuities between the speeches and the methods of argument otherwise in use in fifth-century Greece have been worked out by John H. Finley, Jr., in "The Origins of Thucydides' Style," *Harvard Studies in Classical Philology* 50 (1939): 35–84, (reprinted in John H. Finley, Jr., *Three Essays on Thucydides*). His point is to show that the techniques employed by the speakers in Thucydides were not invented after the time the speeches were supposed to have been given but in fact represented contemporaneous styles of thought and expression, of the kind that appear, for example, in the plays of Euripides.

Notes

1. Thucydides never explains why Corcyra refused to assist the Epidamnians. Since Corcyra was a democracy, one might have expected her to sympathize with the people rather than the oligarchs, but she did not. Her conduct remains a puzzle, one of the many in this text that are never resolved.

2. For a discussion of the composition of the speeches see the Bibliographical Note to this chapter (p. 303, above).

3. Here and elsewhere Thucydides speaks in the plural of representatives, but he gives us the argument in a single speech. My general prac-

tice in such cases will be to write, for reasons of convenience, as if each speech had a single author.

4. The Corinthians in fact speak as though the question of prior wrongdoing had been injected into the proceedings by the Corcyreans, and they profess to take it up reluctantly. I do not take that claim seriously, for it seems obviously meant to make more acceptable their own attack on the character of Corcyra—an attack they planned to make in any event.

5. In modern legal terms we might say that Corinth seeks to deny Corcyra "standing" to use the discourse. This is the most drastic step that a system of rhetoric can take. It is the declaration that one is no longer to be spoken of as a person. Compare the holding in the *Dred Scott* case, 60 U.S. (19 How.) 393 (1857), that a Negro could not become a citizen of the United States and therefore could have no access to its courts; the doctrine of "civil death," once imposed on those sentenced to life imprisonment; and the practice of excommunication from a religious community.

6. This seems to be the meaning of the somewhat unclear passage at 1. 36. 1.

7. On the divisions within Athens, for example, see, e.g., Francis M. Cornford, *Thucydides Mythistoricus* (London: Edward Arnold, 1907), 14–24.

8. I use the term autonomy in its modern sense, meaning independence and self-direction. "Autonomy" of another kind, the right to regulate one's internal affairs, was granted by Athens even to her subject states. See A. W. Gomme, A. Andrewes, and K. J. Dover, *A Historical Commentary on Thucydides*, 5 vols. (Oxford: Clarendon Press, 1945–81), 1:380–85, 388–89.

9. This is not to say that the arguments from justice are wholly without persuasive force on the merits or that the talk about gratitude is solely about anticipated claims of ungratefulness; for, as Corinth's preexisting hatred for Corcyra shows (1. 25, 38), these cities are capable of what can be called moral emotion, a fact that takes on supreme importance in the speech Cleon makes in the Mytilenean debate, discussed above, pp. 72–76. And the terms used here in an argument about justifiability are presumably the same ones that would be used in a conversation about justice, whether that conversation took the form of disinterested philosophy or expressions of blame by a party that felt unjustly injured. What is more, an actor has an interest of another kind in the justifiability of his conduct, for there seems to be a deep human need not to admit that one's conduct is simply unjustifiable.

10. This is what Corinth means when she warns Athens against establishing the precedent (*nomos*) that defection from one side may be supported by the other.

11. One way to restate Corinth's case against Corcyra is to say that her

prior isolation demonstrates Corcyra's immunity to the rhetorical sanctions that alone can give meaning to the practice of alliance. She has shown that she actually prefers the condition that is the worst the community can impose upon her, namely, that of excommunication. This is different from saying that Corcyra has a "bad character"; it describes the nature and consequences of her situation. It is this point that Corcyra is most eager to refute by saying, in effect, that she realizes that she too depends on the community and will therefore, in the future, be meaningfully subject to its sanctions.

12. One commentator believes that Corinth's interpretation of the treaty is "very forced" (A. Andrewes, "Thucydides on the Causes of the War," *Classical Quarterly* n.s. 9 [1959]: 223–27).

13. As Momigliano says, "War was an ever present reality in Greek life; it was a focus for emotions, ethical values, social rules. It was not by chance that Herodotus made war the centre of historical writing, and that his successors accepted his decision. War was the centre of Greek life" (Arnaldo Momigliano, *Studies in Historiography* [London: Weidenfeld & Nicolson, 1966], 120).

14. The Athenians claim that they are not seeking to justify their empire. They say they have not come to debate, still less to litigate, the charges that have been made, but they wish to speak, "lest the Spartans, through their allies' persuasion, lightly decide badly on a matter of great importance, and [they wish] also to show . . . that it is fitting for [them] to hold what they have obtained, and that their city is worthy of consideration" (1. 73). This is an odd beginning, for Corinth and the others have not attacked the Athenian empire; they have only complained about alleged violations of the treaty. Notwithstanding these disclaimers, it is evident from the speech that follows that its main purpose is a kind of justification, and one of its critical subjects is what shall count as a justification.

15. Indeed, Athens says, part of the hostility toward her arises from the very fact that her relations with her allies are in large measure regulated by law, for the allies are resentful whenever she insists on her rights, whenever a judgment goes against them, and whenever they suffer some injury, however small, through the exercise of Athens' superior military power. Being so used to the relationship of equality implied in the practices of law and argument, they resent these things more than if Athens had from the beginning openly put law aside and simply imposed her will.

16. It has been argued that the natural force of this speech, in which Athens brazenly defines herself as ready to go wherever her interests might take her, is not to persuade the Spartans to delay but to provoke them into a hasty declaration of war. See Gomme, *A Historical Commentary on Thucydides*, 1:252–55. Compare J. R. Grant, "A Note on the Tone

of Greek Diplomacy," *Classical Quarterly* 15 (1965): 261–66, who sees its bluntness as an expression of urgency. But, as I say in the text, I think its real purpose is neither to delay nor to hasten the war but to make a declaration of the terms on which Athens is willing to talk about the resolution of differences.

17. Pericles' Funeral Oration is about the glory and greatness of Athens: how the ancestors added to her powers, how she herself uses every talent in the state, and what kind of life she makes available to her citizens, all meant as a way of justifying the sacrifice of life that is the occasion of the speech. There is nothing about limits here. And as a justification it seems to me defective: how does he get from "acquisitiveness and brilliance" to "worth dying for"? Finley says that the speech has no equal in the genre except, perhaps, for the Gettysburg Address (John H. Finley, Jr., *Thucydides* [Cambridge, Mass.: Harvard University Press, 1942], 144). This is an interesting comparison, because for Lincoln, as for the Melians (see above, p. 77), the question is the survival of the community, not its expansion or brilliance. And Lincoln insists on the historically unique interest each person has in the existence of the community and in its survival, not only for himself but for all mankind, on behalf of whom it is an experiment. It is all expressive of an ethic of sharing and recognition, and it is thus altogether different from what Pericles says.

18. The war proceeded much as the Spartan Archidamas (1. 80–85) and Pericles (1. 140–45) had foreseen. The Athenians did not try to stop the Spartans from invading and devastating Attica; retreating behind their walls, they maintained themselves by their supremacy on the sea. It was when Athens was crowded with people from the country that the plague, so vividly described in 2. 48–51, broke out. The people became hostile to Pericles, removed him from office, and subjected him to a fine. But he recovered his power shortly before his death in 429 B.C.

19. Cleon's point here is that Mytilene, by revolting without having even a superficial ground or pretext for doing so, has exhibited a shameless and dangerous disregard for a fundamental convention of the culture: that conduct must be justifiable. We have already seen that principle at work in the Corcyrean debate; and in a part of the *History* we have not discussed Thucydides explains in detail the process by which Sparta and Athens make a further and rather ritualistic (not to say trumped-up) set of countercharges against each other (1. 126–40). Cleon's claim is especially significant because it foreshadows Athens' refusal at Melos to allege a ground on which her own conduct could be justified.

20. The common view that Cleon's speech is grounded in self-interest and that his policy is essentially deterrent (see, e.g., Henry Dickinson Westlake, *Individuals in Thucydides* [London: Cambridge University Press, 1968], 64) seems to me quite wrong. Cleon maintains the estab-

lished convention by which justice, gratitude, and expediency are united, and he is careful to explain the irrelevance of gratitude. That the kind of justice he speaks of provides a coherent, if brutal, basis for action is demonstrated in Sparta's treatment of the captured Plataeans (3. 68). For further scholarship on these speeches, see the Bibliographical Note.

21. On vengeance as a form of justice, see Douglas M. MacDowell, *Athenian Homicide Law in the Age of the Orators* (Manchester, Eng.: Manchester University Press, 1963), chaps. 1, 14.

22. Why does Diodotus concede that justice and compassion are out of the case? One cannot be sure, but one possibility is that he sees so plainly that his arguments under the heading of justice could not prevail; and Cleon's claim that the practices of compassion and gratitude depend on equality may be equally irrefutable. What is more, Cleon's charge (never denied) that Diodotus was paid to speak in the interest of the Mytileneans would greatly impair the standing of Diodotus to make appeals to sympathy, which rest on a common sense of identity between speaker and audience.

23. Diodotus did say that to destroy the people, "who had no share in the revolt," would be to "commit the wrong of killing your benefactors" (3. 47. 3). This contradicts Cleon, who said that all the people attacked the Athenians (3. 39. 7). It is interesting that there is no organized argument on this factual question. Perhaps nothing could be said beyond such assertions. It is also significant that in Diodotus' speech some considerations of justice are invoked. Indeed, the word he uses for "commit wrong" (*adikein*) is the same as that used by Cleon when he says that the Mytileneans have done the Athenians a greater wrong than any other state (3. 39. 1). Does this amount to a demonstration that even the proponent of pure rationality cannot escape his own commitment to justice? Or is it to be read as a skillful insertion of a supposedly omitted topic? On this, as on so many other questions, the text is ineluctably ambivalent.

24. For a discussion of this question in modern terms, see my article "Making Sense of the Criminal Law," *University of Colorado Law Review* 50 (1978): 1.

25. The form of the dialogue between Melos and Athens is different from that of the debates and speeches elsewhere in Thucydides, for it proceeds by question and answer rather than by declamation. This method was an established sophistic form of private discussion, and it is of course familiar to us from the Socratic dialogues. See H. L. Hudson-Williams, "Conventional Forms of Debate and the Melian Dialogue," *American Journal of Philology* 71 (1950): 156–69. See also John H. Finley, Jr., *Thucydides*, 209, and the discussion of Plato's *Gorgias*, above, pp. 102–11. This form is appropriate to negotiations between two parties, each of whom is trying to persuade the other, as opposed to argument by speeches that are competing for the approval of a third party.

26. The Athenian attack on false hopes states a deep and ironic theme of the *History*. For Thucydides, statesmanship itself is the art of fitting one's conduct to actualities and probabilities accurately assessed. This is the art, for example, that both Pericles and Archidamas demonstrate when they predict the character of the war; and the *History* begins with Thucydides' statement of his own prediction, that this would prove to be a great war, which the events subsequently vindicated. This vindication serves as a kind of qualification of the author for the art of which he speaks. One object of the *History* is, accordingly, to train the reader in the perception and estimation of realities; and to speak, as the Athenians do, in favor of this process is to speak in large measure for Thucydides himself. But in the context of the Melian dialogue the words are ironic, for the Athenians are at the same time closing their own minds to the nature and consequences of their conduct. Indeed, the whole dialogue is unrealistic. How could they possibly expect the Melians to capitulate on such terms as these? And the kind of "hope" the Melians demonstrate, unlike the false confidence of the Athenians, is the common human propensity to choose an almost certain death in preference to a fate even worse.

27. In Plato's *Gorgias*, as we noted above, p. 99, one of the charges made against rhetoric is that it is a form of flattery in which the persuader becomes like the object of his persuasion. Athens could be said to exemplify this point, becoming like her hostile and resentful subjects and to that extent becoming their subject rather than their ruler. Whom do Corinth and Corcyra "become like" in the opening argument? Like the ideal audience of their speeches, they become for the moment like one who is moved by a coherent combination of justice, expediency, and gratitude.

28. On the relationship between equality and justice, see Gomme, Andrewes, and Dover, *A Historical Commentary on Thucydides*, 4:162–64. And compare the speech in which the Spartans seek to establish peace after the capture of their men at Pylos, where they say in effect that a reconciliation is most likely to work, not when one side takes full advantage of its superiority and forces an unequal peace, but when the victor is able to conquer through generosity (*aretē*) and will be the more ready to keep the agreement through shame (*aischunē*) (4. 19).

29. My view, that Thucydides' *History* is the history of a deteriorating discourse, would presumably be resisted by some. Andrewes, for example, says that there is in the Melian dialogue "no detectable decline in principle" from the statements the Athenians made at Sparta (1. 76), "only the removal of *onomata kala* [fine words]" (Andrewes, in Gomme, Andrewes, and Dover, *A Historical Commentary on Thucydides*, 4:184). My view is that what Andrewes calls merely the removal of "fine words" is, in fact, the destruction of the culture that gave this world coherence and its principles force. What Andrewes' remark fails to recognize is that

this culture of argument is defined by Thucydides not as mere words but as a social reality, having force and meaning in the real world. It has an existence and a character independent of the motives for its use, which are always assumed to be self-interested.

Another way to put this point is to say that political power is the product of a complicated game, like a perpetual version of chess or Monopoly. The more successful he is, the more power a player acquires; but his power is always defined by the game that others agree to play. What Athens does is to destroy the game from which her power derives.

30. The position of outlawry or excommunication that Corcyra feared has been chosen and admitted by Athens. And Alcibiades, at least, thought that Athens should go from the conquest of Sicily to that of Carthage and presumably then to ruling the entire Greek world (6. 15–18; 6. 90).

31. Thucydides here states his true subject, which is Hellas itself, not Athens alone, and in doing this he also states, I believe, his true allegiance. It is the culture of argument by which the states constituted themselves into a community that enacts what he most values, and it is the destruction of this that is so terrible to him.

32. As even this summary shows, the Archeology states many deep themes of the *History* as a whole. These general ideas—that power is a function of community and exists by agreement; that political stability is an enormous source of wealth and power; and that power is not to be confused with its physical manifestations or monuments—return again and again, in various forms. And, of course, some of the particular observations, such as the importance of sea power and the interconnections between trade, colonization, piracy, and alliance, were all part of the structure of Thucydides' view of the world, as the terms in which Corcyra is attacked make plain.

33. This passage (1. 23. 6) has understandably been the subject of much discussion. The problem is that the word Thucydides uses for "explanation" when he says that the "truest explanation, though least expressed in speech" was Sparta's fear of Athens' growth, is the word *prophasis*, which normally means "pretext." Worse still, when he tells us in the next clause that he will tell us of the "charges" that the two sides had against one another (which led to the war), he uses the word *aitia*, among the normal meanings of which is "cause." What can "truest pretext" mean? Why use the word for "cause" to refer to complaints and charges? To complicate matters further, *prophasis* has another meaning, derived from medical usage, namely, the first sign of disease, or a symptomatic precondition.

But all this is not as bad as it seems. *Aitia* in Greek, like "cause" in English, connects the ideas of causation, responsibility, and blame, even indictment, and the use of *aitia* to refer to the charges the two sides had against each other is perfectly idiomatic. As for *prophasis*, apparently the basic meaning of that term is not "pretext" but "explanation of one's own conduct." The idea is that this is what the Spartans would have said had they spoken to the question. In this sense it is distinguished from the causes that *were* spoken, in the Corcyrean and later debates. *Aitia* is a way of responding to the conduct of another; *prophasis* is a way of explaining one's own conduct. On these points see Gordon M. Kirkwood, "Thucydides' Words for 'Cause,'" *American Journal of Philology* 73 (1952): 37–61; Lionel Pearson, "Prophasis and Aitia," *Transactions of the American Philological Association*, 83 (1952): 205–23; and Andrewes, "Thucydides on the Causes of the War," 223. See also Hunter R. Rawlings, III, *A Semantic Study of "Prophasis" to 400 B.C.* (Ann Arbor, Mich.: University Microfilms, 1970); R. Sealey, "Thucydides, Herodotus, and the Causes of War," *Classical Quarterly* n.s. 7 (1957): 1–12.

34. Much has been inferred from what seems to be Thucydides' use of medical terms and methods, the idea being that he describes recurring patterns of events as a medical writer might describe the symptomatic patterns that define a disease. On this view, the phenomenon of the war is like the phenomenon of disease, with a certain set of preconditions and a definable course, and it is the task of the historian to describe its typical form. Thucydides' description of the plague is thus a model of the *History* as a whole. Similarly, his description of what happens as a result of the civil war in Corcyra becomes a description of the consequences of civil war in general, "which occur and always will occur while human nature is the same, but which are milder or more severe, and varying in their form, as the variations in each circumstance present themselves" (3. 82. 2). For this view, see Charles N. Cochrane, *Thucydides and the Science of History* (London: Oxford University Press, 1929). The medical analogy is challenged in A. Parry, "The Language of Thucydides' Description of the Plague," *Bulletin of the Institute of Classical Studies* 16 (1969): 106–18, and in Kirkwood, "Thucydides' Words for 'Cause'"; and, as I suggest in the text, there is much in Thucydides to support the view that events are controlled as much by policy, character, or luck as by processes analogous to disease.

35. Some books and articles setting forth the views referred to in the text are F. E. Adcock, *Thucydides and His History* (Cambridge, Eng.: At the University Press, 1963) (great admiration for Athenian power; see, e.g., pp. 52–55); R. G. Collingwood, *The Idea of History* (Oxford: Clarendon Press, 1946), 28–31 (the discovery of scientific laws and principles); F. M. Cornford, *Thucydides Mythistoricus* (tragic drama); John H. Finley, Jr., *Thucydides*, 309–10 (goal of text is to educate statesmen); Gomme, *A Historical Commentary on Thucydides*, 1:149–50 (rejects the idea of usefulness to statesmen); Werner Jaeger, *Paideia: The Ideals of*

Greek Culture, trans. Gilbert Highet, 2d ed. (New York: Oxford University Press, 1945), vol. 1, bk. 2, chap. 6 (discovery of the laws of politics through the examination of experience); Richard Jebb, "The Speeches of Thucydides," *Essays and Addresses* (Cambridge, Eng.: At the University Press, 1907), 359, 360 ("It is chiefly by [the speeches] that the facts of the Peloponnesian War are transformed into typical examples of universal laws and illuminated with a practical significance for the students of politics in every age and country"); Momigliano, *Studies in Historiography*, 112–26 (Thucydides "tried to understand the mind of the people who decided to fight"); Westlake, *Individuals in Thucydides* (focuses on character and its consequences in action).

For more on Thucydides' admiration of Athens, see Gomme, Andrewes, and Dover, *A Historical Commentary on Thucydides*, 4:186; A. Andrewes, "The Melian Dialogue and Pericles' Last Speech," *Proceedings of the Cambridge Philological Society* n.s. 6 (1960): 6; John H. Finley, Jr., *Thucydides*, 249; and David Grene, *Greek Political Theory: The Image of Man in Thucydides and Plato* (Chicago: University of Chicago Press, 1950), 91–92.

36. See, e.g., Grene, *Greek Political Theory*, 70–79; John H. Finley, Jr., *Thucydides*, 312–15.

37. Russell Meiggs calls the Pentekontaetia (1. 89–118) "one of the least satisfactory" parts of Thucydides' work, in large part because it omits such important matters as the transference of the Delian treasury to Athens and the so-called Peace of Callias (the supposed peace struck with the Persians in about 450 B.C., which, if it existed, eliminated the defensive purposes of the Athenian empire) and because it stops in 439, several years before the Corcyrean events (Meiggs, *The Athenian Empire* [Oxford: Clarendon Press, 1972], 2–4; cf. Gomme, *A Historical Commentary on Thucydides*, 1:361–413, though Gomme (p. 152) believes that the Pentekontaetia is meant to state the "true cause" of the war).

38. Thucydides manifests an interest in paradox throughout the *History*. For example, it is paradoxical that Athens' original poverty should explain her early wealth and that Cleon's speech should mirror so closely that of Pericles, who was so different a man and leader (see, e.g., A. Andrewes, "The Mytilene Debate: Thucydides 3. 36–49," *Phoenix* 16 [1962]: 64, 75); and Diodotus' speech is based on the paradox that self-interest may lead to mercy. Such paradoxes are a simultaneous enactment of connection and disjunction; they are performances of the ultimate lack of resolution of this text.

39. Andrewes sees the discontinuities as reflecting changes in view as Thucydides matures. See, e.g., his "Thucydides on the Causes of the War" and his remarks in Gomme, Andrewes, and Dover, *A Historical Commentary on Thucydides*, 4:186, where he refers to those "for whom

Thucydides is a secure observer with fixed opinions" and "those for whom the *History* gives an impression of tension and internal struggle," allying himself with the latter. I believe that the discontinuities are deliberate and structural, intended to force the reader to share the struggle of the author. I think it wholly incompatible with the cast of Thucydides' mind to suppose that he would at the end of his life have reordered the text to reflect a new and coherent conception of the world.

40. The Greek verb *historein* meant simply "to inquire."

41. This culture of argument is in fact a kind of law. This is so despite the fact that in many respects it fails to conform to standard modern ideas of law: it is not promulgated by a political sovereign but is made by the parties who are subject to it; there are no formal bureaucracies to interpret, supplement, and enforce it; for the most part it does not take the form of explicit rules but includes materials closer to what we would think of merely as maxims or principles; its terms are so flexible as to permit the justification of a very wide range of conduct in any particular case, making it impossible to talk, as we do today, as if there were a specific state of affairs that the lawmaker wished to bring about, which it is therefore everyone's object to pretend to wish to achieve; and it can be abandoned by any of the parties without any sanctions beyond those that flow from withdrawal itself. But this is not to say that this is not law or that it is unreal or insubstantial. As we have seen, it does impose real limits on conduct—the Athenian treaty with Corcyra is defensive only—and it is a rhetorical system defined with sufficient clarity to be mastered by its practitioners.

In fact I think that this discourse offers us a better model of what law characteristically is, even in our own world, than the usual idea of a system of rules expressing the command of a regularly constituted political sovereign. Think of the way we teach and learn law, for example. Even though in our system we do have sets of legal rules, in law schools we do not devote much energy to teaching or learning them. In most courses the rules the student must learn are very few in number and could perhaps be put on a page or two. Rather, as the brief account of legal education given on pages 9–10 suggests, our attention is given to mastering the arguments that may be made for or against a particular result in a particular case. Our true subject is not the rules but the culture of argument through the operations of which the rules will acquire their life and ultimate meaning, the culture that defines the social and professional universe in which we work. A rule is not self-interpreting, after all, and will always leave open certain aspects of its significance, especially when it is brought to bear in circumstances no one ever thought of. Except in the clear and by definition nonproblematic case the rule can be thought of as establishing not a single necessary result but a range of culturally possible results, among which choices will have to be made by lawyers and by judges. It is the processes of thought and conversation by which these choices are made, the culture of legal argument, that is the law itself.

42. For an elaboration of this principle, see my article "The Fourth Amendment as a Way of Talking about People: A Study of *Robinson* and *Matlock*," *Supreme Court Review* 1974: 165–216.

43. For a recent discussion, see Cass Sunstein, "Public Values, Private Interests, and the Equal Protection Clause," *Supreme Court Review* 1982: 127–66.

44. See, e.g., Edward P. Thompson, *Whigs and Hunters: The Origin of the Black Act* (New York: Pantheon Books, 1975), 258–69.

45. To test this, ask yourself what difficulties the Mytileneans faced when they sought to establish an alliance with Sparta and how you would have addressed those difficulties on their behalf. Then compare what they actually said at 3. 9–14.

46. For other (and rather different) histories of public language, see J. G. A. Pocock, *The Machiavellian Moment: Florentine Political Thought and the Atlantic Republican Tradition* (Princeton: Princeton University Press, 1975), *Politics, Language and Time: Essays on Political Thought and History* (New York: Atheneum, 1971), esp. chap. 1, and Quentin Skinner, *The Foundations of Modern Political Thought*, 2 vols. (Cambridge, Eng.: At the University Press, 1978).

47. On the idea of equality as an invention of the Greek *polis*, see Jean-Pierre Vernant, *The Origins of Greek Thought*, Eng. trans. (Ithaca: Cornell University Press, 1982), 124–32.

CHAPTER FOUR: PLATO'S *GORGIAS*

Bibliography and Background

The *Gorgias* is one of Plato's early dialogues, written probably in the 380s. The standard Greek text is the one edited by Eric R. Dodds, *Plato: Gorgias* (Oxford: Clarendon Press, 1959). A recent English translation, with careful analysis of particular passages, has been done by Terence Irwin (Oxford: Clarendon Press, 1979).

Gorgias of Leontini was born in Sicily early in the fifth century and lived to be over a hundred. He came to Athens for the first time in 427 B.C. and made a great impression with his oratory. He was a contemporary of Protagoras, the sophist about whom Plato wrote a dialogue of that name, and is himself sometimes called a sophist. But Gorgias was less interested in the sophistic devices of reasoning, which made the weaker side appear to be the stronger, than in the power of rhythmic and musical speech. (It was Protagoras who first taught that every question has two sides. See Diogenes Laertius, *The Lives and Opinions of Eminent Philosophers*, 9. 51.) For our purposes, it is best to look to what the text tells us, which is that Gorgias was a "rhetorician," and draw our definition of that term from the text itself. Of Callicles and Polus almost nothing is known beyond what Plato tells us here, except that Polus was a teacher of rhetoric (see Dodds, *Plato: Gorgias*, 6–15; W. K. C. Guthrie, *A History of Greek Philosophy*, 5 vols. [Cambridge, Eng.: At the University Press, 1962–78], 3:262–74. On Gorgias himself, see George Kennedy, *The Art of Persuasion in Greece* (Princeton: Princeton University Press, 1963), 61–68.

The dramatic date of the dialogue is impossible to determine, since evidence within it supports dates ranging from 429 B.C. to 405 B.C. See Dodds, *Gorgias*, 17–18.

On the nature of dialectic, see Richard Robinson, *Plato's Earlier Dialectic*, 2d ed. (Oxford: Clarendon Press, 1953), and Herman L. Sinaiko, *Love, Knowledge, and Discourse in Plato: Dialogue and Dialectic in "Phaedrus," "Republic," "Parmenides"* (Chicago: University of Chicago Press, 1965).

Notes

1. The English word "ethical" comes from a Greek word meaning "habit" and "character."

2. What Plato meant by "dialectic" changed substantially over his life. See, e.g., John E. Raven, *Plato's Thought in the Making: A Study of the Development of His Metaphysics* (Cambridge, Eng.: At the University Press, 1965). We shall be concerned only with the way it is defined in the *Gorgias*.

3. *Kakos* is the masculine nominative singular, and it will be used in my text when a person is referred to; *kakon* is the neuter singular, and it will be used when an object or quality is meant. Other adjectives will be used in the same way.

For a thorough study of the development of the key terms of value in ancient Greek, the reader is (once again) referred to Arthur W. H. Adkins, *Merit and Responsibility: A Study in Greek Values* (Oxford: Clarendon Press, 1960), to which I am largely indebted for the brief discussion of these terms that appears in the text.

4. One who had in this sense "made it" would in Greek terms be *agathos* by virtue of his power (*dynamis*). If he had acquired this power by his brains, he would be *phronimos*; if by guts, he would be *andreios*.

5. In the text Socrates also makes a stronger (but perhaps fallacious) claim, that since the rhetorician must know "just things" he will be just

himself. It follows that there can therefore be no unjust use of rhetoric, and this proves that rhetoric is, after all, not a neutral force, which can be used either for good or for ill, but a way of achieving justice.

This may seem an impossible line of argument in English, and perhaps it is in Greek. It is best taken as a restatement of the well-known Socratic position that knowledge is virtue, i.e., that knowledge of justice necessarily makes one just. This will itself make sense only if it is recognized that the Greek word for knowledge incorporates what we would call "moral" or "emotional" as well as "cognitive" elements and is much more intimately tied to the idea of practice than most uses of "know" are in English. On this, see John Gould, *The Development of Plato's Ethics* (Cambridge, Eng.: At the University Press, 1955), chap. 1, and Michael J. O'Brien, *The Socratic Paradoxes and the Greek Mind* (Chapel Hill: University of North Carolina Press, 1967), chap. 1.

6. Though the translation is traditional, "flattery" is in fact too weak a word to render the sense of the Greek word *kolakeia*; "fawning" or "bootlicking" comes closer.

7. Socrates explains that there are four great arts for the care of the body and soul: gymnastics and medicine, which maintain and cure the body; legislation and justice, which do the same for the soul. Each art has as its object the welfare either of body or soul; each also has a false imitator, which aims not at what is good but only at what is pleasant. These are cosmetics, cookery, sophistic, and rhetoric. They are all knacks, not arts; for they can give no rational account of themselves or their objects, and they do not deal with cause and effect. They are all flatteries, and, because they aim at pleasure without consideration of what is best, "I call that shameful [*aischron*]" (464b–465e).

Notice that here and elsewhere Socrates talks about the soul (what we would call the "self") in terms one would expect to be used of the city, and vice versa. He makes no explicit defense of this usage here. Its fullest development is in the *Republic*, especially book 8.

8. Socrates supports the distinction between "what one wants to do" and "whatever one thinks best" by distinguishing between an activity and its object. People take medicine to get well, make a voyage to get wealthy, and so on. And when a person does something on account of something else, he wants not what he does but what he does it for. Who would want to take medicine or cross the mountains in winter for themselves alone? There are in the world, that is, only good (*agathon*) (in the sense of "advantageous") things, bad (*kakon*) things, and neutral (*metaxu*) things. And when people do neutral (*metaxu*) things on account of the good (*agathon*) things, it is the good (*agathon*) things that they really want. This is how it is possible for a dictator to do "whatever he thinks best" and at the same time "what he does not want"; that is, he can be

wrong about what he really wants, namely, the good (*agathon*). He cannot have much power if he cannot do what he wants (467c–468c).

9. With respect to the desirability of being punished, Socrates leads Polus to agree that, if someone punishes another justly (*dikaiōs kolazein*), the other suffers what is just (*dikaion*); and what is just (*dikaion*) is also *kalon* (admirable; noble; beautiful), and what is *kalon* is *agathon* (good), i.e., either pleasant or useful. Since punishment is no pleasure, it must be beneficial. And the benefit is enormous because it is a relief from the greatest of evils (*kakon*), a miserableness not merely of body or condition but of the very self (477a). All these things being true, to use rhetoric to avoid just punishment is pointless; if it has a proper use, it is only to bring just punishment upon oneself and to deflect it from one's enemies (480c–d).

There is of course a possibility not considered here: that rhetoric might be used to deflect *unjust* punishment from oneself and one's friends. It is characteristic of Polus that he misses the point; it is later raised by Callicles and dealt with by Socrates (see above, p. 101).

10. Socrates demonstrates this by questioning Polus about the terms *agathon* (good: opposed to *kakon*) and *kalon* (admirable or noble or beautiful: opposed to *aischron*). What is *kalon*, he says, and Polus agrees, is so by virtue either of some use to which it may be put, or some pleasure it yields, or both. The opposite of what is *kalon* is *aischron*, which must therefore be characterized by the opposite of use and pleasure, namely, by evil (*kakon*) or by pain. Since it has been agreed that to do injustice is more *aischron* than suffering it, it must exceed in pain or in evil or in both. It is not in fact greater in pain, but less; so it must be greater in evil, i.e., more *kakon*. "I spoke the truth, then, when I said that neither I nor you nor any other man whatever would choose rather to do than to suffer injustice; for it is more *kakon*" (475e).

In my view this proof is, as it seems to be, only a logical or verbal trick. That what is *aischron* must be *kakon* is true (even for Socrates) only for some meanings of the word *aischron*, and such identity as exists rests on more substantial considerations than are revealed here. On the role of false proofs in the dialectic, see above, pp. 105–6. On this section of the dialogue, see Gregory Vlastos, "Was Polus Refuted?," *American Journal of Philology* 88 (1967): 454–60, and W. K. C. Guthrie, *A History of Greek Philosophy*, 5 vols. (Cambridge, Eng.: At the University Press, 1962–78) 4:311–12 (contra Vlastos).

11. If this still seems to the reader an unimaginable position, let me suggest that the question be framed with respect not to oneself but to one's child. Would one prefer that he have a crime committed against him or that he commit a crime? Both are forms of unhappiness, obviously, but the Socratic question assumes that and asks which is worse. And, with

respect to punishment, one might place it in the context of the family: with what sort of love for a child would a parent never punish him? When Socrates speaks of punishment here, it is not just any infliction of pain that he means but pain inflicted with the idea of correction. The practical difficulty of creating a system of socially imposed punishment, rationally based on that principle, does not affect his immediate point. (Similarly, in his final colloquy with Callicles he assumes that there could be a "just" rhetoric, though in fact his arguments seem to demonstrate that this cannot be.) See Herbert Morris, "A Paternalistic Theory of Punishment," *American Philosophical Quarterly* 18 (1981): 263–71.

12. It is a tendency of the dialogues to call whatever kind of bad reasoning is at issue "sophistic" or "eristic" and to label any good reasoning "dialectic." See Richard Robinson, *Plato's Earlier Dialectic*, 2d ed. (Oxford: Clarendon Press, 1953), 70. For our purposes it is the way dialectic is defined in the performance that matters; and it would in any event be inconsistent with the way dialectic is exemplified here to expect a systematic definition.

13. See, e.g., the "proof" that it is more *kakon* to do than to suffer injustice, summarized in the text, page 99.

14. See how easily, for example, Socrates lets Gorgias himself off the hook.

15. See Robinson, *Plato's Earlier Dialectic*, especially chap. 2, for a fuller statement of this process. Consult also Gould, *The Development of Plato's Ethics*; O'Brien, *The Socratic Paradoxes and the Greek Mind*; and Herman L. Sinaiko, *Love, Knowledge, and Discourse in Plato: Dialogue and Dialectic in "Phaedrus," "Republic," "Parmenides"* (Chicago: University of Chicago Press, 1965).

16. For examples, see Arthur W. H. Adkins, *Merit and Responsibility: A Study in Greek Values*, 251, 291; Vlastos, "Was Polus Refuted?"

17. See Adkins, *Merit and Responsibility*, 273–74.

18. For development of this position, see my article "The Ethics of Argument: Plato's *Gorgias* and the Modern Lawyer," *University of Chicago Law Review* 50 (1983): 849–95, esp. 871–95.

Chapter Five: Swift's *A Tale of a Tub*

Bibliography and Background

A Tale of a Tub was written by Jonathan Swift (1667–1745) while he was in the household of Sir William Temple, in 1696 or 1697. During this period he also wrote *The Battle of the Books*, and the two works were published together in 1704. It is important to know both that Swift was a clergyman of the Church of England and that he was possessed of considerable social and political ambition.

In the present chapter all references are to the standard edition by A. C. Guthkelch and D. N. Smith, 2d ed. (Oxford: Clarendon Press, 1958), which reproduces the spelling and typography, as well as the notes and other matter, of Swift's fifth edition (1710).

General Works

Standard works on Swift and the *Tale* include John R. Clark, *Form and Frenzy in Swift's "Tale of a Tub"* (Ithaca: Cornell University Press, 1970); Irvin Ehrenpreis, *Swift: The Man, His Works, and the Age*, 2 vols. (Cambridge, Mass.: Harvard University Press, 1962–67); Phillip Harth, *Swift and Anglican Rationalism: The Religious Background of "A Tale of a Tub"* (Chicago: University of Chicago Press, 1961); Ronald Paulson, *Theme and Structure in Swift's "Tale of a Tub"* (New Haven: Yale University Press, 1960); Ricardo Quintana, *The Mind and Art of Jonathan Swift* (Gloucester, Mass.: P. Smith, 1965); Edward W. Rosenheim, *Swift and the Satirist's Art* (Chicago: University of Chicago Press, 1963); Miriam Kosh Starkman, *Swift's Satire on Learning in "A Tale of a Tub"* (Princeton: Princeton University Press, 1950); Kathleen Williams, *Jonathan Swift and the Age of Compromise* (Lawrence, Kans.: University of Kansas Press, 1959). See also Paul Fussell, *The Rhetorical World of Augustan Humanism: Ethics and Imagery from Swift to Burke* (Oxford: Clarendon Press, 1965).

The third edition of William Wotton's *Reflections upon Ancient and Modern Learning*, published in 1705, contained an appendix attacking the *Tale*. In the Author's "Apology," added to the fifth edition of the *Tale*, Swift characterizes Wotton's work as "*half Invective, and half Annotation.*" Wotton's explanations of the meaning of particular difficulties in the allegory were for the most part accurate enough, and Swift took revenge on him by inserting them as if they were the notes of a serious commentator.

Interpretations of the "Digression on Madness"

The "Digression on Madness" has often been analyzed in detail. See, e.g., Clark, *Form and Frenzy*, 13–20, 30–35, 48–53, 72–79; H. Davis, "Swift's Use of Irony," reprinted in Brian Vickers, ed., *The World of Jonathan Swift* (Cambridge, Mass.: Harvard University Press, 1968), 158–59; Denis Donoghue, *Jonathan Swift: A Critical Introduction* (Cambridge, Eng.: At the University Press, 1969), 47–58; Ehrenpreis, *Swift: The Man, His Works, and the Age*, 1:216–25; F. R. Leavis, "The Irony of

Swift," *Scrutiny* 2 (1934): 372–74; Harth, *Swift and Anglican Rationalism*, 121–37; and Rosenheim, *Swift and the Satirist's Art*, 195–206. None of these writers takes the particular view set forth in the text.

Notes

1. In a well-known article F. R. Leavis attacks Swift's irony on the grounds that it is wholly negative, particularly as contrasted with Gibbon's use of irony to affirm civilized standards. Swift offers us, he says, "probably the most remarkable expression of negative feelings and attitudes that literature can offer—the spectacle of creative powers . . . exhibited consistently in negation and rejection" (Leavis, "The Irony of Swift," *Scrutiny* 2 [1934]: 377). And Robert M. Adams says that, "If there are positive teachings lurking in the book, one is hard put to know what they are" (Adams, *Strains of Discord: Studies in Literary Openness* [Ithaca: Cornell University Press, 1958], 157). But see William Frost, "The Irony of Swift and Gibbon: A Reply to F. R. Leavis," *Essays in Criticism* 17 (1967): 41–47.

2. Each of these pieces can be regarded as training the reader in the art of reading that this text will require. In the third, for example—"The Epistle Dedicatory, to his Royal Highness, PRINCE POSTERITY"—the "author" in a modern voice laments the ravages of time, which so quickly blast and destroy the products of the age. "His inveterate Malice is such to the Writings of our Age, that of several Thousands produced yearly from this renowned City, before the next Revolution of the Sun, there is not one to be heard of: Unhappy Infants, many of them barbarously destroyed, before they have so much as learnt their *Mother-Tongue* to beg for Pity." The real point, of course, is not to lament but to express respect for the processes of collective experience and judgment—here called "Time"—by which what is most worthy among human productions is preserved, what is least worthy is destroyed; that is, for the processes by which a culture is made and maintained.

The other most significant piece is the Preface, in which the "modern author" explains that he has written this tale as a diversion to occupy the "Wits of the present Age," to keep them from picking "Holes in the weak sides of Religion and Government," pending the establishment of a more permanent institution for achieving the same object, namely "a large Academy," in which the "Wits" will be disposed into several schools, there to "pursue those Studies to which their Genius most inclines them." He lists the schools:

> There is first, a large *Pederastick* School, with *French*
> and *Italian* Masters. There is also, the *Spelling* School,

> *a very spacious Building*: The School of *Looking*
> *Glasses*: The School of *Swearing*: The School of *Crit-*
> *icks*: The School of *Salivation*: The School of *Hobby-*
> *Horses*: The School of *Poetry*: The School of *Tops*: The
> School of *Spleen*: The School of *Gaming*: with many
> others too tedious to recount.

Exhibited here is a mind that is mad in at least two respects: it is incapable of distinction and connection in the ordinary way, and it accepts and praises everything. Indeed, the author tells us, "TIS a great Ease to my Conscience that I have writ so elaborate and useful a Discourse without one grain of Satyr intermixt." And later:

> I am so entirely satisfied with the whole present Proce-
> dure of human Things, that I have been for some Years
> preparing Materials towards *A Panegyrick upon the*
> *World*; to which I intended to add a Second Part, en-
> tituled, *A Modest Defence of the Proceedings of the Rab-*
> *ble in all Ages.*

3. John, Lord Somers (or Sommers) (1651–1715), Protestant, lawyer, trusted adviser to King William, draftsman of the Bill of Rights, was a wealthy and powerful patron of the arts. He was made Lord Chancellor of England at about the time the *Tale* was finished, which may partly explain why it was dedicated to him.

4. The bookseller says that he was about to write a dedication in the usual form (that is, by plagiarizing others), giving "your Lordship a List of your own Virtues" and celebrating your "Liberality towards Men of great Parts and small Fortunes, and give you broad Hints, that I mean my self," when he came upon the following instruction with the manuscript: "DETUR DIGNISSIMO." Neither the bookseller nor any of his authors could read it ("tho' I have them often in pay, to translate out of that Language"), but the local curate said it meant "*Let it be given to the Worthiest*; And his Comment was, that the Author meant, his Work should be dedicated to the sublimest Genius of the Age, for Wit, Learning, Judgment, Eloquence and Wisdom." But who should that be? The bookseller called at a poet "(who works for my Shop) in an Alley hard by," and asked him who the author could mean.

> He told me, after some Consideration, that Vanity was a
> Thing he abhorr'd; but by the Description, he thought
> Himself to be the Person aimed at; And, at the same
> time, he very kindly offer'd his own Assistance *gratis*,

towards penning a Dedication to Himself. I desired him,
however, to give a second Guess; Why then, said he, It
must be I, or my Lord *Sommers*.

The bookseller then went "to several other Wits of my Acquaintance" and
"found them all in the same Story, both of your Lordship and themselves."
This convinced him that his lordship must be the person meant, for it is a
"Maxim, that those, to whom every Body allows the second Place, have
an undoubted Title to the First."

So he employed "those Wits aforesaid" to "furnish [him] with Hints
and Materials, towards a Panegyrick upon your Lordship's Virtues." They
brought him ten sheets of paper, written on both sides, claiming to have
ransacked whatever had been said about the wisest and best men of the
world.

> [But] when I came to read over their Collections, there
> was not a Syllable there, but what I and every body else
> knew as well as themselves: Therefore, I grievously
> suspect a Cheat; and, that these Authors of mine, stole
> and transcribed every Word, from the universal Report
> of Mankind. So that I look upon my self, as fifty Shill-
> ings out of Pocket, to no manner of Purpose.

If he could, by altering the title, make the same materials serve for another dedication, it would not be so bad, but "I have made several Persons, dip here and there in those Papers, and before they read three
Lines, they have all assured me, plainly, that they cannot possibly be applied to any Person besides your Lordship."

5. By the "*Strong-Box*" Swift refers to the ancient languages in which
the Scriptures, prior to Martin Luther's great translations, were left
largely unintelligible to the ordinary person. The acquisition of the house
by fraud is the Donation of Constantine, the forged grant of temporal rule
over Rome to the popes.

6. Allusion can be an important mode of poetic thought and expression, functioning rather in the manner of simile and metaphor, and it was
widely practiced by the Augustan poets, who loved the classical world.
See Reuben Arthur Brower, *Alexander Pope: The Poetry of Allusion* (Oxford: Clarendon Press, 1959). The *Tale*'s structure of allusion enacts a
similar value.

7. In the *Preface* Swift's modern author explains why satire is always
more popular than "panegyrick":

> the Materials of Panegyrick being very few in Number,
> have been long since exhausted: For, as Health is but

one Thing, and has been always the same, whereas Diseases are by thousands, besides new and daily Addi-
tions; So, all the Virtues that have been ever in
Mankind, are to be counted upon a few Fingers, but his
Follies and Vices are innumerable, and Time adds
hourly to the Heap.

8. The Aeolists hold that "*Man* brings with him into the World a peculiar Portion or Grain of *Wind*," which is "of a Catholick Use upon all
Emergencies of Life, is improvable into all Arts and Sciences, and may be
wonderfully refined, as well as enlarged by certain Methods in Education." It ought not be "covetously hoarded" but "freely communicated to
Mankind," and therefore the "Wise *Aeolists*, affirm the Gift of BELCH-
ING, to be the noblest Act of a Rational Creature." All learning comes
from the same source:

> Because, First, it is generally affirmed, or confess'd that
> Learning *puffeth Men up*: And Secondly, they proved it
> by the following Syllogism: *Words are but Wind; and
> Learning is nothing but Words*; Ergo, *Learning is
> nothing but Wind.*

9. One is inevitably reminded of Freud's drive-defense psychology, according to which enormous personality variations emerge from different
ways of responding to the same basic drives.

10. For a thorough treatment of the ways in which irony works, see
Wayne C. Booth, *A Rhetoric of Irony* (Chicago: University of Chicago
Press, 1974), esp. 1–31.

11. At least one critic, and an Irishman to boot, thinks we should, and
he also thinks that the man "truly wise," who "creams off nature," is really
Sir William Temple, Swift's patron, friend, and ideal. This is his argument:

> So: is Temple a fool? Yes, but only in a specially defined
> sense. "Fool" is a "complex word" in William Empson's
> sense, and we ought to recall not only his account of
> the ramifications of folly in *King Lear* but also the tradi-
> tion of Stultitia which culminates in Erasmus. But we
> can bring the matter nearer home. [There follows a
> quotation from Temple's own writing, in which he de-
> scribes his retirement to the country, and says that
> "among the follies of my life, building and planting have
> not been the least."]
>   To be a fool among knaves is consciously and cons-
> cientiously to seek the life of the garden, rejecting the

life of the world which, in this Epicurean setting, is the work of knaves. [Denis Donoghue, *Jonathan Swift: A Critical Introduction* (Cambridge, Eng.: At the University Press, 1969), 55–57]

12. For the observation that the wish for "serenity" with which the text primarily deals is the reader's own wish, I am indebted to Donald Quander of the Montana Bar.

13. For more on false questions, see my article "Law as Language: Reading Law and Reading Literature," *Texas Law Review* 60 (1982): 416–19.

14. But see Kathleen Williams, *Jonathan Swift and the Age of Compromise* (Lawrence, Kans.: University of Kansas Press, 1958), 134, for the view that Swift's central ethical value is the "mean": here the mean between reason and passion.

15. Some of the topics here divided into false questions have elsewhere been dealt with seriously. See, for example, Johnson's *Rambler* essays: Number 4 deals with the tension between fiction and truth (as in a different way does Number 60); Number 41, with memory and the imagination; and Numbers 175 and 79, with suspiciousness and credulity.

16. The benevolence of the Houyhnhnms was universal, extending to every member of the species and recognizing no distinction based on mere family connection. That sort of sentiment is incompatible with—indeed, as Swift suggests, it destroys—what we think of as love. Compare Dickens's Mrs. Jellyby in *Bleak House*.

17. My reading of the Houyhnhnm episode is not universally shared. See, e.g., Ricardo Quintana, *The Mind and Art of Jonathan Swift* (Gloucester, Mass.: P. Smith, 1965), 327: the "greatest weakness" of *Gulliver's Travels* is "the sensationalism into which Swift falls while developing the theme of bestiality, a sensationalism which diverts attention from the concurrent statement of the life of reason and comes perilously close to breaking down the perceptions and judgments enforced in this latter statement." And Edward W. Rosenheim, *Swift and the Satirist's Art* (Chicago: University of Chicago Press, 1963), 222, remarks that, "To the devastating portrayal of humanity which brings Gulliver to his final state Swift has offered no mitigating suggestion." But see Hugh Kenner, *The Counterfeiters: An Historical Comedy* (Bloomington: Indiana University Press, 1968), 134–42, to which my own reading is indebted.

18. This is a tension that Swift himself may never have resolved. The plain, reasoning, pragmatic voice, like that of the Will, which is used by Swift in such essays as his "Hints Towards an Essay on Conversation," and the "Proposal for correcting, improving, and ascertaining the English tongue," can by insensible degrees become the voice of Gulliver among

the Houyhnhnms or the sorts of clichés contained in his "Complete Collection of Genteel and Ingenious Conversation," which enacts a kind of personal and social death; but the imagination uncontrolled can lead to the madness of the modern author in the *Tale.* Swift's powerful imaginative drives were checked by powerful corrections toward plainness, and it may be that his only resolution was in writing the texts we have been examining.

19. This is the method Swift uses in *A Complete Collection of Genteel and Ingenious Conversation in Three Dialogues* to parody both the clichés themselves and the ethical conceptions that they (and that method of teaching) embody.

20. This art is of the greatest value when it is applied to one's own productions as part of a process of self-examination and correction. ("Did *I* really say *that?*") The text is a training in the internal processes by which one tests and remakes the productions that express and define the self. But it is also meant to train one to hear differently what others have written, partly as a protection against dangerous persuasion and partly as a real polemic against external forces in the literary and intellectual world.

To consider only one example, a reading of Swift will, I think, forever change the way one responds to such a passage as this, from chapter 5 of Part One of Hobbes's *Leviathan*:

> When a man *reasoneth,* he does nothing else but conceive a sum total, from *addition* of parcels; or conceive a remainder, from *subtraction* of one sum from another; which, if it be done by words, is conceiving of the consequences of the names of all the parts, to the name of the whole; or from the names of the whole and one part, to the name of the other part. And though in some things, as in numbers, besides adding and subtracting, men name other operations, as *multiplying* and *dividing,* yet they are the same; for multiplication, is but adding together of things equal; and division, but subtracting of one thing, as often as we can. These operations are not incident to numbers only, but to all manner of things that can be added together, and taken one out of another. For as arithmeticians teach to add and subtract in *numbers;* so the geometricians teach the same in *lines, figures,* solid and superficial, *angles, proportions, times,* degrees of *swiftness, force, power,* and the like; the logicians teach the same in *consequences of words;* adding together two *names* to make an *affirmation,* and two *affirmations* to make a *syllogism;* and

many syllogisms to make a *demonstration*; and from
the *sum*, or *conclusion* of a *syllogism*, they subtract one
proposition to find the other. Writers of politics add together *pactions* to find men's *duties*; and lawyers, *laws*
and *facts*, to find what is *right* and *wrong* in the actions of private men. In sum, in what matter soever
there is place for *addition* and *subtraction*, there also is
place for *reason*; and where these have no place, there
reason has nothing at all to do.

And in chapter II of the *Leviathan*, "Of Imagination," the reader experiences a shock of recognition when he is told that "IMAGINATION therefore is nothing but decaying sense," which, when "we would express the
decay, and signify that the sense is fading, old, and past," we call "*memory*." "So that imagination and memory are but one thing, which for divers considerations hath divers names." (An even more specific parody of
Hobbes has been observed by Phillip Harth, *Swift and Anglican Rationalism: The Religious Background of "A Tale of a Tub"* [Chicago: University of Chicago Press, 1961], 84.

In the *Tale* Swift parodies what seem to be two opposing tendencies of
mind, both diseased: devotion to mechanistic systems and theories (instruments of universal explanation or universal improvement) on the one
hand, and, on the other, an intoxication of the self with its own sensations
of greatness, in the form of inspiration. In his account of the inspired
Aeolists, who mechanically reduce everything to vapor or spirit, he shows
that the two tendencies, though often expressed in different ways, are
really one, since both are rooted in the same impossible grandiosity of
the self.

Modern examples of such things are of course not wanting, and the
reader who has been trained by Swift should find it amusing and instructive to listen whenever someone seeks to reduce life to system or theory
(to "his own notions"), whether by way of explaining events as a scientist
or controlling them as a politician. Fine examples can easily be found in
the literature of cost-benefit analysis, psychological or educational theory,
university catalogues or foundation reports, the analysis of social systems, theoretical literary criticism ("there are no texts, only interpreta-
tions of texts"), grant applications, degree prospectuses, and so on.

CHAPTER SIX: JOHNSON'S *RAMBLER*

Bibliography and Background

Samuel Johnson (1709–84) published the *Rambler*s as independently
issued papers, twice a week, from March 1750 to March 1752. They were

often hurriedly composed, in part because this was the period when Johnson was at work on his monumental *Dictionary of the English Language* (published in 1755). They constituted one of his first successes as a writer. The standard text of the *Rambler*, from which quotations in this chapter are drawn, is the Yale Edition of his *Works*, edited by W. J. Bate.

For our purposes the best works on Johnson are W. Jackson Bate, *Samuel Johnson* (New York: Harcourt, Brace, Jovanovich, 1977); Paul Fussell, *Samuel Johnson and the Life of Writing* (New York: Harcourt, Brace, Jovanovich, 1971); and two works by W. K. Wimsatt, Jr., *The Prose Style of Samuel Johnson* (New Haven: Yale University Press, 1941), and *Philosophic Words: A Study of Style and Meaning in "The Rambler" and "Dictionary" of Samuel Johnson* (New Haven: Yale University Press, 1948). For a general description of the *Rambler*s see Patrick O'Flaherty "Towards an Understanding of Johnson's *Rambler*," *Studies in English Literature* 18 (1978): 523–36. I am indebted to Wayne Booth for first drawing my attention to the difference between "principle" and "commonplace" in these essays, which is central to my reading of them.

In these essays Johnson addresses the widest range of moral topics: hope, pride, envy, sorrow; forgiveness and revenge, advice and flattery; cowardice, greed, curiosity; hypocrisy and affectation, rashness and timidity; frugality, idleness, and so on; as well as questions usually considered under the heading of manners, such as politeness, peevishness, the qualities of youth and age, the difficulties of marriage and bachelorhood, and the necessity of education. In addition, he includes essays on literary criticism, both theoretical and practical. The essays vary in form. Some are disquisitions in Johnson's own voice, others are fables, still others are letters from imaginary correspondents. I have concentrated on what I regard as the central group of essays, those that are expository in their form and moral in their subject matter. These are the essays, "professedly serious," in which Johnson himself took the greatest satisfaction, as he tells us in the last *Rambler* (No. 208).

The World of the *Rambler*

A general statement of the impression the essays make when read as a whole may be of some use to the reader as background for the more detailed work done in the text.

At the center of the essays is Johnson's sense that all of life is in constant motion. "Nothing terrestrial can be kept at a stand" (No. 85). From the beginning to the end of life, conditions and relations change, expectations form and are disappointed, perceptions shift, all in a swirl of uncertainty. "[T]he present is in perpetual motion, leaves us as soon as it arrives, ceases to be present before its presence is well perceived, and is only known to have existed by the effects it leaves behind" (No. 41). This sense of constant change comes partly from shifts in objective conditions; the experience of youth, for example, becomes that of age, and neither young nor old can understand the other (Nos. 50, 111, 151). (The young man "never imagines that there may be greatness without safety, affluence without content, jollity without friendship, and solitude without peace" [No. 196].) Each stage of life has its particular passions, dangers, capacities, and weaknesses: "to contend with the predominance of successive passions, to be endangered first by one affection, and then by another, is the condition upon which we are to pass our time" (No. 151). And "it is the fate of almost every passion, when it has passed the bounds which nature prescribes, to counteract its own purpose" (No. 53). The conscious self is incompletely aware both of its own motives (No. 87) and of the circumstances that shape them: as we grow older we discover that we have "changed our minds, though perhaps we cannot discover when the alteration happened, or by what causes it was produced" (No. 196). "[E]very step in the progression of existence changes our position with respect to the things about us" (No. 43).

Our perceptions and sentiments are naturally affected by our activities as well as by our years, for every enterprise of man entails habits of thought and feeling that stamp themselves upon the mind, and a man often carries these as a "brand of [his] calling" (No. 173). Our sense of "excellence" itself is so relative "that men may be heard boasting in one street of that which they would anxiously conceal in another" (No. 201). In such ways as this "we are by our occupations, education and habits of life divided almost into different species" (No. 160). But the constancy of change itself constitutes a kind of uniformity, especially when it is recognized that, beneath the surface shaped by the particular objects of our desire and fear, "we are all prompted by the same motives, all deceived by the same fallacies, all animated by hope, obstructed by danger, entangled by desire, and seduced by pleasure" (No. 60).

Our sense of perpetual change has internal roots as well, especially in our ineradicable capacity to form hopes and expectations against the plain facts of reality. No theme more deeply marks Johnson's moral writing than that expressed in the title of his poem "The Vanity of Human Wishes." It is our nature to shape our lives by wishes that are vain either in the sense that they cannot be attained at all or, if seemingly attained, prove not to be what we in fact desire. Of a plan formed by the poet Cowley to go to America, forsaking "this world for ever, and all the vanities and vexations of it," Johnson says:

> It is common for a man, who feels pain, to fancy that
> he could bear it better in any other part. Cowley having
> known the troubles and perplexities of a particular con-

dition, readily persuaded himself that nothing worse
was to be found, and that every alteration would bring
some improvement; he never suspected that the cause
of his unhappiness was within, that his own passions
were not sufficiently regulated, and that he was har-
rassed by his own impatience, which could never be
without something to awaken it, would accompany him
over the sea, and find its way to his American elysium.
He would, upon the tryal, have been soon convinced,
that the fountain of content must spring up in the
mind; and that he, who has so little knowledge of human nature, as to seek happiness by changing any
thing, but his own dispositions, will waste his life in
fruitless efforts, and multiply the griefs which he purposes to remove. [No. 6]

Since religion teaches of an afterlife, true hope toward that end is not only
proper but "the chief blessing of man" (No. 203). But in this world what
Johnson calls "philosophy" instructs us that we should not allow our
"happiness to depend upon external circumstances" (No. 6) and that we
should be sure "not to take pleasure in any thing, of which it is not in our
power to secure the possession to ourselves" (No. 32). The life of man
may be represented as a flotilla of ships that sets out to cross a sea that
has no end, on a journey that can terminate, sooner or later, only with the
sinking of each vessel (No. 102). The wise man "escapes disappointment
because he never forms any expectations" (No. 29).

But these are counsels of perfection that cannot be obeyed. Nature has
made impossible such a confinement of feeling and being. We carry
within us hopes and fears that must find external objects or end by "rav-
aging" the self (No. 120). And for us to overcome our propensity to waste
life in idleness ("the mere repugnance to motion" [No. 134]), or in empty
fantasizing ("this invisible riot of the mind, this secret prodigality of
being" [No. 89]), it is in fact necessary, against the teaching of "philosophy," for every man to "teach his desires to fix upon external things; he
must adopt the joys and the pains of others" (No. 89). We must participate in life by hoping and loving, whether we will or not; and we should
actively do so. Hope, which "begins with the first power of comparing our
actual with our possible state, and attends us through every stage and
period," is "necessary in every condition" (No. 67); the logical counsels of
philosophy, Johnson says, might increase "tranquillity" but not "happiness" (No. 47). "The natural flights of the human mind are not from pleasure to pleasure, but from hope to hope" (No. 2).

We are self-misled not only in our hopes but in our perceptions and judgments as well, especially with respect to ourselves. "It is easy for every man, whatever be his character with others, to find reasons for esteeming himself" (No. 76). The devices by which we do this are familiar enough: "the substitution of single acts for habits" (as "a man concludes himself to be tender and liberal, because he has once performed an act of liberality and tenderness"); or "confounding the praise of goodness with the practice"; or regulating life, "not by the standard of religion, but by the measure of other men's virtue"; and so on (No. 28).

The cost of such self-deception is a change of self. The essays are full of stories by which a quirk of mind becomes a vice, a series of acts becomes a habit, a slip becomes an irretrievable slide. The quick learner, for example, who goes from one pursuit to another, ends in eccentricity (No. 19); the sarcastic wit, who first pleases then wounds his company, ends in isolation (No. 174); acceptance of flattery leads to decay of the character (No. 162); and so on. "Every desire, however innocent, grows dangerous as by long indulgence it becomes ascendant in the mind" (No. 207). Here is what happens, for example, to a man of disputatious mind, who shines by his capacity to object to what others say:

> "The habit of considering every proposition as alike uncertain, left me no test by which any tenet could be tried; every opinion presented both sides with equal evidence, and my fallacies began to operate upon my own mind in more important enquiries. It was at last the sport of my vanity to weaken the obligations of moral duty, and efface the distinctions of good and evil, till I had deadened the sense of conviction, and abandoned my heart to the fluctuations of uncertainty, without anchor and without compass, without satisfaction of curiosity or peace of conscience; without principles of reason, or motives of action." [No. 95]

As we move through life, we acquire a store of experience; the capacity to make this experience real and instructive, "the faculty of remembrance," is what "place[s] us in the class of moral agents" (No. 41). What is past is real, as our hopes are not; and the pleasures that reality affords are "the only joys which we can call our own." Thus, "the time comes at last, in which life has no more to promise, in which happiness can be drawn only from recollection, and virtue will be all that we can recollect with pleasure" (ibid.).

The great enterprise of life, for Johnson, is to act against the circumstances of life and the pressures of the mind, in a constant making and remaking of the essential self and its experience: to "make" (as he says in the last line of "The Vanity of Human Wishes") the "happiness [one] does not find." It is the "reigning error of mankind" not to be "content with the conditions on which the goods of life are granted" (No. 178), and in these essays it is Johnson's constant desire to move himself and his reader toward understanding and acceptance of those conditions. The woman whose extraordinary beauty has been destroyed by disease is told: "Consider yourself . . . born to know, to reason, and to act" (No. 133).

Notes

1. For a general account of the view of life and morality that is reflected in these essays, see the Bibliographical Note for this chapter, just above.

2. This is a phrase from *Rambler* No. 180, where Johnson speaks of the "lustre of moral and religious truth."

3. *Idler*, Nos. 60–61.

4. On the sources for the Minim truisms, W. J. Bate has this to say: "Johnson . . . echoes consecutively here Pope's *Imitations of Horace* (II. 1. 279), Collins' *Epistle to Hanmer* (1. 55), Pope's *Imitations of Horace* (II. 1. 98), Dryden's *Preface to the Fables* (par. 11), and Pope's *Essay on Criticism* (1. 361); in the remarks on Otway immediately below, *Imitations of Horace* (II. 1. 278) and *Spectator* 39. The remark on the Spenserian stanza echoes Johnson's own opinion (*Rambler* 121, par. 14)" (Samuel Johnson, *Essays from the Rambler, Adventurer, and Idler*, ed. W. J. Bate [New Haven: Yale University Press, 1968], 300).

5. Compare the account of a principle, "[S]urely the remembrance of death ought to predominate in our minds, as an habitual and settled principle, always operating, though not always perceived" (No. 78), with that of a commonplace: "'*life is short*,' which may be heard among mankind by an attentive auditor, many times a day, but which never yet within my reach of observation left any impression upon the mind" (No. 71).

In *Rambler* No. 14 Johnson explains how it is that one can have an adequate intellectual grasp of principles but be defeated when it comes to putting them to work.

> [I]n moral discussions it is to be remembred that many
> impediments obstruct our practice, which very easily
> give way to theory. The speculatist is only in danger of
> erroneous reasoning, but the man involved in life has
> his own passions, and those of others, to encounter, and
> is embarrassed with a thousand inconveniences, which
> confound him with variety of impulse, and either per-
> plex or obstruct his way. He is forced to act without
> deliberation, and obliged to choose before he can exam-

ine; he is surprised by sudden alterations of the state of
things, and changes his measures according to superficial appearances; he is led by others, either because he
is indolent, or because he is timorous; he is sometimes
afraid to know what is right, and sometimes finds
friends or enemies diligent to deceive him.

6. In the conditions of existence as Johnson perceives them, where the
world constantly changes around us and we ourselves are always changing, our grasp of fact and language keeps slipping away. "We frequently
fall into error and folly, not because the true principles of action are not
known, but because, for a time, they are not remembered" (No. 175).

Truth finds an easy entrance into the mind when she
is introduced by desire, and attended by pleasure; but
when she intrudes uncalled, and brings only fear and
sorrow in her train, the passes of the intellect are barred
against her by prejudice and passion; if she sometimes
forces her way by the batteries of argument, she seldom
long keeps possession of her conquests, but is ejected
by some favoured enemy, or at best obtains only a nominal sovereignty, without influence and without authority.
[No. 165]

7. This essay is well analyzed, from a somewhat different point of view,
in W. K. Wimsatt, Jr., *The Prose Style of Samuel Johnson* (New Haven:
Yale University Press, 1941), esp. 24–25, 47, 54–62, and in Leopold
Damrosch, "Johnson's Manner of Proceeding in the *Rambler*," *Journal of
English Literary History* 40 (1973): 70–89. Damrosch gets the main
idea—"the heart of Johnson's mission as a moralist is to make us stop
parroting the precepts of moralists and start thinking for ourselves"
(p. 81)—and shows some ways Johnson does this. Wimsatt is good on the
antithetical movement of Johnson's prose (see esp. p. 47).

8. Compare the structure of *Rambler* No. 32, on patience. Johnson
there begins by presenting his reader with a series of arguments in favor
of patience. He states his thesis by saying that there is "nothing more unsuitable to the nature of man in any calamity than rage and turbulence,"
and then proceeds to demonstrate it by considering two pairs of alternative possibilities. First, if "what we suffer has been brought upon us by
ourselves," patience is "eminently our duty," for our sufferings are deserved; if, on the other hand, they are undeserved, patience is "much
easier," since "we have not the bitterness of remorse to add to the asperity
of misfortune." Second, if one's evils are of the class that admit no remedy,

such as deformity or old age, "it is always to be remembred, that impatience can have no present effect, but to deprive us of the consolations which our condition admits"; if, on the other hand, one's evils do admit a remedy, "impatience is to be avoided, because it wastes that time and attention in complaints, that, if properly applied, might remove the cause."

This passage has an unsatisfactory quality; it is too logical and neat, almost forced, and seems not deeply felt. In propounding these arguments, Johnson has assumed an uncharacteristic position as one who is trying to argue the reader into submission rather than talking with him as his friend about the difficulties of life.

9. On this point, and its consequences, see Paul Fussell, *Samuel Johnson and the Life of Writing* (New York: Harcourt, Brace, Jovanovich, 1971) 157–71.

10. This distinguishes Johnson not only from many modern preachers but from devotional writers of the first rank, such as Jeremy Taylor. The several sections of Taylor's *Holy Living and Holy Dying*, for example, are a little like the *Rambler* in that they contain amplifications on the central topics of moral life. But this is a literature of ministration, in which Taylor does not descend from the position of superiority from which he instructs his reader in the considerations that may affect his heart. It is indeed part of the strength of Taylor's writing that the voice that addresses us retains its serenity in the face of its recognition of human suffering. With Johnson, by contrast, we share a struggle that it is Taylor's purpose to put elsewhere, out of his prose.

11. Compare Johnson's *Rasselas*, where the Prince lives in a kind of utopia, the Happy Valley; free from all human cares, he is nevertheless filled with nameless discontents and vague wants: "Man has surely some latent sense for which this place affords no gratification, or he has some desires distinct from sense which must be satisfied before he can be happy." The Prince thus starts in a kind of moral and psychological infancy, without life and experience and hence without a language of self or motive: "If I had any known want, I should have a certain wish." To the world of experience he carries with him, also like an infant, impossible expectations, which his experience will destroy. But the destruction of his expectations does not destroy his preference for life over emptiness: "Do not suffer life to stagnate; it will grow muddy for want of motion: commit youself again to the current of the world."

12. On Johnson's movement by opposition, see Fussell, *Samuel Johnson and the Life of Writing*, 148–49, 171–74; and Wimsatt, *The Prose Style of Samuel Johnson*, 47.

In this connection, compare Johnson's literary judgments: when he categorizes the merits or the faults of a writer, the reader's mind is so filled by the present judgment that he half-forgets the other side; rereading Johnson's movements to conclusion is thus an expansion of the range of feeling, understanding, and judgment. Consider, for example, the turning point in his "Preface to Shakespeare": "*Shakespeare* with his excellencies has likewise faults, and faults sufficient to obscure and overwhelm any other merit." Or, in his "Life of Milton," his remarks on *Paradise Lost*, "a poem which, considered with respect to design, may claim the first place, and with respect to performance the second, among the productions of the human mind." "Before the greatness displayed in Milton's poem all other greatness shrinks away." But: "the reader finds no transaction in which he can be engaged, beholds no condition in which he can by any effort of the imagination place himself; he has, therefore, little natural curiosity or sympathy"; and "no one ever wished it longer than it is. Its perusal is a duty rather than a pleasure."

13. Of course Johnson uses the word "pride" somewhat differently in the two papers, allowing it to maintain in one usage the associations with "dignity" it is the object of the other to strip away. But definition by use and performance (rather than by the statement of equivalence) is a characteristic of Johnson's language, as it is of all literary and ordinary, as opposed to theoretical, language. The partial inconsistencies that this writing tolerates, indeed develops, are a part of its strength, a recognition of the limits of the schematic part of the mind.

14. For example, certain sets of essays similarly complicate Johnson's views of a good-humored disposition (Nos. 141 and 149), of peevishness (Nos. 72 and 74), of politeness (Nos. 98, 147, 157), of advice (Nos. 87, 105, 106, 155), and so on.

15. On the topic of hypocrisy Johnson elsewhere says that it is wrong to call someone a hypocrite for professing "zeal for those virtues, which he neglects to practice." The reason is that "he may be sincerely convinced of the advantages of conquering his passions, without having yet obtained the victory" (No. 14). The key to hypocrisy is insincerity. On affectation, see also note 20, below.

16. Compare Johnson's definition of patience in No. 32: "Patience and submission are very carefully to be distinguished from cowardice and indolence. We are not to repine, but we may lawfully struggle; for the calamities of life, like the necessities of nature, are calls to labour, and exercises of diligence." When we are in distress, we are "not to conclude" that it is our duty to languish under it, "any more than when we perceive the pain of thirst we are to imagine that water is prohibited." The duty of action is a difficult one, especially in disease; but "lest we should think ourselves too soon entitled to the mournful privileges of irresistible misery, it is proper to reflect that the utmost anguish which human wit can contrive, or human malice can inflict, has been borne with constancy." We are so constructed that:

we soon cease to feel our maladies when they once become too violent to be born. I think there is some reason
for questioning whether the body and mind are not so
proportioned, that the one can bear all which can be
inflicted on the other, whether virtue cannot stand its
ground so long as life, and whether a soul well principled will not be separated sooner than subdued.

Patience and principle both have now been defined for us in a new way.
Patience, since it now includes a duty of action and resistance as well as
of submission, can have the standing of a "principle," which is distinguished both from a merely theoretical position (like that of the Stoics)
and from the conclusion of a chain of proper reasoning, like Johnson's
own. The principle of patience is not a set of words but a radical alteration
of the self, a capacity for action and endurance.

17. This is how languages are made, even mathematical ones. Compare "A straight line is the shortest distance between two points" and "$F
= ma$," which at once defines force and mass in terms of each other and
in terms of the third term—the only measurable one—acceleration.

18. On Johnson's *Dictionary* in general see James H. Sledd and Gwin
J. Kolb, *Dr. Johnson's Dictionary: Essays on the Biography of a Book*
(Chicago: University of Chicago Press, 1955), and W. K. Wimsatt, Jr.,
"Johnson's *Dictionary*," in Frederick W. Hilles, ed., *New Light on Dr.
Johnson: Essays on the Occasion of His 250th Birthday* (New Haven:
Yale University Press, 1959), 65–90.

19. Johnson's way of putting this, in the Preface to his *Dictionary*, is to
say that he was "desirous that every quotation should be useful to some
other end than the illustration of a word."

20. Here is a more extended instance of the same sort of writing, in
which, among other things, Johnson works up to a definition of "affectation" by example:

He that stands to contemplate the crowds that fill the
streets of a populous city, will see many passengers
whose air and motion it will be difficult to behold without contempt and laughter; but if he examines what are
the appearances that thus powerfully excite his risibility,
he will find among them neither poverty nor disease,
nor any involuntary or painful defect. The disposition to
derision and insult is awakened by the softness of fop-
pery, the swell of insolence, the liveliness of levity, or the
solemnity of grandeur; by the sprightly trip, the stately
stalk, the formal strut, and the lofty mien; by gestures

intended to catch the eye, and by looks elaborately
formed as evidences of importance.

It has, I think, been sometimes urged in favour of
affectation . . . . [No. 179]

21. Compare Socrates' redefinition of *agathos* to include what no traditional *agathos* man would consider part of his dignity: suffering injustice.

CHAPTER SEVEN: AUSTEN'S *EMMA*

Bibliography and Background

Jane Austen (1775–1817) wrote six novels, of which *Emma*, published
in 1815, was the next to last. The text of *Emma* used here is the standard
edition, edited by R. W. Chapman (3d ed., London: Oxford University
Press, 1933).

The most useful accounts of *Emma* (and of Jane Austen) can be found
in Julia Prewitt Brown, *Jane Austen's Novels: Social Change and Literary
Form* (Cambridge, Mass.: Harvard University Press, 1979); R. W. Chap-
man, *Jane Austen: Facts and Problems* (Oxford: Clarendon Press, 1948);
David Lodge, "The Vocabulary of *Mansfield Park*," in *The Language of
Fiction* (London: Routledge & Kegan Paul, 1966); David Lodge, ed., *Jane
Austen, "Emma": A Casebook* (London: Macmillan, 1968) (especially the
essays by Wayne Booth, Marvin Mudrick, and Lionel Trilling); Norman
Page, *The Language of Jane Austen* (Oxford: Basil Blackwell, 1972); and
Stuart M. Tave, *Some Words of Jane Austen* (Chicago: University of Chi-
cago Press, 1973).

Notes

1. That it is possible for the reader to learn to use Jane Austen's language of reason and value is beautifully demonstrated by Stuart M. Tave
in *Some Words of Jane Austen* (Chicago: University of Chicago Press,
1973). See also David Lodge, "The Vocabulary of *Mansfield Park*," in *The
Language of Fiction* (London: Routledge & Kegan Paul, 1966), 94–113,
and Norman Page, *The Language of Jane Austen* (Oxford: Basil Blackwell, 1972).

2. We can, at least on rereading, see something additionally odd about
the way Emma is defined in this sentence: as one who "unites" various
qualities or attributes that are apparently not an inherent part of her personality but nonetheless, for certain purposes, define her, as though this
were the natural way to describe a person. But by the end of the novel we

shall not be able to imagine Emma being defined by such a series of adjectives (though she is of course still as handsome, clever, and rich as she ever was) nor by her social and psychological circumstances (her wit, her high-class marriage); for by then we shall have learned that the concern of the text is not with matters like these but with the person she has become and the relations she has established with others. Compare, for example, the very different way in which Austen introduces us to Miss Bates, who, though "neither young, handsome, rich, nor married" (that is, without any of Emma's "blessings") was yet a "happy woman," one whom "no one named without good will":

> [S]he loved every body, was interested in every body's
> happiness, quick-sighted to every body's merits; thought
> herself a most fortunate creature, and surrounded with
> blessings in such an excellent mother and so many
> good neighbours and friends, and a home that wanted
> for nothing. The simplicity and cheerfulness of her na-
> ture, her contented and grateful spirit, were a recom-
> mendation to every body and a mine of felicity to
> herself. [P. 21]

Unlike Emma, Miss Bates is defined by her inner nature and by the quality of her relations with others, not by her attributes or possessions.

3. The methods by which Austen tells us what Emma's habits of mind are, and what to think of them, are of course enormously complex, and a full explication of them is beyond our present scope. Consider the following example that contains items from several discourses, representing distinct and contrasting attitudes:

> The real evils indeed of Emma's situation were the
> power of having rather too much her own way, and a
> disposition to think a little too well of herself; these
> were the disadvantages that threatened alloy to her
> many enjoyments. The danger, however, was at present
> so unperceived, that they did not by any means rank as
> misfortunes with her.

In this paragraph identical things are spoken of in very different terms: as "real evils," as "disadvantages," and as "not by any means rank[ing] as misfortunes." We learn here that the narrator's voice may speak of things either as we are ultimately intended to see them, as Emma sees them, or somewhere in between; and that it may shift from one mode to another within a single sentence. A necessary part of learning to read this book

337

will be learning to distinguish these voices, to tell the sound and right language, when we hear it, from the diseased and wrong; and part of the promise made to us is that the text itself will help us learn these things.

4. Actually, Emma's sense of her social position is also distorted, a part of her fantasy. Speaking in Emma's voice, for example, Austen says: "The Woodhouses were first in consequence there. All looked up to them." The truth is that the Woodhouses do enjoy a "superior" social position, but it is not quite the grand and elevated one that Emma describes. Their property is really part of the town, and, though it has a lawn and shrubbery, it has no real grounds. Emma herself is later much amused when Mrs. Elton presumes to speak to her as an equal, on the basis that she is connected with the Sucklings, whose Maple Grove has equally "extensive grounds" with Hartfield (p. 273), and it becomes plain that, on the traditional scale of social status, by far the highest rank in the district belongs to Mr. Knightley, who is possessed of Donwell Abbey, the grounds of which run at least the mile between his house and Hartfield and perhaps much farther.

5. Emma later says, and many critics agree with her (e.g., Marvin Mudrick, "Irony as Form: *Emma*," in David Lodge, ed., *Jane Austen, "Emma": A Casebook* [London: Macmillan, 1968], 114), that she is not "tender-hearted"; but in this she is quite wrong, for she is very tender-hearted toward her father and toward her nephews and nieces. The difficulty is that her tender-heartedness is not always appropriately available.

6. It is significant that he is introduced without mention of his social status. Jane Austen speaks of him according to his qualities and worth, not, in Emma's sometime fashion, according to his "superiority."

7. Much of Mr. Knightley's influence takes the form of correcting Emma's use of language: "No, Emma, your amiable young man can be amiable only in French, not in English. He may be very 'aimable,' have very good manners, and be very agreeable; but he can have no English delicacy towards the feelings of other people: nothing really amiable about him" (p. 149).

8. This helps to explain what some regard as a puzzle of the work: the fact that the reader, at the end, can feel not only that Emma has been corrected but that Mr. Knightley is a very lucky man to have her for a wife. Trollope puts the puzzle this way (in the notes inscribed in his copy of *Emma*): "even at the last we hardly know why Mr. Knightley loves her" (Lodge, *Jane Austen, "Emma,"* 51). I hope that the reader of this book will come to think that he or she sees something that Trollope missed.

9. Emma's conception of marriage in terms of class is likewise a way of making it unreal, reducing it to a game.

10. We are exposed so thoroughly to Emma's insufferable side because it is Austen's object to trace her cure, and in such a story much attention must of necessity be given to the disease itself.

11. Lionel Trilling says that Emma's way of talking is a perversion of Mr. Knightley's because it is not loving, and this is in some sense true. Another way to look at it is to see Emma as trying to work by imitation, and not understanding what she imitates, instead of proceeding from herself. See Trilling, "*Emma* and the Legend of Jane Austen," in Lodge, *Jane Austen, "Emma,"* 148–69.

12. Compare the way Edmund Bertram defines manners in *Mansfield Park*. He is talking to Miss Crawford about the effect the clergy have on society by influencing its manners.

> "And with regard to their influencing public manners,
> Miss Crawford must not misunderstand me, or suppose
> I mean to call them the arbiters of good breeding, the
> regulators of refinement and courtesy, the masters of
> the ceremonies of life. The *manners* I speak of, might
> rather be called *conduct*, perhaps, the result of good
> principles; the effect, in short, of those doctrines which
> it is their duty to teach and recommend." [Jane Austen,
> *Mansfield Park*, ed. R. W. Chapman, 3d ed. (London:
> Oxford University Press, 1934), 93]

On this passage, and the language of manners in Jane Austen generally, see Lodge, "The Vocabulary of *Mansfield Park*," in *The Language of Fiction*, 99–102.

13. In the argument between Mr. Knightley and Emma over the propriety of her conduct with respect to Harriet, they articulate two wholly opposed views of social and moral merit. Emma functions out of her views of class and status, of success and "superiority," Mr. Knightley (and Austen) out of the views (ultimately adopted by Emma) of internal and individual excellence. In this connection, notice that by the end of the novel the meaning of Emma's word "superior" has changed entirely. She then says to Frank Churchill that, by their respective betrothals, they are connected "with two characters so much superior to our own" (p. 478). Mr. Knightley and Mrs. Weston also have an argument on the subject of Emma's friendship with Harriet, in the course of which Mrs. Weston adamantly refuses to accept the possibility that Emma should be criticized in any important way (pp. 36–41). She insists successfully on her own construction of reality and in doing this shows us how powerful is her disposition to indulge Emma, the fruits of which are seen in Emma's present condition.

14. Emma has already demonstrated in an impressive way her capacity to read well and to use her reading to correct her own biases. When she read Mr. Martin's letter to Harriet, for example, she first admitted, against her expectation and wish, that it was good; then she tried to evade this

conclusion by attributing it to one of his sisters; but on rereading it, she conceded it to have been his own: "[I]t is too strong and concise; not diffuse enough for a woman" (p. 51). Harriet, by contrast, is wholly incapable of reading the letter in a critical way; she asks only whether it is too long.

Notice that Emma's standard would lead to a misjudgment of her own expressions, which can, as in this very instance, be very "strong and concise": in the ordinary sense manly, not feminine. Compare Trilling's remark that Emma has "a moral life as a man has a moral life," which he attributes to her "self-love" (Trilling, "*Emma* and the Legend of Jane Austen," in Lodge, *Jane Austen, "Emma,"* 153–54). Does the indulgence that nearly spoils her also contribute, when corrected, to her self-love and her strength of mind?

15. There is at least one other case in which Emma judges more rightly than Mr. Knightley: she foresees, as he does not, how badly Mrs. Elton will treat Jane Fairfax. See pp. 286, 295–96.

16. Emma's capacity to stand up to Mr. Knightley is of course not always to good effect. In their intense argument about Harriet Smith and the propriety of Emma's conduct, referred to above, she refuses to give in even though she is plainly in the wrong. What she has is a strength of mind that may, like other strengths, be put to good ends or bad.

17. Here is the conversation:

> "This is coming as you should do," said she, "like a gentleman.—I am quite glad to see you."
>
> He thanked her, observing, "How lucky that we should arrive at the same moment! for, if we had first met in the drawing-room, I doubt whether you would have discerned me to be more of a gentleman than usual.—You might not have distinguished how I came by my look and manner."
>
> "Yes I should, I am sure I should. There is always a look of consciousness or bustle when people come in a way which they know to be beneath them. You think you carry it off well, I dare say, but with you it is a spirit of bravado, an air of unaffected concern; I always observe it when I meet you under those circumstances. *Now* you have nothing to try for. You are not afraid of being supposed ashamed. You are not striving to look taller than any body else. *Now* I shall really be very happy to walk into the same room with you."
>
> "Nonsensical girl!" was his reply, but not at all in anger. [Pp. 213–14]

18. Another example of the kind of "conversation" that takes place between Churchill and Emma is the interchange in the Bateses' sitting
room, after the arrival of the piano. Frank Churchill, speaking, as usual,
in different ways to Emma and to Jane Fairfax, says that "True affection
must have prompted it." The text goes on:

> Emma wished he would be less pointed, yet could
> not help being amused; and when on glancing her eye
> toward Jane Fairfax she caught the remains of a smile,
> when she saw that with all the deep blush of conscious-
> ness, there had been a smile of secret delight, she had
> less scruple in the amusement, and much less com-
> punction with respect to her.—This amiable, upright,
> perfect Jane Fairfax was apparently cherishing very rep-
> rehensible feelings.
> He brought all the music to her, and they looked it
> over together.—Emma took the opportunity of
> whispering,
> "You speak too plain. She must understand you."
> "I hope she does. I would have her understand me. I
> am not in the least ashamed of my meaning."
> "But really, I am half ashamed, and wish I had never
> taken up the idea."
> "I am very glad you did, and that you communicated
> it to me. I have now a key to all her odd looks and ways.
> Leave shame to her. If she does wrong, she ought to
> feel it."
> "She is not entirely without it, I think."
> "I do not see much sign of it. She is playing *Robin
> Adair* at this moment—*his* favorite." [P. 243]

19. One might compare this to the conversation in which Emma tries
to find out from Mr. Knightley whether there is any truth to Mrs. Weston's
supposition that he may have sent the piano. Emma knows just what to
say to him and just how to read the response she gets. She brings up the
subject by saying that the piano is "very kindly given." Mr. Knightley responds affirmatively but is disapproving toward surprises: "Surprises are
foolish things. The pleasure is not enhanced, and the inconvenience is
often considerable. I should have expected better judgment in Colonel
Campbell." Emma is now confident that she knows the truth: "from that
moment she could have taken her oath that Mr. Knightley had no concern in giving the instrument" (p. 228). She here shows that she knows
who Mr. Knightley is, how to read him, and that she may trust him; and,

341

though she does not know it, this is the exact opposite of the case with Frank Churchill.

20. Notice that in this passage Emma is looking forward from midsummer to winter and from life at a frantic pace (the strawberry party of Donwell and the Box Hill party occur on successive days) to a life that proceeds very slowly indeed. In the autumnal *Persuasion* Jane Austen as it were makes a novel out of this paragraph; for Anne Elliot must face just such a life as that described here, with no consolations beyond those Emma foresees for herself.

21. It is important that we do share, directly and in our own experience as readers, Emma's sense of the tiresomeness of Miss Bates. To read one of her speeches aloud, word by word, is a kind of torture, and this makes us share something of Emma's impulse to shut her up.

22. On the presence of Jane Austen in the text and her friendship with the reader, see Wayne C. Booth, "Control of Distance in Jane Austen's *Emma*," in Lodge, *Jane Austen, "Emma,"* 213–15. Booth quotes Katherine Mansfield's remark: "the truth is that every true admirer of the novels cherishes the happy thought that he alone—reading between the lines—has become the secret friend of their author." My point is that there is a sense in which that happy thought is not an illusion but true.

23. On the unsettled social world of these novels, see Raymond Williams, *The Country and the City* (London: Chatto & Windus, 1973), 112–17; Marilyn Butler, *Jane Austen and the War of Ideas* (Oxford: Clarendon Press, 1975), 272–73; Barbara Hardy, *A Reading of Jane Austen* (London: Owen, 1975), 106–7. On the place of the Woodhouses within it, see above, note 4.

24. In one chapter Emma has two failed conversations, which demonstrate (though she herself does not yet fully perceive it) how limited her opportunity for conversation really is. First she tries an elegantly good-humored pleasantry on Mrs. Elton, which falls completely flat:

> "We cannot suppose," said Emma smiling, "that Mr.
> Elton would hesitate to assure you of there being a *very*
> musical society in Highbury; and I hope you will not
> find he has outstepped the truth more than may be pardoned, in consideration of the motive."
> "No, indeed, I have no doubts at all on that head. I
> am delighted to find myself in such a circle." [P. 277]
> [This is the conversation in which Mrs. Elton refers to
> Mr. Knightley as "Knightley."]

When Emma returns home, she tries to engage her father in conversation, teasing him about his opposition to marriage:

> "But, my dear papa, you are no friend to matrimony;
> and therefore why should you be so anxious to pay your
> respects to a *bride*? It ought to be no recommendation
> to *you*. It is encouraging people to marry if you make so
> much of them." [P. 280]

But Mr. Woodhouse is not equal to the teasing, and she desists. "Her father was growing nervous, and could not understand *her*."

As John Halperin remarks, "Indeed almost all of the major characters of *Emma* live within a reality of their own devising" (John Halperin, "The Worlds of *Emma*: Jane Austen and Cowper," in Halperin, ed., *Jane Austen: Bicentenary Essays* [Cambridge, Eng.: At the University Press, 1975], 202). But Halperin goes on in a somewhat different vein from my own: "the world they see is a function of their own selfish egoism." See also Butler, *Jane Austen and the War of Ideas*, 222.

25. There is this additional consequence: once it is recognized, as Socrates and Jane Austen would both agree, that one's central concern should be for one's character—who one is, who one becomes—it follows that in a story such as this, and, barring accident, in life itself, each person gets precisely what he deserves because he gets what he is. This is one way a fiction can be at once true to life and morally instructive.

26. In his essay "*Emma* and the Legend of Jane Austen," Lionel Trilling says that the social world of *Emma* is idyllic, and there is a sense in which it is (Trilling, in Lodge, *Jane Austen*, "*Emma*," 148–69. But the sense of the idyllic social world is largely the effect of Emma's imagination and force of mind, not Jane Austen's view of how life is or should be led, and it is punctured in Emma's sudden vision of her future.

There is in this novel a sense of perfection of another kind, the "perfect happiness of the union" between Emma and Mr. Knightley. This is not a product of Emma's fancy but something the reader is expected to feel and feel deeply, for it has been Austen's object to portray an ideal of friendship as perfect as she can conceive. On the perfection of the ending, see Booth, "Control of Distance in Jane Austen's *Emma*," 195–217. For a sharply contrasting view of the ending of this novel, see Mark Schorer, "The Humiliation of Emma Woodhouse," in Ian P. Watt, ed., *Jane Austen: A Collection of Critical Essays* (Englewood Cliffs, N.J.: Prentice-Hall, 1963), 98–111.

27. I owe to Howard Sayetta the powerful observation that the central value of this novel is kindness. This value of course also commits it to the virtues necessary to kindness, such as truthfulness, loyalty, and accurate perceptions. Compare Julia Prewitt Brown, *The Novels of Jane Austen: Social Change and Literary Form*, (Cambridge, Mass.: Harvard University Press, 1979), 125: "*Emma* is a novel of human interdependence in

every way"; and see Jane Nardin, "Charity in *Emma*," *Studies in the Novel* 7 (1975): 61–72.

28. This is also the kind of teaching that *Mansfield Park* offers its reader, who is likely to misread Fanny Price (in fact the only person with any real strength) as being timid and weak. And compare Henry Tilney's capacity to see the excellence in Catherine Morland, the awkward adolescent heroine of *Northanger Abbey*.

Chapter Eight: Burke's *Reflections*

Bibliography and Background

Edmund Burke (1729–97) was an Irishman by birth, born probably of a Protestant father and a Catholic mother. He was raised as a Protestant and educated in Ireland. With the publication of *A Vindication of Natural Society* and *A Philosophical Enquiry into the Sublime and the Beautiful* in 1756 he became a well-known literary figure. He entered Parliament in 1765, where he was a constant critic of the Tory government. For our purposes it is significant that he was a supporter of the claims of the American colonists; of the Irish Catholics and of Irish trade; of the people of India, who were being systematically looted by the East India Company; and of those held in slavery within the empire. (He supported abolition of the slave trade and the gradual extirpation of slavery. See, especially, "Sketch of a Negro Code" (1792) in *The Writings and Speeches of the Right Honourable Edmund Burke*, 12 vols. [New York: J. F. Taylor, 1901], 6:262.) He constantly addressed the tension between the dominant and the dominated, and perhaps his greatest achievements were his proposals for reformation of the powers held by the one in greater recognition of the claims of the other.

Burke wrote his *Reflections* just after the French Revolution of 1789, before the Terror and the outbreak of hostilities with England in 1793, and many Englishmen still saw the Revolution as holding out the promise of universal liberty, equality, and fraternity or at least as effecting a benign transformation of a defective government. To some, including the correspondent to whom it was nominally addressed, this text came as a great surprise, for it seemed to speak not for liberty but for repression. Part of Burke's effort in the text is accordingly to define the kind of "liberty" he stands for, and has stood for, and his commitment to the conditions upon which he has done so.

For our purposes the best works on Burke are James T. Boulton, *The Language of Politics in the Age of Wilkes and Burke* (London: Routledge & Kegan Paul, 1963); *The Correspondence of Edmund Burke*, ed.

Thomas W. Copeland, 10 vols. (Cambridge, Eng.: At the University Press, 1958–78); Paul Fussell, *The Rhetorical World of Augustan Humanism: Ethics and Imagery from Swift to Burke* (Oxford: Clarendon Press, 1965); L. Lipking, "Analyzing Burke," *The Eighteenth Century* 20 (1979): 65–95; Conor Cruise O'Brien, Introduction to the *Reflections* (Baltimore: Penguin, 1969); Leo Strauss, *Natural Right and History* (Chicago: University of Chicago Press, 1952), chap. 6; Raymond Williams, *Culture and Society* (London: Chatto & Windus, 1958).

Throughout I have used the Penguin edition of the *Reflections* (Edmund Burke, *Reflections on the Revolution in France and on the Proceedings in Certain Societies in London Relative to That Event* [1790], ed. Conor Cruise O'Brien [Baltimore: Penguin, 1969]).

Notes

1. In *A Philosophical Enquiry into the Sublime and the Beautiful* (1756), Burke drew a distinction between "clear" and "strong" expression: "The former regards the understanding; the latter belongs to the passions. The one describes a thing as it is; the other describes it as it is felt" (*The Writings and Speeches of the Right Honorable Edmund Burke*, 12 vols. [New York: J. F. Taylor, 1901], 1:180). As J. T. Boulton, to whom I owe this reference, says, Burke in the *Reflections* aspires to "strong," not merely "clear," expression. "In other words, he writes not simply as a political philosopher but as an imaginative artist." What that means—what kind of imaginative art he engages in, and what kind of philosophy—is my subject, as, in a somewhat different way, it is Mr. Boulton's (James T. Boulton, *The Language of Politics in the Age of Wilkes and Burke* [London: Routledge & Kegan Paul, 1963]; the quotations are from pp. 120–21).

2. Edmund Burke, *Reflections on the Revolution in France and on the Proceedings in Certain Societies in London Relative to That Event* (1790), ed. Conor Cruise O'Brien (Baltimore: Penguin, 1969), 84. All of my references are to this edition.

The young Frenchman who wrote to Burke has been identified as one Charles-Jean-François de Pont, and his letters to Burke have been published, in translation, in H. V. F. Somerset, "A Burke Discovery," *English* 8 (1951): 171–78. When Burke, for unclear "prudential considerations" (as he styles them in the opening paragraph of the *Reflections*, where he describes the correspondence), held back his first response, de Pont wrote him again, imploring him to write: "Ah! tell me, you whom I look to as a guide and master, tell me that the events which have taken place have been the necessary consequences of a change which the circumstances rendered indispensable! Ah, tell me that I may hope to see my country worthy to enjoy liberty, English liberty! My utmost wishes extend no further." When Burke finally sent him the *Reflections*, de Pont was horrified: "I certainly had no idea that my letter would lead to the publication of the work you so kindly sent me. I will even confess that I should never have made the request, had I been able to foresee its effect." See also *The Correspondence of Edmund Burke*, ed. Thomas W. Copeland, 10 vols. (Cambridge, Eng.: At the University Press, 1958–78), 6:31, 39.

3. It is in part this character of the text that leads Tom Paine, in his response to the *Reflections*, to refer to the "disorderly cast of [Burke's] genius," which renders him "unfitted for the subject he writes upon" (Thomas Paine, *The Rights of Man* [London: Dent, Everyman's Library, n.d.], 53), and Mary Wollstonecraft to remark that "I perceive from the whole tenor of your *Reflections* that you have a mortal antipathy to reason" (Mary Wollstonecraft, *A Vindication of the Rights of Men* [1790; Gainesville, Fla.: Scholars' Facsimiles and Reprints, 1960], 9).

4. There is an instructive example of an attempt to outline the text by subject matter and thesis in the Bobbs-Merrill Library of Liberal Arts Edition of the *Reflections* (T. Mahoney ed., 1955).

5. Compare: "But what is liberty without wisdom and without virtue? It is the greatest of all possible evils; for it is folly, vice, and madness, without tuition or restraint. . . . To make a government requires no great prudence. Settle the seat of power; teach obedience: and the work is done. To give freedom is still more easy. It is not necessary to guide; it only requires to let go the rein. But to form a *free government*; that is, to temper together these opposite elements of liberty and restraint in one consistent work, requires much thought, deep reflection, a sagacious, powerful, and combining mind" (pp. 373–74).

Of the French system of representation, Burke similarly says: "I do not see a variety of objects, reconciled in one consistent whole, but several contradictory principles reluctantly and irreconcileably brought and held together by your philosophers, like wild beasts shut up in a cage, to claw and bite each other to their mutual destruction" (p. 296).

6. "Their purpose every where seems to have been to evade and slip aside from *difficulty*. This it has been the glory of the great masters in all the arts to confront, and to overcome; and when they had overcome the first difficulty, to turn it into an instrument for new conquests over new difficulties; thus to enable them to extend the empire of their science; and even to push forward beyond the reach of their original thoughts, the land marks of the human understanding itself. . . . This amicable conflict with difficulty obliges us to an intimate acquaintance with our object, and compels us to consider it in all its relations. It will not suffer us to be superficial" (p. 278).

7. Burke repeatedly characterizes the French and their allies as violating "nature," including human nature, including that part of human na-

ture that is formed by culture. Dr. Price's use of the pulpit for political purposes is a violation of this kind (p. 94), as is the fact—as Burke sees it—that the government of France treats the nation "exactly like a country of conquest" (pp. 297–98). Compare Burke's claim that "poets, who have to deal with an audience not yet graduated in the school of the rights of men, and who must apply themselves to the moral constitution of the heart, would not dare to produce such a triumph as a matter of exultation" (p. 176); and "Why do I feel so differently from Dr. Price . . . ?—For this plain reason—because it is *natural* I should" (p. 175). The unnatural world of France is irrational and impossible, full of contradiction and paradox: "By following those false lights, France has bought undignified calamities at a higher price than any nation has purchased the most unequivocal blessings! France has bought poverty by crime!" (p. 124). Cf.: "After destroying all other genealogies and family distinctions, they invent a sort of pedigree of crimes" (p. 246).

Compare also the quotation in the text, p. 210, and the following:

> Every thing seems out of nature in this strange chaos of levity and ferocity, and of all sorts of crimes jumbled together with all sorts of follies. In viewing this monstrous tragi-comic scene, the most opposite passions necessarily succeed, and sometimes mix with each other in the mind; alternate contempt and indignation; alternate laughter and tears; alternate scorn and horror.
> [Pp. 92–93]

8. On pages 92–93 Burke makes plain that the world looks different to him and to the partisans of revolution. What is monstrous moral chaos to him is a source of "exultation and rapture" to them. This is a way of saying that his concern is in part with observing the world—with who you become when you read the world accurately, as he does, and who you become when you read it otherwise. In part as a way of offering the reader an exercise in the art, he then starts to tell a story, almost as a novelist might: "On the forenoon of the 4th of November last, Doctor Richard Price . . . ," etc.

9. These attitudes are, of course, not original with Burke. See, e.g., Richard Hooker, *The Laws of Ecclesiastical Polity*, especially his Preface 1593); Sir Matthew Hale, *Considerations Touching the Amendment or Alteration of the Laws*, printed in Francis Hargrave, *A Collection of Tracts Relative to the Law of England* (London, 1787) vol. 1, pt. 2; Shakespeare's *Richard II*, from which Burke borrowed much of his imagery, and *Troilus and Cressida*, especially Ulysses' famous "degree" speech (act I, scene iii). See also Blackstone's lecture "On the Study of Law," ap-

pearing as an introduction to his *Commentaries*, where he describes the various ways in which a gentleman is likely to be a legal actor: as proprietor, representative, landlord, church member, and so on.

10. As Burke elsewhere puts it, the "habits which are communicated by the circumstances of civil life" constitute a "second nature," which operates on the first—the nature of man out of society—and "produce[s] a new combination; and thence [arise] many diversities amongst men, according to their birth, their education, their professions, the periods of their lives, their residence in towns or in the country, their several ways of acquiring and of fixing property, and according to the quality of the property itself, all which [render] them as it were so many different species of animals" (p. 299).

11. In another famous passage on the French destruction of language and culture Burke says:

> On this scheme of things, a king is but a man; a
> queen is but a woman; a woman is but an animal; and
> an animal not of the highest order. All homage paid to
> the sex in general as such, and without distinct views,
> is to be regarded as romance and folly. Regicide, and
> parricide, and sacrilege, are but fictions of superstition,
> corrupting jurisprudence by destroying its simplicity.
> The murder of a king, or a queen, or a bishop, or a fa-
> ther, are only common homicide; and if the people are
> by any chance, or in any way gainers by it, a sort of
> homicide much the most pardonable, and into which
> we ought not to make too severe a scrutiny. [P. 171]

12. Burke's use of the word "prejudice" may owe its origins to a passage in one of the letters that de Pont wrote Burke, pressing him for his views: "Condescend, sir, to satisfy my doubts, and do not leave under the prejudice of party spirit a young man who was taught in England the danger of all prejudices" (from Somerset, "A Burke Discovery," 175).

13. The revolutionary, by contrast, proceeds to improve by destroying, by making a "carte blanche" of his country, upon which "he may scribble whatever he pleases." But "a good patriot, and a true politician, always considers how he shall make the most of the existing materials of his country" (pp. 266–67).

As an example of the sort of "material" out of which a "constitution" could be composed, consider the monasteries that the French destroyed. With all their defects, Burke says, they offered a "power," or what "our workmen call a purchase," for benevolence:

There were revenues with public direction; there were men wholly set apart and dedicated to public purposes, without any other than public ties and public principles; men without the possibility of converting the estate of the community into a private fortune; men denied to self-interests, whose avarice is for some community; men to whom personal poverty is honour, and implicit obedience stands in the place of freedom. In vain shall a man look to the possibility of making such things when he wants them. The winds blow as they list. These institutions are the products of enthusiasm; they are the instruments of wisdom. Wisdom cannot create materials; they are the gifts of nature or of chance; her pride is in the use. [P. 267]

Notice that these materials are the product not of nature alone but of culture as well.

14. Here is a famous passage describing the dissolution of culture that would flow from constitutional instability:

And first of all the science of jurisprudence, the pride of the human intellect, which, with all its defects, redundancies, and errors, is the collected reason of ages, combining the principles of original justice with the infinite variety of human concerns, as a heap of old exploded errors, would be no longer studied. Personal self-sufficiency and arrogance (the certain attendants upon all those who have never experienced a wisdom greater than their own) would usurp the tribunal. Of course, no certain laws, establishing invariable grounds of hope and fear, would keep the actions of men in a certain course, or direct them to a certain end. Nothing stable in the modes of holding property, or exercising function, could form a solid ground on which any parent could speculate in the education of his offspring, or in a choice for their future establishment in the world. No principles would be early worked into the habits. As soon as the most able instructor had completed his laborious course of institution, instead of sending forth his pupil, accomplished in a virtuous discipline, fitted to procure him attention and respect, in his place in society, he would find everything altered; and that he had turned out a poor creature to the contempt and derision of the world, ignorant of the true grounds of estimation. Who would insure a tender and delicate sense of honour to beat almost with the first pulses of the heart, when no man could know what would be the test of honour in a nation, continually varying the standard of its coin? No part of life would retain its acquisitions. Barbarism with regard to science and literature, unskillfulness with regard to arts and manufactures, would infallibly succeed to the want of a steady education and settled principle; and thus the commonwealth itself would, in a few generations, crumble away, be disconnected into the dust and powder of individuality, and at length dispersed to all the winds of heaven. [Pp. 193–94]

15. It is possible for a writer to give "toleration" quite a different meaning, as Gibbon shows in these sentences: "The various modes of worship, which prevailed in the Roman world, were all considered by the people, as equally true; by the philosopher, as equally false; and by the magistrate as equally useful. And thus toleration introduced not only mutual indulgence, but even religious concord" (Edward Gibbon, *The History of the Decline and Fall of the Roman Empire* [London, 1776], chap. 3). In this passage the value of "toleration" is not elevated to a high virtue, to a species of justice and charity, as in Burke, but reduced to mere "mutual indulgence." The enormously powerful term of value, "religious concord," is rendered trivial. To do these things to these words is indeed the point of the sentences. And this passage, like Burke's, derives additional meaning from its larger context. To go no farther than one example, there is here an echo of Gibbon's earlier well-known sentence about the Roman Republic, the form of which, balancing one item against another, imitates the form of the Republic itself: "The principal conquests of the Romans were achieved under the Republic; and the emperors, for the most part, were satisfied with preserving those dominions that had been acquired by the policy of the senate, the active emulation of the Consuls, and the martial enthusiasm of the people" (chap. 1). In the sentence on religious concord we have as it were a negative republic, made of parts that do not interact but ignore each other, united not by shared energies but by mutual indifference. Gibbon in this way says that the best kind of community it is possible to have with respect to religion is a community of disdainful indifference.

Another example of a text giving a meaning of its own to "toleration" is Tom Paine's response to Burke in *The Rights of Man* (London, 1791):

Toleration is not the *opposite* of Intolerance, but is the *counterfeit* of it. Both are despotisms. The one assumes to itself the right of with-holding Liberty of Conscience, and the other of granting it. The one is the pope, armed with fire and faggot, and the other is the pope selling or granting indulgences. The former is church and state, and the latter is church and traffic.

But toleration may be viewed in a much stronger light. Man worships not himself, but his Maker; and the liberty of conscience which he claims, is not for the service of himself, but of his God. In this case, therefore, we must necessarily have the associated idea of two beings; the *mortal* who renders the worship, and the IMMORTAL BEING who is worshipped. Toleration, therefore, places itself, not between man and man, nor between church and church, nor between one denomination of religion and another, but between God and man; between the being who worships, and the BEING who is worshipped; and by the same act of assumed authority by which it tolerates man to pay his worship, it presumptuously and blasphemously sets itself up to tolerate the Almighty to receive it. [P. 74]

16. Others, of course, have also seen Burke as offering a literary rather than a theoretical experience. Raymond Williams, for example, quotes Arnold's remark on Burke, that, "Almost alone in England, he brings thought to bear upon politics, he saturates politics with thought." Williams then continues:

Arnold himself is one of the political heirs of Burke, but again this is less important than the kind of thinking which Arnold indicates by the word "saturates." It is not "thought" in the common opposition to "feeling"; it is, rather, a special immediacy of experience, which works itself out, in depth, to a particular embodiment of ideas that become, in themselves, the whole man. The correctness of these ideas is not at first in question; and their truth is not, at first, to be assessed by their usefulness in historical understanding or political insight. Burke's writing is an articulated experience and as such has a validity which can survive even the demolition of its general conclusions. It is not that the eloquence has

351

survived where the cause has failed; the eloquence, if it were merely the veneer of a cause, would now be worthless. What survives is an experience, a particular kind of learning; the writing is important only to the extent that it communicates this. It is, finally, a personal experience become a landmark. [Raymond Williams, *Culture and Society* (London: Chatto & Windus, 1958), 4–5]

Compare this, from Boulton:

Burke was not only a great thinker, he was also an imaginative writer who requires a response from the reader as a whole man and not simply as a creature of intellect. Consequently his exposition—the play of imaginative insights as well as the statement of logical argument— itself becomes "proof" in this special sense that it communicates, and affirms while communicating, the rich complexity of a philosophy of life; it does not merely demonstrate the truth of a set of propositions. [James T. Boulton, *The Language of Politics in the Age of Wilkes and Burke*, 98]

See also David Weiser, "The Imagery of Burke's *Reflections*," *Studies in Burke and His Time* 16 (1975): 213–34.

The best general statement of the kind of distinction I mean when I talk of "literary" language is Owen Barfield's *Poetic Diction: A Study in Meaning* (London: Faber & Faber, 1952).

17. This is Marie Antoinette:

I saw her just above the horizon, decorating and cheering the elevated sphere she just began to move in,— glittering like the morning-star, full of life, and splendor, and joy. Oh! What a revolution! and what an heart must I have, to contemplate without emotion that elevation and that fall! [P. 169]

This is how the French Assembly conducts its deliberations:

They act like the comedians of a fair before a riotous audience; they act amidst the tumultuous cries of a mixed mob of ferocious men, and of women lost to shame, who, according to their insolent fancies, direct,

control, applaud, explode them; and sometimes mix and
take their seats amongst them; domineering over them
with a strange mixture of servile petulance and proud
presumptuous authority. [P. 161]

18. It is true that Burke can be called "eminently quotable," but if one examines a piece of modern rhetoric larded with Burkean quotations, one usually finds that his statements do not mean much out of their proper context. (This may be what makes him so "quotable.") But the reader of Burke's text is not addressed as one who will make quotations but as one who is capable of mastering a complex system of expression that is not reducible to theoretical summary or excerption. This is one way in which his text respects its reader.

19. This point can be put very simply: it is possible to imagine a country having universal suffrage that is in other respects less happy than one that does not; it may be less prosperous culturally and economically, less stable, less protective of individual rights, and so on.

We ourselves tolerate exceptions to absolute democracy with very little difficulty, as in the extremely unequal basis of representation in our Senate and in the lifetime appointment of judges (and professors). In fact, despite our principled or prejudiced resistance to Burke on the grounds of equality, there is perhaps no country in the world, including England, that is more conscious of the value of its political inheritance and less disposed to tolerate experimental or ideological change than our own. We now instinctively have many of the attitudes that Burke celebrates.

20. It may be instructive in this context to recall that the Melian community, which adhered to its identity in the face of death, was an oligarchy and that the Athenian community, which dissolved for lack of a coherent identity, was a democracy more extreme than our own.

And England does not select the men who will shape her life and laws by confining "power, authority, and distinction to blood and names and titles. No, Sir. There is no qualification for government, but virtue and wisdom, actual or presumptive." But while "everything ought to be open" to every man, it ought not to be open "indifferently." The man ought to be "select[ed] . . . with a view to the duty" (p. 139).

21. Think, for example, of the terms in which you would respond to a suggestion that we call a general constitutional convention next year, to be held in Kansas City. On purely theoretical grounds there can perhaps be no opposition: our present Constitution contemplates its own revision, and there is no reason for those who believe in the legal equality of all people to think that we, today, are less capable of forming a government for ourselves than our predecessors were in 1787. Yet such a convention would pose a terrible risk of destroying the set of understandings and atti-

tudes, of institutions and expectations—the language, the culture—that we have made, that has made us, and that we respect deeply. It would put at risk our very constitution. Here our prejudices are very much like Burke's own.

CHAPTER NINE: AMERICAN LAW

Bibliography and Background

For a recent discussion of the Declaration of Independence and its background, see Garry Wills, *Inventing America: Jefferson's Declaration of Independence* (New York: Doubleday, 1978). (This otherwise good book overargues its case that the primary intellectual tradition of Thomas Jefferson, the draftsman of the Declaration, was the Scottish Enlightment, and it somewhat underrepresents the role of Locke in Jefferson's thought. For more extensive criticism, see Ronald Hamowy, "Jefferson and the Scottish Enlightenment: A Critique of Garry Wills's *Inventing America: Jefferson's Declaration of Independence*," *William and Mary Quarterly* 3d ser. 36 [1979]: 503–23.) Earlier well-known works are Carl Becker, *The Declaration of Independence: A Study in the History of Political Ideas* (New York: Knopf, 1942), and Edmund S. Morgan, *The Birth of the Republic 1765–1789* (Chicago: University of Chicago Press, 1956). An excellent literary analysis of the Declaration, from which I have borrowed in the text, is Stuart M. Tave, "The Creative Teacher—Who Needs Him?" *Illinois English Bulletin* 53 (1966): 6–13. The text used is that of the parchment copy signed by the members of Congress and reprinted in *The United States Code*, vol. 1, pp. xxv–xxvi (1953 ed.).

The best recent book on the period between the Declaration and the Constitution is Gordon S. Wood, *The Creation of the American Republic* (Chapel Hill: University of North Carolina Press, 1969). See also Bernard Bailyn, *The Ideological Origins of the American Revolution* (Cambridge, Mass.: Belknap Press of Harvard University Press, 1967). The best accounts of the Constitution itself are Madison's *Notes of Debates in the Federal Convention of 1787*, ed. Adrienne Koch (Athens: Ohio University Press, 1966) and *The Federalist*, written by Hamilton, Madison, and Jay in support of its ratification. See also Max Farrand, *The Framing of the Constitution* (New Haven: Yale University Press, 1913).

General histories of the Supreme Court, which include some discussion of *McCulloch*, are: Charles Warren, *The Supreme Court in United States History* (Boston: Little, Brown, 1924); Andrew C. McLaughlin, *A Constitutional History of the United States* (New York: D. Appleton–Century, 1935); and Arthur E. Sutherland, *Constitutionalism in Amer-*

ica: Origin and Evolution of Its Fundamental Ideas (New York: Blaisdell, 1965). For more of Marshall's writings, see John P. Roche, *John Marshall. Major Opinions and Other Writings* (Indianapolis: Bobbs-Merrill, 1967).

I owe the felicitous phrase, "declaration of dependence" to Willis Buck.

Other recent works setting forth a humanistic conception of law include Joseph Vining, *Legal Identity: The Coming of Age of Public Law* (New Haven: Yale University Press, 1978) and Milner S. Ball, *The Promise of American Law: A Theological, Humanistic View of Legal Process* (Athens, Ga.: The University of Georgia Press, 1981).

Notes

1. See *Rambler* No. 60, quoted above, p. 328. And cf. Gibbon's famous sentence: "If a man were called to fix the period in the history of the world during which the human race was most happy and prosperous, he would, without hesitation, name that which elapsed from the death of Domitian to the accession of Commodus" (*The Decline and Fall of the Roman Empire* [1776], chap. 3).

2. Stuart M. Tave, "The Creative Teacher—Who Needs Him?" *Illinois English Bulletin* 53 (1966): 6–13.

3. On fame as a motive of the founding fathers see Douglass Adair, *Fame and the Founding Fathers* (New York: Norton, 1974), 3–26.

4. Locke said that the uncertainty of the state of nature makes a man "willing to quit this condition which, however free, is full of fears and continual dangers; and it is not without reason that he seeks out and is willing to join in society with others who are already united, or have a mind to unite for the mutual preservation of their lives, liberties, and estates, which I call by the general name—property" (John Locke, *An Essay Concerning the True Original, Extent and End of Civil Government*, § 123 [1690]). Despite the claims of Garry Wills to the contrary (*Inventing America: Jefferson's Declaration of Independence* [New York: Doubleday, 1978], 172–74), Jefferson was to some degree familiar with this language of Locke's, which indeed seems reflected in the Declaration itself (see Arthur E. Sutherland, *Constitutionalism in America: Origin and Evolution of Its Fundamental Ideas* [New York: Blaisdell, 1965], 143).

5. See the analysis of this section in Wills, *Inventing America*, 69–70. The indictment form is to some degree traditional. The English Bill of Rights of 1688, for example, contained a set of charges defining the occasion, perhaps the "necessity," for the provisions of the Bill itself. See Sutherland, *Constitutionalism in America*, 91.

6. For a discussion of Lincoln's use of the Declaration, see, e.g., H. Jaffa, *The Crisis of the House Divided: An Interpretation of the Issues in the Lincoln-Douglas Debates* (Garden City, N.Y.: Doubleday, 1959).

7. In my reading of the Preamble I have, with his kind permission, borrowed extensively from Professor Craig Lawson's unpublished paper "The Literary Force of the Preamble."

8. The elaborate and explicit design of the Constitution in itself embodies a principle of order that has deeply affected our thinking about it. The quality of this order is not as organic as that of Burke's garden. Characterized by straight lines and bold strokes, it is more akin to French city planning.

9. Presidents have on certain occasions asked their attorneys general for formal opinions, and these have been collected and published. George Washington asked Jefferson and Hamilton to furnish opinions on the constitutionality of legislation, then being proposed, to establish the Bank of the United States. See the text, p. 247.

10. George Washington in fact went to the Senate to consult with the members of a committee about a treaty with certain Indians. He was treated so rudely that he left and never went back (see Andrew C. McLaughlin, *The Constititional History of the United States* [New York: D. Appleton–Century, 1935], 249 ff.).

11. The Jefferson and Hamilton documents are easily accessible in Richard Hofstadter, ed., *Great Issues in American History: From the Revolution to the Civil War, 1765–1865* (New York: Vintage Books, 1958), 160, 164. In *McCulloch* Marshall drew heavily on Hamilton's text. *McCulloch* was not the end of the story, for in 1832 President Jackson vetoed another Bank bill, making a famous statement in explanation of his decision (see Hofstadter, pp. 291–95).

12. *Marbury* involved a federal statute purporting to expand the Court's jurisdiction beyond constitutional limits, and this presents the easiest kind of case in which to justify judicial invalidation of a legislative act. The power of judicial review established by *Marbury* might easily be limited to legislation that improperly expanded the jurisdiction of the Supreme Court or, more generally, to legislation that interfered in any way with the operations of the judicial branch.

13. Prior to Marshall's chief justiceship, the justices followed the English practice of routinely issuing separate opinions. Marshall initiated the practice of an opinion that spoke for the Court as a whole.

14. A similar case can be made for the rhetorical effect of *The Federalist*. These papers establish a quality of analysis and argument that promises to become the standard for constitutional discourse if, but only if, the Constitution is ratified. If it is not, the occasion for this kind of reasoning and speech will disappear.

15. Remarkable as they are, Marshall's claims so accord with our present expectations of a judicial opinion that it is worth pausing to say that this is not the only way the Court might have proceeded to claim and ex-

ercise the power of judicial review, nor is it the most modest or unassuming. For example, the Court might have said merely that the Constitution "requires us to decide this question in favor of the Bank," perhaps adding by way of explanation that the power to incorporate a Bank is necessarily implicit in the congressional powers enumerated in the Constitution and that the Supremacy Clause invalidates the Maryland tax. A document that has something of this character is the early *Correspondence of the Justices* (1793), in which the Court refused to advise Congress on the constitutionality of legislation under its consideration. (This letter is reprinted in *Hart and Wechsler's The Federal Courts and the Federal System*, 2d ed., edited by Paul Bator et al. [Mineola, N.Y.: Foundation Press, 1973], 65–66.) The entire explanation and justification of the Court were contained in the adverb "extrajudicially," which it employed to characterize the way it would be acting if it complied with the request. There are, of course, many reasons that could be advanced for the correctness of their judgment, and some that could be advanced against it, but the Court did not engage in public reasoning of any kind.

The modern lawyer might criticize this kind of opinion for failing to meet our standards of reasoned justification, saying that in thus resting on its bare authority the Court was being rather high-handed, both with the reader and with the other branches of government. But there is a sense in which the kind of opinion Marshall promises to write, which rests not merely on a claim of authority but on its own persuasive reasoning, is even more high-handed than that; for to claim to be guided by reason is to claim the right to go where reason leads. It is of course true that such an opinion will be subjected to criticism of a kind from which an "authoritative declaration" would be effectively insulated, and this involves a submission to communal judgment. But not merely submission: such a writer also necessarily expresses great confidence that his reasoning will withstand such criticism and that the community by which he will be judged will therefore be partly of his own creation.

16. Compare, for example, Marshall's treatment of Maryland's power to tax the Bank, in the second half of the opinion:

> This great principle is, that the constitution and the
> laws made in pursuance thereof are supreme; that they
> control the constitution and laws of the respective
> States, and cannot be controlled by them. From this,
> which may be almost termed an axiom, other proposi-
> tions are deduced as corollaries, on the truth or error of
> which, and on their application to this case, the cause
> has been supposed to depend. These are, 1st. that a
> power to create implies a power to preserve. 2d. That a

> power to destroy, if wielded by a different hand, is hos-
> tile to, and incompatible with these powers to create
> and to preserve. 3d. That where this repugnancy exists,
> that authority which is supreme must control, not yield
> to that over which it is supreme.

Actually, of course, the subsidiary principles that Marshall "deduces" are not implicit in his "axiom" at all but are instead directly expressive of his own highly controversial view of the relations between the state and federal governments, the central tenet of which is that they are essentially hostile. Once that is granted—and only if it is—it becomes obvious that the Supremacy Clause requires the invalidation of a state tax levied on a federal instrumentality. For the power to tax is the power to destroy, and who would place such a power in hostile hands? If, on the other hand, the relation between the two kinds of government were conceived to be one of mutual confidence and trust, their powers could be—and Marshall in his opening paragraph somewhat misleadingly implies that, in his view, they are—genuinely concurrent. This is, in fact, the argument of Maryland, who claims that the Constitution should be construed to leave the power of taxation in the states, "in the confidence that they will not abuse it." See also the text, p. 261.

17. In describing the principle of supremacy in the second part of the opinion, Marshall also works in this mode. He says this is "a principle which so entirely pervades the constitution, is so intermixed with the materials which compose it, so interwoven with its web, so blended with its texture, as to be incapable of being separated from it, without rending it into shreds." He thus defines the Constitution as a kind of fabric, the integrity and coherence of which depend on a particular thread that runs through it all, giving it shape and substance. Without it, the fabric would fall into shreds.

18. To make his result more tenable, Marshall frames the question in terms of the general power to incorporate, not the power to create a bank. He then says, "no particular reason can be assigned for excluding the use of a bank, if required for its fiscal operations." Even if its necessity were less apparent, however, "none can deny its being an appropriate measure; and if it is, the degree of its necessity, as has been very justly observed, is to be discussed in another place." He concludes with a statement of institutional self-restraint and modesty:

> [W]here the law is not prohibited, and is really calcu-
> lated to effect any of the objects entrusted to the gov-
> ernment, to undertake here to inquire into the degree of
> its necessity, would be to pass the line which circum-

scribes the judicial department, and to tread on legislative ground. This court disclaims all pretensions to such
a power.

19. Notice that Marshall prepares for his discussion of the meaning of
"necessary" by using the word three times in the paragraph that just precedes the long passage quoted in the text.

20. Marshall has thus created the rhetorical conditions on which he
can define Maryland's argument on confidence as impossibly unrealistic—"unrealistic," that is, by the standard that is artificially created by
Marshall's own rhetoric. He accordingly characterizes Maryland's argument in these sarcastic and patronizing terms: "But all the inconsistencies [created by concurrent sovereignties] are to be reconciled by the
magic of the word CONFIDENCE."

But is this a case of confidence? Would the people of
any one State trust those of another with a power to
control the most insignificant operations of their State
government? We know they would not . . . . This, then,
is not a case of confidence, and we must consider it as it
really is.

21. Cf. *The Federalist*, No. 78: "[The judiciary] may be truly said to
have neither *FORCE* nor *WILL* but merely judgment."

22. Marshall does not merely adopt the practices of judicial law-
making that preceded him; he profoundly modifies them. Prior to Marshall, the Supreme Court spoke not in a single opinion but (in the current
English fashion) in separate opinions by each justice. Moreover, as is apparent from what we have read, he does not often cite other cases as supporting authority or feel constrained to deal with them if they oppose his
position. Instead, he speaks on the authority of the Constitution itself, expounded in the light of reason and practice. His is a voice that is beginning again, on a new basis; but he intends no general departure from the
practice of obeying precedent, for he certainly expects his successors to
treat seriously the cases he decides.

At a deeper level, the awareness that the people of the law were making something new came to affect the process of common-law decision-
making as well. Over time, the model of the judicial opinion has come to
be no longer the meticulous comparison of precedent against precedent
but the large-minded, energetic, and perpetual reconstitution of language and the world we see displayed here in such dramatic form. Today
the constitutional judicial opinion, with its own more recent modifica-
tions, has taken over a larger and larger segment of American life, and we

happily present our courts with questions about the death penalty, abortion, race relations, voting rights, and so on—questions that in most other countries would be resolved through a wholly different kind of political process.

23. The classic statement is Felix Frankfurter, "A Note on Advisory Opinions," *Harvard Law Review* 37 (1924): 1002.

24. See Lewis H. LaRue, "A Jury of One's Peers," *Washington and Lee Law Review* 33 (1976): 841.

25. If one were excluded from the discourse, as Corcyra feared she would be, one would lack not only equality but juridical existence. See, e.g., *The Cherokee Nation v. Georgia*, 30 U.S. (5 Pet.) 1 (1831); *Dred Scott v. Sandford*, 60 U.S. (19 How.) 393 (1857).

26. The practice of blaming, for example, as it is institutionalized in our criminal law, is a way of insisting that one person recognize the reality of another's experience. See my article "Making Sense of the Criminal Law," *University of Colorado Law Review* 50 (1978): 1.

27. George Eliot, *The Natural History of German Life* (July, 1856), in *Essays of George Eliot* (Edinburgh, 1884), 270.

28. For example, one branch of legal language, the judicial language built up to interpret the Fourth Amendment, defines an essential aspect of the relation between the citizen and his government by defining the set of claims that can be made on both sides when a government official interferes with private security and liberty. This body of law specifies both the intrusions that count as "searches and seizures" that must be justified by an official when made and the justifications that will and will not suffice. Is it enough to support an arrest, for example, for the officer to say that he was suspicious or afraid? Or do we require more and, if so, how much more and what? Enough to demonstrate that the officer's act was rational in the sense that anyone would have done the same? Enough to dispel the suspect's fear that it was discriminatory or bullying? These questions are of course difficult to answer, and I cannot undertake to do so here; but one can see how they emerge from the method of reading exemplified here, and it is significant that the government must justify itself at all. In the world of the law we are defined by our rights, which are in the end always rights to speak in certain ways on certain occasions. For further discussion of these questions, see my article "The Fourth Amendment as a Way of Talking about People: A Study of *Robinson* and *Matlock*," *Supreme Court Review* 1974: 165.

It is also, of course, the law that gives us in a firm and reliable way the practice of contracting that enables us to organize ourselves around our work and property as we do.

29. The political philosopher and policymaker speak in ways that lawyers sometimes use, and they can helpfully criticize or modify the con-

tentions and substance of legal discourse. But in doing so, they speak differently, in a context outside the world created by the law. They will say, "I am someone who has thought about these matters, and I say . . . ."

30. To hear expert legal argument is to experience an expansion of the mind. When one speaker has finished, one wonders what can possibly be said the other way, why we should even bother to listen; but when the second speaker is heard, one forgets the appeal and force of the first and can hardly remember that one was actually affected by it. In the experience of decision, the judge or juror is forced to activate the arguments each way and make them his own, for only then can he say that the case itself, as opposed to some issue within it, has been decided. A lovely example of this capacity of the legal mind is Sir Matthew Hale's essay "Considerations Touching the Amendment or Alteration of the Laws" (in Francis Hargrave, *A Collection of Tracts Relative to the Law of England*, [London, 1787], vol. 1, pt. 2), in which he first sets forth all the reasons that would move one to respect one's legal tradition and hesitate to modify it, then all the reasons why reform may be necessary or desirable. In this way he establishes a complex attitude, uniting veneration for the laws with willingness to change them, as a prelude to his own proposals for reform. Compare Samuel Johnson's literary judgments, described above, pages 333–34.

31. For one example, see Justice Harlan's dissenting opinion in *Poe v. Ullman*, 367 U.S. 497, 539 (1961), where he sets forth the "framework of constitutional principles" in which he thinks that case, involving a state law making it a crime even for married people to use contraceptives, "must be judged." And compare Edmund Bertram's remark to Mary Crawford, in *Mansfield Park*, redefining "manners" as "*conduct*, perhaps, the result of good principles" (Jane Austen, *Mansfield Park*, ed. R. W. Chapman, 3d ed. [London: Oxford University Press, 1934], 93).

32. For a fuller development of these ideas, see my article "The Ethics of Argument: Plato's *Gorgias* and the Modern Lawyer," *University of Chicago Law Review* 50 (1983): 849–95.

33. There are obvious connections here with such modern works about justice as John Rawls, *A Theory of Justice* (Cambridge, Mass.: Harvard University Press, 1971), and Lawrence Kohlberg, "Justice as Reversibility," in Peter Laslett and James Fishkin, eds., *Philosophy, Politics, and Society*, 5th ser. (New Haven: Yale University Press, 1979), 257–73.

Index

Achilles, 24–58 passim; breakdown of meaning for, 7, 49, 51; calls assembly, 33–34; changes in, 44–45; conflict of, with Agamemnon, 32–35, 38; and Priam, 53–54; rejects embassy, 47–51; Shield of, 26. *See also* Agamemnon
—position of: compared with that of reader of *Gorgias*, 106; impossibility of, 54; on margin of world, 38–39
—wrath of: as abstraction, 57; like Athenian ambition, 71; beyond language, 21; without social form, 57; uncontained by system giving rise to it, 48–49
Adair, Douglass, 355 n.3
Adams, Robert M., 320 n.1
Adcock, F. E., 311 n.35
Adkins, A. W. H., 290, 295 n.4, 299 n.25, 302, 315 n.3, 318 nn.16–17
Agamemnon: conflict of, with Achilles, 32–34, 38; political position of, 32–33; shift as characteristic of, 34–35
Agreement on language, necessary to argument, 64, 268
Allusion in Swift's *Tale*, 124, 322 n.6
Andrewes, A., 300, 301, 302, 303, 305 n.8, 306 n.12, 309 nn.28–29, 311 n.33, 312 nn.35, 38–39
Arbitration as fifth-century Greek institution, 61

"Archeology," as mode of history in Thucydides, 83–85
Argument: agreement necessary to, 64; Athenian love of, 72, 74; defines cultural resources by exhaustion, 9–10; *Iliad* as having form of, 41–42; as mode of representation, 198–99; symmetry in, 63; running out, in Johnson, 158, 332 n.8. *See also* Conversation; Culture of argument; Persuasion; Rhetoric
—culture of: as law, 231–74 passim, 313–14 n.41; in Thucydides, 59, 60–82
—legal: criticism as part of, 267–68; experience of, 361 n.30; Iliadic argument like and unlike, 34–35; as mode of constituting reality and culture, 270
—as method: of cultural analysis, 6–7, 9–10, 267–68; of testing ideas, 252–53
—mind given to: Samuel Johnson's, 146, 148, 332–33 n.8; Hale's, 361 n.30
Aristotle, on friendship and justice, 283
Art: civilization as, in Burke, 229–30; cultural activity as, 283–85; of juxtaposition in *Iliad*, 39–44; law as, xi, 263–74
Assembly: called by Achilles, 33–

363

Porter, David H., 297 n.18

Power: of community, 78, 84, 310 n.32; of Congress, 242–43; of judiciary, 246–47, 250–51, 264–65; means for exercising, 257–59; persuasion as, 280. *See also* Persuasion; Rhetoric

Powers, separation of, in Marshall's opinion, 242, 263

Prayer: of Chryses to Apollo, 28–29; compared to ransom, 30; Johnson teaches method of, 161

Prejudices: American, 223–29, 231; in Burke, 212–13; origin of term, for Burke, 348 n.12

Priam and Achilles, 53–54

Pride redefined by Johnson, 158. *See also* Grandiosity

Principles: in Declaration, 233–37; in Johnson and in law, 139, 143–44, 269, 331 n.5, 361 n.31; not a proposition but a change of character, 140–41

Private and public, Burke's integration of, 195–97, 206–7

Property: in Burke, 197–99, 205–8, 214–16; in Declaration, 235

Psychology, Emma's, 170–72

Quander, Donald, 324 n.12

Quintana, Ricardo, 319, 324 n.17

*Rambler*s: No. 2, 145–49; No. 25, 149–52; No. 32, 334–35; No. 60, 355 n.1; No. 185, 157–60. *See also* Johnson

Rasselas, 333 n.11

Raven, John E., 315 n.2

Rawlings, H. R., 311 n.33

Rawls, John, 361 n.33

Reader: as authority in judicial opinion, 263; as ideal reader, 15–17, 270–73; position of, in the *Iliad*, 44, 52, 54. *See also* Ideal reader; Textual community

—as audience implied in: Corcyrean conduct, 62; Declaration of Independence, 231–40

—changes in, as meaning of text, x, 15, 16, 19; in Austen, 163, 165, 169, 174–75, 185–91; in the *Iliad*, 58,

281; in Johnson, 156, 157, 160–62; in Plato, 106–7, 110–11; in Swift, 121, 131–32, 135–36; in Thucydides, 88

Reading: Emma's capacity for, 174–75, 185–86, 339–40 n.14; equality implicit in, 228, 283; expounding as, 254–63; by imaginative participation, 8–10; as interactive process, 18–19; as a kind of writing, 4, 19; as subject of Swift's *Tale*, 117, 124, 132, 320 n.2; summarized, 3–23, 275–85, 286–88; way of, in law, 9–10; as way of learning, x, 3–23

Reality: beyond words, 21. *See also* Words

—and imagination: in the *Iliad*, 54; in Swift, 134–37; in Thucydides, 59, 65, 81, 87, 303–4

Reason: as authority in judicial opinions, 256–57, 262, 356–57 n.15; character necessary to, in Athens, 79, 82; and exhaustion of logical forms, 147; false appearance of, in Declaration, 235; and feeling, equally required by Burke, 193; forms of, in cultural analysis, 12; vs. irrationality, as integration or wholeness, 115–16, 122, 135, 136, 157–60, 213–19; recognition of other as necessary to, 79; sense of limit as necessary to, 79; theory as false, 195, 199, 212, 227; true, includes sense of dignity and proper feeling, according to Johnson, 160. *See also* False question; Integration; Language, literary; Theory

—and epistolary structure: in Burke, 195–97; in Johnson, 144–45

—failure of, regarded as spiritual defect: by Johnson, 158; by Swift, 122–23

—geometric: in Johnson, 151; in Marshall, 256, 357–58 n.16

Reciprocity: between individual and text, 18–19; between text and culture, 260. *See also* Ideal reader; Reader; Reading; Reconstitution; Textual community

—between culture and the self, 3, 8,